CAMBRIDGE NATIONAL

LEVEL 1/2

Health and Social Care

Mary Riley, Judith Adams
& Maria Ferreiro Peteiro

An OCR endorsed textbook

DYNAMIC LEARNING

OCR
Oxford Cambridge and RSA

Although every effort has been made to ensure that website addresses are correct at time of going to press, Hodder Education cannot be held responsible for the content of any website mentioned in this book. It is sometimes possible to find a relocated web page by typing in the address of the home page for a website in the URL window of your browser.

Hachette UK's policy is to use papers that are natural, renewable and recyclable products and made from wood grown in sustainable forests. The logging and manufacturing processes are expected to conform to the environmental regulations of the country of origin.

Orders: please contact Bookpoint Ltd, 130 Milton Park, Abingdon, Oxon OX14 4SB. Telephone: (44) 01235 827720. Fax: (44) 01235 400454. Email education@bookpoint.co.uk Lines are open from 9 a.m. to 5 p.m., Monday to Saturday, with a 24-hour message answering service. You can also order through our website: www. hoddereducation.co.uk

ISBN: 978 14718 9974 4

© Judith Adams, Mary Riley and Maria Ferreiro Peteiro 2017

First published in 2017 by
Hodder Education,
An Hachette UK Company
Carmelite House
50 Victoria Embankment
London EC4Y 0DZ
www.hoddereducation.co.uk

Impression number   10 9 8 7 6 5 4 3 2 1

Year   2021 2020 2019 2018 2017

Cover photo © Jupiter/Getty Images
Typeset in DIN Regular 11/13 by Integra Software Services Pvt. Ltd., Pondicherry, India
Printed in Slovenia

A catalogue record for this title is available from the British Library.

Contents

Acknowledgements

Mary Riley

Enormous thanks to the Hodder editors for their wise advice and many editorial insights.

Also a huge thank you to my very supportive husband, Ian whose IT skills saved many a diagram! Last but not least my two sons, Tom and Joe, and two dogs who kept me sane by allowing me to switch off.

Maria Ferreiro Peteiro

I wish to thank the Hodder and OCR teams for all their ideas and guidance as well as my family, especially my husband, for their encouragement and support ... I couldn't have done it without you all!

Judith Adams

Many thanks to Sundus Pasha, my patient and supportive editor at Hodder, also the welcome guidance from Stephen Halder and Sebastian Rydberg and the other editors involved in the production of this book.

A special thank you to Tony, whose endless support and constant supply of coffee and tea kept me going to the end. Also Jack and Ursula because I don't think I ever thanked you.

Photo acknowledgements

Introduction

The aim of this book is to help you to develop the knowledge, understanding and practical skills that you will need to complete your Level 1/2 Cambridge National Health and Social Care course. The Cambridge National Health and Social Care course will provide you with an introduction to the topics, issues and legislation that it is important to be aware of in health, social care and early years settings.

Each of the units in this book closely follows all the topics required for each unit in the course specification. Case studies from a range of health, social care and early years settings and practical tasks are used to help you to apply the knowledge you have gained in order to complete your assessment tasks.

Mandatory and optional units

All students will need to complete Units R021 and R022, these are the mandatory/compulsory units.

Whatever qualification size you take, you will need to study both mandatory units. In addition, for the National Certificate, you will also need to take two optional units; for the National Diploma this will be six optional units. The optional units are R023 to R031.

Assessment: Examined unit and Model assignments

- Unit R021 is an examined unit where you will sit a one hour examination paper which is set and marked by OCR.
- Units R022 through to R031 are assessed through a series of tasks for a model assignment you have been given. The assignments are set by OCR, marked by your tutor and then moderated by OCR.

All of the examination questions and model assignment tasks contain 'command' verbs. These tell you what you have to do to answer the question or complete the task. Example command verbs might be to 'explain', 'analyse', 'describe' or 'identify'. Definitions of the command verbs are in the OCR Glossary of terms at the end of this Introduction. Always check the command verb before starting a task or answering a question. If you describe something when an explanation is required you will not be able to gain full marks, this is because an explanation requires more detail than a description.

Plagiarism and referencing

Your work for the model assignment assessment tasks, Units R022 – R031, must be in your own words. You must not plagiarise. Plagiarism is the submission of another's work as one's own and/or failure to acknowledge the source correctly. Sometimes you might need to use a diagram or include a quotation from someone else. If you do this it is very important that you always provide a reference for any information you use, that is not your own work. Quotation marks should be placed around any quoted text. You should put the source reference next to the information used. In addition to referencing the picture, diagram, table or quotation, you should explain in your own words why you have used it, what it tells you and how it relates to your work.

Providing a reference means that you will give details of the source, this is where you found the information. You should include the full website address and date you found it, or for a textbook, the page number, the title, author's name, date it was published and the name of the publisher. For newspaper or magazine articles you should give the date of publication, title of the paper or magazine and the name of the author. When producing your work for the assessment you should never use any templates or writing frames, you must always decide yourself how to present your information.

It is also good practice to include a bibliography at the end of your assignment. A bibliography is a list of all the sources of information you have used, whether for background reading, quotations used in your work, or possibly an individual you have interviewed. The bibliography shows how detailed your research has been for the assignment and demonstrates how you have found the information needed to complete your assignment.

Glossary of terms from the OCR specification

Term	Definition
Adequate	Sufficient for the task – meets necessary requirements but does not go beyond this.
Adequately	It is clear that the learner understands the concepts and principles but may not have provided the full details, expansion or examples needed in order to gain the highest marks.
Appropriate/ Appropriately	Relevant to the purpose/task.
Attempt	To make an effort to do, accomplish, solve or effect.
Basic	The work comprises the minimum required and provides the base or starting point from which to develop. Responses are simple and not complicated; the simplest and most important facts are included.
Brief/Briefly	Accurate and to the point but lacking detail/contextualisation/examples.
Clear	Focussed and accurately expressed, without ambiguity.
Coherent	Logical; consistent.
Competent/ Competently	Evidence that meets the necessary standard for the task.
Comprehensive	The work is complete and includes everything that is necessary to evidence understanding in terms of both breadth and depth.
Confident/ Confidently	Exhibiting certainty; having command over one's information/argument etc.
Create	To originate (e.g. to produce a solution to a problem).
Describe	Set out characteristics.
Detail	To describe something item by item, giving all the facts.
Detailed	Point-by-point consideration of e.g. analysis, argument.
Discuss	Present, explain and evaluate salient points e.g. for/against an argument.
Effective	Applies skills appropriately to a task and achieves the desired outcome; successful in producing a desired or intended result.
Explain	Set out the purposes and reasons.
Few	A small number or amount, not many but more than one.
Full/Fully	Completely; containing as much information as possible.
Independent	Without reliance on others.
Informed	Having or prepared with information or knowledge.
Justified/ Justifying	The reasons for doing something are explained in full.
Limited	The work produced is small in range or scope and includes only a part of the information required; it evidences partial, rather than full, understanding.

Term	Definition
List	Document a series of outcomes or events or information.
Little	A very small amount of evidence, or low number of examples, compared to what was expected, is included in the work.
Many	A large number of (less than 'most', see below).
Most/Mostly	Greatest in amount; the majority of; nearly all of; at least 75% of the content which is expected has been included.
Occasionally	Occurring, appearing or done infrequently and irregularly.
Partly	In part, to some extent or degree; partially; not wholly.
Range	The evidence presented is sufficiently varied to give confidence that the knowledge and principles are understood in application as well as in fact.
Reasonable	Enough to complete a task but not flawless, omissions/inaccuracies are present, the work, whilst not ideal, is of a quality and type which is acceptable for the task and level.
Reasoned	Justified, to understand and to make judgments based on practical facts.
Relevant	Correctly focussed on the activity.
Simple	The work is composed of one part only, either in terms of its demands or in relation to how a more complex task has been interpreted by the learner.
Some	About 50% of the content which would have been expected is included.
Sophisticated	Uses refined and complex applications efficiently and effectively.
Sound	Valid, logical, justifiable, well-reasoned.
Thorough	Extremely attentive to accuracy and detail.
Variety	A number or range of things of the same general class that are distinct in character or quality.
Wholly	To the whole amount/extent.
Wide	The learner has included many relevant details, examples or contexts thus avoiding a narrow or superficial approach, broad approach taken to scope/scale; comprehensive list of examples given.

How to use this book

Key features of the book

Learning outcomes

LO1: Understand how to communicate effectively

LO2: Understand the personal qualities that contribute to effective care

Prepare for what you are going to cover in the unit.

How will I be assessed?

You will be assessed through a series of assignment tasks which are set by OCR. The assignment will be marked by your tutor and then moderated by OCR.

Understand all the requirements of the qualification with clearly stated learning outcomes and what you will be assessed on for each learning outcome, fully matched to the specification.

Links to other units

Unit R021: Essential values of care for use with individuals in care settings (LO1–4)

Relevant links to other units and learning outcomes.

Key term

Empathy The ability to understand and share another person's feelings and experiences.

Understand important terms.

Getting started

Communication is not just about what we say verbally but also what we say through our actions. Our bodies and faces can express how we are feeling and what we are saying in

Short activity to introduce you to the topic.

Classroom discussion

Non-verbal communication methods

Discuss the following types of non-verbal communication methods: eye contact and touch. For each method, discuss:

Discuss topics with others and test your understanding.

Stretch activity

Effective communication

1 Name the different types of communication methods that you know about.

Take your understanding and knowledge of a topic a step further with these stretch activities designed to test you, and provide you with a more in-depth understanding of the topic.

Case study

Negative impact of aggression

Tony is 90 years old and has experienced a recent deterioration in his mobility.

See how concepts are applied in settings with real life scenarios.

Group activity

Read through the communication profiles for two individuals: Ken, who is 65 years old,

Work in groups to discuss and reflect on topics, and share ideas.

Research activity

Job roles

Research the personal qualities that are required for the following three job roles:

● mental health nurse

Enhance your understanding of topics with research-led activities encouraging you to explore an area in more detail.

Know it!

1 What are the four different types of communication that care practitioners use?

Test your understanding with this end of unit task.

Question practice

Question

Faiza is a care assistant. She visits Anna in her own home daily. Anna has had a stroke and, while she recovers, she receives help from

This feature appears in Unit R021 where you will be assessed via an exam. This feature includes example questions, mark schemes, additional guidance, and example answers to help you prepare for the exam.

Assessment guidance

Learning Outcome 1: Understand hov

Marking criteria for LO1 part A

Mark band 1	Mark ban
Demonstrates a **basic** understanding	Demonstrates a s

Guidance and suggestions on what you will need to cover for the OCR model assignment and a breakdown of what the command words mean.

Read about it

Weblinks

www.actiononhearingloss.org.uk Action on Hearing Loss – information and factsheets on

Includes references to books, websites and other various sources for further reading and research.

About this unit

This unit provides an introduction to **equality**, **diversity** and rights (see page 3 for definitions), which are issues that affect workers in health, social care and early years settings on a daily basis. The focus of the unit is to examine how health, social care and early years workers, and care services, can support individuals' rights, value their diversity and provide them with equal opportunities in order to meet their needs.

The unit explores how care workers can apply the values of care with individuals who have differing care and support needs such as young children in a nursery, pregnant women at the antenatal clinic and elderly service users at a day centre or retirement home.

You will learn about different types of **discrimination** (see page 3 for definition) that can occur, the effects this can have on individuals and how it should be professionally challenged. Current legislation promoting anti-discriminatory practice will also be introduced, and its impact on care settings and the work of practitioners will be discussed.

It is vital that care environments are safe, healthy and hygienic. This unit outlines the different procedures care workers can use to promote the health and safety of everyone in the care setting.

Learning outcomes

LO1: Understand how to support individuals to maintain their rights

LO2: Understand the importance of the values of care and how they are applied

LO3: Understand how legislation impacts on care settings

LO4: Understand how personal hygiene, safety and security measures protect individuals

How will I be assessed?

You will be assessed through a written examination set and marked by the OCR examination board. The examination paper is worth 60 marks and is 1 hour in duration. The examination paper will consist of section A and section B.

- Section A of the paper consists of three context-based questions. This means that the questions are based on three scenarios, which are different every session. Examples of scenarios could be: in a hospital, retirement home, nursery, primary school setting and so on. You have to apply your health and social care knowledge to the given scenario context to produce a response relevant to that setting.

- Section B of the paper consists of two questions that are fact and knowledge based. The questions will not be based on any particular care setting.

Links to other units

Unit R022: Communicating and working with individuals in health, social care and early years settings (LO1 and LO3)

Unit R026 (optional unit): Planning for employment in health, social care and children and young people's workforce (LO2)

Unit R027 (optional unit): Creative activities to support individuals in health, social care and early years settings (LO3)

Unit R028 (optional unit): Understanding the development and protection of young children in an early years setting (LO3)

Unit R031 (optional unit): Using basic first aid procedures (LO1)

Learning outcome 1

Understand how to support individuals to maintain their rights

Getting started

How are my rights supported?

In small groups, discuss how your school or college supports your rights. Think about ways that confidentiality, choice, consultation and protection from harm are provided.

Share your examples with the rest of your class.

The rights of individuals

Rights are what everyone is legally entitled to. Rights are set out and supported by **legislation** (see page 3 for definition) such as the Children Act and the Equality Act (see LO3 for details of these Acts). Examples of rights are shown in Figure 1.1.

Choice

Choice gives individuals control over their lives and promotes independence. In care settings, individuals should be given the choice of joining in activities or not. For example, in a residential care home, residents should be given a choice of food options that takes account of special dietary

Figure 1.1 Individual rights

needs or religious requirements. In healthcare, individuals should be given their choice of GP, and where and how they receive their treatment. Further information about providing choice can be found in LO2, in the section titled 'The importance of applying the values of care'.

Confidentiality

This is an important right for all service users. Personal information and medical records have to be kept secure. Care workers may have access to a lot of personal information about the people they are caring for, and should always ask if it is all right to pass on any information. Meetings about service users should take place in private where information cannot be overheard by people who do not need to know about that individual. A social worker, for example, should not share details of a service user's finances, bank accounts and property in public as this could put their safety at risk.

If private information is not kept private the service user will lose trust in the care provider as they will not feel valued and respected. Further information about maintaining confidentiality is in LO2, in the section titled 'The importance of applying the values of care'.

Protection from abuse and harm

All care settings should follow safeguarding procedures to protect children and adults. The Health and Safety at Work Act (see LO3) should be implemented in the setting, and fire and risk assessment procedures should be followed (see LO4).

Equal and fair treatment

Individuals should be treated in accordance with the Equality Act and their individual needs. Everyone should be given the same opportunities as others in relation to accessing education, health and social care. It is important to realise that providing the same treatment does not always guarantee equality, because different individuals are in different situations and have different needs.

Consultation

Individuals in health, social care or childcare environments should be asked for their opinions and views about the type of care they would like, and their views and opinions taken account of wherever possible.

Why it is important to maintain individuals' rights

It is important to maintain individuals' rights to:

- make people feel valued and raise their **self-esteem**
- **empower** them and give them control over their lives (see page 4 for definitions)
- instil confidence and trust in care services and in care workers
- feel safe in the care setting
- provide equality of access to services and treatments
- ensure individual needs are met.

Key terms

Self-esteem How much a person values themselves and the life they live. High self-esteem is associated with people who are happy and confident. An individual with low self-esteem experiences feelings of unhappiness and worthlessness.

Empower To give someone the authority or control to do something. The way a health, social care or early years worker encourages an individual to make decisions and to take control of their own life.

How care workers can support individuals, to maintain their rights

By using effective communication

 Key terms

Jargon The use of technical language or terms and abbreviations that are difficult for those not in the group or profession to understand.

Interpreter Converts a spoken or signed message from one language to another.

Translator Converts a written message from one language to another.

PECS Stands for 'picture exchange communication system'. It is a specialist method of communication. It was developed for use with children who have autism and helps them learn to start communicating by exchanging a picture for the item or activity that they want.

Dynavox Speech-generating software. By touching a screen that contains text, pictures and symbols, the software converts those symbols touched into speech.

Lightwriter A text-to-speech device. A message is typed on a keyboard, is displayed on the screen and then converted into speech.

Using vocabulary that can be understood
- no **jargon**
- specialist terminology must be explained
- age-appropriate vocabulary
- simplified language – for example, with young children, individuals with learning disabilities or patients with dementia
- using **interpreters** or **translators**

Adapting communication to meet individual needs or the situation
- emphasising, or stressing important words
- slowing the pace if necessary
- increasing the tone of voice – but not shouting
- repeating where appropriate
- using gestures or flash cards/pictures
- making use of aids to communication, e.g. loop system
- using specialist methods, e.g. Braille, signing, **PECS**
- technological aids, e.g. **Dynavox, Lightwriter**

Not being patronising
- use of positive body language
- no sarcasm or talking down to the person
- being polite
- make them feel they they are being taken seriously
- being patient/listening to repetitions
- do not ignore their views or beliefs because they are different to yours

Listening to individuals' needs
- active listening – demonstrating interest in response to what a person is saying, using body language to show a positive reaction
- ask the person – do not assume you know what they want, need or prefer
- concentrate on what the person is saying, this can encourage them to communicate their needs

Figure 1.2 How to communicate effectively

By using effective communication, care workers will establish good relationships with the people using care services and with other practitioners. This ensures that individuals' rights are supported and that they are provided with appropriate care that meets their individual needs. Figure 1.2 shows some examples of using effective communication.

Case study: Using effective communication

Naz enjoys working with children. She makes an effort to plan activities that they will enjoy as well as making sure that they will help them learn. She thinks it is very important to build up good relationships with the children so that they feel safe and secure in the care setting and will want to attend and take part in all the activities.

1 Consider the picture of the practitioner working in the nursery in Figure 1.3.

2 Identify and explain the ways that the practitioner is using effective communication with the children. Think about body language, facial expression, gestures and positioning.

3 How does the practitioner's effective use of communication benefit the children?

4 Share your thoughts with the rest of your class.

Figure 1.3 Using effective communication

By providing up-to-date information

Table 1.1 How providing up-to-date information supports individuals' rights

Information about	How it supports rights
Times services open/closed	• So that the individual knows when they can access services.
	• So time is not wasted attending when services are not available.
Contact details for the service	• Phone numbers, email, so service users can communicate with the service provider.
Type of care provided	• The individual can choose what is most appropriate for their circumstances.
	• Informed choices can be made.
	• Service users have a say in their treatment or care.
Location	• So service users are aware of where specific services they need are available.
Alternatives available	• Awareness of different options empowers individuals to take control of their own decisions.
	• The individual can choose what type of care or treatment is most appropriate for themselves.
Results of tests/treatments	• So that individuals are able to choose/know the options/know why they are in need of treatment or care.
Complaints procedures	• Service users will know what to do if their rights are not being met.
	• Reassures service users that their concerns will be taken seriously.

Finding up-to-date information

1   Either visit a local care setting or use the internet to find a website for a local care setting – for example, a GP surgery, a dentist, optician or a nursery.

2   Make a list of the types of information provided by the care setting. Examples to look for are shown in Table 1.1.

3   Write an explanation of how the types of information you have found support the rights of service users.

Aim to produce a **thorough** explanation. (Look at the command word definitions to see what **thorough** means in the assessment.)

By challenging discriminatory behaviour

Table 1.2 Examples of how to challenge discriminatory behaviour

Ways to challenge	Action to take
Challenge at the time	● Explain to the individual how they are being discriminatory, to raise their awareness. ● Make the person reflect on their actions/what they have done or said. ● Supervision by senior staff – monitor the person as they carry out their work with the service users.
Challenge afterwards through procedures	● Refer the person to the setting's policies – e.g. equal opportunities, bullying. ● Instigate disciplinary action against the person – this makes them aware of the seriousness of the issue and provides a basis for changing their attitudes. ● Consult with other senior staff to discuss ways the setting can address the issue.
Challenge through long-term proactive campaigning	● Provide equality and diversity awareness sessions for the person discriminating and the other staff on the values of care. ● Provide training on effective communication. ● Send the person who has discriminated on an anger management course. ● Regular staff training over time – to raise awareness of correct ways of working to address the issue if they observe discriminatory practice.

Group activity

Challenging discrimination

1   In groups, write a short role-play script about a situation where a service user has been discriminated against.

2   In turn, each group performs their role play to the whole class.

3   After each role play, have a classroom discussion about the best ways to challenge the discrimination that has been portrayed.

By providing information about complaints procedures

Having this information enables individuals, such as practitioners, service users or their families, to take action about poor care or treatment in health, social care or early years settings. Complaints procedures empower individuals to seek redress (correct or set things right, see page 23 for more information), and can help to protect them from discrimination, abuse and unfair treatment.

Complaints procedures enable individuals to openly raise concerns and complaints. The process of reviewing complaints received enables settings to monitor the quality of their services and to take action to promote high standards. Settings that respond promptly to complaints will show that they are striving to promote good practice. This instils or establishes confidence and trust in those using the services.

When to complain
If rights have not been met. For example:

- A service user in a care home is regularly not given any choices of activities or meals.
- Confidentiality has been broken unnecessarily.
- A service user is injured in the setting or given incorrect medication.
- Unfair and discriminatory treatment due to age, race or gender.
- Treatment or care decisions are made without involving the service user.

Options available
- Choose to make a complaint or not.
- Choose when to make a complaint – straight away or later.
- Who you can complain to – the member of staff, a supervisor, the management or owner of the setting.
- Discuss the problem with senior staff or a manager.
- Write a letter of complaint.
- Start the setting's formal complaints procedure.
- Choose to take up the issue with external input – e.g. police, solicitor, local health authority, Care Quality Commission, Ofsted, Equality and Human Rights Commission.

Steps to take
- Think about what happened, the issue/incident, and gather evidence.
- Find out about the formal complaints procedure.
- Take advice, for example from the local Healthwatch or Citizens Advice Bureau.
- Stay calm – reflect on the situation.
- Talk to someone in authority at the setting.
- Explain how the individual feels/was treated and show evidence.
- Listen to other views/perspectives.
- Pursue further if needed, e.g. take specialist advice.

Procedures to follow
- Write down what happened – describe the issue/incident.
- Retain any evidence.
- Take advice – for example, from family, friends, Healthwatch, CAB, solicitor and so on.
- Follow the steps of the setting or services' complaints procedure.

By providing advocacy
An advocate is someone who speaks on behalf of an individual who is unable to speak up for her or himself. This could be, for example, a young child, an individual with learning disabilities or an older person with dementia (see page 25 for definition). An advocate would represent the individual at a care review meeting, for example, and act in their best interests.

An advocate is independent, and will represent the views, needs and interests of individuals who are unable to represent themselves, without judging them or giving them their own personal opinions.

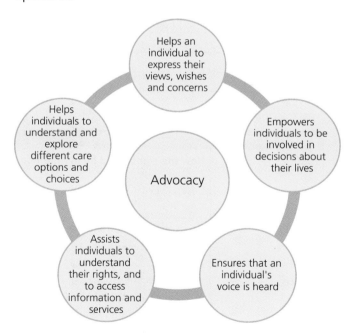

Figure 1.4 Benefits of advocacy

Finding out about advocacy

- Three organisations that provide advocacy services are SEAP (Support, Empower, Advocate, Promote), Empower Me and Mencap.
- Choose one of these organisations and access its website.
- Find out about the advocacy services that it provides.

Know it!

1 State five rights to which everyone is entitled.
2 Give three reasons why it is important to maintain the individual's rights.
3 Describe four main steps to follow in order to make a complaint about receiving poor treatment at a care setting.
4 Give two examples of ways a health centre could ensure that the information it provides is accessible to individuals with visual and hearing impairments.
5 Define the term 'advocate'.

Question practice

Question

Faiza is a care assistant. She visits Anna in her own home daily. Anna has had a stroke and, while she recovers, she receives help from Faiza with bathing, dressing and preparing meals.

Anna has rights. For each right in the table below, give an example of how it could be maintained by Faiza. The first example has been done for you. [3]

Right	How the right could be maintained
Equal and fair treatment	Faiza should carry out an assessment of Anna's needs so that she can have appropriate care.
Choice	
Confidentiality	
Consultation	

Mark scheme and additional guidance

Expected Answers		Marks	Additional Guidance
Right	**How the right could be maintained**	**3** (3×1)	Do not credit: • repeat of the right, it must be qualified, e.g. "offer choices" is too vague • "not tell anyone anything" or similar – confidentiality does have to be broken sometimes
Choice	Faiza should ask Anna: • what she would like to eat for breakfast, lunch and dinner • whether she would like to have a bath or shower • what she would like to wear today • how she would like to be helped today • which GP would she like to have an appointment with		

→

Confidentiality	Faiza should: • make sure Anna's case notes are being stored securely • not discuss Anna where others not involved can hear • not gossip about Anna to her friends • share Anna's personal information on a 'need to know' basis	
Consultation	Faiza should: • discuss with Anna the type of care she would like to help meet her needs, give her a 'say' in her care • ask for and take account of Anna's opinion about the care she receives • be an advocate for Anna • ask for Anna's views about her care and take suggestions from her	

Candidate answer

Right	How the right could be maintained
Choice	Faiza should always ask Anna what she would like to wear or what she would like for breakfast, so she can choose herself.
Confidentiality	Faiza should not discuss Anna with anyone else. She should keep all the information private.
Consultation	Faiza should give Anna her opinion and provide advice on the care that Faiza thinks Anna needs.

Commentary

Question context/content/style

The question is set in the context of a practitioner, Faiza, providing home care for Anna, who has had a stroke.

Three examples of how Anna's rights can be maintained. Three marks available.

Requirements

• Give examples of how to maintain the three rights stated in the question.
• A sentence is needed – one-word answers will not provide enough information.
• The answer must be relevant to Anna in her home care setting.

Marks awarded and rationale: 1/3

• A good example is provided for choice.
• The example given for confidentiality is incorrect. There are circumstances when private information has to be shared on a 'need-to-know' basis. So, it is inaccurate to say 'never discuss Anna with anyone else' as Faiza will need to discuss Anna's progress with other practitioners involved in her care.
• The example given for consultation is incorrect. Consultation involves getting Anna's opinions and views, not receiving opinions and advice from Faiza.
• This response gains one mark.

→

Question practice

Question

Garry attends Progress Primary School. Staff have discovered that Garry has been discriminating against one of the other children.

Describe two ways that the primary school staff could challenge Garry's discriminatory behaviour. [4]

Mark scheme and additional guidance

Expected Answers	Marks	Additional Guidance
Two ways required. **Two marks** each. Methods staff can use to challenge discrimination can include: **Challenge at the time** ● Explain to Garry how his behaviour is discriminating; this will help to raise his awareness and make him reflect on his actions. ● Report the incident to senior staff/supervisor straight away, so that they can deal with the situation. ● Involve parents/guardians to help Garry understand his behaviour is not appropriate. **Challenge afterwards through procedures** ● Refer to the school's policies – e.g. equal opportunities, bullying – so that correct procedures are followed. ● Implement complaints procedures so that the child's parents are aware of how to take action if they have a complaint about discrimination. ● Take disciplinary action against Garry, which makes him aware of the seriousness of the issue; provides a basis for changing his attitudes. ● Consult with senior staff to address the issue. **Challenge through long-term proactive campaigning** To try to change attitudes: ● Provide awareness sessions for children, e.g. assemblies/workshops. ● Have a 'discrimination awareness' campaign for a week; put up anti-discrimination displays/resources and invite guest speakers to talk about the issue. ● Train staff to raise awareness of discrimination and correct ways of working to address the issue.	4 (2×2)	**Two marks** A full description that clearly shows understanding of a way staff could challenge discriminatory behaviour with an example or further detail. **One mark** A basic description that lacks clarity. Wording of answers does not have to exactly match that on the mark scheme. Focus should be on the **'ways'**, i.e. what staff can do. **Example responses:** At the time it happens, staff could ask Garry why he is discriminating against another child (1) and tell him why it is discriminatory behaviour. (1) Report it to senior staff later (1) to alert them about the discriminatory behaviour that is happening, so it can be monitored. (1) Deliver a whole-school training session (1) to make sure everyone is aware of what is meant by discriminatory behaviour. (1)

Candidate answer

1 The member of staff who saw Garry discriminating against the child should challenge him on the spot by telling Garry how his behaviour is discriminatory, so he is aware of exactly what he said or did wrong.

2 The member of staff could report Garry's behaviour to the head of pastoral care so that the child's parents can be contacted and brought into school to discuss the matter. This makes sure the matter is dealt with properly and also demonstrates to Garry how serious his behaviour is, helping him to understand how to behave. →

Commentary

Question context/content/style

The context is a primary school that Garry attends. Garry has been discriminating against one of the other children.

Two ways that staff can challenge Garry's discriminatory behaviour. Two marks for a description of each way.

Requirements

- Two descriptions are required – a list will gain only one or two marks.
- The description should show understanding of the situation.
- The answer must be relevant to a primary school-age child.
- A full description will gain two marks.

Marks awarded and rationale: 4/4

- Both descriptions clearly identify a specific way that staff could challenge Garry's behaviour.
- Both descriptions are fully developed and detailed, with reasons for the actions.
- Both descriptions are appropriate for the primary school context.
- This response gains four marks.

Learning outcome 2

Understand the importance of values of care and how they are applied

Values of care are the guiding principles that underpin the work of those providing care and support in health, social care and early years settings. If staff in a care setting apply the values of care in their day-to-day work the service users will receive a high standard of care and will be treated fairly, with equality and respect. The values of care aim to eliminate (remove) discrimination, reduce inequalities and help to ensure individuals' care needs are met.

Getting started

Read the following statement:

'Equality means treating everyone the same.'

Do you agree or not? Give reasons for your answer. Share your thoughts and have a class discussion guided by your teacher.

The values of care in health and social care

The values of care are core principles that underpin care work. They are ways of working that aim to prevent discrimination, reduce inequalities and help to ensure individuals' care needs are met.

The values of care to be applied in health and social care settings are:

- promoting equality and diversity
- maintaining confidentiality
- promoting rights and beliefs.

The values of care to be applied in early years care and education settings are:

- ensuring the welfare of the child is paramount
- keeping children safe, and maintaining a healthy and safe environment
- working in partnership with parents/guardians and families
- encouraging children's learning and development
- valuing diversity
- ensuring equality of opportunity
- practising anti-discrimination

- ensuring confidentiality
- working with other professionals.

Where the values of care are applied

The values of care should be applied in all types of health, social care, and early years care and education settings. Examples of settings are shown in Figures 1.5, 1.6 and 1.7.

Figure 1.5 Examples of healthcare settings

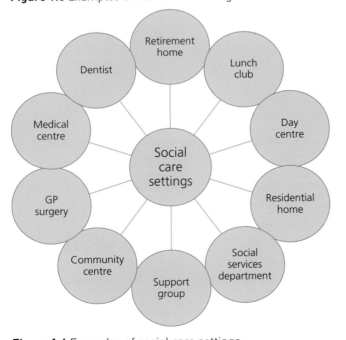

Figure 1.6 Examples of social care settings

Figure 1.7 Examples of early years care and education settings

How the values are applied in health and social care settings

Promoting equality and diversity

Care workers should always use non-discriminatory language and avoid patronising the individuals they are caring for. They should challenge discrimination if they see or hear it happening; whether it is a staff member or another individual using the care setting. Ways of challenging discrimination are explained in LO1.

An important way to promote **equality** is to provide care that meets an individual's specific needs. For example, if a theatre trip is arranged for residents of a care home, it should be to somewhere that has wheelchair access and a hearing loop system for those who need them.

Other examples could be helping someone to take a shower or helping them to get dressed, for example, if they have mobility difficulties (difficulties with moving).

Maintaining confidentiality

Information should be shared only on a need-to-know basis – for example, with other workers involved in the individual's care. You should not share information with anyone else, even the person's family or friends, without the individual's permission. The only exceptions to this are:

- if the person is at risk of harming others
- if the person is at risk of harming themselves
- if the person is at risk of being hurt by others
- when there is a risk of a serious offence being carried out.

Risk of harming others could involve child sex abuse or domestic violence, or if someone is mentally ill with a condition such as schizophrenia and says they are going to harm themselves or others. Risk of harming themselves could also be if someone said they were thinking of committing suicide. A serious offence could be drug dealing or threats of violent assault.

Private information about individuals, such as medical records, should be password-protected on computers or filed in a locked cabinet with restricted access. Staff working in care settings who have access to confidential information should not gossip about the individuals in their care or discuss them with friends and family.

Promoting individuals' rights and beliefs

Care environments such as hospitals and residential care homes could provide access to a prayer room or transport to church to support individuals' religious beliefs. In healthcare, the right to choose of a pregnant woman could be supported by consulting with her about the choice of birth she would like, whether at the hospital or a home birth. Providing a menu with vegetarian, vegan, gluten-free, halal and kosher options caters for all types of dietary needs and provides choice for all.

See page 16 for information on being a reflective practitioner.

 Key terms

Equality Promoting equality means ensuring that people are treated equally. For example, ensuring individuals are treated fairly and given the same choices and opportunities regardless of differences. They are not discriminated against due to their age, race or sexuality, for example. People are treated according to their own, individual needs.

Designated child protection officer A named individual who is the first point of contact for staff in a care setting if they have any concerns about a child, or need advice about the welfare of a child.

DBS checks Criminal record checks carried out by the Disclosure and Barring Service (DBS) to help to prevent unsuitable people working with vulnerable adults or with children.

How the early years values are applied in care and education settings

Ensuring the welfare of the child is paramount

Childcare environments should use a child-centred approach where the child's needs come first. A child must never be humiliated, abused or smacked. Safeguarding and child protection procedures should be in place in all settings – for example, having a **designated child protection officer** and **DBS checks** carried out on all staff.

Keeping children safe, and maintaining a healthy and safe environment

A safeguarding procedure should be in place and all staff should be DBS checked. Staff should wear lanyards for identification. Health and safety procedures and legislation should be followed, which should include regular fire drills, risk assessments and making sure first aiders are available. There should always be an appropriate staff-to-child ratio – this means having enough staff to properly care for the number of children present and for the type of activity that is happening. A bullying policy should be in place so that children know what to do if they experience bullying and who to go to for help.

Working in partnership with parents/guardians and families

A childcare environment could welcome parents/guardians by having open days or evenings where they can meet staff and look around the setting. Daily diaries can be kept by nursery staff to keep parents/guardians informed of progress. Information sessions could be provided on topics such as potty training, dealing with tantrums or picky eaters. Awards certificates could be sent home and parents/guardians could be invited in to discuss behaviour or other issues. Staff could have an informal contact with parents – for example, a chat with them when they bring their child to nursery in the morning.

Encouraging children's learning and development

To encourage a child's learning and development, a range of activities should be provided. Children should experience opportunities for developing physical skills, intellectual skills, creativity and social skills. A well-planned curriculum will meet children's differing needs – for example, language skills as well as numeracy and literacy.

Progress should be monitored so that extension activities, designed to stretch learning, are provided at the appropriate time when the child is able to cope with higher demands. Monitoring progress also ensures that care providers are aware when support is also needed for those with special educational needs. Feedback such as a rewards system (e.g. stars or praise letters sent home) can motivate children's learning. Activities that are stimulating for the children will engage their interest and help them to enjoy learning.

To enable all the children to participate and learn, practitioners should ensure that resources such as toys, games and activities are accessible for all of the children who use the setting. Differentiated worksheets and reading materials for different abilities could be provided; also, having specialist staff available who can use sign language, and teaching assistants who can support children with additional physical or special educational needs and learning disabilities.

Valuing diversity

Teaching children about **diversity** and discrimination helps them to develop an understanding of individual differences, and encourages acceptance of and respect for others.

Displays, toys, and resources such as books, DVDs and food should reflect different cultures, beliefs and needs. A range of different festivals could be celebrated with all the children – for example, Diwali, Christmas, Chinese New Year – so that everyone feels their culture is of equal importance. Welcome signs could be displayed in a range of different languages to reflect the diversity of service users. Meeting individual cultural, communication or mobility needs shows all children that they are valued.

Figure 1.8 Welcome: 'Hello' in 13 languages

Ensuring equality of opportunity

Every area of the setting should be accessible to all – this may require adjustable-height tables to accommodate wheelchairs and ramps to ensure physical access. Activities should be accessible to everyone by using adapted resources if required or providing one-to-one support if needed. Children's individual needs should be met, whether those are cultural, religious, mobility, dietary or communication, for example. All children should be treated fairly, with no 'favourites'. Staff should be aware of, and follow, a setting's equal opportunities policy.

Practising anti-discrimination

Staff should always be good role models by using non-discriminatory language – no racist or sexist comments. Discriminatory comments or behaviour should be challenged with the individual concerned to ensure they know and understand that what they have said or done is unacceptable.

All children should be treated fairly, irrespective of their age, race, gender, religion, disability or sexuality, and staff should not have 'favourites'. No one should be excluded due to a disability and their individual needs should be catered for – this could involve providing a hearing loop, information in Braille or by using PECS, providing a translator or information leaflets for parents in different languages. Dietary needs should be met by providing gluten-free, halal or vegetarian meals.

Ensuring confidentiality

Personal and private information about children, their family circumstances or progress records, for example, should be shared only on a 'need to know basis'. This means that only staff or other individuals who are directly involved in caring for the child should have access to the information. Children's personal information should be kept secure in a locked filing cabinet or password-protected if electronic. It is important that staff do not have conversations about the children where they can be overheard. Such conversations should take place privately in an office, for example.

Working with other professionals

Sometimes practitioners or agencies that support children will need to work together. For example, a nursery school teacher may work with the school nurse, a health visitor or social services to support or meet the needs of a child.

The importance of applying the values of care

In health, social care or early years settings, practitioners who apply the values of care will deliver best practice when caring for their service users. Individuals using care and early years services will feel valued and respected, their needs will be met, they will have equal opportunities and will not be discriminated against.

- **Applying values of care ensures standardisation of care:** practitioners will know how to do their job effectively; service users will receive appropriate care, attention and treatment to meet their individual needs; all of the staff in a care setting will be working to the same high standards.

- **Applying values of care improves the quality of care:** people who use services will have their individual needs met – for example, providing hospital patients with appropriate nutritional meals, providing help to eat and drink, discussing their treatment with them and consulting them about alternative types of treatment potentially available to them.

- **Applying values of care provides clear guidelines to inform and improve practice:** the values of care inform practitioners about the key features of best practice so that they know how to provide effective care; applying the values of care in their work ensures that that the standard of the care provided by practitioners meets legal requirements.

- **Applying values of care maintains or improves quality of life:** service users' rights, beliefs and preferences will be respected and their individual needs met; this ensures that the care they receive is beneficial in every way; examples include: a teaching assistant providing literacy support to a child to enable them to achieve their full potential, an occupational therapist carrying out a home assessment of an older person with arthritis resulting in various kitchen aids such as an easy-grip knife and a special 'bottle and jar opener' being provided – these will enable her to continue preparing her own meals independently.

Being a reflective practitioner

A reflective practitioner is someone who regularly looks back at the work they do, and how they do it, to consider how they can improve their practice. It literally means to 'reflect on the work they have done'.

There are four main aspects involved in being a reflective practitioner:

1 evaluating specific incidents or activities
2 identifying what might be done better next time
3 identifying what went well
4 exploring training and development needs.

The effects on people who use services if the values of care are not applied

Effects on individuals can be **P**hysical, **I**ntellectual, **E**motional and **S**ocial – it can help to remember these as the '**PIES**' effects.

Physical effects relate to an individual's body. Some examples of possible physical effects of not receiving appropriate care include:

- if a nursing home resident with coeliac disease (which causes unpleasant symptoms if gluten is consumed) is not provided with gluten-free food, their digestive health will deteriorate
- a hospital patient who is not given regular drinks, resulting in them becoming dehydrated and their condition worsening.

Case study: Improving patient experience

Read the following information about Oakleaf Surgery.

Jayne is the GP practice manager at Oakleaf Surgery. Part of her job is to regularly check the patient feedback forms completed by people using the surgery.

She finds that, recently, several older patients have written on their patient feedback forms that they feel patronised by the way staff speak to them. Some also feel as though they are being treated as though they are stupid and incapable because their hearing is impaired and they have to ask for things to be repeated.

To address this problem, Jayne reflects on her own practice when speaking with patients and also discusses the issue with other surgery staff. Jayne reaches the conclusion that she, and the other members of staff at the surgery, would benefit from some training in effective communication skills. She thinks that this training will improve everyone's knowledge and understanding about effective communication with patients.

Topics covered by the training Jayne organises include:

- active listening
- adapting communication to the needs of the individual
- not being patronising.

Jayne also arranges for a hearing loop to be fitted at the surgery reception desk so that those patients with hearing impairments do not have to ask for information to be repeated all the time.

Two months later, when checking patient feedback forms again, Jayne finds that there are no complaints about poor communication – in fact there are some very positive comments from patients about how they have been treated with respect and how useful the hearing loop has been.

Questions

1 Write down the following headings:
   - Evaluating specific incidents or activities
   - Identifying what might be done better next time
   - Identifying what went well
   - Exploring training and development needs

2 Under each heading list the actions that demonstrate Jayne's reflective practice.

3 How has Jayne's reflective practice helped to support the rights of service users?

Intellectual effects relate to an individual's thought processes, such as thinking skills, understanding, learning, reasoning, comprehension and knowledge. Some examples of possible intellectual effects of not receiving appropriate care include:

- if a child who has learning difficulties is not given support and learning activities matched to their special needs, their learning will not progress
- staff at a retirement home expect residents to sit and watch television for most of the day and do not provide a range of activities to engage their interest; the residents will lack mental stimulation, which can have negative effects on their health and well-being.

Emotional effects relate to an individual's feelings. Some examples of possible emotional effects of not receiving appropriate care include:

- an elderly woman attends a day centre; she is a vegetarian but at lunch is expected to eat the same meal as the others, just without the meat – this would be unfair treatment and is likely to upset her as she is not being treated as well as the others; she might develop low self-esteem as she feels she is not important enough to be given a proper vegetarian meal; she could also feel embarrassed that she is being a nuisance by expecting a 'special' meal
- an expectant mum would be upset, angry and frustrated if her midwife told her that she cannot have a home birth, without explaining the reasons why or giving her the chance to ask questions.

Social effects relate to an individual's relationship with others. Some examples of possible social effects of not receiving appropriate care include:

- if staff at a primary school do nothing about children laughing at a child who has a birthmark on his face, the child may lack friends, become isolated, withdrawn and refuse to attend

- George, an elderly resident at a retirement home, has an undiagnosed hearing problem; the staff do not bother to talk to him much because they think he just doesn't like socialising and prefers to be by himself; George avoids spending time with other residents as he can't hear properly and has to keep asking for things to be repeated; he doesn't want to bother people so he keeps himself to himself.

Some more examples of effects on individuals of the values of care not being applied in care settings are shown in Figure 1.9.

It is important to realise that these effects do not occur in isolation but are 'interrelated' (they affect one another). For example, a young boy who is being bullied at primary school may suffer physical harm such as bruises. This could lead to him feeling frightened and unsafe, causing him to not attend school so as to avoid the bullies. Not attending school will affect his learning and development of skills such as maths and English, but will also negatively affect his social skills as he will not be mixing with other children.

Physical effects	Intellectual effects	Emotional effects	Social effects
• pain • existing illness gets worse • bruising • cuts and grazes • broken bones • dehydration • malnutrition • injury	• lack of skills development • lack of knowledge • lack of progress • loss of concentration • losing interest • lack of stimulation • will not achieve potential	• low self-esteem • low self-confidence • disempowered • upset • loss of trust • angry • depressed • stress • frustrated • humiliated • self-harm • frightened • feeling unsafe	• withdrawn • isolated • excluded • become antisocial • unco-operative • lack of friends • develop behaviour problems • refusal to use the service

Figure 1.9 Effects on individuals if the values of care are not applied in care settings

Stretch activity

Mrs Talbot's cup of coffee

Two volunteers perform a role play of the following conversation to the rest of your group. The conversation is between Mrs Talbot (a retired grandmother living in a residential home) and Adrianne (a care assistant).

Adrianne: Hurry up Mrs T, your coffee is going cold and we need to get you into your nightie before I go off duty.

Mrs Talbot: It's too hot to drink – you have only just given it to me.

Adrianne: Oh, you are imagining things again Mrs T. I gave it to you 10 minutes ago. Now come on.

Mrs Talbot: I do wish you wouldn't call me 'Mrs T', Adrianne – my name is Mrs Talbot.

Adrianne: Oh, don't be so formal. Mrs T is nice. Anyway let's get this coffee finished and then you can get into your nightie and watch Neighbours. It starts in 15 minutes.

Mrs Talbot: [Sips her coffee] Ugh – you've not put any sugar in it!

Adrianne: Sorry, I forgot. Now come on, I have to get you into that nightie right now.

Mrs Talbot: It's far too early.

Adrianne: No it's not. We always start getting people ready for bed at around 5 o'clock, after teatime.

Mrs Talbot: Oh, well I suppose so then, if I must.

Adrianne: That's my girl.

Questions

These could be discussed by the whole group and then answered as a piece of written work.

1 Explain the ways in which Adrianne has not supported Mrs Talbot's rights.

2 Analyse the effects on Mrs Talbot of Adrianne not applying the care values in this way.

Aim to produce a **thorough** explanation and **detailed** analysis. (Look at the command word definitions to see what **thorough** and **detailed** mean in the assessment.)

Know it!

1 Give two examples of settings for each of health, social care and early years.

2 Name the values of care that apply to health and social care settings.

3 Name three different values of care that apply to early years settings.

4 What is the meaning of the term 'reflective practitioner'?

5 Give three reasons why it is important to apply the values of care.

Question practice

Question

Linda is a nurse working on a busy hospital ward. Identify the three values of care that Linda should apply when caring for the hospital patients.

Mark scheme and additional guidance

Expected Answers	Marks	Additional Guidance
Three required, **one** mark each. Health and social values of care: ● Promoting equality and diversity ● Promoting individuals' rights and beliefs ● Maintaining confidentiality	**3** (3×1)	For values of care you can accept just: ● equality **or** diversity ● rights **or** beliefs on their own, but credit only once. Must state '**promoting**'. Must state '**maintaining**' confidentiality. Do not credit '**confidentiality**' on its own. Do not accept early years values of care.

Candidate answer

1 Promoting equality and diversity
2 Confidentiality
3 Rights and beliefs

Commentary

Question context/content/style

Identification of the three values of care that would apply in a healthcare service context. Three marks, one mark for each value of care.

The command verb is 'identify' so only a short answer is required, no explanation.

Requirements

● Correct identification of the three values of care that would apply in a healthcare service context.
● The words 'maintaining' or 'promoting' must be given to gain the marks.

Marks awarded and rationale: 1/3

● This response demonstrates a common error made by candidates, missing the verb required.
● The first value of care is correct, gaining one mark.
● The second value of care given is not awarded a mark because the verb 'maintaining' has been left out. No mark for confidentiality on its own.
● The third value given also misses out the verb, this time 'promoting'.

Question

Explain the possible **social** effects on a child in a nursery if the value of care 'ensuring equality of opportunity' is not applied. [6]

→

Mark scheme and additional guidance

Expected Answers	Marks	Additional Guidance
Social effects: • become antisocial • behaviour problems • exclusion/left out/unwanted • inability to make relationships • isolated/alone • lack of friends • marginalised • poor social skills/not wanting to interact with others • refuse to attend nursery • unco-operative • withdrawn. This list is not exhaustive, accept other appropriate **social** effects. **Do not accept:** Any emotional effects, e.g.: • not feel safe • not trust staff • upset.	6	This is a 'levels of response' question – marks are awarded on the quality of the response given. The focus of the question is explanation. **Level 2 (4–6 marks)** Answer provides a detailed explanation of at least two social effects on a child if 'ensuring equality of opportunity' is not applied. Answers will be coherent, using correct terminology. **Sub-max of 3** for one effect done well. **Level 1 (1–3 marks)** Answer provides a basic explanation/description of social effects on a child if 'ensuring equality of opportunity' is not applied. List-like answers should be placed in this level. Limited use of terminology.

Candidate answer

If the care value 'ensuring equality of opportunity' isn't applied, a child could become excluded or marginalised, which will make them have a lack of confidence. They may see that other children are more valued. An effect could be that the child's social skills would not develop, leading them to display antisocial behaviour and not make any friends.

If the child doesn't have equal opportunities, they will feel left out and that they are not receiving the correct standard of care. The child will not feel empowered or build trust, which will prevent them from gaining social skills.

Commentary

Question context/content/style

An explanation of possible social effects, on a nursery-age child, resulting from a specific value of care not being applied. Six marks available.

The question requires an explanation, so specific effects need to be identified, with a line of reasoning that demonstrates understanding of the situation. It requires more depth and detail than a description.

Requirements

● An explanation is required – a list will gain only one or two marks
● Two or more effects for Level 2
● The answer must be relevant to a nursery-age child
● Social effects only – not emotional

→

Marks awarded and rationale: 5/6

- The response provides more than two social effects and uses some correct terminology such as 'marginalised' and 'antisocial behaviour'. There is a line of reasoning evident in the first paragraph – cause and effect – and so this places the response into level 2. The examples given are appropriate for a nursery school child.
- However, the second paragraph refers mainly to feelings/emotions, and repeats the point about not developing good social skills. The quality of the response is not at the top of the mark band.
- This response gains level 2, five marks.

Learning outcome 3

Understand how legislation impacts on care settings

Legislation protects all groups of people in society, it provides individuals with rights to which they are entitled through laws passed by parliament. Law is upheld through the courts, it supports an individual's rights and also states their responsibilities to society.

Legislation imposes responsibilities on service providers to promote equal opportunities and to support individual rights.

Legislation:

- provides a framework to maintain and improve quality of practice
- provides guidance for those who work in the health, social care and early years sectors
- sets out the standard of practice and conduct those who work in the health and social care and early years sectors should meet.

Getting started

Visit the Equality and Human Rights Commission (EHRC) website at www. equalityhumanrights.com/en to find out about the laws that protect each of the groups of people shown in Figure 1.10.

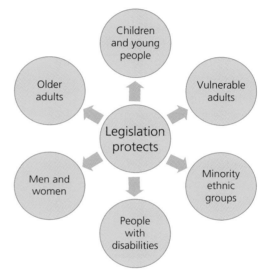

Figure 1.10 Groups of individuals supported by legislation

Although anyone in society can be **discriminated** against, some groups of individuals can be particularly **vulnerable** to discrimination or poor standards of care. Children, for example, are young and so may not be aware of their rights or what they are entitled to, or who to complain to, and so can be taken advantage of or abused. Other individuals may have an illness or condition that affects their ability to stand up for their rights or to complain about poor treatment. An older person with **dementia** (see page 22 for definition) may forget about how they have been treated so it is never reported. Lack of ramps or lifts, information in Braille or leaflets and information in different languages are all examples of discrimination against particular groups of people in society.

Key terms

Discrimination When people judge others based on their differences, and use these differences to create disadvantage or oppression. Discrimination could be based on race, disability or gender.

Vulnerable An individual who is unable to take care of themselves against significant harm or exploitation. This may be because of mental or physical disability or illness.

Dementia A condition that causes memory loss, confusion and difficulty with daily living tasks.

Disabilism Behaviour that is abusive or discriminatory based on the belief that people with disabilities are inferior or less valued members of society.

Sexualism Discrimination or negative attitudes towards a person or group on the basis of their sexual orientation or sexual behaviour – for example, against lesbian or bisexual individuals.

Transphobia Discriminatory behaviour against transgender or transsexual individuals on the basis that they do not conform to society's gender expectations.

Some individuals in society hold strong negative beliefs or views about a particular group of people, which can lead to discrimination. Discrimination against individuals may be based on:

- race/ethnicity – racism
- disability – **disabilism**
- sexuality – **sexualism**, homophobia, **transphobia**
- age – ageism
- gender – sexism.

Discrimination can be 'direct' or 'indirect'. An example of direct discrimination is an 86-year-old, who is in otherwise good health, being refused a hip operation because they are 'too old'. A job advert stating that either men or women are not suitable for the job would be discrimination on the basis of gender. For example, a job condition of 'must be clean shaven', as this would discriminate against men whose religious beliefs prevent them from shaving their beards.

Legislation gives people rights and aims to prevent discrimination and unfair treatment. It also enables individuals to take action against discrimination when it happens through the courts to obtain **redress** (see page 23 for definition).

An overview of the key aspects of legislation

Equality Act 2010

The Equality Act simplified previous laws covering discrimination, such as the Sex Discrimination Act, the Race Relations Act and the Disability Discrimination Act. All of these previous laws were put together in one new piece of legislation, the Equality Act.

The key aspects of the Equality Act are as follows.

- Direct and indirect discrimination on the basis of a **protected characteristic** is illegal. The nine protected characteristics are: age, disability, gender reassignment, marriage and civil partnership, pregnancy and maternity, race, religion, sex and sexual orientation.
- Prohibits or forbids discrimination in education, employment, access to goods and services, and housing.
- Covers **victimisation** and **harassment** (see page 23 for definitions) on the basis of a protected characteristic.
- Reasonable adjustments have to be made by employers or providers of goods or services for those with disabilities. For example, installing a ramp to access a building, aids such as computer software to help a person to do their job or providing information in a large format. Hearing loop systems and information provided in Braille are also reasonable adjustments that can enable individuals to access services.

Key terms

Redress To obtain justice after being discriminated against or receiving inadequate care. This may take the form of compensation awarded by the courts or having your rights restored in some way.

Protected characteristic Refers to nine characteristics identified by the Equality Act. It is unlawful to discriminate against someone on the basis of a protected characteristic.

Victimisation Bad treatment directed towards someone who has made a complaint or taken action under the Equality Act.

Harassment Unwanted behaviour that has the purpose or effect of violating a person's dignity, or intends to intimidate or humiliate them.

Classroom discussion

The Equality Act
Discuss the following.

● How has the Equality Act supported the rights of service users with disabilities?

● Why do you think some organisations or settings do not make 'reasonable adjustments' to improve access for individuals with disabilities? Consider factors such as cost, time, and the age and type of the building.

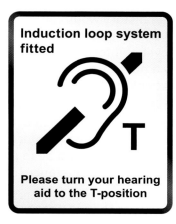

Figure 1.11 Adapting the environment to improve access to services

● Women have the right to breastfeed in public places. It is against the law for a woman to get less favourable treatment because she is breastfeeding. However, there is no right to breastfeed at work.

● The act encourages positive action. One form of positive action is encouraging or training people to apply for jobs or take part in an activity in which people with that protected characteristic are under-represented.

● Discrimination due to association is now an offence. This means that there is now protection from discrimination for carers of an individual who has a protected characteristic.

● Pay secrecy clauses are now illegal.

Children Act 2004

The key aspects of the Children Act are as follows.

● Aims to **protect children at risk** and to keep them safe. This may involve taking a child away from their family using an emergency protection order or care order.

● **Paramountcy principle**: this means that the child's needs must come first. For example, taking a child away from their family may adversely affect the adults but may be in the child's best interests. Children have the right to stay within their wider family circle wherever possible.

● Children have a **right to be consulted**. The act gives children who are mature/old enough a voice. They have the right to express their wishes and these wishes should be taken into consideration.

● Children have a **right to an advocate**. An advocate is someone who represents the child and speaks on their behalf. An advocate acts in the best interests of the child.

● **Every Child Matters (ECM) – 5 outcomes**: ECM states five aims for children's services to support: staying safe, being healthy, enjoying and achieving, make a positive contribution, and economic well-being. These are universal ambitions for every child and young person, whatever their background or circumstances.

- **Encourages partnership working**: practitioners need to ensure that information is shared when appropriate to help avoid miscommunication or lack of communication between services. This is particularly in child protection situations.
- The act created the **Children's Commissioner**, whose role is to raise awareness of the best interests of children and to report annually to Parliament.
- The act also requires each area to set up a **Children's Safeguarding Board** to represent children's interests, and develop policies and procedures for safeguarding and promoting their welfare.

Data Protection Act 1998

This act states that information and data should be:

- **processed fairly and lawfully**: this means that information should be collected only with an individual's permission; the information should be shared only on a need-to-know basis
- **used only for the purposes for which it was intended**: information should be gathered only for a specific and necessary purpose and only used for that purpose
- **adequate and relevant but not excessive**: care workers should collect and use only information that is needed – for example, a detailed case history would be required by a social worker in order to inform a care plan; the same level of information would not be required by a nurse treating someone who had injured their ankle playing football
- **accurate and kept up to date**: inaccurate data should be destroyed or corrected; care workers have responsibility to ensure information is correct and systems should be in place for checking accuracy – for instance, checking with individual patients
- **kept for no longer than is necessary**: information should be deleted or destroyed when it is no longer needed – for example, securely deleting or shredding sensitive or personal data
- **processed in line with the rights of the individual**: 'processed' means how the information is used; individuals have a right to know if information is being held about them and how their information is being used; they have the right to have any errors corrected, and to prevent any data being used for advertising or marketing purposes
- **secured**: non-authorised staff/people should not be allowed access to the information; the information – for example, patient records – should be kept in secure conditions, locked

away or password-protected; settings should have clear guidelines in place for who can have access to the information, and there should be a confidentiality policy

- **not transferred to other countries**: information should not be transferred outside the EU unless the service user has given consent; this is because other countries may not have the same data protection legislation as the EU and so the data may not be secure.

Health and Safety at Work Act 1974 (HASAWA)

There are specific key aspects of the HASAWA for employers (service providers) and for employees (staff and practitioners).

Employers must ensure that:

- the working environment must not put anyone at risk
- the equipment provided must be safe and in good working order
- staff are provided with adequate health and safety training
- a written health and safety policy is provided
- the 'health and safety law' poster is displayed
- there are health and safety procedures in place, such as fire evacuation procedures
- settings have working fire alarms, extinguishers and accessible fire doors
- appropriate health and safety signs are provided
- adequate first aid is available
- protective equipment, if needed, is available free of charge to employees.

Employees must ensure that they:

- co-operate with their employer by following health and safety regulations in the workplace
- report any hazards they come across to the employer
- do not misuse or tamper with equipment provided that meets health and safety regulations, e.g. fire extinguishers
- understand their responsibility to take care of themselves and others in the workplace.

The HASAWA set up the Health and Safety Executive (HSE). This is the regulator for the health, safety and welfare of people in work settings in the UK. The HSE can carry out inspections of workplaces, and investigate accidents or complaints about health and safety issues. The HSE can take action against care settings by issuing cautions and improvement notices. In the most serious cases the HSE can take the organisation, or individuals responsible for breaches of health and safety, to court and they can be fined heavily.

Mental Health Act 2007

The key aspects of the Mental Health Act are as follows.

- It gives a definition of different types of mental disorder.
- It gives relatives and approved social workers and doctors the right to have a person detained under the Act for their own safety or to ensure the safety of others.
- It clearly sets out the circumstances in which a person who has a mental disorder can be treated without their consent.
- The circumstances in which people with mental disorders can be admitted to psychiatric hospitals against their wishes are set out in different sections of the act, so the process of admitting people to hospital against their will is called 'sectioning'.
- Initially, detention is for the purpose of assessment and can be for a period of up to 28 days.
- A longer period of detention can follow, during which patients are required to receive medication.
- The act makes provision for the aftercare and treatment of people who have been discharged into the community; they are entitled to supervised treatment in the community.
- It sets out the safeguards to which the person with the disorder is entitled.
- It established Managers' Hearings, Mental Health Review Tribunals and the Mental Health Act Commission, through which individuals or their advocates can make a legal appeal against being 'sectioned' and kept in hospital for treatment against their will.
- This legislation does not apply to everyone with a mental disorder – only those whose condition is likely to pose a threat to themselves or others.

Case study: Suresh

Suresh has a serious mental illness. He has been prescribed medication for his condition, but often forgets to take it and sometimes refuses to take it. Recently Suresh has become very aggressive and increasingly violent. He is becoming a risk to himself and to his family because of violent outbursts when he accuses people of stalking him and says he can hear voices telling him to attack certain people.

His close family members are very concerned about Suresh and worried he will harm himself or someone else if things continue as they are. They decide to contact his social worker for advice. The social worker goes to see Suresh at his home. Suresh is very angry and aggressive, and refuses to speak to the social worker.

The social worker is an Approved Mental Health Professional and is very concerned about Suresh. He arranges for Suresh to be detained under Section 2 of the Mental Health Act so that he can be kept in hospital for up to 28 days.

Access the mental health charity Rethink's website: www.rethink.org/resources. Find its Mental Health Act factsheet and use it to help you answer the following questions.

Questions

1 What is the purpose of Suresh being detained in hospital for up to 28 days?

2 How many people are needed to agree that someone can be sectioned?

3 Can Suresh be treated against his will?

4 What are Suresh's rights under Section 2 of the Mental Health Act?

5 What do you think are the benefits for Suresh of being detained in hospital for up to 28 days, and what are the negatives?

The impact of legislation in health, social care and early years services

Figure 1.12 The impact of legislation

Legislation has an impact on people who use services, the ways that practitioners deliver the services, and also on the organisation or care setting that provides the services. Here are some examples of the impact on each of these groups.

How legislation impacts on people who use services

● The Mental Health Act provides protection for people who might harm themselves or others, through compulsory admission to hospital, where they are assessed and appropriate treatment provided, or in the community.

● The Equality Act helps to make all settings accessible. It states that health, social care and early years environments have to make reasonable adjustments to accommodate individuals with disabilities. Examples of adjustments include speaking lifts with Braille controls, hearing loops, automatic doors and ramps.

● Individuals can exercise their rights when using care and support services – for example, choice and consultation.

● Individuals are entitled to be treated fairly, and protected from abuse and harm. They can take action through complaints procedures and the courts if their treatment is unsatisfactory.

How legislation impacts on care practitioners

Practitioners are the individuals working in a setting delivering the health and social care or early years service.

- The Mental Health Act makes it clear which practitioners can take decisions for individuals, in which situations and how they should go about it.
- The Data Protection Act provides detailed regulations about how to handle information; this is very important in health, social care and childcare environments as the use of a lot of private, personal information about individuals is necessary.
- The Health and Safety at Work Act informs practitioners of their individual responsibilities for keeping themselves and others safe in the care setting. For example, attending training, wearing protective clothing provided and reporting damaged or dangerous equipment.

How legislation impacts on service providers

'Service providers' refers to the care setting as a whole – the organisation providing the service.

- Organisational policies and procedures have to be produced – for example, confidentiality, data handling, bullying, equal opportunities, and health and safety policies. The setting must monitor that the policies and procedures are being followed.
- Staff have to be provided with training about equality and diversity, health and safety, and data handling, for example.
- HASAWA requires risk assessments to be carried out, personal protective clothing to be provided for employees, and that they should be provided with training before using equipment, such as hoists.

- Staff recruitment procedures must meet the requirements of the Equality Act. For example, the advertisement must not state requirements that discriminate against certain groups, such as women or particular ethnicities; non-discriminatory questions must be asked at interviews. This ensures that an individual with a disability is not asked if they 'are sure they can cope with the job because of their wheelchair'. A woman should not be asked if she is thinking of starting a family, when a male candidate is not asked that question.

Legislation provides a system of redress

Each piece of legislation outlines the rights that individuals are entitled to. If those rights are breached (in other words, if those rights are not upheld, or are not adhered to), then the law can be enforced by taking legal action through the courts so that individuals have their rights restored, or the person or organisation breaking the law is penalised in some way. This may be a fine or imprisonment, or a care setting may be closed down.

Know it!

1. What is the meaning of the term 'legislation'?
2. Identify four groups of individuals that are protected by legislation.
3. List five key aspects of the Mental Health Act.
4. Identify the nine protected characteristics named by the Equality Act.
5. Describe two key aspects of the Health and Safety at Work Act that apply to service providers (employers) and two key aspects that apply to care workers.

Question practice

Question

Listed in the table below are key aspects of four different pieces of legislation. Complete the table by adding the correct piece of legislation from the list below:

- Mental Health Act
- Data Protection Act
- Equality Act
- Health and Safety at Work Act
- Children Act. [4]

Legislation	Key aspects
	Provides the authority to 'section' a person for their own safety.
	States that it is the duty of childcare practitioners to ensure information is shared.
	Identifies nine protected characteristics.
	Requires that the working environment should not put anyone at risk.

Mark scheme and additional guidance

Expected Answers		Marks	Additional Guidance
Legislation	**Key aspect**	**4** (4×1)	No other answers are acceptable.
Mental Health Act	Provides the authority to 'section' a person for their own safety.		If two responses are given for a key aspect: Mark the first response only. **Crossed-out responses:** Where a candidate has crossed out a response and provided a clear alternative then the crossed-out response is not marked. Where no alternative response has been provided, examiners may give candidates the benefit of the doubt and mark the crossed-out response where legible.
Children Act	States that it is the duty of childcare practitioners to ensure information is shared.		
Equality Act	Identifies nine protected characteristics.		
Health and Safety at Work Act	Requires that the working environment should not put anyone at risk.		

Candidate answer

Legislation	Key aspect
Mental Health Act	Provides the authority to 'section' a person for their own safety.
Data Protection Act	States that it is the duty of childcare practitioners to ensure information is shared.
Children Act/ Equality Act	Identifies nine protected characteristics.
Health and Safety at Work Act	Requires that the working environment should not put anyone at risk.

Commentary

Question context/content/style

Choose from the list provided to match the legislation to a key aspect. Four marks available.

Requirements

- Match the correct piece of legislation with the key aspect.

Marks awarded and rationale: 2/4

- The response provides two correctly matched pieces of legislation – the first and last answers are correct.
- The second answer 'Data Protection Act' is incorrect.
- The third answer provides two pieces of legislation: the Children Act and the Equality Act. Although the Equality Act is the correct answer, a mark cannot be awarded as the first answer given is the one that is marked.
- This response gains two marks.

Question practice

Question

Explain the impact of key aspects of the Data Protection Act on the work of care practitioners. [8]

Mark scheme and additional guidance

Expected Answers	Marks	Additional Guidance
Key aspects of the Data Protection Act – it is the practitioner's responsibility that personal data should be: ● **secured so that no unwanted persons can access it**, following the setting's Data Handling Policy ● **used only for the purposes for which it was intended** – practitioner should keep information for a clear purpose and use it only for that purpose unless given permission by the service user ● **adequate and relevant but not excessive** – practitioners should collect only the information that is needed to provide care; do not collect unnecessary information ● **accurate and kept up to date** – practitioners should destroy or correct inaccurate data; it is also a responsibility to record information accurately and it should be checked with the patient/service user ● **kept for no longer than is necessary** – destroyed securely (shredded or deleted) after use or when no longer needed ● **processed fairly and lawfully** – practitioners should not collect personal information without the service user's permission ● **processed in line with the rights of the individual** – practitioners should support the individual's right to be informed about information held on him or her ● **not transferred to countries outside the European Economic Area** – unless that country ensures an adequate level of protection for the rights and freedoms of data subjects; practitioners need to obtain consent for this to happen.	8	This is a 'levels of response' question – marks are awarded on the quality of the response given. The focus of the question is explanation. **Level 3 (7–8 marks)** Answers will include a detailed explanation of at least two key aspects of the legislation and the impact on the work of care practitioners. Answers will be coherent, logically organised and factually accurate. **Level 3 (4–6 marks)** Answers will include a sound explanation of one or two aspects of the legislation and the impact on the work of care practitioners. Answers will be factually correct. **Sub-max of 4** for one aspect done well or two aspects not linked to care practitioners **Level 1 (1–3 marks)** There may be evidence of one or two aspects of the legislation. Explanations may not link to the work of care practitioners. List-like answers should be placed in this band. Answers may be muddled and lack technical detail.

Candidate answer

The Data Protection Act means that practitioners have to keep everyone's personal information (such as medical test results) secure. The Act also protects personal information against not being used for its intended purpose as it cannot leave the UK without permission. Data cannot be kept longer than its intended or legal purpose.

Confidentiality is another key aspect of the act. To help protect the data, practitioners should not talk to others about personal information from service users. When on the phone, practitioners should go to a separate room where you will not be overheard. All personal files should be locked up.

Commentary

Question context/content/style

An explanation of the effect of the Data Protection Act on the work of care practitioners. The answer could relate to a specific care setting of your choice or care settings in general as the question does not state a particular type of setting. Eight marks available.

→

The question requires an explanation, so specific key aspects need to be identified with a line of reasoning that demonstrates understanding of the impact on care workers' practice. It requires more depth and detail than a description.

This is an extended writing question, so give some thought to planning the structure of your answer. Two or three key aspects of the Data Protection Act, a paragraph on each aspect explaining how it affects the way a practitioner works. Lots of key aspects with limited explanation of the impact will not get into the Level 2 mark band.

Requirements

- An explanation is required – a list will gain only one or two marks.
- Two or more key aspects and their impact for Level 2.
- Use of correct terminology from the Data Protection Act for Level 2 mark band.
- The answer must be clearly relevant to care settings.

Marks awarded and rationale: 3/6

- The first paragraph refers to some key aspects of the act, using correct terminology – 'secure', 'intended purpose', 'kept longer than intended', 'cannot leave the UK'.
- The key aspects identified in paragraph one are not developed; there is limited reference to the impact on a practitioner's work.
- Paragraph two is about maintaining confidentiality, which is not relevant here. No key aspects of the Data Protection Act are given in this paragraph.
- Overall, the answer provides some accurate key aspects of the legislation but with very limited reference to the impact on practitioners. Some information is not relevant. This limits the mark to Level 1.
- This response gains Level 1, three marks.

Learning outcome 4

Understand how personal hygiene, safety and security measures protect individuals

Getting started

Think about what you have done so far today. Make a list of everything you have touched since you got out bed this morning.

On your list highlight or underline all the things that someone else could have touched as well.

List any hygiene measures you have used today.

Share and discuss with the rest of your class hygiene measures that could be taken to reduce the spread of bacteria and infections between individuals.

Personal hygiene

Bacteria will grow very easily in most environments that are warm, light and moist. There are lots of opportunities for bacteria to grow and spread in health, social care and early years settings. This is because they are accessed by many individuals over the course of a day, and many different activities take place, such as meals being prepared and served, physical examinations and treatments. This is why it is so important that everyone working in a care setting has high standards of personal hygiene, to prevent the spread of infection.

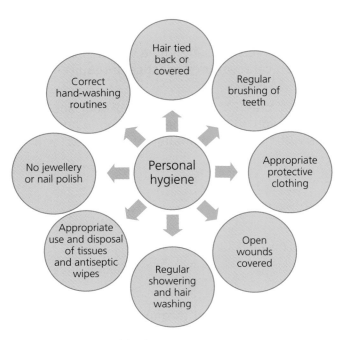

Figure 1.13 Personal hygiene measures

How personal hygiene measures protect individuals

Maintaining good personal hygiene ensures a high level of cleanliness and helps stop the spread of infection. Personal hygiene:

- prevents the transfer of bacteria
- correct hand-washing routines can destroy bacteria
- the individual carries fewer bacteria, which reduces the opportunity to spread infection
- barrier methods reduce and prevent the transfer of bacteria and spread of infection; examples include wearing disposable gloves, wearing a disposable apron and covering open wounds
- not wearing jewellery removes places for bacteria to be trapped
- not wearing nail polish removes the risk of it flaking off and contaminating food or a wound
- if hair is tied back or covered, it can't drop into food and contaminate it with any bacteria that may be present.

Safety procedures and safety measures

Safety procedures provide guidelines about how to deal with emergency situations such as a fire, or how to arrange a safe school trip. A procedure is a set of actions that are done in a particular order; it will inform care workers and service users as to what they have to do and how it should be done.

A safety measure is a specific action such as putting up fire safety notices or 'wet floor' signs.

Emergency procedures

All care settings should have emergency procedures in place for situations such as fire, bomb scares and intruders. Care workers should be made aware of the procedures and their role in an emergency. Service users also need to be made aware of fire evacuation procedures.

There should be regular evacuation practices and fire drills so that everyone is familiar with what to do and where to go, and can do it quickly in an emergency. Figure 1.14 shows a fire evacuation procedure for a nursing home.

Fire safety measures include:

- fire safety notices that are visible throughout the setting
- signs indicating fire doors and assembly points
- fire doors kept clear
- a fire extinguisher available by each exit
- a fire blanket in kitchen areas.

Checkleigh Nursing Home
Fire evacuation procedure

- **If you discover a fire, raise the alarm – alert people in the immediate area, activate alarm system, call 999.**
- **All staff to remove people from their immediate area – direct them to the fire assembly point, use designated fire exits, never use lifts.**
- **Designated staff assist residents with:**
  - **mobility difficulties (use of evac chairs/wheelchairs)**
  - **hearing difficulties (may not hear alarm)**
  - **dementia patients (may be confused/unaware of what is happening).**
- **Staff to close doors and windows, switch off lights as they leave.**
- **Staff evacuating the building must check their locality is clear.**
- **Everyone to assemble at designated external assembly point to await further instructions.**
- **Do not re-enter the building until told it is safe to do so.**
- **Carry out head count to ensure everyone is accounted for.**
- **Senior staff to inform fire brigade if anyone is left in the building.**

Figure 1.14 Example of a fire evacuation procedure

Equipment considerations

Table 1.3 Equipment considerations

Equipment considerations	How they improve safety
Appropriate training of staff for specialist equipment, e.g. hoists, transfer boards	So staff know how to use it correctly
Fit for purpose, appropriate for the task Specialist equipment available	Correct equipment provided for the task, reduces risk of injury to staff and service users
Checked regularly for damage – repaired or disposed of if necessary, e.g. toys, wheelchairs	No worn-out, damaged or potentially dangerous equipment will be in use
The care setting should have a reporting system for damaged or faulty equipment	Action can be taken immediately to take it out of use, reduces risk of accident
Replacement programme for older or worn-out equipment	A good standard of safe equipment is maintained

Moving and handling techniques

Care workers in health, social care or early years settings will often need to move items of equipment such as toys, tables and chairs. In social care and healthcare practitioners may have to assist individuals to move. Scenarios include:

- assisting an older person or an individual with a physical disability to get out of a bed, chair, shower or bath
- transfer from bed to chair
- moving and handling objects, e.g. shopping bags
- use of hoists – when bathing or getting out of bed.

Having staff who are trained in moving and handling techniques is essential if this is part of their job role. The training helps to protect care workers as well as the person receiving care and support.

Protection of care workers:

- gives staff guidance on good practice – they will be aware of the correct posture and position to be in when using equipment for lifting or moving
- the environment, equipment and load will always be risk assessed
- the risk assessment identifies if a second person is needed to assist with the lift
- prevents injury to care workers
- helps care workers to do their job correctly; this results in a safer environment as it reduces risk
- improved knowledge of moving and handling develops the care worker's confidence when moving and handling service users

- the training provides protection from accusations of abuse as correct procedures will have been followed.

Protection of service users:

- prevents injury to service users
- improves the comfort and dignity of service users
- shows respect
- instils confidence, trust, feeling safe as the service user knows that the care worker is trained and qualified to carry out manual handling
- results in a safer environment, reduces risk to service users
- will not feel disempowered by being handled incorrectly.

Security measures

An important aspect of maintaining the safety of a care setting is keeping it secure from strangers and intruders entering the building. Security measures also prevent service users leaving the care setting – for example, toddlers and children from a nursery or individuals with dementia leaving a residential home.

Security measures such as monitoring of keys mean that no one unauthorised can enter the building because they would not have access to the keys. A receptionist can monitor external CCTV to ensure there are no intruders around, and if there are this can be reported to the manager to deal with. A receptionist can control

Figure 1.15 Security measures in care settings

who is allowed in or out, and will know who is in the building. It should also be ensured that visitors sign in and are provided with a visitors' badge; and, to ensure everyone in the care setting can be identified, staff should wear ID lanyards.

Some examples of security measures are shown in Figure 1.15.

How individuals are protected

Methods for reducing the spread of infection

General cleanliness

Different care settings have different types of furniture and equipment. The methods of maintaining general cleanliness will vary depending on the setting. However, some examples of standard ways to maintain a clean and hygienic environment are as follows.

- Floors should be vacuumed or mopped every day.
- Spillages and vomit should be cleaned up immediately.
- Walls, blinds, windows and curtains should be cleaned regularly.

- Coffee tables, dining tables and chairs, and hard surfaces should be cleaned, polished, dusted or disinfected every day.
- Toys, plastic and fabric, should be washed frequently.
- Cleaning items such as dusters and cleaning cloths should be changed regularly.
- Empty bins every day to remove rubbish and avoid cross-contamination.
- Remove and wash dirty crockery.
- Clean worktops, cookers, floors and equipment
- Ensure the setting is free from infestation of pests, e.g. mice.
- Specialist disposal methods, e.g. hard yellow sharps box for used syringes, red bags for soiled bed linen, yellow bags for clinical waste such as used dressings and disposable gloves.

Correct food preparation practices

To prevent cross-contamination and food poisoning:

- use the correct coloured chopping boards to keep raw food separate from cooked food (red for raw meat, white or yellow for cooked meat, blue for fish, green for fruit and vegetables)
- correct food storage methods
- check 'use by' and 'eat by' dates
- cook thoroughly to kill bacteria
- wash fruit and vegetables before use
- cover food to protect it from insects.

Hand washing

This should be done:

- before and after touching raw food or meat
- after visiting the toilet
- after emptying rubbish bins
- after exposure to cleaning materials
- after dealing with soiled bedding or nappies
- before and after undertaking clinical procedures
- after coughing or sneezing.

Research activity

Finding out about hand washing

1   Find a YouTube clip (or information in a textbook) that shows the correct technique for washing hands. One example of a detailed clip is 'A complete hand washing guide', which you can find at www.youtube.com/watch?v=mWe51EKbewk. This short film shows how to wash your hands correctly with both alcohol rub and soap and water within a medical environment. The clip was originally used by medical students at the University of Leicester.

2   Write a set of illustrated step-by-step instructions for the correct method of hand washing.

Wearing disposable gloves

This is a barrier method of preventing the spread of infection. Fresh gloves should be used for each new task. They should be worn in the following situations:

- changing nappies
- changing soiled bed linen
- dealing with body fluids, e.g. blood, urine, vomit
- dressing wounds
- clearing up spillages
- before and after eating
- food preparation and serving.

Protective clothing

Disposable aprons protect your clothing from contamination and other individuals from any bacteria your clothes may carry. A new apron should be used for each person attended to, and disposed of immediately afterwards. In some situations, in hospitals or when preparing food, hairnets, gowns and masks have to be worn to prevent the spread of infection.

Personal hygiene measures have been covered earlier in this section (see pages 31–32).

Methods for reducing risks and dangers

Risk assessments need to be carried out for any activities or visits and trips that care settings organise. They are needed to check that equipment is safe and that the care setting building itself is safe. Risk assessments identify dangers such as potential accidents, trip hazards and risky activities that require more than the usual amount of staff supervision.

Carrying out a risk assessment

Carrying out a risk assessment involves the following steps.

1   Look for hazards.
2   Decide who might be harmed and how.
3   Consider the level of risk – decide on the precautions needed to reduce the risk.
4   Make a written record of the findings.
5   Review the risk assessment from time to time and improve the precautions if necessary.

Reasons for risk assessments

- Risk assessment is a legal requirement under the Health and Safety at Work Act. The written record provides evidence that the risk assessments have been carried out.
- Staff, service users and visitors have a right to be protected and kept safe from harm.
- To check what could cause harm to people using the care setting.
- To prevent accidents, illness and danger.
- Staff, service users and visitors will feel confident using the service knowing that risk assessments are carried out.

Procedures to prevent accidents and promote good practice

The procedures that care settings should have in place to prevent accidents and promote good practice include:

- emergency fire procedures
- emergency evacuation procedures
- equipment considerations, e.g. appropriate training
- specialist training for the use of manual handling equipment
- regular risk assessments
- regular fire drills
- first aid procedures

- food safety procedures
- supervision – children at all times/adults as necessary
- adequate staff to children/patient/resident ratio.

How safety procedures protect service users

The procedures provide guidance for staff so they know what to do to keep service users safe at all times. Knowledge of safety procedures enables them to take quick, efficient action in emergencies. Staff will know how to treat with first aid and how to reduce the risks of cross-contamination to avoid the spread of infection. Training to use equipment prevents accidents, which helps to provide a safe environment.

Service users will feel safe knowing that the procedures are in place, reassured that staff will know what to do in an emergency, and will know that equipment is safety checked and risk assessed for faults or damage so there is little or no risk of being injured.

Case study: Willowfield residential home

Serena is the new manager at Willowfield, a residential home that has 25 residents aged between 75 and 96 years. Serena has been checking the accident book and has discovered that, over the past 12 months, there have been numerous occasions when residents have had falls, including one when a resident had to spend six weeks in hospital because of their injuries. Two staff have had back injuries due to lifting and handling residents.

Serena urgently wants to do something to address the problem and asks the staff for volunteers to be part of an 'accident reduction team'. You are part of the team and have been tasked with producing an action plan to reduce the number of accidents.

You must answer the following questions before creating the action plan.

Questions

1 The residents' bedrooms are personalised with their own furniture and belongings, including ornaments, rugs, lamps and televisions. How can the risk of falls be reduced in the residents' bedrooms?

2 Suggest what could be done at Willowfield to reduce the risk of staff getting injured when moving and handling the residents.

3 Create an action plan to help protect residents and staff, making Willowfield residential home a safer place.

Group activity

Write a quiz

1 In groups, write a quiz about health and safety in care settings. Each group could be allocated a different health and safety topic.

2 Write ten questions and produce an answer sheet.

3 Have a quiz session with the whole class. Which group will score the most points?

Know it!

1 How does good personal hygiene protect individuals in care settings?

2 Give four examples of when a care worker wears disposable gloves and explain why this is important.

3 Describe what should happen during a fire evacuation procedure.

4 What procedures should a residential home have in place for visitors?

5 What are the five stages of carrying out a risk assessment?

Question practice

Question

Maintaining security is very important in all health, social care and early years settings. Identify three different security measures. Describe how each security measure could protect individuals. [6]

Mark scheme and additional guidance

Expected Answers		Marks	Additional Guidance
Security measure	**How it protects**	**6** (3×1 + 3×1)	Examples may relate to any health, social care or early years settings. How individuals are protected must relate to the security method identified Answers must relate to security not safety. **Do not accept:** ● All doors locked ● References to fire safety ● References to data security/ protection ● 'ID' on its own.
Checking/monitoring external entrances	Controls access – only authorised people have access to the setting.		
Monitoring of keys			
Security pads/key pads			
CCTV monitoring exit/ entrance			
Manned reception desk	To control who is allowed into the setting. In a nursery children only released to authorised people.		
Receiving/escorting and monitoring visitors			
Signing in/out book			
Staff wearing ID/lanyards	Easy to identify staff and unauthorised people. Easy to identify visitors.		
Visitor badges			
Window locks/window restraints	To prevent people falling out of windows. Prevents unwanted visitors getting into the setting.		
Reporting of concerns to line managers	Appropriate action / response can be initiated.		

Candidate answer

Security measure: DBS checks

How this could protect individuals: Stops the children being put at risk if someone was applying for a job at a primary school.

Security measure: Fire alarms

How this could protect individuals: These alert people in the care setting that there is fire and they need to leave the building.

Security measure: Signing in and out book for visitors

How this could protect individuals: This makes sure that people coming in to the setting have permission to enter and it keeps a record of who is in the building.

→

Commentary

Question context/content/style

Identification of three different security measures relevant to any type of care setting. Six marks available, three for identification of security measures and three for descriptions of how they protect individuals.

The question requires an identification, so specific security measures are needed. The description must show understanding of how security is maintained.

Requirements

● Identification of three different security measures.
● A description of how each security method protects individuals.
● Your answers may relate to a specific care setting, but do not have to.

Marks awarded and rationale: 2/6

● DBS checks are not security measures – they are a safety procedure. No marks awarded.
● Fire alarms are also safety measures, not security. No marks awarded.

Two marks awarded for visitors signing in and out, along with a correct, clear description of how this security measure protects individuals.

Question practice

Question

Describe how personal hygiene measures can protect individuals in care settings. In your answer you must include:

● some examples of personal hygiene measures
● details of how these personal hygiene measures protect individuals in care settings. [6]

→

Mark scheme and additional guidance

Expected Answers	Marks	Additional Guidance
Personal hygiene measures • Hair tied back/covered • Open wounds covered • No jewellery • No nail polish • Appropriate protective clothing • Appropriate hand-washing routines • Regular showering and hair washing • Regular brushing of teeth • Appropriate use and disposal of tissues/antiseptic wipes. **How it protects staff/service users** • Prevents transfer of bacteria • Destroys bacteria • Care worker carries fewer bacteria/germs • Ensures high level of cleanliness • Reduces opportunity for spreading bacteria/germs • Stops others coming into contact with bacteria/germs • Barrier method reduces/prevents transfer of bacteria • Removes places for bacteria to be trapped. Answers must relate to **personal** hygiene not general cleaning, etc.	6	This is a 'levels of response' question – marks are awarded on the quality of the response given. The focus of the question is description. **Level 2 (4–6 marks)** Answers provide a detailed description of at least two personal hygiene measures and how they protect individuals in care settings. Answers will be coherent, using correct terminology. **Level 1 (1–3 marks)** Answers provide personal hygiene measure(s) and how they protect individuals in care settings. Answers may not be explicitly linked to care settings. List-like answers should be placed in this level. Limited use of terminology. **Sub-max of 3** for only one measure done well. **For Level 2:** must use terminology, e.g. 'bacteria', 'cleanliness', 'disposal', not generic answers such as 'keeps clean'.

Candidate answer

The reason personal hygiene is important in care settings is because it stops the spread of bacteria and micro-organisms that can cause illness and diseases. Many people who are in care settings such as residential homes or hospitals may be vulnerable to infection.

Personal hygiene includes washing hands very thoroughly, using anti-bacterial soap, before eating or preparing food, after sneezing or using the toilet, as this will destroy the bacteria on the hands. Hands should always be washed before moving on to care for another patient or service user to avoid passing on bacterial infections from one person to another.

Also, personal hygiene involves tying up hair and not wearing any jewellery as these can harbour bacteria that could be passed on to others or, for example, infect food. Covering a cut with a clean dressing will avoid cross contamination from blood-borne diseases.

Wearing appropriate protective clothing, for example, a disposable apron or disposable plastic gloves, which are disposed of appropriately immediately after use, will also help to avoid the transfer of bacteria when providing personal care for individuals.

→

Commentary

Question context/content/style

Examples of personal hygiene measures with a description of how they protect individuals in care settings. The examples could relate to a specific care setting or you could give examples for more than one type of setting.

This is an extended writing question, so give some thought to planning the structure of your answer. Two or three personal hygiene measures with a paragraph on each describing how individuals are protected. Lots of examples with limited description of how they protect will not get into the Level 2 mark band.

Requirements

- A description is required – a list will gain only one or two marks.
- Two or more personal hygiene measures must be described for Level 2 mark band.
- Use of correct terminology for Level 2 mark band (e.g. 'bacteria', cleanliness', 'disposal').
- The answer must be relevant to care settings.

Marks awarded and rationale: 6/6

- This response is very well organised. It starts with an introduction about why personal hygiene is particularly important in care settings. Three further paragraphs each focus on different aspects of personal hygiene.
- More than two examples are given, and they are all in the context of care settings.
- There is good use of appropriate terminology throughout: 'bacteria', 'micro-organisms', 'cross-contamination'.
- All of the information is accurate, relevant and detailed.
- This response gains Level 2, six marks.

Read about it

Weblinks

www.equalityhumanrights.com/en Equality and Human Rights Commission – provides comprehensive information on all aspects of equality, diversity and anti-discrimination legislation.

www.hse.gov.uk/index.htm Health and Safety Executive – comprehensive information about health and safety in the workplace.

www.skillsforcare.org.uk/Home.aspx Skills for Care – organisation that provides resources and shares best practice to help raise standards in health and social care services.

www.nmc.org.uk Nursing and Midwifery Council – codes of practice for nurses and midwives.

www.skillsforcare.org.uk/Standards/Care-Certificate/Care-Certificate.aspx – all about the Care Certificate and how to provide quality care

www.scie.org.uk – The Social Care Institute for Excellence.

Reference books

Lindon, J. (2012) *Equality and Inclusion in Early Childhood* (2nd edn), Linking Theory and Practice. Hodder.

Stretch, B. (2007) *Core Themes in Health and Social Care*. Heinemann.

Thomson, H. and Aslangul, S. (2009) *OCR Health and Social Care for GCSE*. Hodder.

Walsh, M. (2009) *GCSE Health and Social Care for OCR*. Collins.

R022 Communicating and working with individuals in health, social care and early years settings

About this unit

Good quality health, social and early years care depends on practitioners having and applying the skills and personal qualities that are essential for effective communication and that impact positively on individuals' health and well-being.

In this unit you will learn about the different types of communication skills that care practitioners use, as well as the reasons why they are important. You will also learn about the barriers to communication that practitioners may face and the different techniques that can be used to overcome these.

You will have an opportunity to explore the many different essential, personal qualities of practitioners that are necessary for positively enhancing individuals' experiences of care. Finally, you will develop your knowledge of the different aspects involved in one-to-one and group interactions and be able to demonstrate the communication skills you have to be able to meet individuals' needs and preferences as well as promote their abilities and strengths.

Learning outcomes

LO1: Understand how to communicate effectively

LO2: Understand the personal qualities that contribute to effective care

LO3: Be able to communicate effectively within a health, social care and early years setting

How will I be assessed?

You will be assessed through a series of assignment tasks, which are set by OCR. The assignment will be marked by your tutor and then moderated by OCR.

For LO1, you need to:

- demonstrate an understanding of how to communicate effectively
- explain the different types of communication methods related to health, social care and early years settings, with examples
- describe the factors that positively influence communication
- describe barriers to communication and ways to overcome them, together with examples.

Note that SPAG is assessed in LO1.

For LO2, you need to:

- describe the different personal qualities that contribute to effective care
- make connections between personal qualities and effective care, and links to how personal qualities are used when caring for an individual in a health, social care and early years setting, using examples.

Make sure you refer to the current OCR specification and guidance.

For LO3, you need to:

- create a plan for the practical tasks of communicating with people who use health, social care and early years settings, both in one-to-one and group situations
- demonstrate effective communication skills, relating positively to the people who use health, social care and early years settings, and be able to maintain a conversation with individuals, applying theory to practice
- use methods of communication appropriate to individual circumstances and that ensure that individuals always feel comfortable.
- consider the use of body language and how it can contribute to effective communication, with examples of the types of behaviour that fail to value people
- consider the importance of adapting language in order to meet the needs of individuals
- draw on skills, knowledge and understanding from other units in the specification.
- make sure that your teacher is up to date with the latest specification and guidance from the awarding body.

Links to other units

Unit R021: Essential values of care for use with individuals in care settings (LO1-3): When demonstrating effective communication with individuals who use a health, social care or early years' service you must ensure that your approach is supportive and patient, promotes individuals' rights and applies the values of safe, fair and effective care. You must also ensure that you listen attentively to individuals and adapt your communication methods to meet their needs. Your plan must also take into consideration individuals' rights such as their choice of preferred communication methods and must also show respect for their confidentiality.

Unit R024 (optional unit): Pathways for providing care in health, social care and early years settings (LO3): When planning for communicating effectively in both one-to-one and group interactions you could consider how your plan meets and is appropriate for the individual and/or group's needs depending on whether they are children, adults, older people, people with disabilities or people with mental health needs.

Unit R027 (optional unit): Creative activities to support individuals in health, social care and early years settings (LO3): Planning for communicating effectively will also involve you taking into consideration the duration of the interaction, the material resources you may need and how you will measure its effectiveness. Encouraging individuals' involvement and checking their understanding throughout are other aspects of your communication that you could also consider.

Learning outcome 1

Understand how to communicate effectively

Getting started

Communication is not just about what we say verbally but also what we say through our actions. Our bodies and faces can express how we are feeling and what we are saying in many different ways.

Without using any words, see if you can use your body and face to convey the following emotions: happy, anxious, in pain, frightened.

Different types of communication

Practitioners working in health, social care and early years settings need to be able to communicate in different ways with individuals and others, including their colleagues, other professionals they work with and individuals' families and **advocates**. There are four different types of communication skills that practitioners must be able to understand and use: verbal, non-verbal, written and specialist.

Verbal skills

Verbal or spoken communication can provide others with clues about who you are and how you are feeling. For example, practitioners who feel confident in their own abilities will tend to speak more clearly and positively than practitioners who do not. Communicating with clarity involves sharing information with others clearly, accurately and in a way that can be easily understood, i.e. by pronouncing words clearly, not mumbling, and using words that are respectful. It also involves being receptive to communications from others, listening attentively and confirming an understanding of what is being expressed. You will learn more about how verbal communication is linked with non-verbal communication below.

Our tone of voice reflects what we are thinking and feeling, and will therefore impact on how we express our words and how they may be received

 Key terms

Advocates Independent people who represent the wishes, views and preferences of individuals who are unable to do so for themselves because of an illness, disability or condition.

Empathy The ability to understand and share another person's feelings and experiences.

by others. A GP who uses a conversational tone of voice when speaking with a nervous patient will be more likely to enable the patient to relax and talk about how they are feeling than a GP who engages with patients using an abrupt or harsh tone of voice.

The pace or speed at which you speak is also very important. Speak too fast and you could prevent others from understanding what you are saying. Speak too slowly and you could risk others being distracted or losing interest in what you are saying. Getting the balance just right therefore is important. A children's centre worker who is able to vary the pace they speak during activities for groups of children will be more likely to encourage their active involvement than a worker who does not.

Being able to convey **empathy** through verbal communication is one of the most important skills practitioners can learn. Being empathetic involves using words that show sensitivity and respect, as well as conveying or showing a genuine interest in how another person may be feeling. A care worker who uses kind and reassuring words when visiting an individual who has experienced the death of someone close to them will be able to convey support and understanding more effectively than a care worker who does not.

Paraverbal skills refer to the feelings and meanings that are expressed to others through our use of verbal communication and the emphasis we put on certain words (or how we stress certain words), for example, through use of clarity, tone and pace. This means that the same words can have different meanings, depending on how we say them. The example below shows how the same sentence used by a support worker in response to a question from an individual who has **dementia** (see page 45 for definition) can have different meanings, depending on the *tone* and *emphasis* placed on certain words.

Question from individual who has dementia: What time is it?

Response 1 from support worker: It's 1.00pm – time for lunch.

Response 1 is spoken clearly, not hurried and with the emphasis on *1.00pm* and *lunch*. The information requested by the individual is conveyed simply and accurately.

Question from individual who has dementia: What time is it?

Response 2 from support worker: It's 1.00pm, time for lunch.

Response 2 is spoken quietly, abruptly and with the emphasis on *It's*. The information conveyed to the individual may not be understood or may lead to the individual believing that they have not been heard and therefore repeating the question again.

Non-verbal communication

Non-verbal communication such as body language, gestures and facial expressions also plays a very important role in the information and meanings we convey to others and in how we interpret the information and messages we receive from others.

Non-verbal communication includes:

- **body language** – how we use our bodies through movement or positioning to

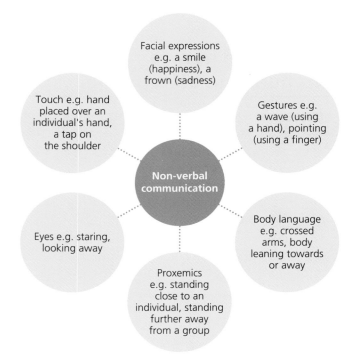

Figure 2.1 Forms of non-verbal communication

communicate, e.g. welcoming an individual with open hands can indicate that you are approachable and have nothing to hide
- **gestures** – how we use parts of our bodies through movement or positioning to communicate, e.g. nodding your head while speaking to an individual can indicate that you are listening and taking a genuine interest in what is being said
- **facial expressions** – how we use our faces to communicate, e.g. smiling when an individual completes an activity can indicate that it has been completed well.

Written communication

Written communication forms an important part of working with individuals in health, social care and early years settings. Practitioners may be asked, for example, to write a **care plan** (see page 45 for definition) or a daily report about the care provided to an individual, or the instructions to follow for a medical procedure or activity; they may need to take minutes of a meeting or to send an email to an individual's family.

💬 **Classroom discussion**

Non-verbal communication methods

Discuss the following types of non-verbal communication methods: eye contact and touch. For each method, discuss:

1 examples of when it can be used
2 examples of how it can convey different messages.

Figure 2.2 What messages do you think the health care worker is giving to this patient?

Good writing skills create good impressions. Pay careful attention to:

- how the text is presented, including the typeface and font size used – a clear and easy-to-read layout will look more professional
- correct grammar, punctuation and spelling – this will instil confidence in the reader
- the style of writing used – formal or informal styles may be required for different situations and will be appropriate for some situations and not others
- the language used – the use of current sector terminology and avoiding **jargon** is important for ensuring that information is understood.

Specialist communication

Practitioners working in health, social care and early years settings have many different interactions with individuals who have a diverse

 Key terms

Care plan A written statement that sets out an individual's preferences, wishes, care and support needs, including the care and support that will be provided, the reasons why, when they will be provided and by whom.

Dementia A term used to describe the symptoms that occur when the brain is affected by specific conditions and diseases; symptoms may include memory loss and difficulties with thinking, problem-solving or language.

Jargon Words or expressions used by professionals that are difficult for others to understand.

range of needs. Knowledge of specialist communications and how to use these may at times be required to enable effective interactions.

Braille

Braille is used by individuals who are blind or visually impaired and are unable to access materials in print. It is important as it enables individuals to read and write independently. Braille uses raised dots to represent the letters of the alphabet, numbers and punctuation marks; these can be read and written by touch. Braille has been adapted to many different languages and is also used for musical and mathematical notation.

The **Royal National Institute of Blind People (RNIB)** is a charity for blind people and those who have sight difficulties that provides support and information to individuals, their families and others who support them. It provides a range of courses, training and resources for learning braille.

Sign language

The most common form of sign language used in Britain is British Sign Language (BSL). It was recognised by the UK government as an official language in March 2003 and is the most widely used form of language after English, Gaelic and Welsh. It has its own grammar and sentence structure that is completely different to that used in English. Sign language is used by individuals who are deaf or hearing impaired. It is a form of communication that uses gestures, facial expressions and body language.

Action on Hearing Loss (formerly known as the Royal Institute for Deaf People) is the largest charity representing individuals who are deaf and have hearing loss in the UK. It estimates that approximately 50,000 individuals use BSL to communicate, and that BSL is the first language of many of them.

Another form of sign language used in Britain is Sign Supported English (SSE). SSE is similar to BSL as it uses the same signs but it is not an official language and does not have its own grammar and sentence structure; it follows the same rules that are used in spoken English. It is mainly used therefore to support spoken English, i.e. in schools with children who are hearing impaired and learning English alongside their signing.

Action on Hearing Loss is a useful source of information if you want to find out more about these forms of sign language.

Makaton

Makaton is a form of communication that uses signs and symbols to help adults and children who have difficulties with speech to communicate. It is designed to support spoken language; the signs and symbols are used with speech, in spoken word order and can be personalised to an individual's needs and preferences.

The Makaton Charity in the UK estimates that over 100,000 children and adults use Makaton. It provides a range of resources, information, support and training sessions for individuals who have learning or communication difficulties or would like to learn Makaton, including individuals' families, carers and professionals.

Voice-activated software

Voice-activated software enables individuals to operate a device, carry out commands or write without having to use a keyboard, mouse or push any buttons. It can be used by individuals who have difficulties with their mobility (their ability to move) or in using a keyboard to type due to a **physical disability**, a **learning disability**, **dyslexia** (see page 47 for definitions) or because they are blind.

Voice-activated software can promote equal opportunities and provide individuals with independence. For example, an adult who has **cerebral palsy** (see page 47 for definition) could use the software in the workplace by instructing the computer to open the internet or search for a document. An older individual who has limited mobility could also use voice-activated software at home, so as to open and close the curtains or turn the lights on and off.

Key terms

Physical disability A physical impairment or weakness that affects an individual's ability to do daily activities.

Learning disability A learning impairment that affects an individual's ability to do daily activities.

Dyslexia A learning difficulty that affects an individual's ability to learn to read or interpret words, letters, numbers and/or other symbols.

Cerebral palsy A condition that affects the body's muscle control and movement, and is usually caused by an injury to the brain before, during or after birth.

Stretch activity

Effective communication

1 Name the different types of communication methods that you know about.

2 Explain to a partner, in as much detail as possible, two different communication methods. (Aim to produce a **thorough** explanation. Look at the command word definitions in the introduction to see what 'thorough' means in the assessment.)

You may have used voice-activated software when using automated phone systems that require you, for example, to say '1' or '2' for the service you require, or when using Siri to ask questions on Apple devices, or Google Voice that allows you to ask questions on your computer, tablet or phone.

As well as technological support, people can also act as aids to communication and interactions with children and adults who have a range of needs.

Advocates
Advocates can support and enable individuals to express their views and concerns when they find it difficult to do so. Advocates are independent and can represent both individuals and groups. Children who are looked after in care can benefit from having an advocate to ensure that their wishes and feelings are taken into account when important decisions about their lives are made. Children who have complex communication needs can have their views represented through an advocate who knows them well. An independent mental health advocate can help an individual who is in hospital to explore their options and rights in relation to their care.

Interpreters
Interpreters can also facilitate communication (or make communication happen) by converting spoken or sign language from one language into another. For example, sign language interpreters can work with individuals who are deaf and attend

meetings. Interpreting can also be carried out over the telephone for individuals and others whose preferred language is not English and who may need to access information about a health, care or early years service that is available in the local area.

Factors that positively influence communication

Effective communication is influenced by a combination of environmental and interpersonal factors. To be able to use the different types of communication you explored in the previous section, it is important to be aware of these different factors, so that you can ensure that all communications are positive, effective and meaningful.

Environmental factors

The physical environments of health, social care and early years settings can have a positive impact on communication. Holding an individual's **care review** (see page 48 for definition) in a room that is not too hot or too cold and that is well-ventilated (i.e. where air circulates freely) will mean that all those present will feel comfortable and be more likely to listen and interact with each other.

The layout of a play room in a children's centre that has been carefully and safely arranged into separate areas for different activities will promote positive, enjoyable and interactive communications with children. Similarly, the layout of the communal lounge area in a residential care home, including the positioning of armchairs and tables, can lead to an increase in individuals participating in conversations, feeling a sense of belonging and being a part of interactions with others.

Lighting and noise also play an important role in positive communication. Using British Sign Language in a well-lit area will mean that individuals' facial expressions, signs and gestures will be visible and therefore easily understood. A doctor that makes arrangements to speak with a patient and their family in a quiet room will be less likely to be interrupted and/or distracted by others; in addition, a quiet environment, free from noise and distractions, is essential for **active listening**.

Interpersonal factors

Relationships
The nature and quality of relationships between individuals and those who provide them with care and support will have a direct impact on communication.

Working relationships that are developed over time and built on mutual trust and respect are the basis of positive communications where honest exchanges of information and ideas can take place. Caring and supportive relationships will have a positive influence on communication, as the participants will feel valued, understood, listened to and respected. Good quality relationships are underpinned by a willingness and commitment to understand the other person's point of view. This is an essential component in positive communications.

Personal space
Observing and respecting an individual's **personal space** can be a good way of influencing **positive communications**. A young person who feels anxious or nervous about meeting new people or visiting new places may prefer to have more personal space around them; respecting this will make them feel more relaxed in these situations. Getting too close to an individual who you do not know may be misinterpreted; the individual may feel threatened by you invading their personal space.

Key terms

Care review Regular meetings where individuals and others supporting them and working with them discuss whether the individual's care plan is effective and meeting their current needs.

Active listening Being able to focus, understand, interpret and respond to what is being said or expressed.

Personal space The physical area that immediately surrounds a person.

Positive communications Communications that are positive, honest and constructive.

Respecting differences in culture
Communications are influenced by cultural differences. Being aware of the communication differences that exist between cultures will avoid misunderstandings and encourage positive communications. It is important to remember that we are all individuals; even if two individuals are from the same culture it does not mean that both individuals will communicate and respond in the same way.

What is seen as respectful and polite in one culture may be disrespectful and rude in another. For example, finger pointing is commonly used in commands but during communications it can be seen as disrespectful and insulting. It is commonly used in Hispanic cultures for objects and animals only, and in Asian cultures it can be perceived as rude; the whole hand is used instead.

Body language
Being aware of the meaning behind the different non-verbal signals that our bodies are constantly giving out enables us to read more easily what another person is saying and feeling. It also helps us to understand the messages and impressions that we are giving out to others.

Body language can therefore also positively influence communications. Here are a few examples.

- A care assistant who smiles and maintains an open posture when approaching individuals for the first time at a new day service will enable the individuals to feel more relaxed and comfortable.
- A home care worker who visits an older person at home is more likely to positively interact with the individual if they sit next to and lean towards the person when speaking.
- A crèche worker who reads with young children will be more likely to actively engage them if they use positive body language such as head nodding.

Active listening

Active listening is a communication technique that requires the listener to:

- understand, interpret and evaluate what they hear, through **paraphrasing** and **summarising**
- find out the true meaning of what is being communicated, through **open questions**, observing facial expressions, gestures, body language
- show empathy, by reflecting feelings.

The SOLER theory was developed by Gerard Egan and is used by practitioners who work in health, social care and early years settings as a technique for active listening:

- **S**it squarely to the individual, at the 5 o'clock position, to avoid the invasion of their personal space
- **O**pen posture – no crossing of the arms or legs to avoid appearing defensive
- **L**ean slightly in towards the individual – show a genuine interest in what the individual is communicating
- **E**ye contact – not too much and not fixed, to avoid making the individual feel uncomfortable
- **R**elax – maintaining a relaxed posture will in turn enable the individual to feel relaxed.

Active listening is an important communication technique because:

- it is central to creating positive communications
- it is the basis of all trusting and respectful relationships
- it enables interactions to happen easily

- it enables communications to be fully understood
- it is a way of avoiding misunderstandings through clear and accurate communications.

Active listening can positively influence communications in a number of different ways. Here are some examples.

- It may help a GP to fully understand a patient's concerns about taking their medication for a prolonged period of time. The GP may then be able to explain to the patient the benefits of continuing to take their prescribed medication for their current health condition.
- It may help an activity worker who works in a residential care setting to influence the nature and range of activities that are provided to the residents. Active listening will enable the activity worker to understand the diverse needs of the residents and their individual preferences through clear exchanges of information.
- Active listening skills can be very effective in an early years setting in enabling workers to communicate and interact with children completing different activities.

🔑 Key terms

Paraphrasing A way of restating what has been said or heard by clarifying.

Summarising A way of concluding and focusing on key points.

Open questions Questions that encourage the expression of opinions and feelings such as *What? Why? How?*

Stretch activity

Factors that positively influence communication

1 How many factors that positively influence communication can you list?

2 Choose one of the factors and describe it in as much detail as possible. (Aim to produce a **thorough** description. Look at the command word definitions to see what 'thorough' means in the assessment.)

Barriers to communication

Positive communications can at times be distorted, or prevented from taking place, by different types of barrier. If barriers to communication are not recognised and overcome, they can prevent positive communications from taking place. Some of the common barriers to effective communication in health, social care and early years settings are included below.

Language

Patronising, inappropriate use of language or differences in language

The type of language used in verbal communications can prevent positive communications from taking place. For example, a message that includes **patronising language** towards an older adult, or the use of complex and technical terms when documenting a child's progress with their learning and development, are both inappropriate and must be avoided. They are disrespectful and can lead to information not being understood.

Other examples of **inappropriate use of language** include swearing and being rude. Using language in these ways can prevent positive communications from taking place and make it more difficult to engage and interact with individuals and others. Using respectful language that meets individuals' preferences is also very important. For example, some individuals may want to be addressed when spoken to as 'Mr' or 'Mrs'; other individuals may prefer to be addressed by their first names.

Language differences, including regional accents and differences in languages spoken, can make it difficult to understand what is being communicated. For example, if an individual and a support worker do not speak the same language, then they will not be able to understand each other fully. This may cause misunderstandings between what is being said and how it is received and interpreted, as well as make communications very difficult. Regional accents can also sometimes make it difficult to understand the message being communicated; the receiver of the messages may rely on their understanding of only key words and phrases, which can lead to communications being misinterpreted.

Inappropriate body language

Non-verbal forms of communication such as inappropriate body language can also result in the intended meanings behind communications being wrongly interpreted. For example, closely hugging a young person who is upset is appropriate if you are their friend or family member, but not if you are a health or social care professional. Similarly, a health or social care professional who sits in a team meeting with their arms crossed may appear to other members of the team as having something to hide, or not being very approachable.

Tiredness

Being tired can also influence how we communicate and interact with others. A health care assistant who has had very little sleep the night before a morning shift may find it difficult to pass on accurate information to others, due to their words and ideas becoming confused and them feeling grumpy and irritable. Similarly, an individual who has **insomnia** will be less likely to focus when participating in communications with others and may appear uninterested and distracted. Tiredness therefore can have a direct impact on how we communicate with others.

Aggression

Verbal and non-verbal aggressive behaviours such as shouting, swearing, name calling, sarcasm, **emotional abuse** and threatening gestures are harmful and can have a negative impact on communications by causing a range of reactions such as frustration, anger, hostility and anxiety.

 Key terms

Patronising language Using language that makes another person feel that they are not very intelligent or important.

Insomnia A condition that involves difficulties with falling asleep and/or staying asleep.

Emotional abuse The emotional maltreatment or emotional neglect of an individual.

Case study

Negative impact of aggression

Tony is 90 years old and has experienced a recent deterioration in his mobility. This has meant that Tony finds it difficult to mobilise (or move) in his flat on his own and is supported to do so by his sister, Molly, who lives with him, and his son, Kevin, who supports him with his personal care tasks every morning and evening. Molly has arranged for a family meeting to discuss Tony's current and future care needs. Kevin does not believe that there is a need for his two other brothers to be involved in his father's care as they both live over 200 miles away and show no interest in their father.

On the morning of the family meeting Kevin telephones Molly and starts shouting and making threats about the arrangements for the family meeting. Molly gets very upset at her brother's aggression and explains to Tony that she feels very anxious and unsure whether she can continue to manage looking after him. Tony feels overwhelmed by this news and is worried that he may no longer be able to continue living in his flat.

Questions

1 What were the effects of Kevin's aggressive communications?

2 How could Kevin have communicated more positively?

Speech difficulties due to disabilities or illness

Every individual is unique. Disabilities or illnesses can therefore affect individuals in different ways and impact on their communication with others.

Dementia, for example, can affect an individual's ability to communicate because they may not understand what has been said, may not remember what has been said or may have lost their cognitive ability to use spoken language.

Deafness, too, can affect an individual's communication with others as the individual may have difficulty fully understanding all parts of a conversation. This may lead to misunderstandings and/or over-reliance (or being very dependent) on non-verbal forms of communication such as facial expressions and body language, which may be misinterpreted.

The environment

Indoor and outdoor environments can also be barriers to positive communications.

● A noisy environment – loud noises and background noises can be unwelcome distractions to communications, e.g. children playing loudly in the same room where a

nursery worker is trying to speak with a child who is feeling upset.

● Inadequate space – environments where space is insufficient or inadequate can make individuals feel crowded and uncomfortable, e.g. conducting a drama session in a very small room can prevent individuals from expressing themselves.

● Poor lighting – environments that are dimly lit or dark can make it difficult for individuals to see each other while communicating; as non-verbal communication is important, facial expressions and body language may not be seen and therefore messages being communicated may be misinterpreted. For instance, a social worker holding a meeting with a child who is deaf in a room that is poorly lit may prevent the child from participating in the communication as the child may not be able to lip read.

● Damaged or unsuitable furniture – environments containing damaged furniture can create a bad first impression and be distracting during communications. Unsuitable furniture, such as shelves that are too high or tables that are too large, can also act as barriers to communication. For example, a shelf that sits at eye level may prevent a care professional from making eye contact with an individual; this could affect how the individual perceives the care professional and can create an air of mistrust.

Group activity

Read through the communication profiles for two individuals: Ken, who is 65 years old, has dementia and lives in a residential care home, and Skye, who is 4 years old, is deaf and accesses the after school club in her local area. Both profiles have been developed to provide information about how each individual communicates.

COMMUNICATION PROFILE: KEN

My name is Ken and this is my communication profile. Please read this as it will help you get to know me and how I communicate.

ABOUT ME

My family and friends are very important to me; I enjoy their company and talking with them. I have been diagnosed with vascular dementia. I am a real chatterbox but my speech is less fluent than it used to be, so you need to be patient and give me more time when communicating with me. I like to talk about my family, places I've visited on holiday, films I've watched on television and my hobbies: birdwatching and gardening.

Please don't finish my sentences for me, I find this annoying. Please don't assume what I am going to say, this is also very annoying!

You can help me by giving me time to respond to any information or questions you share with me, by not interrupting me and by not asking me too much all at once.

COMMUNICATION PROFILE: SKYE

ABOUT ME
I am deaf in both ears and I wear hearing aids. I enjoy painting and writing stories.

COMMUNICATION METHODS I USE
✓ I lip read some words – to help me do this I need you to avoid covering your mouth when speaking to me or standing in a very dark or very bright room.
✓ I use objects and photographs – to help me to use these, I need you to identify the objects you are using clearly by placing them in front of me. The photographs I use are stored in my photo book and are of people I know who are important to me, and also of places I like going to or have visited.
✓ I use Makaton signs and symbols – to help me to use these you need to understand the signs and symbols I use as well as their meanings. I have a Makaton book with these in.

HELPFUL WAYS TO COMMUNICATE WITH ME
✓ Speak clearly.
✓ Use short sentences.
✓ Do not shout.
✓ Give me time to respond.
✓ If I don't respond, find out if I have understood.
✓ Make sure I can see you clearly.
✓ Use facial expressions and gestures.
✓ Get to know the objects, photographs, Makaton signs and symbols I use.

Figure 2.3 Communication profiles: Ken and Skye

1 In small groups, discuss and reflect on how their speech difficulties may affect their communication with others.

2 Share your findings with the rest of the class.

 Case study

How the environment can be a barrier to positive communication

Read through the three different case scenarios below and answer the following questions:

1 What aspects of each environment could act as barriers to positive communications taking place?

2 Why?

Ron (health care)

Ron arrives by himself at the Accident and Emergency department of his local hospital as he is experiencing severe and persistent chest pains. It is very busy and noisy; the waiting room is full and there is a long queue of people waiting to register.

→

Aafia (social care)

Aafia is a wheelchair user and has recently moved into an accessible flat and enjoys cooking and baking with support from her carer. Aafia likes the flat's layout and location as it is close to the High Street, but the kitchen area is not suitable. It contains shelves that are too high for her to reach and she feels that there is inadequate space for her to turn her wheelchair around in the far end of the kitchen. She has also noticed that although one of the worktops can be adjusted to different heights, the other two cannot. The lounge contains a damaged armchair and a table that is far too high for her to use.

Parent and toddler group (early years)

The local parent and toddler group plan to use the small outdoor space located around the back of the village hall for toddlers to play in and explore. One of the parents thinks that although the activities planned sound enjoyable, the space is not big enough. He has also noticed that the poorly lit corridor leading to the outside space, as well as the shadow cast from the large tree outside the back door, mean that the whole area is poorly lit.

Ways to overcome barriers to communication

Ensuring effective communication is crucial for safe, effective, compassionate and good quality care and support in health care, social care and early years settings. Instead of allowing barriers to positive communications taking place, ways to overcome these barriers must be found, such as **adapting the environment**, using **a calm tone** and **training staff**. Table 2.1 provides a number of different suggestions for overcoming communication barriers. Can you think of any others?

Table 2.1 Ways to overcome different communication barriers

Communication barrier	Ways to overcome communication barriers
Language Example: language differences in terms of country/regional accents between children and staff in a **pre-school playgroup** (see page 54 for definition)	• Use photographs and pictures along with spoken and written words • Develop different language activities for children and **training days for staff** and children to explore the different languages that they use • Ask others to interpret what the children are saying
Aggression Example: an older woman who has dementia is verbally and physically aggressive to her home carer	• Respond calmly; use a **calm tone** of voice, do not use an angry tone of voice • Give the individual plenty of space; do not crowd the individual or invade their personal space • Distract the individual; talk about something the individual likes or show the individual an activity or item they like
Tiredness Example: a care assistant who has worked a night shift has been asked to attend a moving-and-handling training session the following morning	• Change the timing of the training for staff; provide a training session that can be attended by the care assistant after they have been able to rest from the night shift • Provide additional staffing so that the care assistant can be released from their night duties to attend the training session • Change the media used for the training session, e.g. use online training, video clips, a distance-learning course

→

Table 2.1 Ways to overcome different communication barriers *(continued)*

Communication barrier	Ways to overcome communication barriers
Speech difficulties Example: a crèche assistant who is unable to understand what a child that **stammers** is saying	• Provide time for communication with the child, so the child has time to communicate and feels comfortable • **Adapt the environment** by creating a calm and relaxed environment, so the child can also feel relaxed • Slow down speech and reduce the number of questions asked, so the child has time to respond
The indoor environment Example: a team of support workers hold their monthly meeting mid-morning in the small office next to the main entrance of the building, which gets very busy	• **Adapt the environment** by holding the meeting in a larger room, so the team feel relaxed and comfortable when meeting • You can also hold the meeting in a quieter area, so the team will be less likely to be interrupted and/or distracted • Change the time of the meeting, so it can take place at a less busy time and the team will be more likely to feel relaxed – this is another way you can **adapt the environment**
The outdoor environment Example: a young man who has a **hearing impairment** is supported by his advocate to complete his work experience in a garden centre; the outside area in the garden centre gets very busy on Saturdays	• Face the individual directly when communicating with him, so the individual can see you • Speak clearly and do not shout, so the individual can understand what you are communicating • Provide key points in writing, so the individual can refer to this when needed

Key terms

Pre-school playgroup A setting that provides early years education and care for children aged 3 to 5, usually for four hours a day, five days a week.

Stammers When an individual's flow of speech is interrupted through the repeating or prolonging of sounds in words.

Hearing impairment A loss of hearing; it can be mild, moderate or profound, and can affect one ear or both ears.

Overcoming barriers to communication is not easy and can at times be quite challenging. To do it successfully requires a number of key skills, including being:

• able to communicate clearly and effectively
• aware of the potential communication barriers that may exist for different individuals and the methods that are the most appropriate to be used in these situations
• committed to consistently checking understanding of information received.

These skills should help to ensure you are a skilled and effective communicator.

Know it!

1 What are the four different types of communication that care practitioners use?
2 Identify the different ways communication can be adapted for an individual who has a learning disability.
3 Why is a quiet environment essential for active listening?
4 What is the meaning of personal space and why is it important?
5 What is the meaning of the acronym SOLER?

Assessment guidance

Learning Outcome 1: Understand how to communicate effectively

Marking criteria for LO1 Part A

Mark band 1	Mark band 2	Mark band 3
Demonstrates a **basic** understanding of effective communication. Produces a **basic** explanation of some of the different types of communication methods related to a health, social care and early years setting. This may be a list of points with only **partly** relevant examples given.	Demonstrates a **sound** understanding of effective communication. Produces a **sound** explanation of most of the different types of communication methods related to a health, social care and early years setting. Examples given are **clear** and **mostly** relevant to a health, social care and early years setting.	Demonstrates a **thorough** understanding of effective communication. Produces a **thorough** explanation of all the different types of communication methods related to a health, social care and early years setting. Examples given are **detailed** and **wholly** relevant to a health, social care and early years setting and link theory to practice.

 The OCR Model Assignment will ask you to:

- Demonstrate an understanding of how to communicate effectively.
- Produce an explanation of, and include examples of different types of communication methods that are used in a health, social care or early years setting, and their purpose.

 What do the command words mean?

- **Thorough understanding:** Your understanding of effective communication will be extremely attentive to accuracy and detail.
- **Thorough explanation:** Your work is extremely attentive to accuracy and detail with regard to the different types of communication methods related to a health, social care and early years setting.
- **Detailed and wholly relevant:** Examples given are a point-by-point consideration and are fully (to the whole amount) relevant to a health, social care and early years setting and link theory to practice.

You should check the glossary in the Introduction for the definitions of each of the command words from OCR.

Marking criteria for LO1 Part B

Mark band 1	Mark band 2	Mark band 3
Produces a **basic** description of some of the factors that positively influence communication.	Produces a **sound** description of most of the factors that positively influence communication.	Produces a **thorough** description of all the factors that positively influence communication.
Produces a **basic** description of barriers to communication and offers limited ways to overcome them, giving **basic** examples, **few** of which will be relevant to a health, social care and early years setting.	Produces a **sound** description of barriers to communication and offers **detailed** ways to overcome them. Examples given are **sound** and **most** are relevant to a health, social care and early years setting.	Produces a thorough description of barriers to communication and offers **detailed** and **effective** ways to overcome them. Examples given are **detailed** and **wholly** relevant to a health, social care and early years setting and link theory to practice.
There will be **some** errors in spelling, punctuation and grammar.	There will be **minor** errors in spelling, punctuation and grammar.	There will be **few**, if any, errors in spelling, punctuation and grammar.

The OCR Model Assignment will ask you to:

- Describe the factors that positively influence communication.
- Include examples of different barriers to communication and the ways to overcome them. These will be relevant to a health and social care and early years setting.

What do the command words mean?

- **Thorough description:** Your description of all the factors that positively influence communication will be extremely attentive to accuracy and detail.
- **Detailed:** You will produce a through description of barriers to communication and the ways to overcome them will be a point-by-point consideration.
- **Effective:** You will produce a thorough description of barriers to communication and the ways to overcome them which will mean you apply skills appropriately to this task and successfully produce a desired or intended outcome/result.
- **Detailed and wholly relevant:** Examples given are a point-by-point consideration and are fully (to the whole amount) relevant to a health, social care and early years setting and link theory to practice.
- **Few:** You may have a small number of errors in spelling, punctuation and grammar (not many, but more than one).

You should check the glossary in the Introduction for the definitions of each of the command words from OCR.

Learning outcome 2

Understand the personal qualities that contribute to effective care

Now that you have learned about the different types of communication methods that can be used in health, social care and early years settings; the factors that positively influence communication; and the barriers to communication and how to overcome them, we will explore in more detail the many different personal qualities that contribute to effective care and are essential for care practitioners to have.

Getting started

To provide effective care you need skills and knowledge, and most important of all the right personal characteristics. Writing down the qualities you have is one way of communicating to a care employer what makes you unique and the right person to care for and support others.

Write down the top five qualities you think you have. In small groups, discuss one situation in which you've used at least one of your qualities.

The qualities that contribute to effective care

We will look at some of the qualities (patience, understanding, empathy, willingness, sense of humour, cheerfulness) that contribute to effective care. First, here are some useful reminders of what effective care is and of the principles that underpin effective practice in health, social care and early years settings.

'By effective, we mean that people's care, treatment and support achieves good outcomes, promotes a good quality of life and is based on the best available evidence.'

Source: Care Quality Commission (CQC), *The Five Key Questions*, 2016

'Care that is clinically effective – not just in the eyes of clinicians but in the eyes of patients themselves.'

Source: NHS England, *What do we mean by high quality care?*, 2016

The principles that guide the work of all early years practitioners and underpin effective practice in the delivery of the Early Years Foundation Stage are grouped into four themes:

1 A unique child – every child is a unique child who is constantly learning and can be resilient, capable, confident and self-assured.

2 Positive relationships – children learn to be strong and independent from secure, positive relationships with parents and/or a key person.

3 Enabling environments – children learn and develop well in enabling environments, in which their experiences respond to their individual needs and there is a strong partnership between practitioners and parents and/or carers.

4 Learning and development – children develop and learn in different ways and at different rates.

Source: Early Education, *Development Matters in the Early Years Foundation Stage (EYFS)*, 2014

To be able to work in health care, social care and early years settings and provide effective care, you need to have a number of personal, unique qualities. Some of the important ones are included in the QUALITIES acronym below:

- **Q**uick thinker and ability to quickly notice changes in others
- **U**nderstanding
- **A**bility to empathise and be patient
- **L**ikeable, cheerful and approachable
- **I**nterested in and willing to care for and support others
- **T**rustworthy and responsible
- **I**ndividual commitment to respect others and promote their rights
- **E**asily communicates and interacts with others
- **S**ense of humour.

How do personal qualities contribute to effective care?

Without personal qualities, it would not be possible to provide effective care and support, to work with individuals who have diverse needs and with others in a range of different settings. Let us look at some of the qualities that contribute to effective care in more detail, including empowerment, reassurance and value.

Patience

Being patient when working with young children in an early years setting is vital. It involves providing the children with time to express what they want to have or do. For example, a child who uses a wheelchair will require more time to mobilise to the outdoors play area than a child who doesn't; a nursery nurse who is patient will empower the child in the wheelchair to mobilise at their own pace and enable the child to be independent and proud of their ability to do so.

Being patient is a quality that also applies when working with adults, children and young people across different settings.

Understanding

Practising good verbal and written communication skills and ensuring all communications are clear will ensure that information is understood. For example, a support worker, in an adult day care centre for individuals who have a range of disabilities, who provides clearly written, signed and spoken instructions for a morning activity will ensure that the purpose of the activity and how it will work is understood by the individuals who are participating, as well as by the team members who will be supporting the activity.

Empathy

Having an awareness of how a hospital patient may be feeling prior to having an operation (anxious, fearful), and being able to show genuine compassion can have a positive impact on that

Figure 2.4 What qualities are being shown in this interaction?

patient's situation by providing reassurance and comfort. This can also have an impact on the patient's overall experience, which will be more positive.

Respect

Knowing about, understanding and respecting individuals' personal religious beliefs is one of the key qualities health care workers are required to have. For example, a health care assistant in a hospital must show respect for the type of food a Muslim patient has indicated they will and will not eat – the individual may only eat hospital food if it is **halal** (see page 59 for definition). Doing so shows the individual that you value and respect the personal religious beliefs that they hold as important to their life.

Willingness

A desire and commitment to care for and support individuals to live their lives how they choose and prefer to do so is an essential quality that involves putting the wishes and preferences of individuals at the centre. For example, a care worker who supports an older individual with personal care, cooking and shopping must always be willing to listen and respect how the individual wishes to be supported with these daily living activities. Doing so will enable the individual to be in control of their life and live their life as fully as possible and according to their preferences.

Sense of humour

Having a sense of humour can be a good way for those who care and support individuals to get to know them and develop trusting, positive working relationships with them. A good sense of humour can also enable children to develop high self-esteem, confidence and **resilience**. For example, a nursery worker working with young children in a nursery can use humour as a way of bonding with the children and creating a happy and relaxed environment. This in turn can impact on the children by enabling them to enjoy and participate in positive experiences and activities, as well as showing them how not to take themselves too seriously.

Cheerfulness

A cheerful and friendly personality is another important quality that underpins the delivery of effective care. For example, a nursery nurse that welcomes the children in the morning in a cheerful manner will not only convey to the children that she is pleased to see them and reassure their parents that they are in **'safe hands'**, but will also enable them to settle in to the activities that have been planned for the morning in a positive manner.

 Key terms

Halal An Arabic term that means lawful in Islam; in relation to food it refers to the foods that can be eaten according to Islamic law.

Resilience The ability to recover quickly from difficulties.

'Safe hands' A term that refers to being cared for or looked after in a skilled way.

Stretch activity

The personal qualities that contribute to care

1 List the personal qualities that are essential for care practitioners to have.

2 Choose one quality and describe in as much detail as possible how it links to effective care. (Aim to produce a **thorough** description. Look at the command word definitions to see what 'thorough' means in the assessment.)

Case study: Choosing a carer

Ingrid has lived in the same village in England for over 40 years. She knows everyone in the local community and makes time to get to know every person who lives there and their family. Ingrid has a neighbour called Eric, whose long-term partner has recently died. Eric's partner used to manage the day-to-day running of their house and Eric is finding it difficult to manage in the house on his own. Due to difficulties with his mobility he finds it difficult to use the stairs as well as complete practical tasks such as changing the bed linen, vacuuming and putting the rubbish bins out.

Eric has decided that he wants to employ a carer, and has asked Ingrid to help him with employing the right carer. Eric explains to Ingrid that he has a local care organisation and is due to meet with two potential carers for the first time on Friday. He would like Ingrid to be present when he does so. Ingrid is very happy to help and agrees to support him.

Upon arriving at Eric's house, Eric asks each carer to introduce themselves and tell him why they are the right person for the job. Read through both carers' introductions below and then answer the questions that follow.

Carer 1

Good morning, I'm Mrs French and I think I'm the right person for the job because I have had many, many years of caring experience and I know what's best when it comes to care. In terms of why I am the right person for the

 →

job, this is because I am a very hard worker and you can be sure that you can always rely on me to get the job done.

Carer 2

Hello Eric, I'm Katy and I am very pleased to meet with you both today. I live very local to you and I think I may have even seen you a few times in the local shops. Thank you for giving me this opportunity for an interview for a job that I really enjoy. What I like most about being a carer is all the different people I meet and get

to know. I am a very patient person and I think it is very important to always show respect and understanding. I enjoy supporting individuals to live their lives how they want to.

Questions

1 Based on these introductions, which carer should Eric employ?
2 Explain the reasons for your choice of carer.
3 How did each carer's introduction make you feel when you read it through for the first time?

 Research activity

Job roles

Research the personal qualities that are required for the following three job roles:

- mental health nurse
- care assistant
- nursery assistant.

You can use the internet to research these job roles or speak with practitioners from different health, social care and early years settings.

What did you find out about the qualities that are common to all three job roles? Were there any differences?

Know it

1 What does the term 'effective care' mean?
2 Identify two qualities required for effective care.
3 For each quality you identified in Question 2, explain why it is important.
4 Identify two consequences of a care practitioner not having the right personal qualities.

Assessment guidance

Learning Outcome 2: Understand the personal qualities that contribute to effective care

Marking criteria for LO2

Mark band 1	Mark band 2	Mark band 3
Produces a **basic** description of the different personal qualities that contribute to care.	Produces a **sound** description of the different personal qualities that contribute to care.	Produces a **thorough** description of the different personal qualities that contribute to care.
Basic connections are made between personal qualities and effective care and there are **limited** links to how these are used when caring for an individual in a health, social care and early years setting.	**Clear** connections are made between personal qualities and effective care and there are **some** links to how these are used when caring for an individual in a health, social care and early years setting.	**Detailed** and in-depth connections are made between personal qualities and effective care and there are **many** links to how these are used when caring for an individual in a health, social care and early years setting.
Basic examples are used which **partly** illustrate relevant application with **some** justification of personal qualities to be used and why.	**Sound** examples are used which **mostly** illustrate relevant application, with **clear** justification of personal qualities to be used and why.	Excellent examples are used which **wholly** illustrate relevant application, with **clear** and **detailed** justification of personal qualities to be used and why.

The OCR Model Assignment will ask you to:

- Describe the different personal qualities that contribute to effective care.
- Include examples of the different personal qualities that contribute to care and how these are used when caring for an individual in a health, social care and early years setting.

What do the command words mean?

- **Thorough description:** Your description of the different personal qualities that contribute to care will be extremely attentive to accuracy and detail.
- **Detailed:** The connections you make between personal qualities and effective care will be in-depth and be a point-by-point consideration.
- **Many:** There will be a large number of (at least 75% of the expected content) links to how these are used when caring for an individual in a health, social care and early years setting.
- **Wholly, clear and detailed:** Excellent examples are used which to the whole amount/extent illustrate relevant application, with focussed and accurately expressed and point-by-point considered justification of personal qualities to be used and why.

You should check the glossary in the Introduction for the definitions of each of the command words from OCR.

Learning outcome 3

Be able to communicate effectively within a health, social care and early years setting

Having a good understanding of how to communicate effectively and of the personal qualities that contribute to effective care is essential for you to be able to demonstrate how you can communicate effectively within a health, social care and early years setting. In this section, you will learn more about how to plan and communicate effectively in one-to-one and group interactions.

Getting started

To be an effective communicator in health, social care and early years settings you need to have the right skills to communicate in both one-to-one and group situations, and with a range of different people and groups, including individuals, their families, your colleagues and other professionals. Employers in care settings are keen to employ people who are able to interact with others clearly and confidently.

Make a list of your strengths and your weaknesses when communicating with others. What did you find out about the skills you already have and the ones that you want to improve?

How to plan for a one-to-one and group health, social care or early years interaction

Planning one-to-one and group health, social care or early years interactions involves being prepared to find out about the needs and preferences of others, as well as being aware of your own skills and knowledge, including the support you may require to be able to carry these out effectively.

Table 2.2 provides examples of one-to-one and group health, social care and early years interactions that require planning.

Table 2.2 Examples of one-to-one and group interactions

Examples of one-to-one interactions	<ul><li>A hospital patient discussing her dietary preferences with a nurse.</li><li>A support worker holding a meeting with an individual who has mental health needs to discuss an aspect of their treatment.</li><li>A childminder reading a book with a child.</li></ul>
Examples of group interactions	<ul><li>A healthcare assistant reassuring a patient and their family about the patient's recovery following an operation.</li><li>A care assistant supporting three individuals to take part in a coffee morning.</li><li>A crèche assistant singing a song with a group of young children.</li></ul>

Effective planning of one-to-one and group interactions involves taking account of a number of important aspects.

Time

Being realistic about how much time the interaction may take is an important first step; not enough time and the interaction will be rushed and may not achieve all of its agreed **aims** and **objectives** (see page 63 for definitions). Allowing too much time may mean that your own and others' time may be wasted, and you may unintentionally convey an unprofessional approach to others. If it is the first time you are taking part in this interaction then you will need to plan how you are going to find out more about the individual's or group's needs, i.e. by speaking with the individual(s) and with others who know the individual(s) well.

Your plan will also need to confirm with all those involved the time you have set aside for the interaction. It is important that you agree this with all those involved beforehand as not doing so may result in an individual or others not being able to participate in the whole interaction, arriving late or leaving before the end of the interaction. The planning process will also enable you to confirm whether the time you have set aside is sufficient, realistic and suitable to meet the individual(s) and/or others' needs.

Key terms

Aims Desired outcomes, i.e. what you want to achieve.

Objectives How you intend to meet desired outcomes, i.e. how you are going to achieve what you want.

Environmental factors

A good plan must also take into account where the one-to-one or group interaction will be taking place. For example, a nursery can be a very noisy environment and so an allocated quiet, private area may be required and this will need to be planned for.

The type of lighting and the amount of space available will also need to be taken into account. An area that is too dark or too bright may make participants feel uncomfortable and act as a barrier to their participation. For example, a young child who is deaf may not be able to see others' facial expressions in a dark room and may therefore not feel part of the interaction or feel able to contribute.

It is also important to take the space available into consideration. Insufficient space may make participants feel uncomfortable, and they may become distracted and lose interest. Too big a space may also result in participants feeling uncomfortable and lost, and less likely to bond. Arranging the environment in a way that enables positive interactions can make a difference.

For example, a support worker who accompanies an individual who has a learning disability to their GP may find it easier to communicate directly with their GP if the chairs have been arranged in a manner that allows the individual to sit facing the GP. Similarly, a care assistant that facilitates a reminiscence session with a group of older people at a day care centre may find it easier to engage and actively listen to all the group members if they are seated in a semi-circle.

Activity or topic of conversation

Planning an activity or a topic of conversation requires knowledge of the individual(s), including their interests, needs and preferences. In this way, you can be sure that the activity or conversation you have planned is relevant to the individual(s) and the setting they are in.

For example, a nursery worker in a playgroup may plan a one-to-one play activity such as painting or sand and water play, or a group activity such as singing, number and word games. A community care worker who supports older individuals to live independently in their homes may provide one-to-one support to an individual with cooking, or arrange for a healthy lifestyles discussion group with a number of different individuals and their families. A healthcare assistant in a hospital may have a one-to-one conversation with an individual who is in pain in order to make them comfortable, or arrange for several patients to go for a walk in order to improve their mobility.

Figure 2.5 What factors would you have to take into account for outdoor activities?

Case study: A day in the life of Marie, a community care worker

8 a.m. Team meeting in the office

Marie listens attentively to the update provided by the community care manager, Lisa, and her senior colleagues about the two individuals she will be visiting this morning at their homes. Marie clarifies with the team the changes that there are now with Mrs Parkes' morning routine and also the additional Makaton signs and symbols that Mr Howard has requested, via his advocate, be used when helping him to prepare his lunch.

10 a.m. Call to Mrs Parkes

Marie greets Mrs Parkes with a big, friendly smile and asks her how she is. Mrs Parkes explains that she's keeping well and pleased to see Marie as she now also requires assistance with getting out of bed and making a cup of tea. Marie explains that this is not a problem as the office has already informed her of this and provided her with an additional half an hour. While assisting Mrs Parkes, Marie turns towards her and asks her how her visit from her grandson at the weekend went. During the conversation, Marie nods, leans slightly towards Mrs Parkes and makes frequent eye contact with her.

12 p.m. Call to Mr Howard

Marie greets Mr Howard using the 'Hello' Makaton sign and smiles. Mr Howard shows Marie the new Makaton signs and symbols to be used when preparing his lunch. Marie sits down next to Mr Howard and turns slightly towards him while he is showing her these and, after checking with him the meaning of each one, points to the 'Thumbs up' picture in his **communication book**. Mr Howard smiles and walks over to the kitchen with Marie to start preparing his lunch.

On her way home, Marie reflects on the day's activities and the reasons why the interactions today were effective.

Questions

1 What communication skills are being used by Marie?

2 How did Marie's communication skills benefit the one-to-one interactions she has?

3 How did Marie's communication skills benefit the group interaction she has?

 ## Key term

Communication book A way for individuals to communicate through the use of pictures, photographs, signs, symbols and words.

Skills to be used

A knowledge and awareness of verbal and non-verbal communication skills is required for facilitating both one-to-one and group interactions. You may find it useful to review your learning from LO1: Understand how to communicate effectively.

The reasons why practitioners and individuals who use the service need to communicate clearly

One-to-one and group interactions should be underpinned by effective communication between practitioners and individuals, to make sure that individuals' unique needs and preferences are fully met.

Practitioners and individuals who use the service need to communicate clearly in order to:

- give information – giving accurate and clear information promotes understanding, e.g. about who will be providing support to the individual
- obtain information – obtaining accurate information avoids misunderstandings and conflicts from occurring, e.g. about how an individual communicates
- exchange information – exchanging information enables mutual and shared understanding between practitioners and individuals, e.g. about the effectiveness of an individual's care.

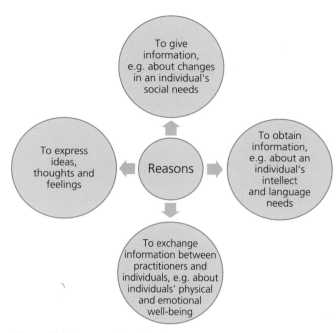

Figure 2.6 Reasons for effective communication

Figure 2.6 summarises the key reasons why practitioners and those who use the service need to communicate clearly.

Clear and effective communication enables the individual to feel valued as a whole person and have all of their needs met, i.e. physical, intellectual, language, emotional and social.

Ensuring the comfort of the individual

When planning interactions the unique comfort preferences of the individual(s) must also be taken into account. For example, an individual who has a learning disability can be supported in different ways when planning how to spend their day. Some individuals may prefer to do this over a coffee with their support worker; others may prefer to discuss it the day before over the telephone; others, on the day, just prior to going out. Knowing this beforehand will ensure the interaction is a positive and effective one.

Similarly, when organising a group activity such as a crafts session, it is important to find out beforehand what seating, layout and room temperature each individual finds comfortable, and what crafts the group enjoy and would like to participate in. In this way you can ensure that you are taking into account the personal preferences of each individual when designing and planning the group activity, to ensure their comfort.

Showing value and respect for the individual

Valuing and respecting each individual is a must in all one-to-one and group interactions. Read through the different ways you can show value and respect for the individual. Can you think of any others?

- Leading by example, i.e. being positive in your communications with the individual, and avoiding the use of disrespectful verbal and non-verbal communication, such as shouting and crossing your arms.
- Listening attentively, i.e. showing a genuine interest in an individual's and group's preferences when planning an activity.
- Recognising differences, i.e. finding out and taking into account an individual's and group's differences when planning an activity.

Creating an accurate and detailed plan will enable you to prepare effectively for all one-to-one and group interactions. This in turn will create a good and professional impression – an essential aspect for contributing to effective care and positive communications.

Stretch activity

Planning for one-to-one and group situations

1 What aspects are important to consider when communicating in one-to-one and group situations?

2 Develop a plan for how to use one of these aspects when planning for a one-to-one communication with a person using the service. (Aim to create a **thorough** plan. Look at the command word definitions to see what **thorough** means in the assessment.)

How to communicate effectively in a one-to-one and group situation

Now that you have created an appropriate plan for how to participate in a one-to-one and group interaction, you are ready to put into practice all the communication skills you have learned.

Active listening

Review your learning of Gerard Egan's SOLER theory, which is used by practitioners who work in health, social care and early years settings as a technique for active listening. You may like to look back at where active listening was discussed in LO1: Understand how to communicate effectively.

Appropriate body language

As you have learned, active listening is not the only important skill you need in order to be an effective communicator; being aware of your own and others' body language is also very important.

Maintaining eye contact

As you will have read earlier in this unit, how long and how frequently you maintain eye contact during an interaction will depend upon the individual's preferences and the situation. Too much and this could be interpreted as quite intimidating, too little could indicate that you are not interested and not to be trusted.

For example, when discussing a care plan with an individual who lives in a residential care home, you will need to find out the individual's preferred method of communicating, including how to use eye contact and how much should be maintained during the interaction. It may be that when discussing specific parts of the care plan, such as the individual's social and religious needs, it is helpful to maintain eye contact to show the individual that you are actively listening to what they are saying, but when discussing other aspects, such as their physical care needs, it is best to avoid making eye contact so as not to embarrass the individual. Remember, every

---

Group activity

Role play

Read the case study, 'A day in the life of Marie, a community care worker', again. Discuss how SOLER is used by Marie to:

- concentrate on what is being said – how does Marie focus her attention on the information being given to her by her colleagues and the individuals she supports?
- understand what individuals and key people are trying to convey – what are the different methods that Marie uses to ensure she has fully understood the information provided to her by her colleagues and the individuals she supports?
- interpret the information being given – how does Marie make sense of the information being given to her by the individuals she supports?
- repeat information if necessary – what techniques does Marie use to repeat and clarify information?
- respond to information appropriately – what verbal and non-verbal communication methods does Marie use to ensure her responses to each person she communicates with are suitable for their needs?
- actively encourage others to communicate – how does Marie enable the individuals she supports to participate in communications with her?
- reflect – how does Marie think back over her day's activities?

Now, role play Marie's case study in a small group and ensure that each person involved in the interactions with Marie also uses the SOLER theory. Then swap roles within the group.

Were there any differences between how these were role played? How did this impact on the effectiveness of the group interaction with the team and the one-to-one interactions with Mrs Parkes and Mr Howard?

individual is unique and so are their preferences for the use of eye contact during interactions.

Using hand gestures

Hand gestures, similar to eye contact, can also have different meanings depending on how they are used. For example, a nursery manager needs to be able to communicate effectively at all times with the staff who work in the nursery, the children who attend, their parents and families, as well as external agencies such as **Ofsted** and **social services**.

When talking to members of staff, it is important that the hand gestures that accompany their words also indicate that they are friendly, approachable and can be trusted, i.e. open arms rather than folded arms, and avoiding finger pointing and covering their mouth with their hand while speaking.

Appropriate facial expressions

It is also very important to be aware of your own facial expressions and how to control them in certain situations. For example, if a child discloses to their childminder that they are being abused by a family member it is important that the childminder does not look shocked. Doing so may make the child think that they are to blame, or feel awkward or embarrassed.

Similarly, when a nurse informs a patient's family that their relative has passed away during the night, their facial expressions are just as important, if not more important, than the words they use to convey their compassion and empathy. A caring, understanding facial expression can be demonstrated where the eyebrows are pulled in and up, the lips are pressed together and the head is in a position where it leans forward slightly.

Adapting and using appropriate language

Effective communication also involves being able to use appropriate language, and knowing how to adapt language to ensure that all communications are respectful, understood and interpreted in the way that they were intended.

Allowing pauses

Pauses in communications can impact positively on your understanding and that of others.

Allowing pauses can enable you to:

- think before you speak, i.e. to choose the correct and appropriate words
- read others' body language, i.e. to ascertain whether they understand and are interested in what you are saying; if not, then this gives you an opportunity to adapt your communication.

Allowing pauses can enable others to:

- think about what you are saying, i.e. it provides them with time to understand what you are saying and respond
- listen attentively to what you are saying, i.e. it provides them with time to clarify their understanding.

For example, when a **radiography assistant** explains to a patient how to position themselves for an x-ray, the use of pauses when giving instructions will enable the patient to think about what they are being asked to do and be able to follow the instructions they are being given accurately.

 Key terms

Ofsted (the Office for Standards in Education, Children's Services and Skills) Inspects and regulates services that care for children and young people, and services providing education and skills for learners of all ages.

Social services A range of public services provided by the UK government and private organisations, such as in relation to housing, healthcare and social care.

Radiography assistant A practitioner who works under the supervision of a radiographer to diagnose a patient's illness, disease or condition, and treat medical conditions through the use of x-rays and imaging.

Tone and pace

Tone of voice and pace when speaking are very important, particularly with children, who begin to notice changes in tone of voice from an early age. For example, a nursery assistant who reads a story to a group of children can inject tones of happiness, excitement, fear and sadness into their story-telling by changing the tone of their voice and the pace at which they speak. A high tone of voice can portray happiness, a hurried pace can portray excitement, a low tone and slow pace can portray fear, and a low, hesitant tone with pauses could portray sadness.

Clarity of information

The use of clear, explicit language will ensure that all information provided is understood by the individual. This needs to be adapted for each individual so it is appropriate to their needs. For example, when a support worker provides information to a group of individuals who have learning disabilities about healthy options for food and drink, the information will need to be presented in a variety of ways to ensure every member of the group understands the options available. For some individuals this may include short words and pictures of foods, for others photographs of foods and/or an audio version of what the support worker says may be required. For some, the support worker may need to repeat the information; for others, the individuals may need to discuss the information presented to them with an advocate.

Use the individuals' preferred means of communication

Using the individuals' preferred means of communication is crucial for communicating effectively in both one-to-one and group situations in health, social care and early years settings. It is important to find out what an individual's preferred means of communication is and not make any assumptions about what these may be. Remember too that individuals' preferred means of communication may change depending on the situation.

You can find out about individuals' preferred means of communication from:

- the individual
- the individual's representative, i.e. advocate
- others who know the individual well, i.e. your colleagues, the individual's family and/or friends
- their care or support plan
- their communication profile.

Case study: Meeting individuals' communication needs

Read about the work that Liza, Pierre and Shamilee do, and then answer the questions that follow.

Liza

Liza works as a volunteer befriender in a **hospice** (see page 69 for definition), providing companionship and social interaction to patients who have a life-limiting illness and/or palliative care needs. Liza is currently using photographs of familiar places, activities and people that are important to one individual who has **Down's syndrome** (see page 69 for definition). Doing so has enabled Liza to build up a trusting relationship with this individual and enabled the individual to develop their self-confidence and emotional well-being.

Pierre

Pierre works in a day care centre as an activities worker providing care and support to individuals who have dementia. When supporting individuals to enjoy their day, either through social activities such as gentle exercise or gardening, or by pursuing their own interests and hobbies, Pierre always ensures he uses the individuals' preferred means of communication. For example, Ella has dementia, is bilingual and speaks both Italian and English but prefers to communicate in English when at the day care centre. John prefers Pierre to use short sentences and non-complex words when speaking with him.

Shamilee

Shamilee works in a pre-school with children aged between three and five as an early years teacher. Her responsibilities include developing children's social and communication skills, and maintaining good working relationships with →

others who work in the pre-school, as well as with the children's parents and families. When working with the children, Shamilee ensures that she finds out the preferred means of communication for every child. She then uses this information to ensure that the activities she develops meets their unique needs – for example, by ensuring that all stories, songs and games that she develops and uses with the children appeal to the five senses: sight, hearing, taste, smell and touch.

Questions

1 How did the practitioners in each of the case scenarios adapt their communications to meet individuals' preferred communication methods?

2 What positive impacts did Liza's adapted communications have on the individual she supported as a befriender?

Key terms

Hospice A service that provides treatment and support to patients who have a life-limiting illness and/or palliative care needs, and their families.

Down's syndrome A genetic condition that typically causes learning disabilities and some physical characteristics.

As you will have learned, being able to communicate effectively in a one-to-one and group situation involves many different skills, up-to-date knowledge and numerous personal qualities. Being an effective communicator can bring about exciting and positive outcomes not only for those individuals who use health, social care and early years services but also for those who work within these.

Stretch activity

The ability to communicate effectively

1 Describe the verbal and non-verbal communication skills that are essential for communicating confidently and competently. (Aim to demonstrate these skills **effectively**. Look at the command word definitions to see what **effective** means.)

2 Choose one situation and demonstrate how the use of verbal and non-verbal communication methods can contribute to effective communication. (Aim to show a **clear** consideration of the use of these communication methods. Look at the command word definitions to see what **clear** means in the assessment.)

Know it!

1 Describe two important requirements for planning a group interaction.

2 Identify two reasons why care practitioners need to communicate clearly.

3 Give one example of how a care practitioner can show respect for an individual.

4 Describe how the tone of your voice can give out different messages to others.

Assessment guidance

Learning outcome 3: Be able to communicate effectively within a health, social care and early years setting

Marking criteria for LO3 Part A

Mark band 1	Mark band 2	Mark band 3
Creates a **basic** plan for the practical tasks of communicating with people who use the service, both in a one-to-one and in a group situation.	Creates a **sound** plan for the practical tasks of communicating with people who use the service, both in a one-to-one and in a group situation.	Creates a **thorough** plan for the practical tasks of communicating with people who use the service, both in a one-to-one and in a group situation.

 ### The OCR Model Assignment will ask you to:

- Create a plan of how to communicate effectively with people who use a health, social care and early years service.
- Include two plans for communicating in both a one-to-one and in a group situation.

 ### What do the command words mean?

- **Thorough plan:** You will produce an extremely accurate and detailed plan of the practical tasks involved in communicating with people who use the service, both in a one-to-one and group situation.

You should check the glossary in the Introduction for the definitions of each of the command words from OCR.

Marking criteria for LO3 Part B

Mark band 1	Mark band 2	Mark band 3
May need guidance and support when demonstrating **basic** communication skills, but relates positively to the service users and maintains, at a **basic** level, a conversation with them. Shows **some** application of theory into practice.	Demonstrates confident and **competent** communication skills requiring little support, relating positively to the people who use the service, **effectively** maintaining a conversation with them.	Demonstrates confident, clear and **coherent** communication skills **independently**, relating positively to the people who use the service, **consistently** maintaining a conversation with them. Clearly applies theory to practice.

→

Marking criteria for LO3 Part B (continued)

Methods of communication used are **sometimes** appropriate to the individual circumstances, but people who use the service may not always feel comfortable.

Basic consideration shown of the use of body language and how it can contribute to effective communication.

Basic examples are given of the types of behaviour that fail to value people.

Basic consideration is shown of the importance of adapting language in order to meet the needs of people who use the service.

Draws upon **limited** skills/knowledge/understanding from other units in the specification.

Shows the ability to apply theory to practice.

Methods of communication used are **mostly** appropriate to the individual circumstances, and people who use the service mainly feel comfortable.

Clear consideration shown of the use of body language and how it can contribute to effective communication.

Sound examples are given of the types of behaviour that fail to value people.

Clear consideration is shown of the importance of adapting language in order to meet the needs of people who use the service.

Draws upon **some relevant** skills/knowledge/understanding from other units in the specification.

Methods of communication used are **wholly** appropriate to the individual circumstances, and people who use the service always feel comfortable.

Thorough consideration shown of the use of body language and how it can contribute to effective communication.

Detailed examples are given of the types of behaviour that fail to value people.

Clear and **comprehensive** consideration shown of the importance of adapting language in order to meet the needs of people who use the service.

Clearly draws upon **relevant** skills/knowledge/understanding from other units in the specification.

 The OCR Model Assignment will ask you to:

- Give a practical demonstration of how to communicate appropriately with people who use a health, social care or early years service.
- Show that you can use methods of communication appropriate to the individual circumstances, and ensure people who use the service feel comfortable.
- Show consideration of use of body language and how it can contribute to effective communication.
- Include some supplementary work about the types of behaviour that fail to value people.
- Show consideration of the importance of adapting language to meet the needs of people who use the service.
- Draw upon skills, knowledge and understanding from other units.

 What do the command words mean?

- **Coherent, independent and consistent:** You will demonstrate confident, clear, logical, and consistent communication skills without relying on others. The skills you demonstrate should relate positively to the people who use the service, and you will be able to consistently maintain a conversation with them, and clearly apply theory to practice.
- **Wholly:** The methods of communication you use will be wholly (to the whole amount/extent) appropriate to the individual circumstances and people who use the service will feel comfortable.
- **Thorough:** You will be extremely attentive to accuracy and detail when using body language and how it contributes to effective communication.
- **Detailed:** This will include a point-by-point consideration of the examples of types of behaviour that fail to value people.

→

- **Clear and comprehensive:** You will show focussed and accurately expressed consideration (without ambiguity) of the importance of adapting language in order to meet the needs of people who use the service. This will be complete and include everything that is necessary to evidence understanding in terms of both breadth and depth.
- **Clearly and relevant:** You will draw upon skills/knowledge/understanding from other units in the specification in a focussed, accurately expressed way (without ambiguity) and this will be correctly focussed on the activity.

You should check the glossary in the Introduction for the definitions of each of the command words from OCR.

Read about it

Weblinks

www.actiononhearingloss.org.uk Action on Hearing Loss – information and factsheets on communicating and supporting people who are deaf, deafblind or have a hearing loss.

www.makaton.org The Makaton Charity – information on Makaton and how it is used with young children and adults.

www.rnib.org.uk Royal National Institute of Blind people – information on using assistive technology and specialist forms of communication for people who have sight loss, blind or are partially sighted.

www.scie.org.uk Social Care Institute for Excellence – e-learning resources including content on good communication skills and how to apply them.

Reference books

Butler, S. J. (2004) *Hearing and Sight Loss – A Handbook for Professional Carers*, Age Concern England.

Morris, C., Ferreiro Peteiro, M. and Collier, F. (2015) *Level 3 Health and Social Care Diploma*, Hodder Education.

Moss, B. (2015) *Communication Skills in Health and Social Care* (3rd edition), Sage Publications Ltd.

Snow, A. and Telling, A. (2011) 'Video Analysis. Developing good practice with people who have sensory impairment and limited communication skills: a framework for reflective practice', Sense. Also available at: www.sense.org.uk/sites/default/files/Developing_Good_Working_Practice_Video_Analysis_0.pdf

R023 Understanding body systems and disorders

About this unit

Studying this unit will give you an introduction to three major body systems: the cardiovascular, respiratory and digestive systems. You will develop a broad knowledge and understanding of how the body works and keeps us alive through the functions of major organs and the interaction of the three body systems.

You will learn what happens when the body systems do not function correctly, by exploring the symptoms of disorders and looking at how these affect the health and well-being of an individual. You will discover the methods and techniques used to diagnose different types of disorder.

By studying this unit you will find out about methods that can be used to assess how well the cardiovascular, respiratory and digestive systems are working. You will also have the opportunity to carry out basic measures of health and learn how to analyse the results.

Learning outcomes

LO1: Know how body systems work

LO2: Understand disorders that affect body systems

LO3: Be able to interpret data obtained from measuring body rates with reference to the functioning of healthy body systems

How will I be assessed?

You will be assessed through a series of assignment tasks, which are set by OCR. The assignment will be marked by your tutor and then moderated by OCR.

For LO1, you need to:

- demonstrate knowledge of how the cardiovascular, respiratory and digestive systems work
- provide information to illustrate the structure of the cardiovascular, respiratory and digestive systems, making links between structure and function
- describe the functionality of each of the systems.

For LO2, you need to:

- describe the symptoms of one disorder associated with the cardiovascular system, one associated with the respiratory system and one related to the digestive system, giving reasons for the symptoms
- provide a list of the methods of diagnosis for each disorder
- make links between the disorder and the structure and/or functionality of the system.

For LO3, you need to:

- demonstrate measuring body rates
- interpret data obtained from measuring body rates and compare against the norms, making reference to the functioning of healthy body systems
- draw on relevant skills/knowledge/ understanding from other units in the specification.

Note: SPAG is assessed in this learning outcome.

Make sure you refer to the current OCR specification and guidance.

Links to other units

Unit R022: Communicating and working with individuals in health, social care and early years settings (LO1): You could explain how you used your verbal skills such as tone of voice and clarity when working with an individual to take their body measurements.

Unit R025 (optional unit): Understanding life stages (LO3): You could describe how you used your knowledge of medical conditions such as heart disease to inform your work about the symptoms, diagnosis and effects of disorders of the cardiovascular system.

Unit R029 (optional unit): Understanding the nutrients needed for good health (LO2): You could explain how you used your understanding of special dietary requirements for different dietary conditions to help explain links between disorders and the functioning of the digestive system.

Learning outcome 1

Know how body systems work

Getting started

Write down the names of the body systems you know.

Under each body system, list the organs you can think of that are part of the system.

Compare your lists with those of the rest of the class.

Research activity

Finding out about body systems

Carry out some internet-based research into body systems. Explore how they work. Focus on the cardiovascular, respiratory and digestive systems.

Healthline.com and BBC Bitesize are good places to start. They have interactive diagrams that show how the body systems work. For example, look at:

● www.healthline.com/human-body-maps

● www.bbc.co.uk/schools/gcsebitesize/ pe/appliedanatomy/0_anatomy_ circulatorysys_rev1.shtml

 Key terms

Cardiovascular system Cardio = heart and vascular = blood vessels. The heart pumps blood around the body, which is transported by blood vessels.

Deoxygenated blood Blood that has no oxygen, but does contain carbon dioxide.

Oxygenated blood Blood that contains oxygen.

Valves Valves are found in veins and ensure a one-way flow of blood.

The cardiovascular system

The **cardiovascular system** is also known as the circulatory system.

The structure of the cardiovascular system

The heart is a muscle that pumps blood around the body. The blood delivers oxygen, nutrients, hormones and antibodies to the cells that make up the body. Blood also removes carbon dioxide and other waste products. The heart is made from specialised cardiac muscle that does not tire like other muscles around the body.

Figure 3.1 shows the structure of the human heart. The heart is split into four chambers: the two upper chambers are called the right and left atriums; the two lower chambers are called the right and left ventricles. The left ventricle has the thickest muscular wall as it has to pump blood from the heart to the rest of the body. Each of the four heart chambers has a major blood vessel entering or leaving it.

Figure 3.1 also shows the other main parts of the heart.

● The aorta is the main artery of the body. It leaves the heart from the left ventricle

● The pulmonary artery carries the **deoxygenated** blood from the heart to the lungs

● The superior (anterior) vena cava is one of the largest veins in the body. This carries blood from the head, arms and upper body into the heart

● The inferior vena cava carries blood from the lower body into the heart

● The pulmonary vein carries **oxygenated** blood from the lungs to the left atrium of the heart.

There are four **valves** in the heart. The valves permit blood to flow one way only.

● The *tricuspid* is the first valve that blood encounters as it enters the heart; it allows blood to flow only from the right atrium to the right ventricle

● The *pulmonary* valve is at the opening from the right ventricle and stops blood going back from the pulmonary artery into the heart

● The *mitral* (*bicuspid*) allows blood to flow from the left atrium to the left ventricle.

● The *aortic* valve is found at the exit of the left ventricle where the aorta begins.

Anatomy of the Human Heart

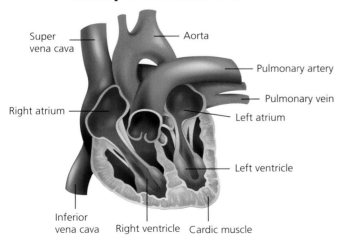

Figure 3.1 The structure of the human heart

Table 3.1 Comparing arteries and veins

Arteries	Veins
Blood is carried away from the heart.	Blood is carried towards the heart.
The blood being carried is oxygenated.	The blood being carried is deoxygenated.
The blood flows quickly under high pressure.	The blood flows slowly under low pressure.
The blood flows in pulses.	The blood flows smoothly with a squeezing action.
The artery walls are thick, elastic and muscular.	The vein walls are thin and they have little muscle.
Arteries do not have valves, except at the base of the large arteries leaving the heart.	Veins have valves.
The internal diameter is small.	The internal diameter is large.
An artery cross-section is round.	A vein cross-section is oval.

Arteries, veins and capillaries are the three different types of blood vessels that together comprise the transport system for the blood.

Figure 3.2 shows the structure of arteries and veins.

Now have a look at Table 3.1, which compares the structure and function of arteries and veins.

Capillaries are the smallest blood vessels and have walls made of a single layer of cells. The thin walls of capillaries allow the exchange of water, oxygen, carbon dioxide, nutrients and waste between blood and the surrounding tissues.

The function of the cardiovascular system
Circulation of blood around the body
The heart is a 'double pump'.

- The right-hand side pumps deoxygenated blood from the veins to the lungs for oxygenation.
- The left-hand side pumps oxygenated blood from the lungs to the body.

The dividing wall between the two sides is called the septum. This keeps the two halves completely separated, and through this the cardiac impulses that make the heart beat are carried. As we saw in Table 3.1, arteries carry oxygenated blood away from the heart and veins carry deoxygenated blood to the heart.

Figure 3.3 on page 77 summarises how the human circulatory system works. Red represents oxygenated blood and blue shows deoxygenated blood.

ARTERY AND VEIN

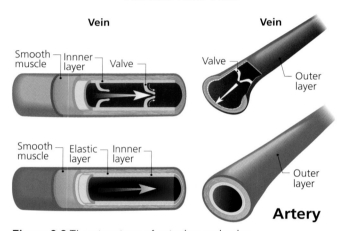

Figure 3.2 The structure of arteries and veins

Here is how blood flow through the heart takes place.

- Blood from the lungs, which is oxygenated, returns to the heart via the pulmonary vein and enters the left atrium.
- Blood passes through the mitral (bicuspid) valve into the left ventricle.
- Blood is forced out of the aorta and carries the oxygenated blood to the rest of the body.
- Deoxygenated blood returns from the body to the right atrium via the superior and anterior (or inferior) vena cava.
- The blood is then squeezed through the tricuspid valve into the right ventricle.
- Blood is forced through the pulmonary artery, which carries the deoxygenated blood to the lungs.

The respiratory system
The respiratory system enables us to maintain a supply of oxygen to the body, which is essential for life.

Case study: Martin

Martin has been diagnosed with a heart condition called atherosclerosis. This condition is caused by the build-up of fatty material in the lining of the artery walls. This narrows the arteries so not enough blood can flow through them.

Martin's doctor has told him that atherosclerosis can affect all of the arteries, but particularly those that supply blood to the heart, the neck arteries that supply blood to the brain, and the arteries that supply the legs.

Martin does not really understand how the blood circulation in his body works or why his blocked arteries affect his circulation. He has asked you to help explain it to him.

Questions

1 Martin does not know what an artery is. Produce a factsheet for him with an illustration to show how an artery works and how it is different from a vein.

2 How does blood flow through the body? Write an explanation for Martin that includes a simple labelled diagram to illustrate the blood flow through the body and why arteries are so important.

HUMAN CIRCULATORY SYSTEM

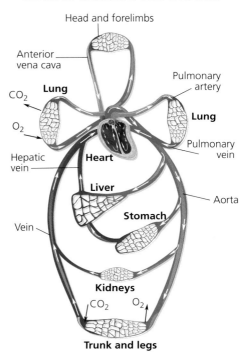

Figure 3.3 How the human circulatory system works

Group activity

Blood flow

● In groups, decide the correct order of the following blood vessels for the flow of blood through the heart:
  ● vena cava
  ● pulmonary vein
  ● pulmonary artery
  ● aorta.
● Then produce a poster to illustrate blood flow through the heart. Label each of the blood vessels with a description of its function.

The Respiratory System

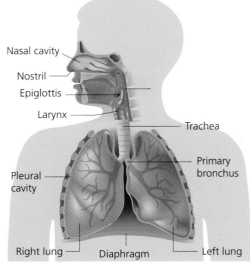

Figure 3.4 Structure of the respiratory system

The structure of the respiratory system

Figure 3.4 shows the structure of the respiratory system.

Trachea

The trachea is also known as the windpipe; it connects the nose and mouth to the lungs. It starts at the back of the throat (pharynx) and divides into two bronchi, each leading into one of the lungs, where they continue to divide to form smaller bronchioles (described in more detail below).

The trachea is a tube of bone, and bronchi are tubes that have rings of **cartilage** along their length, joined together with stretchy tissue called ligaments, to stop the tube collapsing. The rings are 'C' shaped in the trachea with a gap at the back to allow food to travel down the oesophagus (the 'food pipe' see page 79 for more information), which needs to stretch as food passes down.

Lungs

There is one lung on each side of the **thorax** (chest). The lungs are enclosed in the thoracic cavity by the ribs, which are attached to the **sternum** (shown in Figure 3.5). The lungs are cone shaped. The right lung is larger than the left because there is more room for it; the left lung has to share space with the heart. The lungs consist of a network of branching tubes called bronchioles – think of these as the branches of an upside-down tree. At the end of the smallest bronchioles are tiny sacs called alveoli (shown in Figure 3.4).

On the outside, the lungs are covered with a thin, moist membrane known as the pleura. The pleura lines the chest cavity so that the two pleural layers will slide over each other when breathing in and out. This enables the lungs to move with the chest wall as breathing occurs.

Alveoli

As mentioned above, at the end of the tiniest bronchioles are the microscopic alveoli. They are arranged in clusters in the lungs. There are about 300 million alveoli in your lungs.

🔑 Key terms

Cartilage A strong and stretchy connective tissue between bones. It is not as hard and rigid as bone, but is stiffer and less flexible than muscle tissue.

Thorax The part of the body just above the abdomen and below the neck; it includes the ribcage, which encloses the heart and lungs.

Sternum A narrow bone connected with the ribs, also known as the breastbone.

The function of the respiratory system

The function of the respiratory system is to deliver oxygen into the body by breathing in (inhaling) and to remove the waste carbon dioxide gas by breathing out (exhaling).

As air is breathed in through the nose (nasal cavity) it is warmed, moistened and cleaned. Tiny hairs called cilia collect any dust particles, which prevents these getting through to the bronchioles. The cells lining the nose and trachea make slimy mucus, which traps the dust and germs. The cilia 'beat' to carry the mucus and make it flow towards the nose where it exits the body.

When sucking in air from the atmosphere (inhalation), the **intercostal muscles** pull the ribcage upwards and outwards and the **diaphragm** expands (see page 79 for definitions). The result of these two movements is an increase in volume and decrease in pressure, which forces air into the lungs so that they inflate.

When breathing out (exhalation), the reverse happens. The diaphragm relaxes and the intercostal muscles pull the ribcage inwards and downwards. These two movements force carbon dioxide out of the lungs and they deflate.

Figure 3.5 shows the process of inhaling and exhaling.

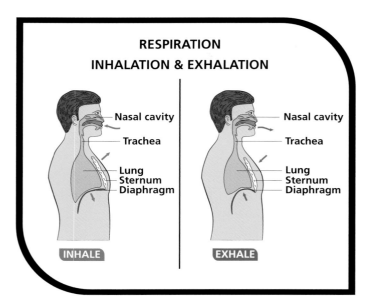

RESPIRATION
INHALATION & EXHALATION

Nasal cavity
Trachea
Lung
Sternum
Diaphragm
INHALE

Nasal cavity
Trachea
Lung
Sternum
Diaphragm
EXHALE

Figure 3.5 Inhalation and exhalation

Stretch activity

How do they work?

- Produce a flow chart that shows the process of breathing. Include pictures of the key parts of the respiratory system involved in the process.
- Add an explanation of how the structure of alveoli helps to carry out gaseous exchange.
- Find information in this chapter and other sources such as GCSE Bitesize:

http://www.bbc.co.uk/schools/gcsebitesize/science/triple_ocr_gateway/the_living_body/respiratory_systems/revision/3/

(Aim to produce a **detailed** and **coherent** explanation. Look at the command word definitions to see what **detailed** and **coherent** means in the assessment.)

Gas exchange in the alveoli

The exchange of oxygen and carbon dioxide takes place in the alveoli, which were mentioned above. The walls of the alveoli are very thin (one cell thick) and each alveoli is surrounded by capillaries through which gases are exchanged.

Alveoli look like bunches of grapes – this increases their surface area, which allows the maximum crossover, or diffusion, of the two gases back and forth to make the process very efficient. As you can see in Figure 3.6, diffusion allows the oxygen to move out of the alveoli to the capillaries and into the bloodstream, and the carbon dioxide to move out of the capillaries into the alveoli and to the lungs to be exhaled.

Key terms

Intercostal muscles Muscles found between the ribs.

Diaphragm A muscle anchored to the lower ribs, which separates the chest from the abdomen.

The digestive system

The digestive system processes the breakdown and absorption of food, and the removal of waste food materials from the body. The four stages of the digestive process are shown in Figure 3.7.

The structure of the digestive system

As Figure 3.8 illustrates, the digestive tract starts with the mouth and ends at the anus.

Oesophagus (or esophagus)

The oesophagus is a muscular tube about 25–30 centimetres long. It begins at the back of

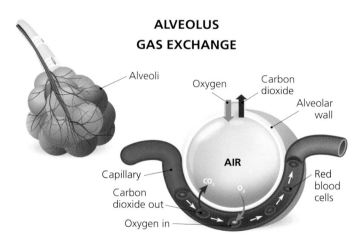

ALVEOLUS GAS EXCHANGE

Alveoli

Oxygen

Carbon dioxide

Alveolar wall

AIR

Capillary

Carbon dioxide out

Oxygen in

Red blood cells

Figure 3.6 Gas exchange in the alveoli

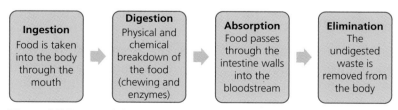

Ingestion
Food is taken into the body through the mouth

Digestion
Physical and chemical breakdown of the food (chewing and enzymes)

Absorption
Food passes through the intestine walls into the bloodstream

Elimination
The undigested waste is removed from the body

Figure 3.7 Stages of the digestive process

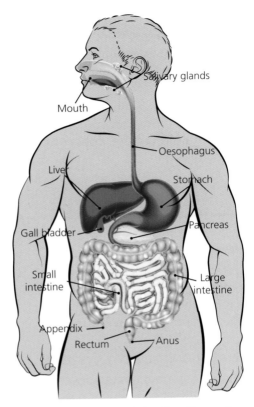

Figure 3.8 Structure of the digestive system

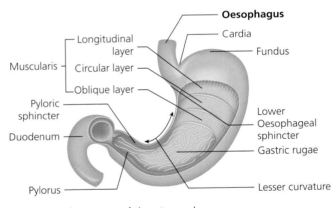

Figure 3.9 Structure of the stomach

Stomach
Figure 3.9 shows the structure of the stomach.

The stomach is sac (bag) shaped and has muscular walls. In an adult it expands during digestion of food to hold up to about one and a half litres, although this does vary from person

> ### 🔑 Key terms
>
> **Cardia** Where the contents of the oesophagus empty into the stomach.
>
> **Sphincter** A circular muscle that narrows a body passage. Examples are the pyloric sphincter at the lower end of the stomach and the anal sphincter.

to person. As mentioned above, the oesophagus enters at the top of the stomach. The duodenum leaves from the lower end of the stomach.

Two **sphincters** keep the contents of the stomach in place – the oesophageal sphincter and the pyloric sphincter. These sphincters are ring-like muscles that close the opening and can relax when necessary to allow contents to pass through.

The fundus is formed by the upper curved area at the top of the stomach. The pylorus is the lower section of the stomach where the contents empty into the small intestine.

The lining of the stomach consists of large folds called gastric rugae (wrinkles). When empty, the surface is wrinkled. The folds reduce because they expand when the stomach fills.

As Figure 3.9 shows, the main body of the stomach consists of three muscular layers that contract and churn food, turning it into chyme (partly digested food), which passes through the pyloric sphincter into the duodenum.

Intestines
In the digestive system, there is the small and large intestine.

- The small intestine consists of the duodenum, jejunum and the ileum. It is a muscular tube about seven metres long. The walls of the intestine are covered with small finger-like structures called villi. Once nutrients have been absorbed, the remaining food moves through to the large intestine.
- The large intestine (colon) is the last part of the digestive system. It is a two-metre-long muscular tube that connects the small intestine to the rectum.

the mouth and joins the top of the stomach at the **cardia**. Food moves down the oesophagus and then enters the stomach.

The function of the digestive system

The main functions of the digestive system are to break down food to absorb the nutrients and minerals required by the body, and to remove waste from the body. When you are looking at the section below, you may find it useful to refer back to Figure 3.8.

Ingestion

Food enters the digestive tract through the mouth, where it is chewed and broken up into particles small enough to be swallowed. As the food is chewed it is mixed with saliva, which contains an **enzyme** called amylase. This starts to break down **carbohydrates** from food into sugars. The food and saliva form a soft mass called a bolus.

When the bolus is swallowed, it then moves down the throat (pharynx) into the oesophagus. The movement of the food is helped by wave-like muscular movements in the oesophagus called peristaltic contractions, or peristalsis.

Digestion

From the oesophagus, the food enters the stomach. The layers of stomach muscle churn and break down the food further using gastric juices and bile from the liver, which helps to digest fat. Bile is made in the liver and stored in the gall bladder, releasing it when needed.

Absorption

After about four to five hours of processing, the food moves into the first part of the small intestine, the duodenum, where digestion continues for about four hours. Enzymes released by the pancreas further break down the food so nutrients can be used.

The ileum is specially adapted. It has many tiny villi lining the small intestine walls, increasing the available surface area and making absorption of nutrients from the food very efficient. At this stage the nutrients are small enough to be absorbed through the wall of the small intestine into the bloodstream.

Elimination

After about seven to nine hours, food that has not been digested will move into the large intestine, where any remaining water is absorbed from it. This leaves the faeces, which are stored in the rectum before being expelled through the anus. The anus is a sphincter, which relaxes at a convenient time to release the faeces.

🔑 Key terms

Enzymes Chemical substances found in the body; they cause key chemical reactions to happen, such as during the digestion of food.

Carbohydrates Essential nutrients from food that provide energy.

Stretch activity

What happens next?

● Stephen has just eaten a cheeseburger and chips. Write a detailed description of how this meal is digested.

● Your description needs to show that you know how the parts of the digestive system work together to perform the digestive process.

(Look at the command word definitions to see what **comprehensive**, **effectively**, **clear** and **thorough** mean in the assessment.)

Know it!

1 Name the three different types of blood vessel and explain the differences between them.

2 What is the function of the aorta?

3 How does the structure of alveoli make them very efficient at their job?

4 What is the function of the respiratory system?

5 What are the four stages of the digestive process? Explain briefly what happens at each stage.

Assessment guidance

Learning outcome 1: Know how body systems work

Mark band 1	Mark band 2	Mark band 3
Demonstrates **basic** knowledge of how the cardiovascular/respiratory/digestive systems work.	Demonstrates **sound** knowledge of how the cardiovascular/respiratory/digestive systems work.	Demonstrates **detailed** knowledge of how the cardiovascular/respiratory/digestive systems work.
Provides **basic** information to illustrate the structure of each body system making **few** links between structure and function. Provides a **basic** description of the system functionality, making **limited** use of terminology but demonstrating a **basic** understanding.	Provides **clear** information to illustrate the structure of each body system making **some** links between structure and function.	Provides **detailed** and **coherent** information to illustrate the structure of each body system making **many** links between structure and function.
	Provides a **clear** description of the system functionality, making **some** effective use of terminology and demonstrating a **sound** understanding.	Provides a **comprehensive** description of the system functionality, **effectively** using terminology, which demonstrates a **clear and thorough** understanding.

Note: You will not cover all of these systems in one go.

Marking criteria for LO1 Part A: For Part A, you will need to look at the cardiovascular system.

Marking criteria for LO1 Part B: For Part B, you will need to look at the respiratory system.

Marking criteria for LO1 Part C: For Part C, you will need to look at the digestive system.

If you are unsure about any of this, you should speak to your tutor or refer to the OCR specification for clarification and further guidance.

 ### The OCR Model Assignment will ask you to:

- Provide information about how the cardiovascular, respiratory and digestive systems work.
- Provide written information, with illustrations, of the structure of the cardiovascular, respiratory and digestive systems.
- Make links between the structure and function of the body systems.
- Describe the functionality of each of the systems to show your understanding.

 ### What do the command words mean?

- **Detailed knowledge:** Your work will show that you have a point-by-point knowledge of how the cardiovascular/respiratory/digestive systems work.
- **Detailed, coherent and many:** You will provide point-by-point, logical and consistent information to illustrate the structure of each body system. You will make a large number of links between structure and function.

  Your work will show that you know how the structure of the body system helps it to function efficiently to perform the system's job – circulation, respiration or digestion.
- **Comprehensive description:** You will provide a description of the system functionality which includes everything that is necessary to evidence understanding in terms of both breadth and depth.
- **Effectively using terminology:** You will use terminology appropriately and successfully which will show that you have a focussed understanding that is extremely attentive to accuracy and detail.

→

- **Clear and thorough understanding:** You will demonstrate a focussed understanding that is extremely attentive to accuracy and detail.

You should check the glossary in the Introduction for the definitions of each of the command words from OCR.

Learning outcome 2

Understand disorders that affect body systems

Getting started

Think about a time when you were ill – such as having a cold or flu, nausea, an asthma attack or food poisoning.

Ask yourself the following questions:

- What were the symptoms of the illness?
- How was the illness diagnosed?
- Which body system did it affect?

Share your experiences with the rest of the group.

Disorders of the cardiovascular system

Examples of heart **disorders** are:

- angina
- heart attack
- heart failure.

Symptoms of heart disorders

Table 3.2 shows the **symptoms** and reasons for these different heart disorders.

 Key terms

Disorder A state where part of the body is not functioning correctly and is causing ill-health.

Symptoms An indication of a disease or disorder.

Diagnosis An investigation of the symptoms of an illness to identify what is the cause of the problem.

Diagnosis of cardiovascular disorders

This section discusses a range of different methods that are used for the **diagnosis** of cardiovascular disorders. Not all methods of diagnosis are included in this section – you may be able to think of others.

Electrocardiogram (ECG)

An ECG is a test that checks the rhythm and electrical activity of the heart. Sensors are attached to the skin and detect electrical signals produced by the heart each time it beats. The signals are recorded by a machine and then checked to see if there is anything unusual. An ECG can help to detect coronary heart disease where the blood supply is blocked or restricted by a build-up of fatty deposits.

Echocardiogram

An echocardiogram uses high-frequency sound waves that reflect against structures of the heart; it is similar to the ultrasound scans used in pregnancy. It can give information about the

Table 3.2 Symptoms, causes and explanations for angina, heart attacks and heart failure

Heart disorders	
Symptoms	Biological explanation
A raised pulse, with other symptoms such as dizziness or tightness in the chest, can be a sign of a heart problem. **Angina:** ● breathlessness ● nausea ● dizziness ● chest pain ● a feeling of tightness in the chest, which may spread to the arms, neck and jaw. **Heart attack:** ● light-headedness ● feeling weak ● sweating ● shortness of breath ● chest pain that can radiate from the chest to the jaw, neck, arms and back. **Heart failure:** ● breathlessness even when resting ● raised heart rate ● feeling tired most of the time ● swollen ankles and legs.	**Angina:** walls of the arteries become blocked with fatty deposits, a process called atherosclerosis. **Heart attack:** when arteries become completely blocked they can cause a heart attack, which can permanently damage the heart muscle. If not treated straight away, it can be fatal. **Heart failure:** the heart becomes too weak to pump blood around the body. This can cause fluid to build up in the lungs, making it increasingly difficult to breathe.
Causes ● Coronary heart disease is usually caused by a build-up of fatty deposits on the walls of the arteries around the heart. ● The risk of heart disease developing is significantly increased by smoking, lack of regular exercise and obesity; or if a person has a high cholesterol level, high blood pressure or diabetes.	

structure of the heart and its pumping action, so can detect any abnormalities in the structure of the heart that could be a cause of the symptoms.

Chest x-ray
An x-ray gives a visual image of changes within a body system. A chest x-ray will show if the heart is bigger than it should be (which indicates a disorder is present), whether there is fluid on the lungs, or whether a lung condition could be causing the symptoms.

Blood tests
Sometimes an individual will have a blood test. The sample is tested to detect chemical imbalance. This provides an indication of potential problems or the effectiveness of treatments.

Cardiac enzyme tests can tell whether there is any damage to the heart. The more severely a heart is damaged by a heart attack, the more enzymes are released. The levels are measured from a series of blood samples taken over a few hours.

Other blood tests check for abnormal levels of chemicals that can indicate abnormal heart rhythms, or for thyroid problems, low haemoglobin levels or high cholesterol levels.

Pulse rates
A normal resting heart rate for an adult should be between 60 and 100 beats per minute, though it can be lower. An irregular pulse could be a sign of arrhythmia (an abnormal heart rhythm).

Blood pressure

Blood pressure is measured using a sphygmomanometer. A cuff is wrapped around the upper arm and inflated until it tightens, then it gradually deflates. If the blood pressure measurement is 140/90 or higher it will probably have to be rechecked several times.

Sometimes a 24-hour blood pressure (BP) monitor is worn to get a more accurate result over time.

- The first number is the highest that the BP reaches when your heart contracts and pumps blood through the arteries – called systolic blood pressure.
- The second number is the lowest that your BP reaches as the heart relaxes between beats – called diastolic blood pressure.

Disorders of the respiratory system

Examples of respiratory disorders are:

- asthma/allergies

Research Activity

Taking your pulse

1 Access the British Heart Foundation website and find the 'Checking your pulse' section: www.bhf.org.uk/heart-health/tests/checking-your-pulse
2 Watch the clip of a senior cardiac nurse demonstrating how to check your pulse.
3 Now, try taking your pulse, or that of a friend.

- pneumonia
- chronic obstructive pulmonary disease (including chronic bronchitis and emphysema).

We will look at each of these disorders in turn.

Table 3.3 summarises the symptoms, reasons for and causes of asthma and allergies.

Table 3.3 Symptoms, causes and explanations for asthma and allergies

Respiratory disorders - asthma and allergies	
Symptoms	Biological explanation
• Recurring episodes of breathlessness; tightness of the chest and wheezing • Asthma 'attacks' – episodes of wheezing that require using an inhaler to open the airway • Allergic reactions such as sore, red, itchy eyes, shortness of breath, coughing, skin reactions, runny nose	• Inflammation of the bronchi (which carry air in and out of the lungs), causing the bronchi to be more sensitive than normal • Contact with something that irritates the lungs, known as a trigger (e.g. cigarette smoke, dust or pollen), makes airways become narrow, the muscles around them tighten, and causes an increase in the production of sticky mucus (phlegm)

Causes

The exact cause of asthma and allergies is not known; it is likely to be a combination of factors.

- It may be genetic, as it often runs in families, and people who have allergies are at higher risk.
- A number of environmental and social factors are thought to play a role in the development of asthma and allergies, e.g. dust, air pollution and chemicals such as chlorine in swimming pools.
- A food allergy is a reaction produced by the body's immune system when it encounters a normally harmless food. This reaction tends to happen very quickly and will happen even with a tiny amount of that food. Examples are peanut or shellfish allergies.

Table 3.4 looks at the symptoms, explanation and causes of pneumonia.

Table 3.4 Symptoms, causes and explanation for pneumonia

Respiratory disorders – pneumonia	
Symptoms	Biological explanation
<ul><li>Can develop suddenly over 24–48 hours, or may develop more slowly over several days</li><li>A cough that may be dry or produce thick yellow, green, brown or blood-stained mucus (phlegm)</li><li>May cause breathing difficulties (rapid, shallow breaths, may feel breathless even when resting)</li><li>Rapid heartbeat</li><li>Fever, sweating and shivering</li><li>Loss of appetite and feeling generally unwell</li></ul>	<ul><li>Pneumonia is inflammation and swelling of the tissue in one or both lungs</li><li>The alveoli in the lungs become inflamed and fill up with liquid; this makes it harder for the lungs to work and get oxygen into the bloodstream</li></ul>

Causes
- It is usually caused by a bacterial infection; the most common is streptococcus pneumoniae.
- The number of cases increases in the winter because infection with flu can lower the immune system, which increases the risk of picking up pneumonia.
- It can also be picked up in hospital due to weakened resistance to the germs that can cause pneumonia.

Table 3.5 summarises the symptoms, reasons for and causes of chronic obstructive pulmonary disease (COPD), which includes bronchitis and emphysema.

Table 3.5 Symptoms, causes and explanations for COPD

Respiratory disorders – COPD	
Symptoms	Biological explanation
The term COPD covers a range of lung diseases including chronic bronchitis, emphysema and chronic obstructive airways disease. Symptoms include: <ul><li>shortness of breath and wheezing</li><li>yellow sputum</li><li>a persistent cough that never seems to go away</li><li>frequent chest infections.</li><li>These symptoms get worse over time.</li></ul>	<ul><li>The airways of the lungs become inflamed and narrowed. As the air sacs get permanently damaged, it becomes increasingly difficult to breathe out.</li><li>There is currently no cure for COPD, but the sooner the condition is diagnosed and appropriate treatment begins, the less chance there is of severe lung damage.</li></ul>

Causes
- The lifestyle choice of smoking is the main cause of COPD and is thought to be responsible for around 90% of cases.
- Some cases of COPD are caused by certain types of fumes, dust and chemical exposure at work, so there can be an occupational cause.
- There can also be a genetic tendency, but this is extremely rare.

Diagnosis of respiratory disorders
Different methods are used to diagnose respiratory disorders.

MRI and CT scans
MRI and **CT scans** (see page 87 for definitions) can provide high-resolution detailed images of the chest. They can be repeated over time to

Key terms

CT scan A computerised tomography scan used for internal organs, blood vessels or bones (sometimes called a CAT scan).

MRI scan A magnetic resonance imaging scan; a strong magnetic field and radio waves are used to produce detailed images of almost all parts of the body.

Group activity

Quiz time!

1 In groups, write a quiz, consisting of ten questions, about the disorders of the respiratory system. Also produce an answer sheet.

2 Your quiz can focus on a specific disorder, or all of them, or it could be about symptoms or methods of diagnosis.

3 Have a quiz session with the class. Which group will score the most points?

monitor changes in a condition. A high-resolution CT scan is the most sensitive method of detecting emphysema.

An MRI scan can take 15–90 minutes depending on the size of the area being scanned. The person has to lie very still throughout the scan.

A CT scan is where several X-rays are taken at different angles and a computer puts the images together. A special dye has to be injected or taken as a drink before the scan. The scan takes 10–20 minutes, during which the person has to lie very still.

X-rays

An X-ray gives a visual image of changes within the respiratory system. For instance, it can show whether there is fluid on the lungs, or whether a lung condition could be causing an individual's symptoms. A doctor can diagnose a disorder such as pneumonia based on the symptoms and by examining the chest, although a chest X-ray is probably needed to confirm it.

Lung function tests

The main lung function tests are spirometry and the peak flow test.

● Spirometry is carried out to measure the breathing capacity of the lungs. It measures the volume of air expired (breathed out) in total and the force of the expired air in the first second of breathing out. It is used to diagnose

and monitor a range of lung conditions such as asthma, COPD and cystic fibrosis. The individual will have a clip on their nose, have to blow into a mouthpiece, having inhaled, and then repeat this at least three times. The test takes around 30–90 minutes.

● In the peak flow test, a peak flow meter is used. This consists of a tube that has a mouthpiece that is blown into (there is a scale down the side that gives a measurement). The test can be used to measure how fast an individual can blow air out of their lungs. This is called your peak expiratory flow (PEF). It is usual to take the best of three readings. In LO3, we will look at how to measure peak flow and interpret the results.

Disorders of the digestive system

Examples of digestive disorders are:

● irritable bowel syndrome
● heartburn
● ulcers.

We will look at each of these disorders in turn.

Table 3.6 summarises the symptoms, reasons for and causes of irritable bowel syndrome (IBS).

Table 3.6 Symptoms, causes and explanations for irritable bowel syndrome

Digestive disorders - Irritable Bowel Syndrome (IBS)	
Symptoms	Biological explanation
<ul><li>Stomach pain and cramping</li><li>Changes in bowel habits, such as diarrhoea or constipation, or both</li><li>Bloating and swelling of the stomach</li><li>Excessive wind, known as flatulence</li><li>Feeling that the bowels have not fully emptied after going to the toilet</li><li>Mucus passing from the anus</li></ul>	With **IBS**, food moves through the digestive system either too quickly or too slowly: <ul><li>if the food moves too quickly, it causes diarrhoea because not enough water is absorbed by the intestines</li><li>if it moves too slowly, it results in constipation because too much water is absorbed by the intestines and this makes the faeces hard.</li><li>It is possible that problems with the absorption of bile during the digestive process may be a cause of IBS in some cases.</li></ul>

Causes
- Believed to be linked to an increased sensitivity of the gut to certain foods.
- Thought to be related to problems with digesting food.
- In many people the symptoms seem to be triggered by something they have had to eat or drink. Triggers vary but can include fatty or fried food, processed snacks such as biscuits or crisps, drinks that contain caffeine such as tea, coffee or cola, alcohol and fizzy drinks.
- Changes in diet and lifestyle can be important in managing and controlling the condition.

Table 3.7 looks at the symptoms, explanation and causes of ulcers.

Table 3.7 Symptoms, causes and reasons for ulcers

Digestive disorders - ulcers	
Symptoms	Biological explanation
<ul><li>A burning or gnawing pain that develops in the abdomen, though not always</li><li>Loss of appetite and weight loss</li><li>Feeling and being sick</li><li>Indigestion and heartburn</li><li>Ulcers can bleed and lead to vomiting blood or passing dark, sticky tar-like **stools** – these symptoms require urgent medical attention</li></ul>	<ul><li>Gastric ulcers are open sores that develop on the lining of the stomach.</li><li>Duodenal ulcers develop in part of the small intestine just beyond the stomach.</li><li>Bacteria or non-steroidal anti-inflammatory drugs (**NSAIDs**) break down the stomach's defence against the acids produced to digest food. This allows the stomach lining to become damaged and an ulcer forms.</li></ul>

Causes
- Usually caused by *Helicobacter pylori* bacteria (*H. pylori*) or by taking NSAIDs for another condition such as arthritis.
- Smoking increases an individual's risk of developing an ulcer.

🔑 Key terms

IBS or irritable bowel syndrome affects the large intestine (colon) and causes diarrhoea, constipation and bloating for example.

Stools Body waste called faeces.

NSAIDs are neosteroidal anti-inflammatory drugs, and are one of the most common pain relief medicines.

Helicobacter pylori A type of bacteria that can cause the stomach to inflame, and ulcers.

Table 3.8 summarises the symptoms, explanation and causes of heartburn (also known as gastro-oesophageal reflux disease).

Table 3.8 Symptoms, causes and explanation for heartburn

Digestive disorders - heartburn	
Symptoms	Biological explanation
• An uncomfortable burning sensation in the chest, usually just below the breastbone but can spread to the throat; usually worse after eating, when bending or lying down	• The sphincter at the bottom of the oesophagus becomes weakened and does not close fully.
• Acid reflux, where acid or other stomach contents are brought back into the throat or mouth; this gives a sour, unpleasant taste in the mouth	• After food is let into the stomach by the oesophageal sphincter opening, it does not close properly.
• Bad breath, sore throat, pain when swallowing	• This allows stomach acid to leak back into the oesophagus.
• Bloating and belching; vomiting	

Causes

- Being overweight can increase the pressure on the stomach and weaken the muscles at the bottom of the oesophagus.
- Smoking and alcohol can relax the muscles at the bottom of the oesophagus.
- Eating a lot of fatty foods (it takes longer to get rid of stomach acid after digesting a fatty meal, so some excess acid may leak up into the oesophagus).
- Pregnancy – temporary hormone changes and increased pressure on the stomach.

Stretch activity

How does it happen?

1 Copy out the diagram of the stomach shown in Figure 3.10.

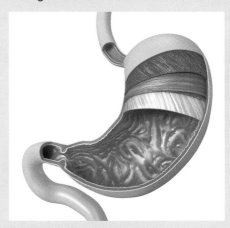

Figure 3.10 The stomach

2 Use the diagram to illustrate a detailed description of the reasons for heartburn (gastro-oesophageal reflux disease) developing.

3 Describe the symptoms and how they are caused by what is happening in the stomach.

(Look at the command word definitions to see what **detailed description** and **detailed reasons** mean in the assessment.)

Diagnosis of digestive system disorders

A range of different methods are used to diagnose digestive disorders.

Medical history and physical exam
A GP will be able to diagnose heartburn/reflux disease based on the symptoms and other information provided by the patient. A GP would suspect an ulcer based on the symptoms but would probably do further tests to confirm this diagnosis.

X-rays
To help diagnose IBS, a barium enema test can be carried out. This is when the colon is filled with a

liquid that then shows up on an x-ray. It highlights the large intestine.

However, it is more usual for endoscopes (see below) to be used.

Body mass index (BMI) tests
The body mass index is a calculation used to find out whether someone is a healthy weight for their height. If not, this could be an indication of weight loss or weight gain linked to a disorder or illness affecting the person's health.

Learning objective 3 has details of how BMI is worked out and what the results mean.

Blood test
Blood can be tested for antibodies to the *H. pylori* bacteria (antibodies fight infection) but this is usually checked by a stool antigen test.

Ultrasound
An ultrasound can be used to examine the liver and other organs in the abdomen and pelvis. A lubricating gel is used on the skin to allow smooth movement of a small hand-held probe, which is moved over the body part that is being examined.

Gastroscopy using an endoscope
A gastroscopy examines the oesophagus, stomach and duodenum. The procedure uses a long, flexible tube called an endoscope. The tube has a light and a video camera at one end. Endoscopes are inserted into the body through a natural opening such as the mouth or anus. It can be uncomfortable so a local anaesthetic spray is used to numb the throat. It takes around an hour to carry out. It is used to investigate symptoms such as difficulty swallowing, persistent abdominal pain and suspected ulcers.

Classroom discussion

What is the disorder?

1 In pairs, choose a cardiovascular, respiratory or digestive disorder. Find out about all the symptoms of the disorder.
2 Take it in turns to perform a role play to the class – one student is the patient, the other a GP. The GP is asking the patient questions about their symptoms to try to make a diagnosis. (Do not tell the rest of the class what the disorder is.)
3 Have a class discussion about the symptoms and decide what the disorder is.
4 Discuss any specialist diagnostic methods that might be needed to confirm the diagnosis.

Case study: Kiran's IBS story

When I was ten years old I was getting a lot of unexplained diarrhoea and feeling sick. I couldn't go anywhere without wanting to go to the toilet. As I grew older it carried on, but I also got constipation, headaches and I felt tired all the time. Sometimes I would wake up at night and sit on the toilet for an hour sweating, with really bad cramping and a pain in my gut. Then suddenly I would have a gush of diarrhoea. I was exhausted all the time.

My GP sent me for a barium enema (see page 89 for more information) and a blood test. They didn't really find anything wrong so were able to rule out anything serious or life threatening, which was a relief. Because of my symptoms my GP thought I might have IBS. He suggested a non-dairy diet; I had to substitute milk and cream with soya products. He prescribed an anti-diarrhoeal drug called codeine phosphate.

This has worked. I feel as though I have got my life back. I can't resist trifle (my favourite), but if I eat it I end up on the toilet for an hour, feel lethargic and my stomach distends. So it is just not worth it. I have to use my willpower to resist temptation.

Questions

1 What symptoms did Kiran have before his IBS was diagnosed?
2 How did the tests lead to a diagnosis of IBS?
3 Kiran describes feeling 'lethargic' and having a 'distended' stomach. What do these words mean?

Know it!

1 Describe four symptoms of a heart attack.
2 Explain a method that could be used to diagnose emphysema.
3 Describe how and why an endoscope would be used.
4 What is the difference between a gastric and a duodenal ulcer?
5 What are the biological reasons for irritable bowel syndrome?

Assessment guidance

Learning outcome 2: Understand disorders that affect the body systems

Mark band 1	Mark band 2	Mark band 3
Provides a **basic** list of the symptoms for a disorder associated with the cardiovascular/respiratory/digestive system giving **basic** reasons for **some** of the symptoms.	Provides a **sound** description of the symptoms for a disorder associated with the cardiovascular/respiratory/digestive system giving reasons for **many** of the symptoms.	Provides a **detailed** description of the symptoms for a disorder associated with the cardiovascular/respiratory/digestive system, giving **detailed** reasons for **most** of the symptoms.
Provides a **basic** list of the methods of diagnosis.	Provides a **sound** list of the methods of diagnosis.	Provides a **comprehensive** list of the methods of diagnosis.
There may be **few**, if any, links made between disorders and the structure and/or functionality of the system.	There may be **some** links made between disorders and the structure and/or functionality of the system.	There are likely to be links made between disorders and the structure and/or functionality of the system.

Note: You will not cover all of these systems in one go.

Marking criteria for LO2 Part A: For Part A, you will need to look at the cardiovascular system.

Marking criteria for LO2 Part B: For Part B, you will need to look at the respiratory system.

Marking criteria for LO2 Part C: For Part C, you will need to look at the digestive system.

If you are unsure about any of this, you should speak to your tutor or refer to the OCR specification for clarification and guidance.

 The OCR Model Assignment will ask you to:

- Describe and give reasons for the symptoms of one disorder of the cardiovascular system, one disorder of the respiratory system and one disorder of the digestive system.
- Give full details of the methods used to diagnose the three disorders.
- Make links between the disorders and how the structure and/or function of the system causes the disorder.

 What do the command words mean?

- **Detailed description with detailed reasons and most of the symptoms:** You will provide a point-by-point description of the symptoms, making sure that you identify the symptoms of one disorder for each body system. You will provide point-by-point reasons for the majority of the symptoms.
- **Comprehensive list:** You will provide a list of the methods of diagnosis which will be complete and include everything that is necessary to evidence understanding in terms of both breadth and depth.

You should check the glossary in the Introduction for the definitions of each of the command words from OCR.

Learning outcome 3

Be able to interpret data obtained from measuring body rates with reference to the functioning of healthy body systems

Getting started

As we saw in LO2, 'peak flow' is a way of measuring how efficient an individual's lungs are, in other words how well they work.

● With a partner, discuss what factors could have a negative effect on an individual's lung efficiency.

● Share your ideas with the class.

Ways of measuring function in the body systems

There are different ways of measuring body function and all of them produce data about the individual whose body rates are being measured. Interpreting this data can provide important information about an individual's state of physical health.

For each of the three body systems there are different methods to measure body function. We will look at the different ways of measuring body rates in detail below, but first let's summarise the method used for each system.

Cardiovascular system

A wave passes along the artery walls each time the heart beats to pump blood. This wave is called the pulse and it can be felt at any point in the body where a large artery crosses a bone just beneath the skin. The pulse is usually checked at the carotid artery in the neck or at the radial artery in the wrist.

Respiratory system

As we saw at the start of this section, to measure how efficiently an individual's lungs are performing a peak flow test can be carried out.

This measures the maximum speed at which air can flow out of an individual's lungs.

Digestive system

The body mass index (or BMI) is used to calculate whether an individual is within the healthy weight range for their height.

How to measure pulse rate before and after activity

Resting pulse rate

The resting pulse rate is taken when someone is relaxed. They will not have recently done any exercise or activity that would increase their heart rate. The resting pulse rate is the number of heartbeats per minute.

Here is how to take someone's resting pulse.

1 Hold the person's arm so it is straight. They should be sitting down and relaxed.

2 Use your index (first) finger and middle finger.

3 Place two fingers at the base of their thumb, between the bone and tendon over the radial artery.

4 Using a clock that counts seconds, count how many beats you feel in a minute, or count for 30 seconds and multiply by 2.

This measure should be taken three times on different occasions. Then an average result should be calculated, to ensure accuracy.

Pulse rate after activity – recovery rate

Exercise causes the pulse rate to increase. The faster the pulse rate returns to the person's normal resting pulse rate after exercise, the fitter they are.

To measure recovery rate, the person will need to do some form of mild exercise appropriate for their age, level of health and fitness. This could be running on the spot, walking up and down the stairs, or stepping on and off one step a few times.

Note: you should **not** attempt to carry out the recovery after exercise measure if the person has any health disorders, breathing difficulties or a heart condition.

Here is how to measure someone's recovery rate.

1 Take the person's pulse rate immediately after exercise (for 30 seconds and double it). Record the number.
2 Take the pulse again two minutes after stopping exercising. Record it.
3 Subtract the second pulse rate from the first to get the recovery rate number.
4 Compare the result with standard measures (see Table 3.10).

You could record the pulse rates in a chart like the one shown in Table 3.9. This measure should be taken three times on different occasions. Then an average result should be calculated, to ensure accuracy.

Compare results against normal/ maximum pulse rates for age

The average normal resting pulse rate for an adult is between 60 and 80 beats per minute. Generally, a lower heart rate means a more efficient heart function and better cardiovascular fitness. The faster the heart rate recovers,

or slows down, after exercise, the fitter and healthier the person is.

Tables of resting heart rates linked to age can be found using this link: www.topendsports.com/testing/heart-rate-resting-chart.htm

The result of the recovery rate test should be compared with those in Table 3.10.

How to measure peak flow of an individual before and after activity

A peak flow meter (see Figure 3.11 on page 94) measures lung function. It has a disposable cardboard mouthpiece and a calibrated scale of measures down the side, with a needle to indicate the result. The person blows as hard as possible into the mouthpiece. The speed at which air is exhaled gives an indication of the width of the bronchial tubes.

This measure should be taken three times. The highest measure should be taken as the result.

Compare results against normal/maximum peak flow rates for age, height and weight

A peak flow recording chart is shown in Figure 3.12 on page 94. This is called a PEF, or 'peak expiratory flow' rate chart. It enables the results to be compared with normal peak flow rates for age and height, and for males and females. The lower the result, the more breathing is restricted.

Research by Asthma UK has shown that children who are obese are more likely to have a low peak flow rate and get a diagnosis of asthma. People who have asthma and lose weight are likely to find that their symptoms improve. So peak flow should be considered alongside an individual's BMI result.

Table 3.9 Chart used for measuring recovery rate

	Name		
	Pulse rate immediately after exercise	Pulse rate 2 minutes after exercise	Recovery rate number
1			
2			
3			
Average			

Table 3.10 Recovery rates: what they mean

Difference	Body age indicator	Fitness level
Less than 22	Slightly older than your actual age	Below-average fitness levels – unfit
22–52	About the same as your actual age	Average level of fitness
53–58	Slightly younger than your actual age	Slightly above average
59–65	Moderately younger than your actual age	Good level of fitness
66 or more	A lot younger than your actual age	Excellent level of fitness

Figure 3.11 A peak flow meter

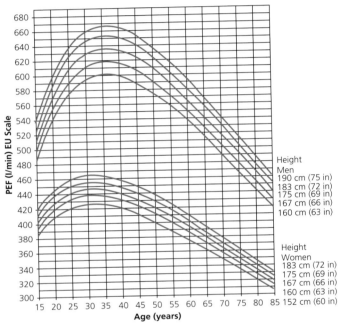

Figure 3.12 Recording peak flow measurements

Source: adapted from www.peakflow.com/pefr_normal_values.pdf

How to calculate BMI

To calculate someone's BMI, use the following formula:

BMI = weight (kg) divided by height (m)²

Here is an example.

Height is 1.752, squared (1.75 × 1.75) = 3.06

Weight is 80 kg

BMI calculation: 80 divided by 3.06 = 26.14

So the BMI result is: 26.14

Compare the results against healthy weights for height

A BMI result is compared against weights and heights using a chart like the one in Table 3.11. The significance (meaning) of the result is shown in the second column. It is thought that an adult BMI of 19–22 is the healthiest.

The example calculation shown above gave a result of 26.14. Compared with the BMI results in Table 3.11, the individual would be classified as overweight.

People with a BMI of 25 and over have a higher-than-average risk of health problems like diabetes, heart disease and some cancers.

BMI	Significance
Less than 18.5	Underweight
18.5–24.9	Healthy
25–29.9	Overweight
30–39.9	Obese
40+	Morbidly obese

Table 3.11 BMI measures: what they mean

There are limitations to the significance of the BMI as some individuals have a high level of muscle and are likely to get an overweight result, when in fact they are fit and healthy because they exercise regularly.

Interpreting data obtained from measuring body rates

To interpret the data you obtain, you have to do more than just state the results.

For each of the three measures we have discussed, you should consider:

- what the result tells you about the function of the body system when compared with the standard norms
- whether the results indicate that the functioning of the body system could be improved, or if it is working well.

Stretch activity

BMI results: what do they mean?

1 Calculate the BMI of the people listed in the table. They are all adults.

Name	Weight (kg)	Height (m)	BMI	Ideal BMI
Naz	56	1.62		
Peter	71	1.69		
Alan	94	1.85		
Priya	47	1.59		

2 Comment on each BMI result. Is each individual underweight, overweight or an ideal healthy result?

3 Complete the final column of the table by calculating each individual's healthy BMI.

4 Work out approximately how much weight each person should gain or lose to become a healthy weight for their height.

Look at the command word definitions to see what **thorough interpretation** of data means in the assessment.

 ## Case study: Interpreting Jason's data

Jason is 18 years old. His height is 1.73 m and he weighs 81.5 kg. He lives in a ground-floor flat. His favourite food is hamburger and chips, and as a treat he often has a milkshake. He snacks during the day on crisps, sweets and biscuits. He likes sport and watches it on TV as often as he can.

Recently Jason has been feeling unwell. He is finding that he gets breathless when he has to run for a bus or climb stairs. He has a resting pulse rate of 89 and a recovery rate of 19. He is also getting indigestion symptoms, with an uncomfortable burning feeling in his chest after he has eaten.

Questions

1 Work out Jason's BMI. What is the significance of the result?

2 How do you think Jason's pulse rate compares with the norms for an adult?

3 The symptoms Jason is getting could indicate health disorders. Suggest which disorders he could be at risk of.

4 Write a conclusion about Jason's body rates results and comment on the functioning of his body systems.

 ## Classroom discussion

BMI: when should it be a cause for concern?

1 In groups find out more about weight measurements and BMI. You could use the weblinks below as a starting point, or do your own research:
  ● www.nhs.uk/chq/Pages/3215.aspx
  ● www.bupa.co.uk/health-information/directory/h/healthy-weight
  ● http://extras.bhf.org.uk/bmi/BMI_Calc.html

2 Use the information you have found out to inform a classroom discussion entitled 'Should a high BMI be a cause for concern?'

Know it!

1 What do the initials BMI stand for? How would you calculate someone's BMI?

2 What is the purpose of a peak flow meter?

3 Write a description of how to take someone's resting pulse rate.

4 What conclusions would you reach if someone had a BMI of 34 and a resting pulse rate of 86?

5 Identify the ideal BMI, pulse rate and peak flow rate for an average adult female.

Assessment guidance

Learning outcome 3: Be able to interpret data obtained from measuring body rates with reference to the functioning of healthy body systems

Marking criteria for LO3

Mark band 1	Mark band 2	Mark band 3
Demonstrates **limited** confidence in measuring body rates.	Demonstrates **some** confidence measuring body rates.	Demonstrates **confidence** and **competence** measuring body rates.
A **limited** interpretation of data obtained from measuring body rates and comparing against the norms making **limited** reference to the functioning of healthy body systems.	A **reasonable** interpretation of data obtained from measuring body rates and comparing against the norms making **some** reference to the functioning of healthy body systems.	A **thorough** interpretation of data obtained from measuring body rates and comparing them against the norms making **detailed** reference to the functioning of healthy body systems.
There will be **some** errors in spelling, punctuation and grammar.	There will be **minor** errors in spelling, punctuation and grammar.	There will be **few**, if any errors in spelling, punctuation and grammar.
Draws upon **limited** skills/knowledge/understanding from other units in the specification.	Draws upon **some relevant** skills/knowledge/understanding from other units in the specification.	**Clearly** draws upon **relevant** skills/knowledge/understanding from other units in the specification.

The OCR Model Assignment will ask you to:

● Measure body rates – pulse, peak flow and BMI.
● Interpret the data obtained from the measurements.
● Compare the results with norms for healthy body systems.
● Include some supplementary written work about skills or knowledge you have used from other units.
● Ensure that your spelling, punctuation and grammar are error free.

What do the command words mean?

● **Demonstrate confidence and competence**: You will be able to show evidence that you know how to measure body rates and show certainty as you demonstrate this.

● **Thorough interpretation and detailed reference**: You will be able to interpret data that you obtain from measuring body rates and you will be extremely attentive to accuracy and detail when doing this. You will also compare them against the norms and make point-by-point reference to the functioning of healthy body systems. You will do this for all three body systems.

● **Few errors:** There will only be a small number, if any errors in spelling, punctuation and grammar.

● **Clearly draw upon relevant skills/knowledge/understanding from other units**: In a focussed manner, you will draw upon the right or correctly focussed skills/knowledge/understanding from other units in the specification.

You should check the glossary in the Introduction for the definitions of each of the command words from OCR.

Read about it

Weblinks

www.bhf.org.uk/heart-health British Heart Foundation – comprehensive information about all aspects of heart health and heart disease

www.blf.org.uk British Lung Foundation – information about asthma, COPD, emphysema and other respiratory conditions, including causes, symptoms and treatments available

www.bbc.co.uk/education/guides/z6h4jxs/ revision BBC Bitesize – information and interactive resources about the respiratory system

www.bbc.co.uk/schools/gcsebitesize/pe/ appliedanatomy/0_anatomy_circulatorysys_ rev1.shtml BBC Bitesize – information and interactive resources about the circulatory system

www.bbc.co.uk/education/guides/zwqycdm/ revision BBC Bitesize – information and interactive resources about the digestive system

www.healthline.com/human-body-maps Healthline – an interactive website that covers all the body systems, and shows their structure and how they work

www.nhs.uk/Conditions/Pages/hub.aspx NHS Choices – the Health A–Z of conditions and treatments produced by the NHS; detailed and up-to-date information about virtually all health disorders, their symptoms and diagnosis

www.theibsnetwork.org IBS Network – extensive information about IBS

Reference books

Fisher, A. et al. (2012) *Health and Social Care A2 Student Book for OCR*. Oxford.

Stretch, B. (2007) *Core Themes in Health and Social Care*. Heinemann.

Waugh, A. and Grant, A. (2014) *Anatomy and Physiology in Health and Illness*. Churchill Livingstone.

R024

Pathways for providing care in health, social care and early years settings

About this unit

There is a wide range of health, social care and early years services and types of support available to meet people's diverse needs.

In this unit you will learn about the different types of services that are available and the different professionals and organisations that provide support. You will also learn about the referral process to access different services and the barriers that may prevent individuals from accessing care pathways.

You will explore the support pathways available to meet the needs of the diverse groups of people who use services. You will also learn how to identify the steps needed to offer an appropriate care pathway and how to develop a good-quality care plan.

Learning outcomes

LO1: Understand the different forms of support available in health, social care and early years settings

LO2: Know the access routes and barriers to care pathways

LO3: Be able to produce care pathways for individuals

How will I be assessed?

You will be assessed through a series of assignment tasks, which are set by OCR. The assignment will be marked by your tutor and then moderated by OCR.

For LO1, you need to:

- understand about the services funded by the government in the statutory sector and about the services that are privately funded
- provide information about the organisations in the third sector (non-profit agencies)
- explain the contribution made by informal carers
- understand how the sectors work in partnership to provide support for individuals.

Note: SPAG is assessed in this learning outcome.

For LO2, you need to:

- provide information about the roles of health, social care and early years professionals,

with examples of how they provide access to support services

- demonstrate knowledge of the referral process to access different forms of services
- provide a description of the different types of barriers that prevent individuals from accessing services, with examples.

For LO3, you need to:

- know how to recognise the groups of people who use services, and their needs
- understand how to identify the steps needed to offer an appropriate care pathway
- explain the purpose of a care plan in organising support for an individual in a health, social care or early years setting
- produce a care plan for an individual using health, social care or early years provision, with examples of services and support, and justifications.

Make sure you refer to the current OCR specification and guidance.

Links to other units

Unit R021: Essential values of care for use with individuals in care settings (LO2):

You must show your understanding of applying the values of care in relation to, for example, promoting individuals' rights and beliefs.

Unit R022: Communicating and working with individuals in health, social care and early years settings (LO1- 3):

You will need to be able to apply your skills for obtaining and giving clear information and showing respect for the individual's needs and preferences (RO22, LO3) whilst ensuring that the communication methods you've used meet individuals' specific needs (unit RO22, LO1). Your approach to gathering information must include involving the individual and all those others who know the individual well and reflect your personal qualities such as empowerment, understanding and value (unit RO22, LO2).

Unit R022: Communicating and working with individuals in health, social care and early years settings (LO1) and Unit R026 (optional unit): Planning for employment in health, social care and children and young people's workforce (LO1):

Your knowledge of the different types of barriers that individuals may experience when accessing support and services could also include different communication barriers such as practitioners' use of language, individuals' specific communication needs and different environments (unit RO22, LO1) as well as the hazards and risks present (unit RO26, LO1).

Unit R024 (optional unit): Pathways for providing care in health, social care and early years settings (LO3):

When producing a care plan for an individual you could also consider its purpose and areas of content.

→

Unit R026 (optional unit): Planning for employment in health, social care and children and young people's workforce (LO1):

When showing your knowledge of the different types of services provided by the health, social care and early years sectors you could also demonstrate your understanding of the different organisations and job roles that exist within these and that provide support and services to a range of groups and individuals.

Learning outcome 1

Understand the different forms of support available in health, social care and early years settings

Getting started

There is a wide range of support available in health, social care and early years settings. This can include information about the services provided as well as specialist guidance from professionals.

Where can you find out about the different forms of support available in your local area? Discuss this in small groups and list as many as you can in five minutes.

People use health, social care and early years services throughout their lives. They will access support from these services at different times and for different durations, depending on their needs and any conditions they may have. Health, social care and early years services can be divided into four main groups, as Figure 4.1 shows.

Figure 4.1 Types of health, social care and early years services

Key terms

Taxes Money deducted and paid to the government for services funded by the government.

National insurance contributions Money deducted and paid to the government for the cost of state benefits such as the state pension.

Services funded by the government in the statutory sector

The statutory sector is also referred to as the public sector because it is funded by the public through the payment of **taxes** and **national insurance contributions**. It consists of organisations and services that are established, managed and led by the government, such as the National Health Service (NHS) and social services.

National Health Service (NHS)

The NHS provides healthcare services and support to children and adults in a variety of settings based in hospitals and in the community. Table 4.1 provides some examples.

Table 4.1 Examples of NHS services used by adults and children

NHS services for adults	GP-led health centres, physiotherapy departments, pain management clinics, occupational therapy services, family planning services
NHS services for babies and young children	GPs, health visitors, nurses, maternity services, speech therapy services, child psychology services

Research Activity

NHS services in your area

From the examples of services provided in Table 4.1, research two NHS services for adults and two NHS services for babies and young children that are available in your local area. For each service you could also find out what healthcare and treatments are provided, as well as who they are for.

Healthcare is usually grouped under primary, secondary and tertiary care services.

- Primary healthcare services are usually the first services that provide treatment to people when they are unwell. They may include GP-led health centres, pharmacists and dentists.
- Secondary healthcare services are used by people who have been referred for the continuation of their treatment. Examples are hospitals, accident and emergency (A&E) departments and mental health services.
- Tertiary healthcare services such as hospices and rehabilitation clinics provide people with access to specialised healthcare and treatment.

Social services

Social services are provided by local authorities or councils and funded through the government in the UK. For example:

- children and their families may access support from early education settings, fostering and adoption services
- adults who have a disability may access support from **domiciliary care services** and **advocacy** services (see page 102 for definitions)

- children and adults may access care and support from domestic/care at home services
- older adults may access support from community services and day care centres.

Primary care trusts (and Clinical Commissioning Groups)

Up to 2013, primary care trusts (known as PCTs) were part of the NHS and were responsible for providing, managing and improving health services. The Health and Social Care Act 2012 saw the replacement of primary care trusts with Clinical Commissioning Groups (CCGs) on 1 April 2013. There are more than 200 CCGs commissioning healthcare services in England and each one is responsible for a population total of approximately a quarter of a million people.

CCGs are:

- responsible for planning the healthcare services that are needed in their local area such as planned hospital care and community health services
- responsible for commissioning healthcare services for the population in their local area such as rehabilitative care, emergency care, mental health services and learning disability services
- responsible for improving health outcomes for the population in their local area such as through visiting clinics on stopping smoking and pre-natal classes
- independent, statutory and NHS-led – i.e. members include GPs, nurses and consultants
- accountable to the Secretary of State for Health and work closely with NHS England and local authorities.

Mental health trusts

CCGs are also responsible for commissioning mental health trusts that provide health and social care services to individuals in England who have mental health illnesses. There are approximately 50 NHS mental health trusts in England. The government has stated that all mental health trusts must become foundation trusts; independent and not-for-profit organisations that are regulated by **Monitor**, rather than the Department of Health.

Mental health services are also provided by privately funded and third-sector organisations; you will learn more about these types of services later in this unit.

Most mental health services that are commissioned through mental health or foundation trusts are based within the community. They are made up of teams of professionals that provide specialist treatment and support to individuals who experience mental health illnesses. Figure 4.2 includes examples of some of the mental health services on offer.

Children's trusts

Lord Laming's inquiry into the death of Victoria Climbié, who died tragically in 2000 as a result of serious abuse and neglect, highlighted the need for improved accountability and joint working between different organisations involved in caring for children and young people. The government's response to Lord Laming's inquiry, along with the Children Act 2004, means that local authorities work closely with all organisations that plan, commission or deliver services to ensure children's safety and well-being, and prevent a case like Victoria Climbié's from happening again.

Children's trusts were established and are a partnership of different organisations that provide services for children, young people and their families (pre-birth to age 19) within a local authority. Children's trusts may include a range of different partners. Examples include:

- the local authority or local council
- the police

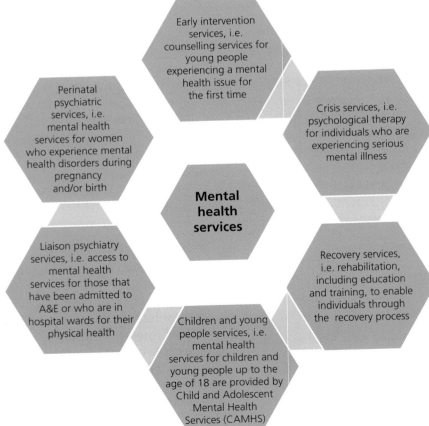

Figure 4.2 Examples of the range of mental health services available

- the Safeguarding Children's Board
- the Clinical Commissioning Group
- pre-natal groups
- schools
- colleges
- youth groups.

The Common Assessment Framework (CAF) for children and young people is an assessment tool used by different services and agencies in England. It is designed to help practitioners develop a shared understanding of a child or young person's needs so that these can be met quickly and effectively. It aims to:

- promote early intervention
- provide support to families
- identify a child's additional needs
- promote the co-ordination of support to meet the needs of children
- reduce the number of different assessment processes that children and young people have to go through.

Services that are privately funded

The private sector consists of the organisations and services that are not owned or managed by the government and that are run to make a profit.

Private residential/nursing care

There are a wide variety of privately funded services that are available to provide care and support to children, and young and older adults, depending on their needs.

- **Housing with a warden**: also known as sheltered housing. This consists of self-contained accommodation with shared communal areas for older adults who would like to continue to live independently but with some support. Support is usually provided through a 24-hour emergency alarm system by a warden or housing manager who may live on- or off-site.
- **Residential home**: there are many different types of residential home that provide care to individuals, and support with activities such as washing, dressing, meals and medication. Residential homes are staffed 24 hours a day. There are residential care homes that provide care for older adults, residential homes that

provide care and support to younger adults with learning and physical disabilities, and residential homes for children of all ages, although most children in residential homes are aged over 12 and have additional needs such as emotional difficulties, or learning and physical disabilities.

- **Nursing home**: this type of home provides nursing care to individuals in addition to support for personal care needs, assisting with meals and medication. Nursing homes are staffed 24 hours a day and have qualified nurses.
- **Care homes**: offer specialist care for individuals who require extra care and support, such as for dementia. These types of homes have qualified nurses and staff trained in dementia care. Other homes are registered to provide both personal care and nursing care.
- **Homecare**: also known as domiciliary care, this service offers care and support to individuals who wish to remain living in their own homes and do not want to move into, for example, a residential care home. Homecare can involve support with washing and dressing, cooking, housekeeping, nursing care and companionship. Homecare can be provided for individuals who require 24-hour care, or for those who require daily assistance with activities, or when their **informal carer** needs a break.

🔑 Key term

Informal carer Usually a family member or friend who provides care and support to an individual without getting paid.

Stretch activity

Privately funded services

1. Research services that are privately funded in the health, social care or early years sector.
2. Describe two privately funded services that provide care and support to adults or children.
3. For one service, describe to a partner how it is funded. (Aim to produce a detailed description. Look at the command word definitions to see what detailed means in the assessment.)

Private day nurseries

Private day nurseries are run by private individuals, community groups or organisations that offer both full-, part-time and **sessional day care services** for children from six weeks to five years. The age varies between nurseries, and some may not provide services for babies and toddlers. Most nurseries are open all year round, except for public bank holidays, usually between 7 a.m. and 7 p.m. Some nurseries also provide out-of-school childcare for school-age children. In England, all day nurseries must be registered with Ofsted.

Private day nurseries provide a range of services, including:

- learning activities
- opportunities for children's emotional and social development
- play activities such as sand and water play, adventure play and construction activities
- arts and crafts
- music and movement
- reading and stories.

Figure 4.3 What support is available from early years settings?

Key term

Sessional day care services Day care offered to pre-school children for a total of not more than 3.5 hours per session.

Hospitals

Private hospitals are funded through payment for healthcare by medical insurers such as the PPP Medical Healthcare Trust, or by patients themselves. The private healthcare company British United Provident Association (BUPA) runs its own private hospitals and also provides health insurance policies. BUPA is the largest international provider of residential and nursing care for older people and of specialist care for individuals who have dementia.

Third-sector organisations

Third-sector organisations are not for profit and are independent of the government – for instance, charities, community groups and self-help groups. Table 4.2 gives some examples of third-sector organisations that are registered charities, and provides information about the health, social care and early years services they provide.

Informal carers

Informal carers provide care and support to individuals who may have an illness or a disability, without getting paid. They can be family members and friends, volunteers and/or neighbours.

For example, a community-based volunteering initiative called Shared Lives is a service that is available to young people and adults who may require support or accommodation, i.e. for individuals who have learning disabilities, mental health needs, older people, young people leaving care, individuals who misuse substances and offenders. Individuals using these services either move in and live with a Shared Lives service approved carer or visit an approved carer regularly, i.e. during the day or overnight for support. In this way both parties share their lives, and the individual is provided with companionship and support that meet their individual needs.

Table 4.2 Examples of third-sector organisations and the services they provide

Third-sector organisation	Services
British Red Cross	• Provides aid to people and communities in the UK and internationally who experience conflicts, natural disasters and emergencies, e.g. the summer floods in the UK in 2007, and currently abroad to countries such as Syria • Provides health and social care services, e.g. support to people who wish to live independently at home including transport and mobility aids
Age UK	• Provides services for older people; the largest charity in the UK that specialises in support to older people • Provides information and advice on a range of topics, e.g. health, finances, housing • Raises awareness of issues faced by older people, e.g. accessing public services, living in safe communities • Provides independent living aids such as personal alarms and stair lifts • Provides training for those who support and provide services to older people • Carries out research about adults in later life, e.g. the Disconnected Mind research project
Barnardo's	• Provides support to children, young people and their families in the UK • Provides and leads a range of specialist services, e.g. counselling for children who have been abused, fostering and adoption services • Provides information, advice and education, e.g. supporting children and young people with developing their reading and writing skills, advising individuals who are homeless on services available in the local area • Runs residential special needs schools for vulnerable young people
Alzheimer's Society	• Provides information and advice on living with dementia and a range of other topics such as accessing services and managing finances • Provides practical and emotional support to individuals who have dementia and their families and carers • Provides training and resources for those who support and provide services to individuals who have dementia • Raises awareness of issues faced by people who have dementia and their carers, e.g. around rights and quality healthcare and support • Carries out research about dementia, e.g. the causes and prevention of dementia
National Autistic Society	• The leading UK charity for children and adults who have autism and their families • Provides specialist information, training and advice to individuals, their families and professionals, i.e. on all aspects of living with autism • Provides specialist care and support including autism services, e.g. residential homes, one-to-one support, support at work, home, in further and higher education

How the sectors work in partnership to provide support to individuals

Health and social care needs vary across different individuals and their life stages. It is not uncommon therefore for individuals to access different types of care and support, which may be provided through more than one type of provision or a combination of several, i.e. through statutory services, privately funded services, charities and/or informal carers. To ensure that individuals' health and care needs are met fully and responded to quickly, the different sectors work together in partnership to provide support to individuals.

Multidisciplinary working

This involves a group of professionals from different organisations, and with specialist skills and expertise, working together as one team to meet an individual's physical and psychological needs, and to provide the best possible outcomes for that individual.

For example, a multidisciplinary team working with an individual who has cancer may include the following members: GP, social worker, nutritionist, physiotherapist, specialist surgeon, cancer care nurse and chemotherapy nurse.

Interagency working

Interagency working is essential to ensure individuals can access the support they require and that meets their specific needs. It involves different agencies working together in a planned and formal way to provide high-quality healthcare and support. For example, to safeguard the welfare of children it is essential that local authorities, health trusts, schools, charities, community groups and the police work closely together.

Services forums

Services forums can consist of individuals and their families who are using health, social care and early years services, as well as professionals from a range of different statutory, private and voluntary organisations. Their aim is to improve the health, well-being and services outcomes for individuals, provide support and advice, share good practice, and influence the delivery and future of services being provided. Most local areas will have health and social care forums.

Case study: Working together to support Leon and his children

Leon is 36 and has recently separated from his wife. He has moved to a new area with his two children: Aidan, aged four, and Ben, aged six. Leon is registered with his local GP surgery and he is continuing his treatment for depression with the health services team. Aidan has learning difficulties and receives support from a carer who visits him at home. Ben has asthma and so visits the asthma nurse at the local GP surgery. A neighbour has been very welcoming and, as they also have two children of a similar age, they have met up for play dates. Leon has also joined a local support group for families of children with additional needs.

Questions

1 What professionals and agencies are working together to support Leon and his children?

2 What different types of support are Leon and his children receiving?

3 What do you think are the potential impacts of multidisciplinary working on Leon and his children? Why?

4 What do you think the potential consequences for Leon and his children would be if these different types of services and support were suddenly not available? Why?

Know it!

1 Give two examples of services in the statutory sector.

2 BUPA is an example of which type of service?

3 What do you understand by the term 'third-sector organisation'?

4 Give two examples of the support that informal carers can provide.

5 Name one difference between multidisciplinary and interagency working.

Assessment guidance

Learning outcome 1: Understand the different forms of support available in health, social care and early years settings

Marking criteria for LO1 Part A

Mark band 1	Mark band 2	Mark band 3
Provides a **basic** description of each health, social care and early years sector to show the types of services provided by each and may include how **some** are funded, with a few specific examples.	Provides a **sound** description of each health, social care and early years sector to show the types of services provided by each and includes how **many** are funded, with **some** specific examples.	Provides a **detailed** description of each health, social care and early years sector to show the types of services provided by each and includes how **most** are funded, with **many** specific examples.
Provides a **basic** explanation of the tasks undertaken by a member of the informal sector.	Provides a **sound** explanation of the tasks undertaken by a member of the informal sector.	Provides a **thorough** explanation of the tasks undertaken by a member of the informal sector.

 ### The OCR Model Assignment will ask you to:

- Describe the types of services provided by the health, social care and early years sector, include details about how they are funded, and include specific examples.
- Explain the care and support tasks undertaken by a member of the informal sector such as an individual's family, friend, neighbour or a volunteer.

 ### What do the command words mean?

- **Detailed description**: Your description will be a point-by-point consideration of each health and social care and early years sector to show the types of services provided by each.
- **Most and many:** Your description will include how the majority or nearly all of these are funded and you will include a large number of examples.
- **Thorough explanation**: Your explanation of the tasks undertaken by a member of the informal sector (e.g. an individual's family, friend, neighbour or volunteer) will be extremely attentive to accuracy and detail.

You should check the glossary in the Introduction for the definitions of each of the command words from OCR.

Marking criteria for LO1 Part B

Mark band 1	Mark band 2	Mark band 3
Demonstrates a **basic** understanding of the different types of support available.	Demonstrates a **sound** understanding of the different types of support available.	Demonstrates a **thorough** understanding of the different types of support available.
Provides a **basic** description of how the sectors work in partnership to provide support to individuals.	Provides a **sound** description of how the sectors work in partnership to provide support to individuals.	Provides a **detailed** description of how the sectors work in partnership to provide support to individuals.
There will be **some** errors in spelling, punctuation and grammar.	There will be **minor** errors in spelling, punctuation and grammar.	There will be **few**, if any, errors in spelling, punctuation and grammar.

→

The OCR Model Assignment will ask you to:

- Demonstrate an understanding of the different types of support available.
- Describe how the health, social care and early years sectors work in partnership to provide support to individuals.
- Your work will contain only a few, if any, mistakes in spelling, grammar and punctuation.

 What do the command words mean?

- **Thorough understanding**: Your work demonstrates an understanding of the different types of support available which will be extremely attentive to accuracy and detail.
- **Detailed description**: Your description is a point-by-point consideration of how the sectors work in partnership to support individuals.
- **Few errors**: Your work will contain a small number (if any) of errors in spelling, punctuation and grammar.

You should check the glossary in the Introduction for the definitions of each of the command words from OCR.

Learning outcome 2

Know the access routes and barriers to care pathways

Now that you have explored the different types of services and support that individuals can access, you will learn more about the different roles of professionals who provide access to health, social care and early years services.

Getting started

The term 'professional' can have different meanings for different people. In small groups, discuss your understanding of the term 'professional'.

How did your understanding compare to that of others? What similarities and differences were there?

The roles of professionals who provide access to health, social care and early years services

Table 4.3 outlines the roles of a range of professionals who provide access to health, social care and early years services.

The referral process to access different forms of services

There are three different ways for individuals to access different forms of services:

1 self-referral
2 professional referral
3 third-party referral.

Let's take a look at each of these in more detail.

Self-referral

Individuals can refer themselves to health, social care and early years services that accept self-referrals. Figure 4.4 on page 110 shows the self-referral journey that Simon took, when he referred himself to his GP and then to a stop smoking clinic.

Stretch activity

Health, social care and early years professionals

1 Provide **detailed** and **coherent** information about the roles of three different professionals who provide access to health, social care and early years services.

2 For one professional, give examples of how they provide access to support services through referral processes.

(Aim to produce a **thorough** account of the referral processes used. Look at the command word definitions to see what **detailed**, **coherent** and **thorough** mean in the assessment.)

Table 4.3 Summary of the roles of a range of professionals who provide access to health, social care and early years' services

Professional	Role
General practitioner (GP)	• First point of contact for individuals who live in the local community and require medical care • Provides advice and information on illnesses and/or conditions • Diagnoses illnesses and/or conditions • Recommends further treatment required for illnesses or conditions • Refers individuals to specialist services and professionals
Social worker	• Assesses individuals' needs • Provides information and advice on the services that individuals require • Provides support to individuals with managing their lives • Arranges access to services that individuals require
Hospital consultant	• Provides treatment and care to individuals accessing hospital and outpatient services • Monitors individuals' conditions and treatment • Refers individuals to other professionals for further treatment and investigations • Works alongside other professionals and specialist services to provide quality care and treatment
Counsellor	• Enables individuals to explore the changes they would like to make in their lives • Enables individuals to improve their lives and access the support they require to do so • Refers individuals to other services and professionals
Mental health professional	• Assesses an individual's mental health needs • Ensures individuals' views and rights are represented, i.e. through use of an advocate • Provides specialist mental healthcare and treatment • Arranges access to services that individuals require

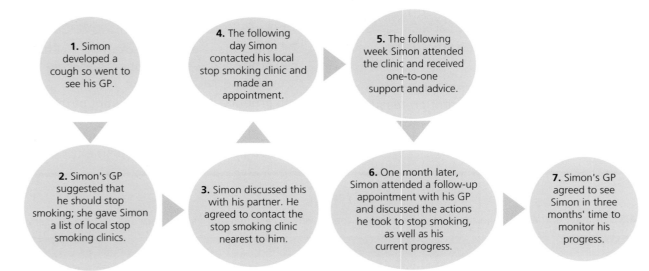

1. Simon developed a cough so went to see his GP.

4. The following day Simon contacted his local stop smoking clinic and made an appointment.

5. The following week Simon attended the clinic and received one-to-one support and advice.

2. Simon's GP suggested that he should stop smoking; she gave Simon a list of local stop smoking clinics.

3. Simon discussed this with his partner. He agreed to contact the stop smoking clinic nearest to him.

6. One month later, Simon attended a follow-up appointment with his GP and discussed the actions he took to stop smoking, as well as his current progress.

7. Simon's GP agreed to see Simon in three months' time to monitor his progress.

Figure 4.4 Simon's self-referral journey

Professional referral

Professionals such as care practitioners can also make referrals on individuals' behalf to specialist services or to other professionals. For example, a GP or nurse may refer an individual to a hospital for tests, to a mental health professional for emotional support, or to a dietician for advice on nutrition. A social worker who has concerns over a child's health, for example, may make a referral to a health specialist for children.

Third-party referral

Third-party referrals usually take place when a non-professional such as a family member, friend or neighbour refers the individual to a service because the individual is not able to do so themselves. For example, a nursery teacher may have concerns over a child and refer them to social services, a daughter may arrange for her frail mother who is having difficulties walking unaided to visit the GP, or an employer may refer a member of staff to their occupational health service if the employee's performance at work has deteriorated due to health reasons.

The barriers that can prevent individuals from accessing services

There are a range of barriers or factors that can act as obstacles and prevent individuals from accessing health, social care and early years services. Individuals may face one or more of these barriers. If the barriers are not dealt with appropriately and sensitively, they can prevent individuals from gaining access to the services they need.

'Ask not what disease the person has, but rather what person the disease has.'

William Osler

Financial

Individuals may not be able to access services because of the costs associated with doing so; charges and fees may deter and exclude individuals. For example, a parent may not be able to pay for childcare provision, or an individual who has a disability may not be able to pay for the cost of a taxi to access a social group that is available in another area.

Geographical

The services that individuals require may not be in close proximity to their home. This is often the case with specialist health or children's services, which may be located in another part of the country. There may be a lack of public transport, or a long bus or car journey may be required to get there. The costs associated with travelling to these locations and the arrangements that need to be made in relation to work and family members may make it difficult to access them. Similarly, an individual who lives in a rural area may find it difficult to find a **domiciliary care agency** (see definition on page 112) that has carers available to work in that area.

Cultural

It is important for services to be aware of the different cultural beliefs that individuals may have about who should provide care and how it should be provided. For example, in the Muslim faith, some women believe that they must be examined only by female nurses and doctors; not having a female professional available could therefore prevent a Muslim woman from accessing healthcare.

Cultural beliefs can also affect perceptions about how illness and social difficulties should be dealt with, including their causes, treatment and prevention. Culture can affect the practices that are used when providing support to individuals at different stages of their lives, such as during pregnancy, birth, during childhood, adulthood, through illnesses and death. For example, in Arabic and Chinese cultures it is common for female relatives instead of the husband to be present at the birth of a child. In some cultures, family members may become very upset if a hospital consultant shares their concerns about a relative's ill-health directly with the individual instead of with their family.

Language

Language interpreters are necessary for individuals to be able to understand and receive information and advice about how services could be of benefit to them. Similarly, not having written information available in a range of formats may exclude some individuals from accessing the services and professionals that are available.

Professionals that do not speak the same language as individuals may not be able to communicate with them effectively, and may also be viewed by individuals as not to be trusted.

Time

Time factors can make it difficult for individuals to access health, social care and early years services. For example, those who work variable shift patterns or have childcare or family commitments may be unable to access services that run only when they are working or caring.

Physical access

The type of building or the location of services can prevent access for some individuals. For example, if a service is in a building where there are stairs to its entrance, a lack of lifts and a lack of adapted toilet facilities, individuals with mobility difficulties may not be able to access it. Ramps and wide doorways can make areas accessible to individuals who have mobility difficulties and/or mobilise using a wheelchair.

Figure 4.5 How can buildings be made more accessible for individuals?

Psychological

Individuals' prior experience and attitudes towards requesting help for care and support may also prevent them from accessing services. For example, an older individual may fear losing their independence and not being able to continue to live in their own home if they request help with their care and support. An individual with mental health needs may fear being discriminated against if they access a **mental health crisis house** or **psychological therapies** for their depression, or may be too unwell to appreciate that they have a mental health need that needs to be treated. Some individuals may fear or not want to depend on strangers to provide their care and support, and prefer to manage by themselves as best they can.

Disability

In addition to the difficulties caused by lack of appropriate physical access to buildings, individuals who have disabilities may also find it difficult to access services where information and communication is not available in alternative formats. Examples include Makaton (for individuals who have learning disabilities), British Sign Language (for individuals who have hearing impairments) and Braille (for individuals who have visual impairments): see page 46 for more information.

Using appropriate terminology is important and not doing so may deter individuals who have disabilities from using services. The terminology used may cause individuals not to understand the service, misinterpret what the service provides, or create an impression that the service is patronising or will not be suitable to meet individuals' needs.

A lack of **assistive technology** can mean that individuals who have disabilities cannot access services. For example, an individual may need a mobility aid such as a wheelchair to be able to leave their home and access a local health centre. A child may need an **adaptive switch** to participate in games at a crèche. A young person with a hearing impairment may not be able to access their local youth group if the room where the evening sessions are held does not have a **hearing loop system**.

Key terms

Domiciliary care agency An organisation that provides care and support to individuals in their own homes.

Mental health crisis house Residential setting that offers intensive, short-term support for individuals experiencing a crisis and who are not able to remain living safely in their own homes.

Psychological therapies Techniques used to support individuals to manage their mental health and overcome any difficulties they are experiencing.

Assistive technology Devices or technologies that support individuals to maintain or improve their independence and safety.

Adaptive switch A device that allows an individual to use assistive technology.

Hearing loop system A specialist type of equipment that transmits sounds to individuals who use hearing aids or cochlear implants.

Group activity

What barriers do individuals with learning disabilities face?

In small groups, find out about the different types of barriers that individuals with learning disabilities may experience when accessing services in their local communities. In what ways can these barriers be overcome?

You may find it useful to refer to Mencap's website during this activity: www.mencap.org.uk

Accessibility of advocacy

Some individuals may not be able to speak up for themselves or make their wishes and needs known to others due to, for example, a learning disability, or a mental health need or a condition such as Alzheimer's.

Advocacy is essential to enable individuals to access services and find out information. As all individuals are unique and have different wishes, needs and preferences, so too there is a range of different advocacy models that individuals can access, depending on:

- their needs
- the type of advocacy they require
- how long the advocacy is required for
- who is able to provide the advocacy.

Here are the six main models of advocacy.

1 Self-advocacy: when an individual speaks up for themselves.
2 Peer advocacy: when an advocate who has experience of using services themselves supports another individual.
3 Citizen advocacy: a long-term partnership between the individual and the advocate.
4 Group advocacy: when a group of like-minded individuals speak up for themselves, such as People First.
5 Independent advocacy: a short-term partnership between the individual and the advocate, often provided by paid advocates and also referred to as case advocacy.
6 Statutory advocacy: where there is a statutory duty in law to provide advocacy, such as Independent Mental Health Advocacy and Independent Mental Capacity Advocacy.

Non-instructed advocacy is another approach that you need to be aware of. It is used for those individuals who, due to lack of capacity, are unable to instruct their advocates.

The type of advocacy required by an individual may not be available in the individual's particular area or to meet an individual's specific needs.

Case study: Barriers – and how to overcome them

Amy is the project co-ordinator for a parents' group in her local area that supports people living with depression. She is going to undertake a home visit to a parent, Tessa, she is concerned about. Recently Tessa has stopped attending the group, having done so for many months previously.

Upon arrival at Tessa's house, Amy notices that she seems upset and a little distracted. Amy begins by asking her how she is, as she hasn't seen her at the support group for some time. Tessa apologises for her non-attendance. She says there have been so many things happening in her life that she doesn't feel she has the time any longer to visit the group. She says she misses it because she used to get so much personally from it. Amy says that the other parents ask after Tessa all the time and are also missing her being there, as she always had so many positive suggestions.

Tessa explains that her mother has been unwell and is in hospital. As Tessa doesn't drive, she uses the local buses to go and visit her; public transport can be unreliable and time-consuming. To then go to the group would mean catching yet another two buses, which she thinks would be too much. Also, Tessa feels that she will be treated differently by members of her family if they find out about her going to the support group. Her sister has already made derogatory comments. Finally, Tessa explains to Amy that she is in the process of having further tests for high blood pressure; this was detected at a routine health check appointment at her doctors.

Questions

1 Identify the different barriers that are preventing Tessa from attending the support group.
2 Describe the effects that these barriers are having on Tessa.
3 Explain how Amy could help Tessa to overcome one of the barriers.

Know it!

1 Describe the role of a social worker.

2 Referrals to access different forms of services can be made by the individual themselves, a professional, and by who else?

3 Name two barriers that can prevent individuals from accessing healthcare services.

4 How can advocacy help individuals to overcome difficulties they may be experiencing in accessing services that meet their needs?

Assessment guidance

Learning outcome 2: Know the access routes and barriers to care pathways

Marking criteria for LO2 Part A

Mark band 1	Mark band 2	Mark band 3
Provides **basic** information on each health, social care and early years professional, giving **few** examples of how they provide access to support services. Gives a **basic** account of the referral processes used.	Provides **sound** information on each health, social care and early years professional, giving **many** relevant illustrative examples of how they provide access to support services. Gives a **sound** account of the referral processes used.	Provides **detailed** and **coherent** information on each health, social care and early years professional, for most giving **relevant** illustrative examples of how they provide access to support services. Gives a **thorough** account of the referral processes used.

 The OCR Model Assignment will ask you to:

- Provide information about the role of health, social care and early years professionals, giving examples of how they provide access to support services.
- Give an account of the referral processes used.

 What do the command words mean?

- **Detailed, coherent information and relevant examples**: Your work includes information that is a point-by-point consideration of each health and social care and early years professional, and it will be logical and consistent. You will provide examples that are correctly focussed on this and they will illustrate how each professional provides access to support services.
- **Thorough account**: Your account of the referral processes used will be extremely attentive to accuracy and detail.

You should check the glossary in the Introduction for the definitions of each of the command words from OCR.

→

Marking criteria for LO2 Part B

Mark band 1	Mark band 2	Mark band 3
Provides a **basic** description of the different types of barriers that prevent individuals from accessing services, with a **few** examples.	Provides a **sound** description of the different types of barriers that prevent individuals from accessing services, with **some** appropriate examples.	Provides a **thorough** description of the different types of barriers that prevent individuals from accessing services, with **many** appropriate examples.

 ## The OCR Model Assignment will ask you to:

● Describe the barriers that prevent individuals from accessing support services.
● Include examples of different types of barriers.

 ## What do the command words mean?

● **Thorough description**: Your description of the different types of barriers, which prevent individuals from accessing services will be extremely attentive to accuracy and detail.
● **Many examples**: Your description will include a large number of appropriate examples. This will not be the most (i.e. the majority of these) but will be a large number.

You should check the glossary in the Introduction for the definitions of each of the command words from OCR.

Learning outcome 3

Be able to produce care pathways for individuals

Getting started

As you have seen, there is a wide range of health, social care and early years services available to meet individuals' unique needs.

In pairs, discuss what you think makes an individual unique. Then note down the differences that exist between your partner and you, as well as the differences that exist between you and someone else you know.

How to recognise the groups of people who use services and their needs

Many different groups of people use health, social care and early years services. Each of these groups consists of people who have diverse needs that can vary throughout their lives.

Children

Children with disabilities and specific additional needs, and their parents or carers, may need access to services such as care in the home, play schemes or a **residential short break** (see page 116 for definition). Children with special educational needs, such as difficulties with reading and writing, socialising with other children, or concentrating, may need to access services that provide them with support to be able to attend nursery or school.

> ### Key term
>
> **Residential short break** A holiday where children can socialise and take part in activities to give their family or carers a break from caring.

Children who care for family members who are chronically ill, or who have a disability or a mental health need, may need to access services so that they can have a break from their responsibilities, and are able to relax and socialise with others. Children who live in households with adults who have substance misuse issues or where domestic violence is taking place may also need to access services for both practical and emotional support.

Services and support may also be needed for children who show signs of abuse and/or neglect, and for children who begin to carry out anti-social or criminal behaviour at a young age.

Accessing services and specialist support early on can enhance the quality of life experienced by children and their parents or carers, and make sure their needs are met.

Adults

'Adults' refers to those who are aged 18 and over.

Some adults may have social care needs and require social care services such as short-term support, up to a maximum of six weeks. This is referred to as reablement support and is aimed at restoring a person's independence, for example following a fall at home.

Long-term support, also called additional support, is required by some adults after six weeks, to help them continue to live their lives independently. Adult carers who look after a vulnerable person may also require access to services and support.

Adults may also require access to healthcare services in relation to their emotional needs, communication, mobility, nutrition, continence as a result of a disability, accident or illness.

It is important to remember that adults' needs may vary through their lifetime and may therefore reflect the needs of people who have disabilities, mental health needs and older people – three groups you will learn more about below.

Older people

There is a range of services available for older people who are at home, in residential settings in the community (such as residential and nursing homes) and in hospital. Figure 4.6 provides you with more information about some of these.

The National Service Framework for older people, published in 2001, introduced the Single Assessment Process (SAP) that requires health and social care professionals to deliver good-quality care and support services to adults and older people. It includes:

- the assessment of older people's needs
- the delivery and review of care and support to older people
- better services and outcomes for older people
- effective sharing of information between different agencies and health and social care professionals.

Figure 4.6 Services for older people

Stretch activity

People with disabilities and their needs

1 Name three different reasons why a person with a disability may require access to services or support.

2 For one service or support, include **detailed** information about how it can help with promoting the person's well-being.

(Aim to provide **detailed** information. Look at the command word definitions to see what **detailed** means in the assessment.)

People with disabilities

Individuals who have disabilities as a result of physical impairments, sensory impairments, cognitive impairments (impairments relating to learning, remembering and problem-solving for example), conditions or illnesses may require access to services for support and information. For example, individuals may need to know about:

- accessible housing
- accessing adaptations, aids and assistive technology
- benefits and funding
- accessible community facilities and other services and support that are available to them to promote their physical and mental health and well-being.

People who have disabilities have the right to ask their local authority for a care and support needs assessment so that they can find out about the services and support that are available to meet their needs, and whether any funding is available to meet these needs.

People with mental health needs

'Mental health problems affect about 1 in 10 children and young people. They include depression, anxiety and conduct disorder, and are often a direct response to what is happening in their lives.'

Source: Mental Health Foundation, 2016

'1 in 4 people in the UK will experience a mental health problem each year.'

Source: Mind, 2016

People with mental health needs can access the specialist treatment and support they require from community-based services, which include teams of professionals with specialist skills in mental healthcare, such as community psychiatric nurses and psychologists. Other services are specifically designed to work with children and young people who experience mental ill-health for the first time, and provide information, treatment and support to both individuals and their families.

Specialist wards in hospitals are also available for individuals who experience serious mental illness and who would benefit from treatment in hospital; day hospitals and crisis houses also offer support and care to people who are experiencing serious mental illness. Recovery colleges are a new type of service that provide individuals who have mental health needs with opportunities to access education and training programmes to enable their recovery.

People who have mental health needs are offered a mental health assessment to ascertain their needs, and the services and support they may require to benefit them. As well as finding out about the person's mental health symptoms and experiences, the assessment will also build a profile of the individual's lifestyle, their background, culture, strengths, abilities, wishes and preferences for the future.

How to identify the steps needed to offer an appropriate care pathway

Offering an appropriate care pathway involves following best practice when providing care and support to an individual who has a specific disability, illness or condition, or particular needs. There are four key steps involved in setting out the care and support journey an individual can expect.

Step 1: Outlining the individual's journey through a health, social care or early years provision

Getting to know and understand each individual as a unique person is crucial to offering an appropriate pathway to provide care and support to the individual. Best practice involves gathering information from the individual and the other people and services who know the individual well, so that an accurate picture of the whole person can be built about their:

- likes
- dislikes
- strengths
- abilities
- interests
- beliefs
- culture
- views
- physical, intellectual, language, emotional and social needs.

Care, support and particular services can then be looked at in the context of which will meet the individual's needs and how these will be provided.

Step 2: Identifying the role and responsibilities of the professionals involved

Once the particular service and the type of care and support has been identified, it is important to identify the roles and responsibilities of the different professionals involved. They may work across a number of different teams and/or services in order to co-ordinate a planned and consistent approach that is suitable for the individual.

Case study: Maisie and the professionals who work with her

Maisie is three years old and has a heart condition. She attends a local nursery and lives at home with her parents, two older brothers and grandfather. Figure 4.7 gives more information about the roles and responsibilities of some of the different professionals involved in Maisie's care journey profile.

Healthcare professionals
- Community child nurse – provides nursing care at home and arranges for Maisie's family to have short breaks from caring for Maisie
- Dietician – provides dietary advice on foods that Maisie can eat, and advises on supplements Maisie can have when she has difficulties eating and drinking
- Consultant paediatrician – provides specialist care, support and treatment for Maisie's heart condition

Social care professionals
- Care co-ordinator – ensures that all care and support services being provided are co-ordinated; provides Maisie's family with information and support, and acts as the link between the different services
- Support group worker – provides support to Maisie's family and other families who are going through similar experiences with their children who have an illness
- Music therapist – promotes Maisie's emotional well-being and provides her with an outlet to have fun and relax

Early years' professionals
- Nursery nurse – works in the nursery Maisie attends and supports the early stages of Maisie's development
- Special educational needs co-ordinator – assesses Maisie's additional needs and provides support to Maisie while in the nursery, to meet her needs
- Play specialist – supports Maisie to express how she is feeling about her condition and the treatment she is undergoing, through age-appropriate play activities

Figure 4.7 Maisie's care journey profile

Questions

1 For one healthcare professional, describe the support provided to Maisie and her family.
2 How does the music therapist contribute to Maisie's care?
3 Identify the role and responsibilities for one early years professional involved in Maisie's care.

Step 3: Recognising the importance of consultation

It is very important for individuals to be involved in the decision-making process for their own care and support by working in partnership with the professionals involved in their care and support, either directly or through a representative such as a family member or advocate.

Having a shared decision-making process between individuals and professionals has many benefits:

- increased well-being, self-confidence and self-esteem
- increased independence for the individual
- increased choices and control of one's life
- opportunities for individuals' views to be heard
- increased understanding and sharing of knowledge between individuals and professionals of the treatments and options available
- increased **self-awareness**
- more likely to lead to high-quality care and support
- more likely to ensure that the individual achieves their goals and aspirations.

 Classroom discussion

'No decision about me, without me.'
Source: NHS England, 2016
What do you think this statement means for individuals and groups of people accessing NHS services? Discuss in small groups and then share your thoughts with the rest of the class.

 Key term

Self-awareness The ability to know one's own character and feelings.

Step 4: Choosing the methods of communicating information according to an individual's needs

When choosing how to communicate information, consider whether the information should be provided in person to the individual and/or their family, over the telephone, or in writing via the post or an email. This will depend on the individual and their family's needs.

The format is important if the information is to be understood. Information may have to be simplified, i.e. by removing jargon, using short sentences and key words. It may need to be made available in the individual's preferred language. Alternative formats may also need to be available, such as large print for those who have visual impairments, photographs, Makaton and/or symbols for those with learning disabilities, or British Sign Language (BSL) for those who have a hearing impairment.

A Care Pathway for an Individual with Dementia

Before Diagnosis
- Individual visits GP with their daughter who is worried that her father has the symptoms of dementia; the individual has also noticed the difficulties he is having with his memory.
- GP conducts an assessment with the individual and his daughter i.e. finds out about the individual's past history and current health
- GP undertakes a physical examination and organises blood tests and an ECG
- GP refers the individual to a specialist memory clinic. A community based eldercare facilitator from the memory clinic meets with the individual and his daughter at home and completes the individual's assessment

At Diagnosis
- The Eldercare Facilitator and the Consultant Psychiatrist meet with the individual and his daughter at a Memory Clinic where further assessment is undertaken involving an MRI (magnetic resonance imaging) scan and a more detailed assessment of their memory and thinking processes. →

Figure 4.8 An example of a care pathway

- A diagnosis of dementia is confirmed.
- A plan to meet the individual's current and future needs for care, support and treatment is discussed and agreed
- Confirmation of the agreed plan is communicated in writing to the individual and his GP

After Diagnosis

- The Eldercare Facilitator and the Consultant Psychiatrist begin to co-ordinate the agreed plan for the individual in relation to the care, support and treatment that will be provided.
- On-going monitoring of the provision of care, support and treatment is completed with the individual and his daughter at regular intervals at home.
- Information and advice continues to be provided by the Memory Clinic to the individual and his daughter.
- The Memory Clinic's team also liaise and review the provision of care and treatment with all the other relevant agencies involved.

Figure 4.8 An example of a care pathway (continued)

The purpose of a care plan in organising support for an individual in a health, social care or early years setting

A care or support plan is an effective way of establishing how an individual's care or support needs will be met, including the roles and responsibilities of all those involved. It must be developed with individuals, or those acting on individuals' behalf. The plan must be able to be understood by the individual and others involved in their lives.

It is unique to the individual and about the whole of the individual's life, including:

- strengths and abilities
- wishes and preferences
- goals and aspirations
- views and beliefs
- needs
- the support required for daily living such as, for example, personal care, household management, socialising and relationships, who will provide it, when and how

- the services required
- the professionals involved.

Care and support plans must also identify:

- what goals the individual wishes to achieve (outcomes)
- how the individual wishes to achieve their goals (actions)
- what support the individual requires in relation to, for example
  - communicating with other people
  - daily activities
  - taking their medicines as prescribed
  - being aware of dangers to their health
  - eating healthily and exercising regularly.

A care and support plan must also include details in relation to who is in charge or responsible, who will provide the support, where it will be provided and when it will be provided.

Care plans need to reflect individuals' changing needs. When areas of support do not work, this needs to be amended on the individual's care and support plan so that all those involved in supporting the individual to achieve their goals can provide consistent and high-quality care that is unique to the individual and meets their needs. It is very important that care plans are updated regularly and remain up to date; this includes having emergency numbers and contact details for all those involved in an individual's care.

Figure 4.9 shows an example of a care plan form. Note the use of 'I' throughout. Why do you think this is important?

Know it!

1 Give two examples of groups of people who use services.
2 Identify the needs of one group of people who use services.
3 Name one reason why it is important to involve an individual in making decisions about their own care.
4 Define the term 'care plan'.
5 Name two areas of support a care plan should cover.

Personal details

Name:
Address:

Tel:
Emergency contact details:

What is important to me?
(My likes, interests, strengths, abilities, wishes, preferences, views, beliefs, the people involved in my life)

What support do I need around personal care?
(What do I want to achieve and how? Who will provide this, how and by when?)

I need…

Actions to take

What support do I need around medication?
(What do I want to achieve and how? Who will provide this, how and by when?)

What support do I need around eating?
(What do I want to achieve and how? Who will provide this, how and by when?)

What support do I need around exercising?
(What do I want to achieve and how? Who will provide this, how and by when?)

What support do I need around socialising?
(What do I want to achieve and how? Who will provide this, how and by when?)

Signatures from those the plan has been agreed with:

Date the plan was prepared:
Date the plan will be reviewed:

Figure 4.9 An example of a care plan form

Assessment guidance

Learning outcome 3: Be able to produce care pathways for individuals

Marking criteria for LO3 Part A

Mark band 1	Mark band 2	Mark band 3
Produces a **basic** care plan for an individual using health, social care or early years services. May need guidance and support to produce the plan. **Few** examples are given to illustrate the services and support suggested. The relevance of choices made is **partly** justified. Provides a **basic** description of an individual and their circumstances.	Produces a **sound** care plan for an individual using health, social care or early years services with little need for support. **Some** examples are given to illustrate the services and support suggested. The relevance of choices made is **mostly** justified. Provides a **clear** description of an individual and their circumstances.	Independently produces a **detailed** care plan for an individual using health, social care or early years services. **Clear** examples are given to illustrate the services and support suggested. The relevance of choices made is **wholly** justified. Provides a **detailed** description of an individual and their circumstances.

 The OCR Model Assignment will ask you to:

- Produce a care plan for an individual using health, social care or early years services.
- Give examples to illustrate the services and support suggested.
- Justify or give reasons for how the choices you have made are relevant.
- Include a description of an individual and their circumstances.

 What do the command words mean?

- **Independently produce a detailed care plan**: Without relying on others, you will produce a care plan. This will be for an individual using health, social care or early years services. The care plan will be set out point-by-point.
- **Clear examples:** The examples you give to illustrate the services and support will be focussed and you will express these accurately.
- **Wholly:** You will make sure that that you justify the relevance of your choices completely, i.e. to the whole extent.
- **A detailed description**: You set out the main characteristics, point by point, about an individual and their circumstances.

You should check the glossary in the Introduction for the definitions of each of the command words from OCR.

→

Marking criteria for LO3 Part B

Mark band 1	Mark band 2	Mark band 3
Provides a **simple** care and support pathway, recognising the needs of the group of people using the services. Includes **basic** information for a chosen individual, detailing, with a **few** examples, the expected journey through provision, the professionals involved, and the consultation and communication methods.	Provides a **sound** care and support pathway, recognising the needs of the group of people using the services. Includes **clear** information for a chosen individual, detailing, with **some** examples, the expected journey through provision, the professionals involved, and the consultation and communication methods.	Provides a **detailed** and coherent care and support pathway, recognising the needs of the group of people using the services. Includes **detailed** information for a chosen individual, detailing with **many** examples the expected journey through provision, the professionals involved, and the consultation and communication methods.
Draws upon **limited** skills/knowledge/understanding from other units in the specification.	Draws upon **some relevant** skills/knowledge/understanding from other units in the specification.	**Clearly** draws upon **relevant** skills/knowledge/understanding from other units in the specification.

 ## The OCR Model Assignment will ask you to:

- Provide a care and support pathway that recognises the needs of the people using the services.
- Include information about the individual including their care journey, detailing with examples the expected journey through provision, the professionals involved, and the consultation and communication methods used.
- Draw on skills, knowledge and understanding from other units.

 ## What do the command words mean?

- **Detailed and coherent care and support pathway**: The care and support pathway you provide will be logical and consistent. It will be a point-by-point consideration recognising the needs of the group of people using the services.
- **Detailed information, and many examples:** Your work includes point-by-point considered information for an individual. You will include a large number of examples, the expected journey through provision, the professionals involved and the consultation and communication methods.
- **Clearly and relevant:** You will draw upon skills/knowledge/understanding from other units that are correctly focussed on the activity at hand. You will do this in an accurate and focussed manner.

You should check the glossary in the Introduction for the definitions of each of the command words from OCR.

Read about it

Weblinks

www.ageuk.org.uk Age UK – information about services and support it provides for older adults

www.alzheimers.org.uk Alzheimer's Society – information about the services and support provided by the UK's leading dementia support and research charity

www.autism.org.uk The National Autistic Society – information about the services and support provided by the UK's charity for people who have autism

www.barnardos.org.uk Barnardo's – information about the services and support provided by the UK's largest children's charity

www.bupa.co.uk BUPA – information about the British United Provident Association

www.mencap.org.uk Mencap – information, advice and support provided by this UK charity for people who have a learning disability, their families and carers

www.mind.org.uk Mind, otherwise known as the mental health charity – information about the support and mental health services available

www.nhs.uk NHS – information about the most common services provided by the NHS in England

http://www.nhs.uk/Conditions/social-care-and-support-guide/Pages/direct-payments-personal-budgets.aspx for more information on working with people who receive direct payments and/or personal budgets.

www.redcross.org.uk British Red Cross – information about the services and support it provides

Reference books

Bradley, A., Murray, K. and Cowan, L. (2007) *My Life Plan: An Interactive Resource for Person Centred Planning*. Pavilion Publishers.

McIntosh, B. and Whittaker, A. (2011) *Personal Planning Book*. Foundation for People with Learning Disabilities.

Stalker, K., Duckett, P. and Downs, M. (1999) *Going with the Flow: Choice, Dementia and People with Learning Disabilities (Research into Practice)*. Pavilion Publishers.

Wrycraft, N. (2016) *Assessment and Care Planning in Mental Health Nursing*. Open University Press.

R025 Understanding life stages

About this unit

This unit examines the life stages from 5 to 65 years, through childhood, adolescence and adulthood. Everyone's life is different. Many different factors affect life stages in varying ways.

In this unit you will look at the changes associated with the development from childhood to adulthood and the factors that can influence this development. You will look at the ageing process for older adults. You will also learn about birth defects and non-birth medical conditions that may affect progress through the life stages. You will have the opportunity to develop a support plan for an individual at a particular life stage.

Learning outcomes

LO1: Understand the stages of development from young people to adulthood

LO2: Understand the ageing process in older adulthood

LO3: Know which medical conditions may affect progress through the life stages

LO4: Be able to create support plans

How will I be assessed?

You will be assessed through a series of assignment tasks, which are set by OCR. The assignment will be marked by your tutor and then moderated by OCR.

For LO1, you need to:

- explain physical, intellectual, language, emotional and social (P.I.L.E.S.) changes associated with young people's transition into adulthood, with examples to illustrate key points
- explain the factors that affect key developmental changes, with examples to justify your thoughts on the effects of life events.

For LO2, you need to:

- describe the ageing process, using examples to illustrate the effects on development
- explain how a person's role in life changes.

Make sure you refer to the current OCR specification and guidance.

Note: SPAG is assessed in this learning outcome. For LO3, you need to:

- provide an overview of birth defects and non-birth medical conditions that affect progress through the life stages
- describe the chosen conditions and discuss the effects of these on the health and social well-being of the individual and their family.

For LO4, you need to:

- provide a support plan for a person with specific medical requirements, showing understanding of their life stage and addressing the specific medical conditions
- be able to communicate the plan to the care user, understanding their needs
- draw upon skills/understanding/knowledge from other units in the specification.

Links to other units

Unit R021: Essential values of care for use with individuals in care settings (LO1 and LO2): As RO25 is about development throughout the life stages you need to know about the rights of individuals (e.g. consultation) as covered in RO21 LO1. LO2 covers the early years care values which could relate to the factors that affect developmental changes for children and young people.

Unit R022: Communicating and working with individuals in health, social care and early years settings (LO1, LO2 and LO3): This unit links into the development of language throughout the life stages. In RO25 LO4, good communication skills will help you to present your plan to the care user in an appropriate manner, for example you may have to use Makaton to communicate your ideas.

Unit R023 (optional unit): Understanding body systems and disorders (LO1 and LO2): LO1 and LO2 provide you with an understanding of how the different body systems work, helping you to understand the ageing process on physical development. This knowledge will also help your understanding of birth defects and non-birth medical conditions that affect progress through the life stages.

Unit R024 (optional unit): Pathways for providing care in health, social care and early years settings (LO2 and LO3): Work that you have completed for this unit will help you to draw up an appropriate support plan for your care user. From LO2 you will know the roles of professionals. You will also be aware of barriers which may prevent care users from accessing services. LO3 will provide you with the knowledge to draw up a support plan.

Learning outcome 1

Understand the stages of development from young people to adulthood

Getting started

Think back to when you were five years old.

- How have you changed physically and intellectually?
- How have your language skills improved?
- What emotional and social changes have you gone through?

The changes associated with the transition from young people to adulthood

Table 5.1 shows the life stages covered in the 5–65 age range.

Table 5.1 Life stages (5–65)

Life stage	Age	Key features
Childhood	5–10	Child starts school.
Adolescence/ young person	10–18	This is the period of **puberty** The child's **peer group** is of great importance.
Adulthood	18–65	At 18, an individual can vote, go to university, get a job, get married, etc.

 Key terms

Puberty The process of physical changes through which a child's body matures into an adult body capable of sexual reproduction.

Peer group A group of people (usually of similar age, background and social status) with whom a person associates, and who are likely to influence the person's beliefs and behaviour.

Gross motor skills The larger movements of arms, legs, feet or the entire body (for walking, running, skipping and jumping).

Fine motor skills Smaller actions, such as grasping an object between the thumb and a finger when holding a paintbrush or pencil.

Physical (childhood)

Development of the body
Between five and ten years of age, the body grows taller and gains weight. As children take part in physical activities both muscles and bones become stronger. Strength and muscle co-ordination improves rapidly in these years. Children lose their baby teeth and replace them with their permanent teeth.

Gross/fine motor skills
During this period of growth, both **gross** and **fine motor skills** develop rapidly. By the age of five, most children can hop, skip, jump and stand on one foot for a few seconds. They are able to throw and catch a ball, usually with two hands.

As they move towards ten years of age, children can combine gross motor and fine motor skills more easily; for example, they can turn, spin and jump, such as in basketball or netball. Children also demonstrate stronger hand–eye co-ordination. They are better able to kick a ball into a goal or throw a ball at a target, for example. They can demonstrate improved agility, speed, co-ordination and balance.

Children continue to advance their fine motor skills, such as those needed for clearer handwriting and detailed artwork. By the age of ten, many will be able to draw and write with better control. Working on the computer or playing videogames will also be taken to a new level, with many children of this age having the co-ordination and heightened reflexes to perform more difficult tasks than ever before. It is a good time for a child to be introduced to a musical instrument.

Physical appearance
A child looks taller and slimmer, and their facial features look more adult as they lose the baby-face look.

Physical (adolescence/young person)

Development of the body
Between the ages of 10 and 12, most girls go through puberty. Figure 5.1 shows the physical changes that take place in girls during puberty.

Boys usually go through puberty between the ages of 12 and 14. Figure 5.2 on page 128 shows the changes that boys go through during puberty.

Case study: Should Chloe be worried?

Chloe is 15 and is very small for her age. She is worried because her periods haven't started and she is still the same shape as she was when she was a child. Her mother says she shouldn't worry as she is a late developer.

Questions

1 Do you think Chloe should be concerned? Why or why not?

2 What advice would you give Chloe?

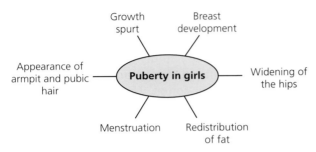

Figure 5.1 Puberty in girls

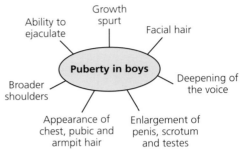

Figure 5.2 Puberty in boys

Boys and girls may experience skin problems such as acne during puberty, due to hormonal changes.

Gross/fine motor skills

By the age of ten, most children have developed their gross and fine motor skills but they may develop them further by practice, for example when playing sports.

Physical appearance

As shown in Figures 5.1 and 5.2, young people's appearance will change considerably during adolescence and they will begin to look like adults.

Physical (adulthood)

Development of the body

By the time people reach adulthood they have reached their full height and have stopped growing. As people age and move towards their sixties, they may experience early symptoms of ageing such as grey hair, wrinkles and long-sightedness which means they need glasses for reading. They may also suffer from poor health such as cancer or heart disease.

Women usually go through the menopause between the ages of 45 and 55. This means their periods stop so they are unable to have children.

Gross/fine motor skills

As people age, they may find difficulty with fine motor skills due to arthritis. For example, knuckles and joints swell and become painful, making it difficult to hold paintbrushes or icing bags for long periods. Muscle strength decreases and reactions become slower.

Physical appearance

In adulthood, skin elasticity lessens, skin wrinkles and muscles slacken, so people may develop a double chin. Men can also lose their hair. Posture can be affected as muscles become less flexible.

 Research activity

The menopause

Find out more about the menopause here: www.nhs.uk/Conditions/Menopause/Pages/Introduction.aspx

1 Explain what is meant by the menopause.

2 Explain the causes of the menopause.

3 Describe the symptoms of the menopause.

4 Analyse why women might feel a sense of loss at the time of the menopause.

Intellectual

Building up of concepts, especially mathematical ones

Although children can count by the age of seven, usually they do not understand how the logic of mass, volume and number works. Maths requires a wide range of skills, and involves a broad vocabulary and variety of concepts. Mathematical skills often build on one another. Some children are strong in some types of maths but weak in others.

By the time children are ten, they are usually skilled in addition and subtraction, and are building skills in multiplication, division and fractions. They are at the stage where logical thinking is limited to what they can actually see.

Aged 11 and over, children have started to use logic and **abstract thinking** to think through complicated ideas. This is adult thinking. This continues to develop throughout adolescence and into adulthood, where people develop more ways of thinking.

Self-esteem

Self-esteem refers to the feelings individuals have about themselves – their confidence in who they are. Self-esteem is based on the judgement of others of ourselves and on our own judgement. If someone is happy about themselves, they will have high self-esteem.

Adolescence is the time when young people begin to think about themselves and wonder what others think about them. If they are unhappy and do not like themselves, they will have low self-esteem and little confidence. This can carry on into adulthood.

Development of ability to understand, reason and learn

Most children start to develop verbal reasoning skills from four or five years of age. When they go to school, teachers help them to develop these skills. From five to ten they develop a capacity to concentrate on one thing (directed thinking). At school they carry out a variety of activities, which helps them to learn and to understand the world around them. Even when they have to learn the concepts of courses like physics or mathematics, verbal reasoning comes into play. Adolescents continue to learn and develop their skills, and this continues into adulthood.

Learning to read and write and, later on, taking exams

Between the ages of six and ten, most children should be able to write legibly and with ease. At this age they are learning to read fluently. By 11 they become more fluent writers, increasing in speed; handwriting becomes more automatic as they develop their own style. By 11–13 they are reading to learn about their hobbies and other interests, and to study for school. They comprehend more fully what they've read. They read fiction, including chapter-based books, and non-fiction, including magazines and newspapers.

They learn to revise for examinations and know that, to do well, they have to memorise and be able to use facts. They may continue to use their examination techniques all through their adult lives, particularly if they go on to study for academic qualifications.

Memory

Memory is the ability to acquire, store and recall information or experiences across time. A person's memories form the basis for their sense of self, guide their thoughts and decisions, influence their emotional reactions, and allow them to learn. As such, memory is central to **cognitive development**. Memory performance generally improves with age up until around 25–30 years.

Key terms

Abstract thinking Being able to solve problems using concepts and general principles.

Cognitive development The construction of thought processes (including remembering, problem-solving and decision-making) from childhood through to adulthood.

Group activity

Memory game

- Put 10 to 20 objects on a tray, then cover them with a towel or cloth.
- Tell your class that you have a number of objects on the tray and that you want them to remember as many items as possible. They will have only one minute to view them.
- Then take the cover off the tray and start timing one minute.
- After one minute, cover the tray again.

Ask the class to write down all the items that they can remember. Could they remember all of the items? Are there any items that were forgotten by all the class? Discuss the implications for someone who remembered none of the items.

Language

Communication skills/being able to hold a conversation

Often by five or six years, children have good communication skills. Usually by the age of five to seven children can speak using full adult grammar. They can use language in a range of social situations. By the age of ten most children can talk easily with people of all different ages. They will keep a conversation going by giving reasons and explaining choices. They will have speech patterns that are nearly at an adult level. Communication skills develop throughout life as people learn to have a better command of language.

Developing language

Children at the age of five can use their language skills to learn to read, write and spell.

They learn that the same word can mean two things, such as 'orange' the fruit and the colour 'orange'. At this age, children's vocabulary will be between 2,000 and 3,000 words.

By the age of ten, some children enjoy reading. They may seek out magazines and books on subjects of special interest.

Vocabulary will be added to at all ages through the lifespan.

Emotional

Family influences

For most people, whatever their age, the family is important for providing emotional stability (or an emotionally stable environment). People should feel secure within the family home. It is a place where family members can relax and be themselves. Young people should be able to test out relationships without fear of rejection.

Positive and negative emotions

Hormones can cause surges (or rushes) of positive and negative emotions known as mood swings; for example, the 'terrible twos' (where children throw tantrums if they don't get their own way), and adolescence, where one minute a young person can be feeling very positive and the next they are feeling very down with negative emotions (for example, that they are very unpopular and that no one likes them). Adolescence is the time of life when a young person learns to regulate and control emotions, and to form secure relationships ready for adulthood.

Self-concept

Self-concept is the view or perception that we have of ourselves – our strengths, weaknesses, status and so on. As people age, self-perceptions become much more detailed and organised, as they form a better idea of who they are and what is important to them.

Stress

As children become older, they start to experience stress. When children start secondary school, they may feel stressed because of the new environment. They may be worried about examinations.

As children become adults there is even more to worry about – for example, keeping their job, having enough money to pay the bills. Later there is retirement and ill-health to consider.

The environment

The environment, or surroundings, that a person lives in can affect their emotions. If it is unpleasant, with noise, pollution or poor housing, it can make someone feel very unhappy and stressed. However, a positive atmosphere will have the opposite effect. The environment can affect people regardless of their age.

Social

Development of relationships
By the time a child is nine years old they will have developed special friendships. They learn about friendships and social roles from within their family. During adolescence, young people are more influenced by their peer group than by their family. They may become friends with members of the opposite sex.

In early adulthood, friendship groups are still very important but as people marry and have families of their own, they may have less time for socialising with friends outside their home.

Social interaction
Social interaction is a social exchange between two or more individuals. It is any conversation, be it a lengthy catch-up between friends or a casual swapping of toys in a playgroup. Social interaction is important for any age group, as people need to feel part of society whatever their age. Otherwise they may feel isolated.

Environment
Where a person lives can have a bearing on their social lives. If they live in an urban area in or near a town, they are going to be within easy reach of cinemas, coffee shops, leisure facilities and so on. However, if someone lives in a rural location, they may have to depend on public transport to get them where they want to be, especially if they don't drive. This will add time and money to their outing. Children and teenagers may have to rely on their parents to drive them everywhere.

Status is the position of an individual in relation to another or others, especially in regard to social or professional standing. The higher up the cultural ladder a person is, the more they are in control of their environment as they can afford to pay for what they want. They can make choices. People can alter their cultural status as they age. For example, someone might be born into poverty but could, by education or hard work, better their opportunities and become financially better off.

Factors that affect development

Education
Education is important for everyone as it helps people to make the right choices – for example, regarding the foods to eat to keep them healthy, or to go to screening to help prevent illness or disease.

Children start school at four or five years of age. It is important that they attend regularly so they do not fall behind. As they become adolescents they have the opportunity to do GCSEs or Cambridge Nationals, then on to Cambridge Technicals and A-levels, then perhaps university, college or work to complete an apprenticeship.

A good education with good qualifications will help people to get a good job that pays more than the minimum wage. Older people often continue their education by going on short courses – for example, some adults will do computer courses to keep them up to date with technology.

Stretch activity

Factors that affect key developmental changes
Harry was born into a comfortable lifestyle. His father was a banker and his mother was a barrister. He was brought up by his grandmother while his parents worked. She died when he was 16. His school holidays were spent in the family's holiday homes in Bermuda and Italy. He can speak three languages fluently. He was educated privately and achieved excellent A-level results. He went to his father's old college in Cambridge, where he achieved a first-class degree. He got a well-paid job in the City and married his childhood girlfriend. After three years of marriage, their first son was born with cerebral palsy.

Give an explanation of the factors that have affected development for Harry. Remember to give examples to illustrate the key points.

(Aim to produce a **thorough** explanation. There should be a **wide** variety of appropriate examples. Look at the command word definitions to see what **thorough** and **wide** mean in the assessment.)

Culture/religion

The culture/religion in which a person grows up can influence everything from developmental milestones and parenting styles to what kinds of hardship they are likely to face. Children learn the customs of their family's religion/culture during their childhood.

While biological milestones such as puberty tend to be the same across cultures, social milestones, such as the age at which children begin formal schooling, or adolescents can go out without their parents, can differ greatly from one culture to the next. Some cultures believe in arranged marriages, where girls are married to a male of their parents' choice; in some cultures, this may be during adolescence. Culture and religion affect individuals throughout their lifespan unless an individual decides to abandon them, but it is often difficult to do so.

Puberty (e.g. hormonal)

During puberty physical changes happen due to the increased production of sex hormones, as described below.

Oestrogen in girls

Oestrogen is a hormone. It is responsible for promoting the development as well as the maintenance of the female reproductive parts. If there is not enough oestrogen in a young girl's body, she will not be able to menstruate properly. A girl will menstruate throughout life (unless pregnant) until the menopause, when the ovaries produce so little oestrogen that the lining of the womb fails to thicken up and so periods stop altogether. For most of a woman's life, oestrogen helps to protect the heart and bones, as well as maintaining the breasts, womb, vagina and bladder in their healthy state. The marked loss of oestrogen in a woman's body that occurs around, and after, the menopause can, therefore, have detrimental effects on her health.

Testosterone in boys

Testosterone is 'a male hormone' and levels of it rise during puberty, peak during the late teen years and then level off. After the age of 30 or so, it's normal for a man's testosterone levels to decrease slightly every year. This can cause physical changes later on in older adults, like increased body fat, reduced muscle bulk and strength, and decreased bone density.

Home/school/work

If an individual is unhappy at home, school or work, it can affect their emotional or social development, or even physical development. For example, if a child is neglected at home they could fail to thrive or gain weight. If a child or young person is bullied at school then they may not want to go to school and could become physically ill with the worry of how to deal with it.

An adult can also be bullied at home or work or be passed over for promotion, which could have a detrimental effect on their self-esteem and confidence.

Relationships (e.g. significant others, marriage, civil partnership, divorce)

Secure relationships, whether through marriage or civil partnership, are essential to provide a safe social base for the family to grow and develop. Relationships also help to prevent stress – for example, if an individual has had an awful day at school/work they know they will feel better when they get back home to people who care about them.

Relationships help individuals to maintain their self-esteem, which can prevent physical illness and help with mental and social well-being. Sometimes, however, divorce is the only answer when a relationship breaks down and cannot be repaired.

Pregnancy

A child's development can be affected during pregnancy if the mother smokes, drinks or takes drugs. The baby could have a low birth weight and more serious defects. If the mother has an unhealthy diet during pregnancy, this can also result in the baby having a low birth weight and a lifetime of poor health.

Infections such as rubella or chickenpox can be dangerous to the foetus, particularly during early pregnancy.

Birth of children

Although most babies are delivered in good health, birth is a traumatic experience and there are many things that can go wrong. Babies suffering from oxygen deprivation (before, during or after birth) often develop disabilities, such as **cerebral palsy**, **autism**, **attention deficit hyperactivity disorder (ADHD)**, seizures and behavioural problems. Most of these conditions will affect the person for life.

Menopause

For some women the menopause is a relief as they know they will no longer have periods. Others feel sad that their child-bearing years are over, even if they had no intention of having any more children. This can cause feelings of depression.

Physically, changes in hormones during the menopause can lead to a bone-weakening disorder called osteoporosis. Osteoporosis describes the reduction in bone density that can cause bones to weaken. As a result, the risk of fractures increases. Women need to ensure that they have enough vitamin D, which will help with the absorption of calcium in the diet, in order to reduce the risk of this disorder. They also need to do weight-bearing exercise such as running, skipping, dancing or aerobics.

Redundancy

Apart from the financial implications, job loss or redundancy can mean a significant loss of identity, and an individual's self-confidence may be eroded. In addition, a person may feel excluded from society. Depending on the age, personality type, family and financial circumstances, individual reactions may range from mild to moderate to severe. The most common reaction to job loss is physical shock, accompanied by some of the classic symptoms associated with grief – disbelief, denial, anger, feeling stunned, becoming withdrawn, loss of confidence and a feeling of low self-esteem. This is especially true if the individual is a younger adult who will then have to find another job in order to support themselves and their family.

With the retirement age rising, an older person who is made redundant may find it difficult to find alternative work. However, if the person is near retirement age they may not be as distressed, if they had intended to retire soon.

Bereavement

The death of someone close to you is a traumatic and painful event for most people. It is often very difficult for children to put their feelings into words. The lowered self-esteem of bereaved adolescents is linked to problems such as withdrawal from social activities, acts of aggression, and impaired performance in school or in their work. Bereaved children also tend to suffer from increased levels of anxiety, depression and guilt. Others may rebel or go into an adult role that is premature and overwhelming. Children and adolescents may experience other losses such as a lack of financial support, and disrupted familial routines and plans for the future.

Loss through **bereavement** is a major stress for older people and can reduce their ability to cope and be independent.

Read the case study on page 134 and write down the answers to the questions that follow.

 Key term

Cerebral palsy Affects body movement, muscle control, muscle co-ordination, muscle tone, reflex, posture and balance. It can also impact fine motor skills, gross motor skills and oral motor functioning.

Autism A lifelong developmental disability that affects how people perceive the world and interact with others.

Attention deficit hyperactivity disorder (ADHD) A group of behavioural symptoms that include inattentiveness, hyperactivity and impulsiveness.

Bereavement Coping with change following the loss of someone very close, such as a partner, wife, husband, etc.

An overview of the ageing process

The effect of ageing on physical development

As people age, they can see physical changes that become more obvious in old age. Table 5.2 summarises the effect of ageing on physical development.

The effect of ageing on intellectual development

Memory loss
Forgetfulness is common among older adults. As people age, they experience physiological changes that can cause slowness in brain function. It takes longer to learn and recall information. People often mistake this slowing of

Table 5.2 The effect of ageing on physical development

Part of body	Physical development due to ageing
Skin	● Wrinkles ● Looseness because of loss of elasticity ● Dryer skin
Hair	● Thinning ● Growth slows ● Men may go bald
Hearing, smell and taste	● Senses deteriorate ● May lose appetite
Eyesight	● Long sightedness may develop ● Cataracts and glaucoma may cause blindness if not treated
Teeth	● May be decay and gum disease
Lungs and respiratory system	● Lungs less elastic ● Respiratory muscles weaken ● Less able to take part in strenuous exercise due to lack of lung capacity ● More likely to be affected by disorders such as influenza or pneumonia, so should be vaccinated
Heart and blood vessels (cardiovascular system)	● Heart efficiency decreases ● Blood pressure may be raised ● Blood vessels less elastic; can lead to cardiovascular disease such as strokes, heart attacks, etc.
Digestive system	● Saliva and digestive juices decrease with age, causing indigestion or heartburn ● Food takes longer to go through system as muscles are weaker and less efficient; this leads to constipation
Urinary system	● Kidneys less efficient at filtering waste products ● May need to pass urine more frequently ● May be prone to urinary infections
Reproductive system	● Menopause marks end of reproduction for women
Skeleton and muscles	● People shrink in height; total bone mass is reduced ● In women, osteoporosis may result in fractured or broken bones ● Knee and/or hip problems can cause mobility issues ● Muscles become less flexible; balance can be affected; posture and mobility likely to alter

the mental processes for true memory loss. Many mental abilities are unaffected by normal ageing.

There are a number of causes of age-related memory loss.

1   The hippocampus, a region of the brain involved in the formation and retrieval of memories, often deteriorates or weakens with age.

2   Hormones and proteins that protect and repair brain cells and stimulate **neural growth** also decline with age.

3   Older adults often experience decreased blood flow to the brain, which can impair memory and lead to changes in cognitive skills.

Not all older people will develop dementia.

Employment/retirement

Many older people are not retiring at 65 but choosing to work for longer. Some people feel they lose their status and a sense of who they are when they retire; that they have lost their place in society and their purpose. People also have to cope with the loss of income, which often falls significantly during retirement. Most people's income will drop by half, or even more.

Key term

Neural growth Refers to any growth of the nervous system.

Older adults may also lose friends when retiring, as they no longer see their work colleagues every day. Retirement can also be a source of relationship stress. For example, a partner may be used to being at home by themselves during the day and both parties could find it difficult to adjust to a new routine.

Research activity

Dementia

In pairs, research dementia and find out what the symptoms are. As a starting point, you may find it useful to look at this link on the Age UK website: www.ageuk.org.uk/health-wellbeing/conditions-illnesses/dementia/what-is-dementia

Then read the two profiles below. Decide which person is likely to have dementia and which one has memory loss. Explain why. Share your answers with the rest of the class.

1   Colin is 69. His partner has noticed that he has difficulty getting washed and dressed in the morning. He has started to repeat stories several times during the same conversation. Last week he set off to his daughter's house and got lost. He had his satnav device but couldn't follow the directions.

2   Archie is 72. He has difficulty occasionally in finding the right word to use in conversation but he has no problem with following and holding a conversation. He recently forgot his wedding anniversary.

Case study: Bernie's retirement

Bernie has looked forward to his retirement for the last two years. He has been planning to stay in bed until late every day, go fishing most weekday mornings and generally enjoy life.

The reality now that Bernie has retired is very different. He still wakes up at the same time each morning and cannot get back to sleep. He misses his work friends, who he now sees only occasionally. Fishing during the week is lonely

as often he is the only one at the riverbank. His wife has her own group of friends who she likes to go out with.

Question

1   In small groups, discuss how Bernie could change his current situation. How can he start to enjoy his retirement?

The effect of ageing on emotional and social development

Change in relationships within the family

After bringing up their own children, many older people have a role in looking after grandchildren, often in the form of childcare when parents are at work. They may also help the family with chores around the house or garden, or sometimes financially. This can be a time of enjoyment for grandparents as they have all the fun but none of the responsibility.

The ageing process can also bring about a role reversal, where the 'children' (now adults) of the family start to look after their parents as they age and become frail.

Bereavement

When a partner dies, there can be confusion about practical issues like financial matters or how to run the home, in addition to all the upset and sorrow. The remaining partner could feel lonely and isolated, particularly if they depended on their partner to take them shopping or out in the car. They may feel that they do not have anyone to go out with. If the couple were together for many years, the remaining partner may become depressed and not want to leave the house.

There is upset too for the children of the deceased, as they realise they have lost a parent. They may then have to be involved with looking after the remaining parent, who could find it difficult to cope after their loss.

For an older person, losing a sibling or a good friend can be a life-changing event, as they may feel that all their support has gone.

The change of role in life

From parent to grandparent

Having grandchildren can give grandparents a sense of continuity and reassurance that life goes on. Their life can have added meaning and purpose, giving them a renewed confidence in their usefulness and value. They get the pleasure of being involved in their grandchildren's lives without the full responsibility of looking after them all the time. However, grandparents must remember that they are not in charge and should respect any decisions that the parents make, even if they disagree with them.

From carer to cared for

Many older people worry that they will lose their health and become a burden to their family. An older person may become totally dependent on one or more of their children. This is a difficult role reversal for many parents because now their son or daughter is in charge and has authority over them. They may feel upset by this if they have the capacity to realise what is happening to them.

Stretch activity

The ageing process

Abdul is 45 and would like to know more about getting older.

Produce a description of the ageing process that will help him.

Use a wide range of relevant examples to discuss the effects on all areas of development. (Remember to give a **thorough** description. Look at the command word definitions to see what **thorough** description means in the assessment.)

Know it!

1 Why are older people more likely to have cardiovascular disease?
2 Explain why mobility may be a problem for older people.
3 Some older people do not want to retire. Why is this?
4 Discuss why grandparents may be keen to look after grandchildren.

Assessment guidance

Learning outcome 2: Understand the ageing process in older adulthood

Marking criteria for LO2

Mark band 1	Mark band 2	Mark band 3
Provides a **basic** description of the ageing process using a **limited** range of examples to illustrate the effects on some areas of development.	Provides a **clear** description of the ageing process, using a **range** of examples to illustrate the effects on most areas of development.	Provides a **thorough** description of the ageing process, using a **wide range** of relevant examples to discuss the effects on all areas of development.
A **basic** explanation is given on how a person's role in life changes with learners **partly** explaining their thoughts.	A **sound** explanation is given on how a person's role in life changes with learners **mostly** explaining their thoughts.	A **thorough** explanation is given on how a person's role in life changes, with learners **wholly justifying** their thoughts.
There will be **some** errors in spelling, punctuation and grammar.	There will be minor errors in spelling, punctuation and grammar.	There will be **few**, if any, errors in spelling, punctuation and grammar.

 The OCR Model Assignment will ask you to:

- Give a description of the ageing process and include examples to discuss the effects on all areas of development.
- Provide an explanation of how a person's role in life changes and explain/justify your thoughts.
- Check spelling, punctuation and grammar carefully.

 What do the command words mean?

- **Thorough description**: Your description of the ageing process will be extremely attentive to accuracy and detail.
- **Wide range:** Your description of the ageing process will include many relevant details, and a comprehensive list of examples to discuss the effects on all areas of development.
- **Thorough explanation, and wholly justifying:** Your explanation of how a person's role in life changes will be extremely attentive to accuracy and detail, and you will explain your thoughts and reasons for this to the whole amount.
- **Few:** There will only be a small number of spelling, punctuation and grammar errors in your work, not many but more than one.

You should check the glossary in the Introduction for the definitions of each of the command words from OCR.

Learning outcome 3

Know which medical conditions may affect progress through the life stages

Getting started

'Underweight celebrities encourage young people to copy their body shape.'

Discuss this statement in small groups. Then open up the discussion to the whole group.

An overview of conditions that may affect progress through the life stages

Birth defects

Birth defects can contribute to a range of health problems and some can be fatal. They are often long-term conditions that cannot be cured, but the symptoms and complications can usually be controlled with treatment. All birth conditions can affect physical, intellectual, language, emotional and social development.

Genetics

Genetics play a significant role in the development of certain birth defects. Every living being has cells containing chromosomes. When a human embryo is fertilised, it gets half of its chromosomes from the father and the other half from the mother. Birth defects may occur if the number of chromosomes passed on to the child is more or less than is required. Problems may also arise if any one of the chromosomes is faulty. Genetic birth defects in babies can occur even when both parents are healthy.

Examples of genetic disorders include **spina bifida**, heart defects and Down's syndrome (which we will discuss later in this section). Table 5.3 outlines some of the possible effects of genetic birth defects on physical, intellectual, language, emotional and social development (P.I.L.E.S.) through the main life stages.

Key terms

Birth defects Problems that affect the structure or function of organs or systems in the body from birth.

Genetics The study of the traits people inherit from their family through DNA.

Spina bifida A type of birth defect called a neural tube defect; it occurs when the bones of the spine (vertebrae) don't form properly around part of the baby's spinal cord.

Table 5.3 Possible effects of genetic birth defects on P.I.L.E.S. across life stages

	Childhood	Adolescence	Adulthood
Physical	• Could have seizures, abnormal speech, visual and/or hearing impairments • Slow at physical development milestones	• Seizures often improve • Starts to catch up with physical development with physiotherapy and training	• Seizures sometimes return • More likely to catch infections
Intellectual	• Could have short attention span • Mild to moderate intellectual disability	• Improvement of attention span through training • With ongoing support and interventions, adolescents with an intellectual disability can learn to do many things but could find learning/academic study challenging	• May be able to work
Language	• Speech/language delay	• Begins to catch up with speech/language	• Language/speech at acceptable level to cope with day-to-day life
Emotional	• May be very immature and have inappropriate behaviour	• Dismay/frustration/anger at not being able to do the same as others	• May be embarrassed/stressed/depressed/angry • Loss of self-esteem and confidence
Social	• Find it harder to build friendships because they are different	• More difficult to socialise as they can be less independent than others	• Few friends, so less opportunity to socialise

Sensory problems

Sensory birth defects affect the development and function of the sensory organs, including the eyes and ears, and can contribute to visual impairment and hearing loss. Many of these problems are caused by syndromes or inherited conditions, and often people with certain conditions experience problems with particular senses. Examples of sensory birth defects include cataracts, other visual conditions, blindness, hearing loss and deafness.

For possible effects of sensory problems on intellectual, language, emotional and social development, see Table 5.3.

Down's syndrome

Down's syndrome is a set of physical and mental traits caused by a gene problem that happens before birth.

- Normal cells contain 46 chromosomes. A child inherits 23 from the mother and 23 from the father.
- In children with Down's syndrome, all or some of the cells in their bodies contain 47 chromosomes.

Children who have Down's syndrome tend to have certain features, such as a flat face and a short

Table 5.4 Possible effects of Down's syndrome on P.I.L.E.S. across life stages

	Childhood	Adolescence	Adulthood
Physical	<ul><li>Poor muscle tone</li><li>Other physical disorders including autism spectrum disorders, problems with hormones and glands</li><li>Hearing loss</li><li>Vision problems</li><li>Heart abnormalities</li><li>Delayed milestones</li><li>Susceptible to infections</li><li>Important to monitor growth and development in babies and children</li><li>When babies' teeth develop, they need regular dental checks</li></ul>	<ul><li>Need regular medical follow-ups</li><li>Important to monitor for heart problems, hearing problems and eye problems</li><li>A healthy, balanced diet and exercise should be encouraged to reduce the risk of weight gain and obesity</li></ul>	<ul><li>Go through the normal physical changes of ageing more rapidly</li><li>Average age of death is 50–55</li><li>Most common cause of death is heart disease</li></ul>
Intellectual	<ul><li>Cognitive impairment</li><li>Short attention span</li><li>Problems with thinking and learning – usually ranges from mild to moderate</li></ul>	<ul><li>Steadily improve in all their independence skills</li><li>Achieve a high degree of independence in personal care by late adolescence</li></ul>	<ul><li>May be independent as adults and able to work successfully</li></ul>
Language	<ul><li>Delayed communication/language skills</li><li>May find it challenging to give a verbal response</li><li>May rely on body language such as gestures and signs</li></ul>	<ul><li>Can start conversations, participate in conversations, talk about past and future events, ask questions and use the telephone</li><li>Some individuals have problems being understood</li></ul>	<ul><li>Vocabulary continues to improve but still may have difficulty being understood</li></ul>
Emotional	<ul><li>May be immature and have inappropriate behaviour</li><li>Impulsive behaviour</li><li>Poor judgement</li></ul>	<ul><li>Increase in confidence and independence</li></ul>	<ul><li>Few adults with Down's syndrome have behavioural difficulties</li></ul>
Social	<ul><li>Most children have appropriate social behaviour and good social skills, but some develop difficult behaviours that cause family stress and affect social inclusion</li></ul>	<ul><li>The opportunity to establish friendships may be affected by lack of social independence, and by speech, language and cognitive delay</li></ul>	<ul><li>Continue to develop good social skills and appropriate social behaviour</li></ul>

neck. They also have some degree of intellectual disability. This varies from person to person, but in most cases it is mild to moderate. Table 5.4 outlines some of the possible effects of Down's syndrome on P.I.L.E.S. through the main life stages.

Non-birth medical conditions

Non-birth medical conditions such as paralysis (when you lose the ability to move your body or part of your body, see page 144 for more information) can affect anyone at any time of their life, for instance if they are injured in an accident. Some conditions do not usually occur during childhood. For example, coronary heart disease normally affects older adults as the trigger is often an unhealthy lifestyle or smoking. However, other conditions such as anorexia, mental ill-health, paralysis, epilepsy and loss of senses could happen in childhood and carry through to adulthood. Other examples of non-birth medical conditions, not discussed in this section, include cancer, asthma and diabetes.

Anorexia

Anorexia nervosa is an eating disorder where a person keeps their body weight as low as possible. It is a serious mental health condition.

Individuals limit the amount of food they eat and exercise excessively. The condition often develops out of an anxiety about body shape and weight that originates from a fear of being fat. Many people with anorexia have a distorted image of themselves, thinking they are fat when they are not (see Figure 5.3). There is also a theory that anorexia is about control – sometimes people with anorexia feel that the only thing they can control is their weight. The condition can affect people throughout their lives; they can recover and then relapse.

Anorexia affects people physically, intellectually, emotionally and socially.

- Physically, periods stop, hair becomes thin, bones become brittle, etc.
- Intellectually, there could be loss of interest in school work (or work and home in adulthood).
- Emotionally, there could be anxiety, depression, mood swings and loss of self-esteem.
- Socially, there could be a total social withdrawal from friends. The condition has a huge effect on family and friends, who are anxious and desperate to get the person to eat.

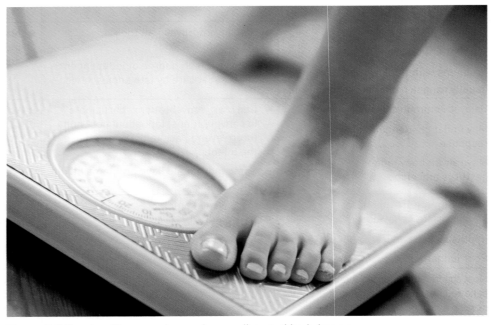

Figure 5.3 People with anorexia may have a distorted body image

Case study: Georgie's anorexia

Georgie is 14 and is studying Health and Social Care. When they were taught about BMI she was shocked to find her BMI was classified as overweight.

She resolved to lose weight. She started to throw her sandwiches away at lunchtime and just ate the fruit in her lunchbox. She told her parents she was going to have breakfast in the school's breakfast club and then skipped breakfast. She started to lose weight. She weighed herself daily. Georgie's friends have commented that she was getting thin and she told them what she was doing. She begged them to do nothing.

She started to walk the six miles to school and back every day when she used to get the school bus. Her parents didn't realise what Georgie was doing, as they left for work early and didn't get home until after 6 p.m. – this also allowed Georgie to cook the evening meal and eat none of it herself.

Questions

1 What should Georgie's friends do next?

2 Anorexia, an eating disorder, is classified as a mental health need. Why do you think some people don't agree with this?

Mental ill-health

Mental illness refers to a wide range of mental health conditions – disorders that affect mood, thinking and behaviour. Examples include depression, anxiety disorders, schizophrenia, eating disorders and addictive behaviours. Many people have mental health concerns from time to time. A mental health concern becomes a mental illness when ongoing signs and symptoms cause frequent stress and affect the person's ability to function in everyday life.

Mental health can affect people physically, intellectually, emotionally and socially.

- Physically, a person might neglect themselves – for example, by not washing or eating.
- Intellectually, an individual may not be able to concentrate on anything, as they feel confused, anxious or depressed.
- Emotionally, they may feel very angry or scared, or be full of self-doubt.
- Socially, friends could be looked on with suspicion or they may shout abuse at them.

Coronary heart disease

Look back at Unit R023 (LO2) for more information about coronary heart disease.

 ## Classroom discussion

Mental health – can we talk about it?

Years ago, mental health was not discussed. If someone had a mental illness it was not spoken about. Psychiatric hospitals were known as 'lunatic asylums'.

In recent years, celebrities have brought mental health issues into the open. People like Patsy Palmer, Ruby Wax, Stephen Fry, Sheryl Crow, Britney Spears and Elton John have spoken about their mental health problems.

1 How do you think the perception of mental health issues has changed over the years?

2 Generally, do you think people are willing to talk about their mental health issues, or is there still a stigma attached to discussing mental ill-health? Give reasons for your answer.

Paralysis

Paralysis is loss of the ability to move one or more muscles. It may be associated with loss of feeling and other bodily functions. It is not usually caused by the muscles themselves, but by problems with the nerves or spinal cord the brain uses to control the muscles. A person with paralysis will usually have some form of nerve damage.

The most common causes of paralysis are:

- stroke
- head injury
- multiple sclerosis
- spinal cord injury.

As well as having a huge physical effect on the body, paralysis causes emotional, social and intellectual problems.

- In emotional terms, the person affected is likely to feel angry, frustrated and helpless, full of grief and depressed.
- Socially, the person may not want to go out, as they don't want others to see them or feel sorry for them.
- Intellectually, an individual may not be able to think beyond their immediate situation of not being able to move. They may be too self-absorbed by their condition.

Epilepsy

Epilepsy is a condition that affects the brain. When someone has epilepsy, it means they have a tendency to have epileptic seizures. Electrical activity is happening in the brain all the time, as the cells in the brain send messages to one another. A seizure happens when there is a sudden burst of intense electrical activity in the brain. This causes a temporary disruption to the way the brain normally works. The result is an epileptic seizure.

There are many different types of seizure. What happens to someone during a seizure depends on which part of their brain is affected. During some types of seizure the person may remain alert and aware of what's going on around them while, with other types, they may lose awareness. They may have unusual sensations, feelings or movements. Or they may go stiff, fall to the floor and jerk.

Research activity

First aid procedures for epilepsy

Watch this video to learn the correct first aid procedure for someone who is having an epileptic seizure: www.epilepsy.org.uk/info/firstaid

In groups, discuss how you could educate all the students in your school about the correct procedures for epileptic seizures. Then share your findings with the class.

Apart from the physical effects of seizures, there are intellectual and emotional/social impacts.

1 Intellectually, the person may have memory loss.

2 When first diagnosed, an individual may be frightened to leave the house in case they have another seizure. They could be anxious, as they do not know when their next seizure might happen. After the diagnosis they may be unable to drive because of their medication. This could mean that they are unable to socialise as much as they did in the past, or get to work as easily.

Loss of senses

Loss of any of the senses can be traumatic, but loss of hearing or sight has the most impact on everyday life, as carrying out tasks becomes more difficult. There can be many causes of loss of senses, ranging from an infection to an accident. In the case of hearing loss, working with loud equipment can cause deafness, as can regularly listening to music at a high volume through headphones.

Loss of sight can affect a person in the following ways.

1 Physically, if the person cannot see they may be afraid of falling.

2 Emotionally, they may feel scared to go out in case they fall.

3 Socially, they may feel helpless and useless, and want to cut off any social contact that involves leaving the house.

Loss of hearing can also affect a person socially, emotionally and intellectually.

- Socially, an individual may not want to mix with other people, as they may feel they cannot communicate properly.
- Emotionally, a person may feel cut off from people as they cannot hear what is going on around them.
- Intellectually, an individual may feel that they appear to be unintelligent if they are unable to keep up with conversations.

The effect of medical conditions on health and social well-being

Financial

Any medical condition, whether it is there from birth or not, can cause the family expense. It could be extra costs for a special diet, heating, medication, clothing, laundry, transport or equipment. For example, if a person is paralysed and wants to go out they may have to use a taxi as the transport in their area is unsuitable for them. They might have to pay transport costs to travel back and forth to the hospital or surgery.

The person with the condition may not be able to work so they have to rely on benefits. They may also need a parent or partner to look after them, so that person cannot do paid work either.

Children with Down's syndrome are at a higher risk of certain health conditions than the general population. Eating nourishing foods can help reduce some of the physical symptoms and increase overall health.

The cost of a holiday goes up when a family member has a medical condition, especially insurance.

Social

Sometimes it is difficult for someone with a medical condition to socialise fully with other people outside the home. There are many reasons for this.

For example, if a person has epilepsy then they would not be able to go with friends to a bar that had flashing lights in case a seizure was triggered. A person who was blind may find it difficult to get to a venue to socialise. An individual in a wheelchair may have issues accessing a venue.

Some families of Down's syndrome children feel 'different' when out in the world and this can make them reluctant to do things other families do. Some families resent stares; others become accustomed to them. Someone with a mental illness may feel that everyone is looking at them and talking about them.

Emotional

People with long-term medical conditions can suffer from depression and other mental health issues. They may experience shock when they are first diagnosed with a condition and have difficulty coming to terms with the implications this might have for them; for example, having to take daily medication, make lifestyle changes, or the realisation that there may be no cure. There could be a lack of understanding from family, friends or employers, which can lead to feelings of isolation and loneliness.

People can become socially excluded if their condition leads them to lose contact with their social networks or they have to give up work. They may feel a range of emotions including:

- fear of what the future may bring
- frustration, anger and resentment
- loss of self-esteem as they are more reliant on other people, because the condition changes their view of themselves or the way others see them.

Families and friends may also feel upset and perhaps resentful.

Physical

Physical health is affected by long-term medical conditions. Individuals may no longer be able to do physical things such as walking along the beach. This could affect family holidays and days out, as parents/carers have to ensure that a venue is accessible for a wheelchair.

People with epilepsy may feel really tired and need to sleep after a seizure, so a planned shopping trip for the family may have to be cancelled. Anorexia may cause the person to have little energy through lack of food or be hospitalised. As we saw earlier in this section, Down's syndrome can cause issues with hormones and glands, hearing loss, vision problems and heart abnormalities. Individuals with Down's syndrome may also have a low immune system, meaning it is easier for them to pick up infections and bugs. People with coronary heart disease have to be careful that they do not get influenza as they can develop life-threatening complications, so they must always have the flu jab.

Stretch activity

How conditions can affect transition through the life stages

Josh has Down's syndrome, Omar has epilepsy and Carly has anorexia.

1 Provide an overview of each condition and how it will affect the transition through the life stages. (Aim to produce a **detailed** and **coherent** overview of the three conditions. Look at the command word definitions to see what **detailed** and **coherent** overview means in the assessment.)

2 Discuss how each condition might affect the health and social well-being of the individual and their family.

(Aim for a **thorough** description and a **thorough** discussion. Look at the command word definitions to see what **thorough** means in the assessment.)

Know it!

1 Explain what is meant by a birth defect.

2 What are the possible effects of genetic birth defects on physical development through the life stages?

3 What are the possible effects of Down's syndrome on language development through the life stages?

4 Describe some of the possible financial implications of having a long-term medical condition.

5 List three emotions a person with epilepsy may feel if they have to give up work.

Assessment guidance

Learning outcome 3: Know which medical conditions may affect progress through the life stages

Marking criteria for LO3

Mark band 1	Mark band 2	Mark band 3
Provides a **basic** overview of a **limited** range of conditions that affect the transition through the life stages.	Provides a **clear** overview of **a range** of conditions that affect the transition through the life stages.	Provides a **detailed** and **coherent** overview of the effect of a **wide** range of conditions that affect the transition through the life stages.
Provides a **basic** description of the chosen conditions with a **basic** discussion of how they might affect the health and social well-being of the individual and their family.	Provides a **detailed** description of the chosen conditions, with a **detailed** discussion of how they might affect the health and social well-being of the individual and their family.	Provides a **thorough** description of the chosen conditions with a **thorough** discussion of how they might affect the health and social well-being of the individual and their family.

→

The OCR Model Assignment will ask you to:

- Provide an overview of a range of conditions that affect transition through life.
- Give a description of the chosen conditions.
- Provide a discussion of how these conditions may affect the individual and their family.

 What do the command words mean?

- **Detailed and coherent overview**: You should provide a point-by-point overview of the conditions that affect the transition through life, which is logically and consistently expressed.
- **Wide range:** You will include many relevant examples of conditions that affect the transition through the life stages.
- **Thorough description and thorough discussion:** Your description of the chosen conditions and discussion of how they might affect the health and social well-being of the individual and their family will be extremely attentive to accuracy and detail.

You should check the glossary in the Introduction for the definitions of each of the command words from OCR.

Learning outcome 4

Be able to create support plans

Getting started

Work in pairs. One of you should wear a pair of ear plugs and the other should try to communicate a verbal message. For example, try asking what they are going to have for lunch or what they are doing at the weekend. You can use any body language you need to help you get the message across.

How successfully was the message passed on?

Swap places (use new ear plugs).

Did it get any easier to communicate? What lessons did you learn?

A support plan sets out how a person's care and support needs will be met. Everyone's needs for care and support are different, and their needs can be met in different ways. The care and support planning process is there to help decide the best way to meet the person's needs. It considers a number of different things, such as what needs the person has, what they want to achieve, what they can do by themselves or with the support they already have, and what types of care and support might be available to help them.

How to communicate information clearly, sensitively and appropriately to different audiences

It is essential to ask an individual how they would like to be communicated with. They may require:

- manual/sign languages such as British Sign Language, Makaton, Braille, etc.
- simplified language
- larger-size type
- symbols or pictures
- audio tapes/DVDs
- text translated into languages other than English.

As well as asking for an individual's preferred method of communication, you must impart the information clearly.

- Make sure they can see, hear and are comfortable.
- Talk clearly and allow the person to be able to lip-read if necessary.
- The environment should be quiet, with no distractions.
- The plan must be physically accessible to the individual.

Case study: Usha's hospital review

Before Usha was discharged from hospital, she had to have a review from the hospital social worker, who was arranging the support needed to allow Usha to go home. Usha was on a busy stroke ward and the social worker had to speak very loudly for her to be able to hear what she was saying. She discussed Usha's financial and family situation on an open ward during visiting hours. Usha was too tired (and has vascular dementia) to take in any information that the social worker was saying, but was expected to sign the forms to say she understood the situation.

Questions

1 Did the social worker communicate Usha's information appropriately, sensitively and clearly? Why, or why not?

2 How could the situation have been improved?

You may want to look back at Unit R022, which has more detailed information on communicating effectively.

- The information must be communicated in a sensitive manner so time is allowed for a response from the service user.
- Concentrate on the individual and ensure there are no barriers to communications about the proposed plan.
- Be sensitive to the individual's feelings. For example, as we will see in the case study later in this section, Alice is coming to terms with needing support when she had been independent.

How to match care and support provision to specific individual needs

As part of the initial preparations for putting together a support plan, an individual will have a comprehensive needs and risk assessment from their local authority. This will involve asking them about their personal needs, and will include questions about all aspects of their life including mobility, medication and their general safety within the home. Having ascertained an individual's needs, the required resources will be identified.

There will be a huge variation in the support needed, depending on the individual's circumstances. Some people, like Clive (who we find out about in the stretch activity on page 149), need a minimum of support to remain in their own home. Others, like Alice, who we will learn about later in this section, have complex needs and will need a lot more support.

How to adapt care and support to reflect the progression of individuals through different life stages

Care needs evolve throughout a person's life. If a child is born with a severe physical disability they will be dependent on their parents, just like any other baby. However, as they grow older and reach adolescence, the parents may need more support in order to meet their child's physical, intellectual, language, emotional and social needs. The child will become bigger and heavier, and therefore more difficult to move, and they may need equipment such as a hoist.

As the child becomes an adult at 18, they will move from child health and social care services into adult services. If they are able to, they may wish to leave their parents' home and have a home on their own. In order for this to happen the individual will need to be assessed. If they are living on their own, they will need support from the health and social care services.

How to link care and support to specific medical conditions for different life stages

As we have mentioned above, care needs change as individuals grow and get older. Children's needs differ from those of adults.

Table 5.5 shows the care and support that 45-year-old Louis, who is paralysed, has received through childhood and adolescence into adulthood.

Table 5.5 Care and support provided to Louis through his life stages

Life stage	Care	Support
Child/ adolescent	• Personal care – help going to bed/ getting up in morning to give parents a break, especially as he got older • Sitters/befrienders • His family	• Aids and equipment such as stair climbers, buggy, wheelchair, etc. • After-school club • Short breaks for disabled children • Taxi to school
Adult	• Personal assistant to help with day-to-day tasks	• Purpose-built house • Mobility car • Aids and adaptations within the house • Assistive devices such as hoist, electric wheelchair, etc. • Blue Badge parking permit

To help identify how to match care and support provision to the specific needs of an older adult, let's have a look at Alice's story.

Alice is an 83-year-old widow. She is recovering from a stroke, which has left her struggling with mobility, and because of this she is prone to falls. Her memory has been affected and so has her eyesight. She needs help with all personal care.

Table 5.6 shows some of the information that would be needed to produce a support plan for Alice.

Table 5.6 Alice's personal information

Personal information	
Title	Mrs
First name	Alice
Surname	Campbell
Date of birth	05/08/1933
Address	43 Goodge Street, Ferryhill, Co. Durham
Telephone number	01234 567890
Religion	Roman Catholic
Next of kin	Naomi Higgins
Relationship	Daughter
Address	89 Tenby Avenue, Bishop Auckland, Co. Durham
Telephone number	01234 997765

Stretch activity

Clive's needs

Clive is 42 and broke his neck in a motorbike accident. He needs help to get up, shower and get dressed in the morning. He needs the same help to go to bed. However, during the day he can go out and meet friends. He also plays wheelchair rugby. He often meets friends in the pub in the evening.

1 Produce a support plan for Clive that would meet his P.I.L.E.S. (Aim for a detailed support plan. Look at the command word definitions to see what detailed means in the assessment.)

2 Communicate the plan to Clive in the most suitable way that would meet his needs.

(Aim to communicate the plan in a **clear** and **appropriate** way. Look at the command word definitions to see what **clear** and **appropriate** means in the assessment.)

Table 5.7 outlines Alice's medical history.

Table 5.7 A summary of Alice's medical history

GP	Dr Katherine Broderick
Telephone number	01234 778643
Diagnosis	Mini strokes
Comments	Very unsteady on feet, memory poor, urinary incontinence, cannot be left on her own, danger of falls
Medication	Heparin, Plavix, Lescol
Allergies	Penicillin
Comfort and mobility	Needs help walking, poor balance
Communication	Easily confused, forgets things
Activities	Day centre to meet friends, cannot go out on her own
Clothing	Easily accessible for changing and using toilet
Personal care	Needs help dressing, washing, brushing hair, cutting nails, toileting and cleaning teeth
Hygiene	Daily wash, brush teeth, shower once a week
Mental alertness	Some days brighter than others
Diet	Can feed herself but struggles to eat as has little appetite, small portions to tempt appetite, must be encouraged to eat and drink
Continence	Urinary incontinence, wears pad
Anxieties	Being left alone, scared of dark, likes low light in bedroom
Sleep	In bed by 8 p.m. and wants to stay there all the time, sleeps very well
Past occupation	Housewife
Social worker	Patsy Anderson

Table 5.8 summarises Alice's daily physical tasks.

Table 5.8 Alice's daily physical tasks

Task	Carried out by
Get up, toileting, wash, change pad, dress, give breakfast (around 8 a.m.)	Daughter-in-law
Company during morning, toileting, change pad, make drinks, household tasks such as washing, ironing, cleaning	Daughter-in-law
Lunch (12.30 p.m.)	Daughter-in-law
Company during afternoon, toileting, change pad, make drinks, household tasks	Daughter
Tea (4.30 p.m.)	Daughter
Supper – hot drink of milk and biscuit (7.30 p.m.)	Daughter
Get ready for bed, toileting, change pad, wash (8 p.m.)	Daughter

Alice also has some regular routines, as follows.

- Once a week, Alice has a shower and her fingernails cut, helped by her daughter and daughter-in-law.
- Her medication is on repeat prescription.
- She has a hospital appointment for her eyesight every three months; she goes to the appointment with her daughter, who drives her there.
- Her GP visits as and when needed or every month.

- A physiotherapist visits her every month to see if her mobility is improving.
- The district nurse checks her blood pressure, takes blood samples and assesses her continence.
- Every day the care agency arrives at 8.30 p.m. when Alice is going to bed and stay with her until 8 a.m. She is toileted only if necessary during this period.
- Alice goes to the hairdressers every week to get her hair washed and set, as she has done throughout her life.
- A podiatrist cuts her toenails every month.

Meeting Alice's specific needs

As can be seen above, Alice's physical needs are met by her daughter-in-law and daughter, as well as the GP, hospital and care agency.

Alice has been asked about what she wants to happen in her life. She wants:

- her family to look after her at home
- to stay in touch with her friends and go for coffee as she always has
- to meet up at the day centre for a singalong
- to keep getting her hair done every week
- to go out for short walks, so she gets some fresh air and stays mobile.

Intellectual/language needs
Unfortunately, Alice's eyesight is now too poor for her to be able to read. Also, her memory loss causes her to forget the plot in television programmes, so she can't be bothered to watch TV. Talking books have the same effect as she loses track of the story and gets frustrated with it.

However, she does like to sing along to music if it is from her younger days as she can remember the words. Her son has compiled a selection of songs and he plays them for her every morning. She also likes musicals on the television as she can sing along. She enjoys looking at old family photographs and never tires of talking about her memories.

Emotional/social needs
Alice loves meeting friends and every Thursday one of them will come and pick her up to go out for coffee. She has known her friend for years and she can find lots of memories to talk about with her. She is always happy when she's going out for coffee. On Tuesday mornings, her daughter takes her to the hairdressers and she socialises there. On Monday she goes to the day centre for a couple of hours in the afternoon, after lunch. She does get frustrated as she cannot do things herself and finds her lack of progress annoying as she wants to be back to normal. If the weather is fine, her son takes her for a short walk down her road every day, where she meets neighbours.

Spiritual needs
Her priest or a eucharistic minister brings Alice holy communion every two weeks.

How to present the support plan to Alice
Alice has difficulty reading or following information. So the best way of presenting all the information to her would be talking her through the plan so she could ask as many questions as she needs to with her daughter or daughter-in-law present. It would be a good idea to leave a copy of the plan with her daughter/daughter-in-law so they could repeat the plan to her if necessary.

If Alice could remember and follow information, another way of presenting information to her would be by audio recording.

Know it!

1 Explain what is meant by a support plan.
2 List different ways of presenting a support plan to an individual.
3 Discuss in general terms how an individual's needs change as they age.
4 When someone like Alice has immediate physical needs how could you ensure that her emotional and social needs are not overlooked when planning a support plan?

Assessment guidance

Learning outcome 4: Be able to create support plans

Marking criteria for LO4

Mark band 1	Mark band 2	Mark band 3
Produces a **basic** support plan for a person with specific medical requirements.	Produces a support plan for a person with specific medical requirements.	Produces a **detailed** support plan for a person with specific medical requirements.
The plan is communicated to the care user in a manner that displays **limited** understanding of the audience needs.	The plan is communicated to the care user in a manner that reflects the audience needs.	The plan is communicated to the care user **clearly** and **appropriately** and reflects the audience needs.
The support plan will show **limited** relevance to the specific medical conditions of the user.	The support plan will address the specific medical conditions of the user and show **some** understanding of their life stage.	The support plan will **effectively** and **clearly** address the specific medical conditions of the user and reflect their life stage.
Draws upon **limited** skills/knowledge/understanding from other units in the specification.	Draws upon **some relevant** skills/knowledge/understanding from other units in the specification.	**Clearly** draws upon **relevant** skills/knowledge/understanding from other units in the specification.

 ## The OCR Model Assignment will ask you to:

- Produce a support plan for a person with specific medical needs.
- Communicate the plan to the person concerned and reflect their needs.
- Ensure the support plan addresses the specific medical conditions of the user and reflect their life stage.
- Draw upon skills/knowledge/understanding from other units in the specification.

 ## What do the command words mean?

- **Detailed support plan**: Your support plan provides a point-by-point consideration of all the person's (specific medical) needs and how they could be met.
- **Clearly and appropriately**: The plan is communicated to the care user in a focussed way, accurately expressed, and relevant to the purpose.
- **Effectively and clearly**: You will apply your skills appropriately to the task in ensuring that the support plan addresses the specific medical conditions of the user and reflects their life stage. You will do this in a focussed and accurately expressed way.
- **Clearly and relevant**: You will draw upon skills/knowledge/understanding from other units (that are focussed on this activity), in an accurate way.

You should check the glossary in the Introduction for the definitions of each of the command words from OCR.

Read about it

Weblinks

www.nhs.uk/Conditions/Osteoporosis/Pages/Introduction.aspx NHS Choices – information about osteoporosis (causes, symptoms, treatment and prevention)

www.alzheimers.org.uk/site/scripts/documents_info.php?documentID=123 Alzheimer's Society – factsheet about coping with memory loss

www.b-eat.co.uk/about-eating-disorders Beat – facts and case studies about eating disorders

www.mind.org.uk/information-support/types-of-mental-health-problems/mental-health-problems-introduction/#.V7inLzXGDT8 Mind – information about different types of mental ill-health, diagnosis and the treatments available

www.epilepsysociety.org.uk Epilepsy Society – information about diagnosis, managing seizures and living with epilepsy

www.nhs.uk/conditions/Paralysis/Pages/Introduction.aspx NHS Choices – information about paralysis (causes, diagnosis and treatment)

www.ageuk.org.uk Age UK – for information on ageing, dementia and the menopause.

Reference books

Fisher, A., Blackmore, C., McKie, S., Riley, M., Seamons, S. and Tyler, M. (2012) *Applied AS Health & Social Care Student Book for OCR*. Oxford.

Moonie, N., Aldworth, C., Billingham, M. and Talman, H. (2010) *BTEC Level 3 National Health & Social Care Book 1*. Pearson.

R026 Planning for employment in health, social care and children and young people's workforce

About this unit

There are many careers within health, social care and the children and young people's workforce. Within these sectors a variety of organisations provide services for the public. A key component of all three sectors is the strong ethos of values, which underpins the way the service is delivered.

In this unit you will learn about the careers in the different sectors, the entry points needed, the qualifications needed and the sources of information about career opportunities. You will learn about the skills and attributes needed to work in the sectors, and investigate the health and safety issues, and the rewards and challenges of working in health, social care and the children and young people's workforce.

You will then have the opportunity to plan for your career in your choice of sector. You will plan development goals that will help you to improve your behaviours, skills and attributes.

Learning outcomes

LO1: Know about careers in health, social care or the children and young people's workforce

LO2: Understand the nature of working in health, social care or the children and young people's workforce

LO3: Be able to plan for careers in health, social care or the children and young people's workforce

How will I be assessed?

You will be assessed through a series of assignment tasks, which are set by OCR. The assignment will be marked by your tutor and then moderated by OCR.

For LO1, you need to:

- demonstrate knowledge of careers within health, social care or the children and young people's workforce
- outline employment opportunities in a range of service providers
- describe the entry points and qualifications needed for health, social care or the children and young people's workforce roles
- describe sources of information about career opportunities in health, social care or the children and young people's workforce.

For LO2, you need to:

- demonstrate an understanding of the personal attributes and skills necessary for careers in health, social care or the children and young people's workforce
- understand the health and safety issues in the three sectors, such as hazards and risks, and accident prevention
- demonstrate an understanding of the rewards and challenges of working in health, social care or the children and young people's workforce.

Note: SPAG is assessed in this learning outcome.

For LO3, you need to:

- research career opportunities in health, social care or the children and young people's workforce
- prepare career plans to inform your development
- produce a plan of development goals to improve behaviours, skills and attributes
- draw upon skills/knowledge/understanding from other units in the specification.

Make sure you refer to the current OCR specification and guidance.

Links to other units

Unit R021: Essential values of care for use with individuals in care settings (LO2): This unit will provide you with the values of care which are essential for anyone who wishes to follow a career in this sector. You will also have covered how personal hygiene, safety and security measures protect individuals.

Unit R022: Communicating and working with individuals in health, social care and early years settings (LO2): You will have covered all the personal qualities that contribute to effective care. You will also have covered effective communication.

Unit R024 (optional unit): Pathways for providing care in health, social care and early years settings (LO1): This unit will help you to examine the different areas in support services for career opportunities.

Unit R028 (optional unit): Understand the development and protection of young children in an early years setting (LO3): In order to prepare for employment in the sector you will need to understand about safe environments which were covered in this unit. You will also need to know how to carry out a risk assessment.

Unit R030 (optional unit): Research – a project approach (LO1 and LO2): If you have completed a project plan this will help you to plan your career plan as you will understand the importance of setting objectives and reviewing your progress.

Learning outcome 1

Know about careers in health, social care or the children and young people's workforce

Getting started

Divide the class into three groups and give each group a different sector: health, social care or the children and young people's workforce.

Each group should list all the careers they can think of for their sector.

Come back together as one group and discuss the number of careers you came up with.

The employment opportunities available within health, social care or the children and young people's workforce

Sectors/organisations

The services in health, social care and the children and young people's workforce are provided by the statutory, private or third sector (see unit R025, LO1 for more information on these). Table 6.1 gives examples of the provision of services within these three sectors. Unit R024 has more detailed information – look back at this unit now if you want to refresh your knowledge.

Within all of these sectors there are many different job opportunities. For example, if someone trained as a nurse they could work in the NHS (statutory service), BUPA (private) or in a Marie Curie hospice (third sector). They could also span health and the children and young people's workforce. For example, they could work in a school as the resident school nurse, or they could travel to schools giving injections to the children.

Examples of employment opportunities in health include:

● doctor

● nurse

● physiotherapist

● occupational therapist (works with service users to help them lead full and independent lives after an accident or illness)

Table 6.1 Examples of provision of services within health, social care, early years and young people's sectors

	Sector		
	Statutory	Private	Third sector
Health	● NHS (including hospitals, GP services, clinics, etc.) ● Mental health services ● Public Health England (PHE) ● Dental services ● Optician services ● Physiotherapy ● Podiatry	● Private hospitals such as BUPA, Nuffield ● Dental services ● Podiatry, e.g. StEPS ● Acupuncture, e.g. WhatClinic ● Physiotherapy, e.g. Physio2u ● Mental health, e.g. BACP	● Marie Curie hospices ● British Association for Cancer Research ● British Heart Foundation ● Cancer Research UK ● Focus on Disability
Social care	● Social services ● Homeless, e.g. soup kitchens ● Individuals with disabilities, e.g. supported living for people with disabilities ● Domestic abuse, e.g. women's hostels	● Residential homes ● Nursing homes	● Alzheimer's Society ● Age UK ● Crisis
Children and young people's workforce	● The Children's Trust ● Adoption, e.g. local authority adoption service ● National Agency of Young Offenders, e.g. Youth Offending Partnerships ● National Careers Service	● Nurseries ● Schools	● Action for Sick Children ● Together for Short Lives ● National Autistic Society ● Save the Children ● Barnardo's ● NSPCC

Research activity

What's in your area?

1 Your teacher will divide the class into three groups and give each group a different sector: health, social care or the children and young people's workforce.

2 In your group, research the services in your local area for the chosen sector. (Each group should have a map of the immediate area around the centre.)

3 Come back together as one group and share your findings. Put the services on a map. Is your area well provided for across this sector?

4 Share your findings with the class and put all the services on a map. Is the area well provided for across the three sectors?

- dietician
- midwife
- healthcare assistant
- pharmacist
- radiographer (uses different kinds of radiation to help diagnose or treat patients who are ill or injured)
- speech and language therapist
- paramedic
- clinical scientist (uses knowledge of science to help prevent, diagnose and treat illness; develops the techniques and equipment used by medical staff)
- medical physicist (researches and develops techniques and equipment used by medical staff to diagnose illness and treat patients)
- biomedical scientist (tests samples from patients to support doctors in the diagnosis and treatment of disease).

Examples of employment opportunities in social care include:

- family court adviser (works directly with vulnerable children and families to advise the family courts on the best course of action for the child or young person)
- children's joint commissioning manager (makes sure that children's, young people's and families' needs are met effectively by ensuring that services are safely and appropriately commissioned)
- facilitator (offers support and help across a wide area in health, social care and early years and the children's workforce, e.g. they may run groups for abused women or study support groups for school children)

- social worker
- drugs/alcohol well-being worker
- family intervention officer (supports families to keep children out of care)
- tenancy support adviser (gives advice and helps families resettle into affordable, good-quality accommodation)
- residential worker
- home manager
- therapist
- support worker
- activities co-ordinator (this role might range from organising quizzes, outings, etc., in a residential home to helping people with a disability to live independently)
- patient and public involvement co-ordinator (allows service users – patients and carers, including the public – to have their say about care and treatment and the way services are planned and delivered)
- home carer
- fundraising development officer.

Examples of employment opportunities in the children and young people's workforce are:

- teacher
- adoption assessment and support social worker (this role can start at the beginning of the adoption process, where the prospective adoptees are assessed for suitability; they will then support the adoptees through the adoption process and beyond)
- youth justice practitioner (works with young people who have broken the law, been arrested and charged with an offence)

- pupil support assistant
- classroom support assistant
- conduct mentor (usually works with students who have social, emotional and attachment difficulties, particularly challenging behaviour and/or additional complex needs)
- drama practitioner
- youth programme leader
- pupil support assistant
- educational psychologist
- music freelancer
- education welfare officer
- nursery nurse.

The entry points and qualifications needed for job roles within health, social care or the children and young people's workforce

Entry points

Organisations

Most organisations will require similar entry points and qualifications for similar job roles. Entry points and qualifications for job roles will be dependent on the seniority and responsibility associated with the role. Many employers offer on-the-job training and qualifications in order to upskill the workforce. This also encourages older people with no formal qualifications to come back into work.

Direct entry

It is very unlikely that lower-level health, social care and children and young people's workforce jobs could be accessed by direct entry. This is because hands-on experience of working with people is needed. For example, if a young person has just left sixth form with a Cambridge Technicals qualification or A-levels and wants to work in residential care, they would still have to start with a Level 2 apprenticeship. This is because, although they have Level 3 equivalent qualifications, they do not have the competence skills needed to work in the sector.

However, in higher-level jobs direct entry means that someone who has no experience of a particular job can apply to go into top jobs. For example, the police force is advertising superintendent jobs where the applicants do not have to be police officers. People who have no experience of teaching can apply to be head teachers. Obviously, they would have to have a certain level of education (degree level) and top-level experience in other job roles.

Apprenticeship schemes

This is training on the job, with the slogan 'Get in, go far'. Apprenticeships can go up beyond Level 6, which is degree level.

Most school leavers start Level 2 at the age of 16 while working in a job. They probably go to college for one day each week for the theoretical part of the course. Level 3 then follows if they wish to progress with promotions.

There is a wide range of subjects to choose from. As well as completing subject-related work, apprentices have to pass Level 2 Mathematics and English if they do not have a grade C or above at GCSE (grade 4 or above for the new GCSEs).

 ## Case study: Rebecca's apprenticeship

Rebecca is 18. She stayed on at school and got a Distinction in her Cambridge Technical Extended Diploma (Level 3). She decided that she did not want to go to university. Instead, she applied for an apprenticeship in Health and Social Care. She assumed she would start a Level 4 apprenticeship, so was shocked when she was told she would have to do a Level 2 apprenticeship.

Questions

1. Why did Rebecca have to start at Level 2 for the apprenticeship?
2. Think of reasons why Rebecca might not have been able to cope with a Level 4 apprenticeship.

Graduate fast-track schemes

Graduate fast-track schemes are designed to attract people who have completed their degrees to reach leadership positions quickly.

One of these schemes, called Teach First, encourages graduates into the teaching profession, with the promise of a head teacher's role within two years. Graduates spend two years training in the classroom, finishing with a master's degree. They are also paid for the time they are training.

There is a similar system for mental health social work called Think Ahead, and Frontline for children's social work.

Voluntary roles

A voluntary role offers good experience for anyone wanting to work in health, social care or the children and young people's workforce, allowing them to see what the job entails.

For example, sometimes young people want to work with babies and young children but, having spent time in a nursery, decide it is not for them. They might find it very stressful when more than one baby is crying at the same time, as they do not know which one to go to first. It is much better to find this out before starting training.

Table 6.2 shows examples of the entry-point requirements for jobs in the children and young people's workforce.

Qualifications

Mandatory/role-specific qualifications

Mandatory means compulsory, or something that is a requirement and not an option for a specific role. For example, most roles ask for GCSE Maths and English at grade C or above.

Many roles in health, social care and the children and young people's workforce require different qualifications and experience, according to the seniority and responsibilities of the position. Some professional roles – for example, social work, teaching and physiotherapy – ask for

Table 6.2 Example of requirements for jobs in the children and young people's workforce

Job role	Entry points	Direct entry	Apprenticeship	Fast track	Voluntary
Nursery assistant	• No set entry • Good level of literacy and numeracy	At 16, could train in nursery for L2 qualification	L2 Apprenticeship as early years worker	Not applicable	Experience of childcare, which could be voluntary or paid, could be within the family or babysitting
Nursery nurse	Examples of courses completed: • CACHE Level 3 Diploma in Child Care and Education • BTEC National Diploma in Children's Care, Learning and Development • Level 3 Diploma in Children's Care, Learning and Development plus GCSE Maths and English, as well as 2 more GCSEs at A to C • Paediatric first aid certificate • Food hygiene certificate	At 18, after completing childcare courses in entry points	L3 Apprenticeship as nursery nurse or nursery teaching assistant	If person had completed good A-levels and had lots of experience in nursery schools, they could start apprenticeship	Must have experience in nursery but would have if vocational courses completed
Nursery teacher	Minimum of 5 GCSEs, including: • Maths and English at A–C (or grade 4 or above for the new GCSEs) • 3 A-levels at C in National Curriculum subjects • Degree (teaching) or with PGCE	Not applicable	Not applicable	Could join Teach First with idea of becoming head within two years	Before applying for degree, must have experience in schools

degrees. However, there are still roles within the sectors that do not require a degree or a higher qualification.

The same values and personality traits or characteristics are needed in every role across the sectors. A social worker, support worker, midwife or nursery nurse all need good communication skills; these are the basis of all human interaction.

Post-employment qualifications

Although someone might be highly qualified to carry out their job role, they still need to be updated on developments within their sector. Most employers are keen to send their employees on training courses to ensure their practice stays up to date. This also benefits the organisation in a competitive world.

Some people complete further qualifications, such as degree courses, in their own time, to improve their chance of promotion both within and outside of the organisation.

Essential

'Essential' means absolutely necessary. So if a job advertisement says a particular qualification is essential, there is no point applying for the job unless you have that qualification. If there is an 'essential' component, then any applicants who do not have the qualification will not be considered.

When shortlisting for interview, many employers go through the applications and remove the applicants who do not have the essential requirements.

Desirable

'Desirable' means worth having and is ideally wanted by an employer. However, if a job advertisement says it is desirable to have a particular qualification, then it would still be worth applying even if you don't have it.

Qualifications that can be taken during employment

Figure 6.1 shows an example of a person specification from a job description, with essential and desirable components. Two of the qualifications are desirable, which means that a person could take the job without having them and then train for the qualifications during their employment.

In most jobs people learn while they are doing the job. In this case, the new employee would observe others practising paediatric first aid and hygiene in their daily role. This would stand them in good stead for taking the qualification themselves.

Qualifications	Essential	Desirable
Level 3 childcare qualification	✓	
Valid paediatric first aid certificate		✓
Valid Level 2 food hygiene certificate		✓
Knowledge and experience		
Experience of working with children aged 0–5 years		✓
Experience of providing personal care		✓
Experience of working within EYFS framework		✓
Knowledge and understanding of health and safety	✓	
Knowledge and understanding of equal opportunities	✓	
Knowledge and understanding of safeguarding	✓	
Knowledge and understanding of confidentiality	✓	
Knowledge and understanding of EYFS statutory framework	✓	
Skills		
Competent level of literacy and numeracy	✓	
Able to communicate effectively	✓	
Able to use IT		✓
Able to prioritise		✓
Able to problem solve		✓
Able to make quick, accurate decisions		✓
Able to work under pressure	✓	
Able to meet deadlines	✓	
Behaviours		
Smart personal appearance	✓	
Reliable team member	✓	
Flexible	✓	
Honest and trustworthy	✓	
Caring	✓	
Willing to undertake professional development	✓	
Approachable	✓	
Able to form warm relationships	✓	

Figure 6.1 A person specification showing examples of the essential and desirable components for a nursery nurse role

Sources of information about career opportunities in health, social care or the children and young people's settings

Internal sources

HR

HR (or human resources) is the part of a company that is focussed on activities relating to employees. These activities normally include recruiting, hiring of new employees and training of current employees. HR should know if there are going to be any future vacancies or if the company is going to expand and will need more employees.

Training and development

Following on from the information from HR, the training and development department would know if current staff are suitably qualified for any new job roles or if they will need further training. They could help to advise someone on how to progress to the next step on the career ladder. They would be able to recommend any further training courses that would help progress.

Intranet

An intranet is the internal or private network of an organisation, based on internet technology and accessed over the internet. An intranet is meant for the exclusive use of the organisation and its employees, and is protected from unauthorised access.

Intranets provide services such as email and are usually where policy manuals and internal directories are available for employees. New jobs within the organisation are often put on the intranet before being advertised more widely.

Publications

Many organisations publish an internal newsletter (i.e. it is not distributed outside of the organisation), which gives details of any job vacancies or possible promotion opportunities. This means that insiders (people who work in the organisation) are the first to learn about any jobs.

If no one from inside the firm applies or is suitable for a position, then the job is advertised externally (is open to people outside the company), if there is a vacancy.

Coaches and mentors

A coach is an individual who has a short-term relationship with an employee, usually while training them to do something. For example, the coach might train a new member of staff to use a computer package. The coach is often the employee's immediate team leader as they have skills they can teach the employee.

A mentor usually has a longer-term relationship with an employee (to build trust) and provides a safe environment for an employee to discuss issues beyond work. For example, the employee may be concerned about their work/life balance as they are spending time working at home outside of their contracted hours. Or they may feel that they lack self-confidence in the job. Mentors do not teach the mentee skills but offer advice and guidance.

External sources

Internet

The internet is an excellent source of information for job opportunities, further training and changes of career in health, social care and the children and young people's workforce. The internet can also be used to complete online qualifications such as the L2 Food Hygiene Certificate. There is a wealth of information on the internet that can help an individual plan their next career move or help them to decide which qualification they need to study for next.

In terms of job vacancies, there is a wide range of agencies to look at online, as well as details of roles on websites such as BUPA's.

Trade unions and staff associations

Trade unions and staff associations provide advice and support for people in different professions. They can also help their members advance their careers by offering free training courses.

Media recruitment campaigns

Organisations sometimes run national television advertising campaigns to encourage people to look at a job in a new way, or to highlight incentives for joining the profession. This happens when recruitment to a profession is lower than the numbers needed.

Sometimes the aim of a campaign is to highlight careers that people may not have thought about. For example, most people when asked to name a career associated with working in a hospital would say nurse, doctor, midwife or physiotherapist. They would usually not say medical engineer, clinical photographer or art therapist.

 Classroom discussion

Can an advert change your mind?

As a class, do the following.

1 Watch this advert: www.tes.com/news/school-news/breaking-news/will-new-tv-advert-solve-teacher-recruitment-crisis

2 Does it make you look at teaching in a new way? After watching the advert, would you consider teaching as a career? Why, or why not?

Publications

Journals related to health, social care or the children and young people's workforce usually have job advertisements. For example, the *Times Educational Supplement* (TES) advertises teaching jobs, Community Care has jobs in the social care sector and the Nursing Times has health vacancies. These journals also have valuable articles on current issues, which develop an individual's knowledge of the sector. This is useful to provide information for future job or higher education interviews. National and local newspapers also have job advertisement sections.

Employment agencies

These are companies that attempt to match the employment needs of an organisation with a registered worker who has the required skill set and interests. Some agencies are privately owned while others are sponsored by government. Employment agencies also recruit staff on behalf of an employer.

Sometimes the jobs on offer are short-term or contract work rather than a full-time permanent post. Employment agencies are not allowed, by law, to charge the employee a fee for finding them suitable employment.

> ### Know it!
>
> 1 Explain what is meant by an apprenticeship.
> 2 Explain the value of voluntary roles to the employer and the volunteer.
> 3 Explain the differences between desirable and essential qualifications, skills and attributes.
> 4 Explain the differences between a mentor and a coach.
> 5 How do employment agencies help employers and employees?

Assessment guidance

Learning outcome 1: Know about careers in health, social care or the children and young people's workforce

Marking criteria for LO1 Part A

Mark band 1	Mark band 2	Mark band 3
Demonstrates limited knowledge of careers within health, social care or the children and young people's workforce. Learner can outline employment opportunities available in a **limited** range of different service providers, and has a **basic** description of sources of information about career opportunities.	Demonstrates **sound** knowledge of careers within health, social care or the children and young people's workforce. Learner can outline employment opportunities available in a range of different service providers, with a **detailed** description of sources of information about career opportunities.	Demonstrates **thorough** knowledge of careers within health, social care or the children and young people's workforce. Learner can outline employment opportunities available in a **wide** range of different service providers, with a **thorough** description of sources of information about career opportunities.

 The OCR Model Assignment will ask you to:

- Demonstrate knowledge of careers within health, social care or the children and young people's workforce.
- Outline employment opportunities in a range of different service providers.
- Describe sources of information for career opportunities.

→

What do the command words mean?

- **Thorough knowledge**: You will demonstrate knowledge of careers within health, social care or the children and young person's workforce that is extremely attentive to accuracy and detail.
- **Wide range:** You will be able to outline employment opportunities available in a range of different service providers and will include many relevant details, examples or contexts and thus avoid a narrow approach. You will include a comprehensive list of examples.
- **Thorough description**: Your description of the sources of information about career opportunities will be extremely attentive to accuracy and detail.

You should check the glossary in the Introduction for the definitions of each of the command words from OCR.

Marking criteria for LO1 Part B

Mark band 1	Mark band 2		Mark band 3
A **basic** description of entry points and qualifications needed for health, social care or the children and young people's workforce roles.	A **detailed** description of entry points and qualifications needed for health, social care or the children and young people's workforce roles.		A **thorough** description of entry points and qualifications needed for health, social care or the children and young people's workforce roles.

 ## The OCR Model Assignment will ask you to:

- Describe the entry points and qualifications needed for health, social care or the children and young people's workforce roles.

 ## What do the command words mean?

- **Thorough description**: Your description of the entry points and qualifications needed for health, social care or the children and young people's workforce roles will be extremely attentive to accuracy and detail.

You should check the glossary in the Introduction for the definitions of each of the command words from OCR.

Learning outcome 2

Understand the nature of working in health, social care or the children and young people's workforce

Getting started

Have you ever been in hospital as a patient? Did you go to a nursery as a child? Have you observed carers in a residential home looking after the residents?

As a group, list all the skills and **attributes** needed to work in these settings.

The skills and attributes needed to work in health, social care or the children and young people's workforce

Honesty

The definition of honesty is refraining from lying, cheating or stealing. It means being truthful and trustworthy. Honesty is a very important **quality** to have, particularly if you are working with people. For example, a nurse may have to look after the valuable possessions of an individual who has dementia, so they have to be trusted to be honest. Similarly, a patient may ask if their cancer will be cured by chemotherapy and the doctor has to tell them the truth even if it is not what they want to hear. It is essential that

 Key terms

Attribute A feature or characteristic of a person.

Quality An expression of personality and temperament, e.g. honesty.

practitioners tell the truth so the patient can trust them. However, when revealing the truth professionals can be sensitive.

Respect for equality and diversity

Anyone working in the caring professions must have respect for equality and diversity. In practice, this means that all service users are treated fairly and do not face discrimination. This could be achieved by making sure there is equal access for everyone to participate in what is on offer. Respect for others' cultural beliefs should be observed throughout the health, social care and early years sectors. For example, all signs in a hospital should reflect the languages of the individuals who use the hospital.

All health, social care and early years environments (for example, a nursery, residential home or hospital) should ensure that issues of race, colour, ethnicity, nationality, social background, religion, culture, gender, language, sexual orientation and disability do not prevent any individual from accessing services. They should promote understanding, respect and awareness of diversity and equal opportunities issues when planning and implementing their programme of

Case study: Anjou's further education prospects

Anjou is 16 and is currently at school. She goes to the local comprehensive but has always been in the lower sets.

Recently, at a parents' evening, a new member of the teaching staff told Anjou's mother that there was no point in Anjou staying on at school for sixth form, as she would never achieve anything worthwhile. Anjou's mother is very upset.

Questions

1. Although the new member of staff was being truthful about Anjou's ability to achieve good academic grades, could she have handled the situation in a different way? Explain how.

2. Write out a possible conversation between the teacher and Anjou's mother, which is truthful but positive.

Research activity

Cultural diversity

1 In small groups, research key festivals for one of the following religions: Christianity, Buddhism, Hinduism, Islam, Sikhism.

2 Plan a programme of events for a residential home using your chosen religion. Present your ideas to the rest of the group.

3 Put all your ideas together to form a multicultural plan for the year for the residential home.

activities/services, so that different cultures are represented as appropriate. They should help all individuals to celebrate and express their cultural and religious identity by providing a wide range of appropriate resources. By recognising and valuing differences between individuals, services are treating them all as individuals.

Respect for confidentiality

All workers in health, social care or the children and young people's workforce will be given confidential information by service users. Confidentiality is essential to protect the interests of any individual. The service user's permission must be obtained before information is passed on to people outside the care team. Obviously if the person is in danger, then the worker should inform them that they have to pass on the information for their own safety.

Workers often receive very sensitive confidential information from vulnerable service users. For example, a child who has been abused by his father may start nursery, or a woman who is HIV positive will use services in her local hospital and perhaps have social care help in her own home. It would be unprofessional to talk about any of these cases outside of the workplace. It is also breaking the law and all the values of care practice. Service users lose trust in a worker who discusses their private affairs.

Politeness

Politeness is behaving in a way that is socially correct and shows understanding of, and care for, other people's feelings. It is showing good manners towards others in the way you behave or speak. Working in the health, social care or children and young people's sector involves working with people, and politeness can help build relationships.

It is always a good idea to greet someone, for example when a patient comes into a clinic, as it shows respect for the other person. Always say please and thank you. In a nursery, this encourages small children to do the same as they will copy the adult. When speaking to others always use appropriate language – be respectful of race, religion, gender and so on. Always be polite and listen attentively to other

Case study: Herbie's experience of confidentiality at the health centre

Herbie is 77 and in poor health. He is at the medical centre for a check-up when he overhears the practice nurse telling the receptionist that Herbie has the symptoms of bowel cancer. Herbie is very distressed as he feels his GP has not been truthful – she had said that Herbie needed to undergo some tests but bowel cancer was not mentioned. When he goes in to see the GP he is very angry.

Questions

1 What do you think should happen at the medical centre to improve confidentiality?

2 Do you think the GP might have had valid reasons for not being honest with Herbie?

3 Do you think Herbie will be able to trust the GP to look after his treatment?

people when they are speaking. Do not interrupt or get distracted. For example, when a patient is describing their symptoms to a GP, they should let them finish before they start asking questions.

Team working

In its simplest terms, teamwork is working together for a purpose or a goal. For example, in football or netball all the team work together to score a goal and win a match. In health and social care, it could be a small team working together to move someone out of bed and help to get them dressed. To be able to work successfully as a team, each member has to understand, respect and value the roles and contributions of all members of the team. Teamwork improves interpersonal skills as the members learn to compromise and work together. It is important that all team members are reliable and contribute fully in any task, otherwise it could cause resentment within the team. For example, in a residential home there could be a team of four to get all of the 20 residents out of bed and dressed in a morning. Resentment will soon build up if one of the team gets one resident dressed while the other team members manage four during the same length of time. However, if the member is new to the team, they may need tips and advice on how to go about the task, to help them improve. When working in a team, each member will be communicating effectively, sharing information and working to meet the team's shared goals in the best interests of the service user.

A team might not necessarily work together on a daily basis. For example, a pregnant mother is sometimes looked after by a large team of different professionals. The team could consist of the GP, midwife, **obstetrician**, **anaesthetist**, **paediatrician**, **sonographer** and health visitor, but they do not necessarily meet up. They contact one another by email or patient records or referrals, but not usually face to face. Nevertheless, they all have a goal in mind, which is the safe delivery of a baby.

Key terms

Obstetrician A doctor who specialises in the care of women during pregnancy, childbirth and after birth.

Anaesthetist A doctor who specialises in pain relief.

Paediatrician A doctor who specialises in the care of babies and children.

Sonographer Specially trained to carry out ultrasound scans.

Objectivity

Objectivity means being able to examine something without bias, feelings, judgement or prejudice. It is being able to look at a situation factually and not emotionally.

- For example, a nurse or doctor may advise parents that their child is brain dead and that there is no hope of recovery. The doctor would be able to give the parents the facts about the situation based on evidence, with no opinions offered. This is because the doctor is not emotionally involved with the patient.
- A nursery teacher might advise parents about which junior school would best suit their child's needs. Again, they should offer facts and show no prejudice against any of the schools.

People who are objective will work to the same high standard with everyone they work with. It should not matter to them what the person is like as an individual, what colour or religion they are, or how they live their life. All individuals are worthy of respect and the best efforts from the staff.

Integrity

Integrity is when someone has the quality of being honest. The individual has strong moral principles, and a sense of justice and standing up for what they believe in.

A **whistleblower** (see page 168 for definition) will not cover up wrongdoing to protect an organisation. They feel that their loyalty should

Key term

Whistleblower Someone who reveals wrongdoing within an organisation to the public or to those in positions of authority.

be with the person who is using the service. The following weblinks give examples of workers with integrity who put their own jobs and reputations on the line to disclose examples of poor practice:

- NHS whistleblowers – www.telegraph.co.uk/news/health/news/11398148/The-NHS-whistle-blowers-who-spoke-out-for-patients.html
- Winterbourne View abuse scandal – www.bbc.co.uk/news/uk-england-bristol-20078999

If a nursery nurse suspected child abuse but knew the parents, she might feel embarrassed. But if she was concerned about the child's safety she would have to raise her concerns with her line manager, even though it could make her relationship with the parents awkward. It is so important to do what is right to protect a service user, taking into account all aspects of equality and diversity.

Impartiality

Impartiality means not taking sides or being biased in an argument but being scrupulously (or thoroughly) fair and examining both viewpoints. For example, a line manager in a residential home may have two conflicting views over an incident; she should listen to both views and weigh up the evidence before making any decisions. An early years teacher should not take the side of one child against another until all the facts are known. Ofsted must inspect schools and nurseries with impartiality, having no preconceived judgements. They must make decisions about the school purely on the evidence they see.

Sensitivity to the needs of others

Every service user is an individual with real feelings and emotions. When working with people, staff should think about how the person may be feeling and then decide what the most appropriate response is to their situation. When a member of staff is sensitive to the needs of others, they treat the service users and their relatives politely, while being aware of the situation they are in and their reactions to it. For example, a service user may be feeling confused, angry or frustrated because they have been given some bad news. It is important that staff are sensitive to this and do not take their reactions personally.

Avoiding conflict with others

When working in a sector that deals with people, there will inevitably be conflicts, either between service users or members of staff.

Conflict avoidance is one way of dealing with conflict, which attempts to avoid directly confronting the issue at hand. Methods of doing this can include changing the subject, putting off a discussion until later, or simply walking away from the conflict. Conflict avoidance can be used as a temporary measure to buy time or as a way of allowing the participants time to cool down so they are not boiling over with emotion. The idea is that when they return they will be calm and more able to see reason.

Dealing with conflict early is usually easier than avoiding it. The best way to address conflict in its early stages is through negotiation between the participants – getting them to identify the issue and talk about it.

Stretch activity

Personal attributes and skills

Malachy wants to work as a probation officer.

Produce a piece of work that demonstrates your understanding of the skills and attributes necessary for a career in the probation service.

(Aim for a **thorough** understanding. Look at the command word definitions to see what **thorough** means in the assessment.)

The health and safety issues in health, social care or the children and young people's workforce

Hazards and risks

A hazard is something that has the potential to cause harm. A risk is the chance (high or low) that someone may be harmed by the hazard. Hazards can be found anywhere, for example, in your own home, in a shopping centre or in a school or nursery. In a care setting, service users are often vulnerable because of age (young or old), illness or lack of awareness. It is the duty of the care setting to provide a safe environment to protect the service users, staff and visitors. Each setting has its own particular hazards.

Organisations such as schools, residential homes or hospitals should have:

- a health and safety officer who will ensure that the organisation's health and safety policy is followed
- a system for reporting defective equipment, e.g. a hoist that is damaged
- an accident book for recording accidents and injuries.

Risk of workplace violence

Most people think of violence as a physical assault. However, workplace violence is a much broader problem. It is any act in which a person is abused, threatened, intimidated or assaulted in their employment. Most staff working in health, social care and the children and young people's workforce will encounter violence or threats in their work at some point. This is because their jobs involve working with the public when they are stressed or feeling under pressure. Real examples (taken from the Health and Safety Executive website) include:

- a carer being bitten by a person with learning disabilities in the course of the normal care of that person

- an irate or angry visitor verbally abusing a ward manager because he considers that his relative has not been properly treated
- a nurse being verbally abused and threatened by a patient who is unwilling to take the prescribed medication.

Stress

Stress is one of the biggest health issues at work. The true extent of stress-related problems is largely hidden because very few people are prepared to admit that they are suffering from stress, or to seek help. It is not surprising, therefore, that every year staff working in health, social care or the children and young people's workforce become ill through work-related stress. This is at least in part due to constant changes in the public sector, arising from fundamental policy changes in delivery, structures and funding. Another cause is the nature of the job, which is working with people. Most workers take their worries home with them. For example, if they are involved in social work it is difficult to switch off from a demanding case. Stress can cause different symptoms ranging from anxiety, lack of sleep and high blood pressure to digestive problems and mood swings.

Mental health

Good mental health is not simply the absence of diagnosable mental health problems; it is about positive well-being, feeling valued at home and at work, and generally feeling relaxed and positive about life. People who experience well-being in the workplace perform well and are therefore more effective in their roles. Organisations with large numbers of stressed, demoralised and anxious staff are not able to function efficiently. This can mean days off work due to the inability to cope with the demands and pressures of the job. This will have a knock-on effect on other staff and service users. Stress can lead to mental illness.

Case study: Gita's heavy workload

Gita is a newly qualified teacher (NQT). She teaches mathematics in her local comprehensive school. For the past three months she has felt anxious and depressed as she has an excessive workload due in part to her NQT status. Some of the pupils she teaches have behavioural issues and she has found herself losing her temper with them, which adds to her worries. She has poor concentration and cannot sleep at night. Sometimes she cannot think at all.

Questions

1 Do you think Gita has good mental health? Explain your answer.

2 What advice would you give to Gita?

Physical requirements

Many individuals who work in health, social care or the children and young people's workforce need to be physically fit. For example, a nurse, midwife or care assistant can spend long hours on their feet during each day's work. They may be required to move and position individuals as they get out of bed, wash and dress, or move on and off the toilet. They may need to help turn people in their beds because they are unable to do this for themselves. This may be because they are paralysed, unconscious following an accident or a stroke, or they are suffering with a severe illness.

Although all staff have training about how to lift correctly, injuries can still happen through human error. For example, the wrong hoist sling could be used, causing the service user to fall out of the sling. This may cause injury to both the member of staff and the service user. No one should move a service user on their own, even if using a hoist, as this is against health and safety guidance. Bending over service users to feed them, wash them and so on, can cause musculoskeletal injuries. Every member of staff in a nursery working at child height is at risk of musculoskeletal injuries.

Accident prevention

The most common types of accident in any workplace are slips, trips and falls. The ideas presented in Figure 6.2 suggest ways to avoid these types of accident. Employers should carry out regular risk assessments to ensure they are doing all they can to prevent accidents. It is also the duty of an employee to report a potential accident so it can be dealt with. The second most common type of accident is muscular strains from manual handling. Staff should always follow the organisational procedure and use a hoist.

Different settings have different types of potential accident. For example, in a hospital there is more likelihood of a **sharps injury** than there would be in a nursery.

Health and Safety Executive (HSE) guidance

The Health and Safety Executive (HSE) (www.hse.gov.uk) is the national independent watchdog for work-related health and safety. It acts in the public interest to reduce work-related death, serious injury and occupational disease across Great Britain's workplaces.

Key term

Sharps injury When the skin is punctured by a needle, blade (such as scalpel) or any other medical instrument.

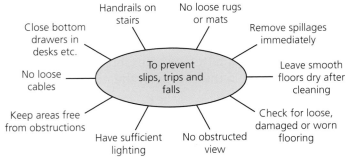

Figure 6.2 Ideas to prevent slips, trips and falls

The rewards and challenges of working in health, social care or the children and young people's workforce

Rewards

Serving the community

The key word to consider when contemplating a career in this sector is 'care'. People who work in this sector truly care about helping other people in their community. Without that level of concern and desire to make a difference, it is impossible to succeed in the health, social care and early years world. Often, people working in these sectors are involved in local projects such as setting up a playgroup or organising a fête to raise money for a community project.

Serving the community often means that employees in these sectors feel they are helping the people around them. As such, they are often well-respected and popular members of their local community. People who use the services often feel reassured if they meet the professional outside of the work environment.

Job satisfaction

When someone works in a helping role, they can get great job satisfaction from knowing that their efforts can help to improve people's lives. They could improve people's physical or mental health or well-being, help people during difficult times or teach people new skills. They might help someone get the qualifications they need to move on to a new life. These are all great achievements. If someone is a 'people person' and gets satisfaction from helping others, then working in health, social care or early years could be a good career choice. Job satisfaction can help improve staff retention rates and workplace morale.

Opportunities for progression

There are many different jobs in health, social care and the children and young people's workforce – it is a broad career sector. There are also lots of opportunities for progression for all different academic backgrounds.

Careers in healthcare are much more likely to require a combination of further study and on-the-job medical training, whereas careers in social care are more likely to start with on-the-job training and allow individuals to work towards professional qualifications later on in their career. Careers in the children and young people's workforce can start with a degree or on-the-job training. The opportunity for on-the-job training allows the individual to advance up the career ladder without having to take time off work to study.

Prestige

Prestige is not just about the money earned by a person; it is also about the respect and admiration felt for the person for their achievements. So jobs that help others in the caring professions are often seen as prestigious. Careers in health, social care and the children and young people's workforce are some of the most important in the world. Employees in these sectors not only help people on an individual basis, but make a difference to society as a whole.

Pay and working conditions

There are too many jobs across the health, social care and children and young people's workforce to list all of the pay and working conditions. Pay in some of the sectors may seem low but professionals do have extra benefits in that they receive an index-linked pension when they retire. They also receive full pay for up to six months if they are absent from work with a serious illness. Tables 6.3 to 6.5 provide a sample of the pay ranges and working conditions for different roles in each sector. These pay ranges are taken from nationalcareersservice.direct.gov.uk and you may want to visit this website for the latest and most up-to-date information.

Table 6.3 Examples of pay and conditions for the early years and young people's workforce

Job role	Pay range (2015–16)	Working conditions
Teaching assistant	£12,000 to £17,000	• Usually school hours five days a week
Teacher (classroom)	£22,023 to £37,418	• School hours but will have marking and preparation to do at home • Five days a week but sometimes Saturday mornings
Head teacher	£43,232 to £150,000 depending on size of school	• School hours but with lots of out-of-school meetings before and after school • Five days a week but sometimes Saturday mornings
Nursery nurse (junior)	£10,000 to £14,000	• Nurseries open 7 a.m. until 6 p.m. Monday to Saturday – will usually work 40 hours across the week
Nursery nurse (experienced)	£15,000 to £22,000	• Nurseries open 7 a.m. until 6 p.m. Monday to Saturday – will usually work 40 hours across the week
Nursery manager	£22,000 to £35,000	• Nurseries open 7 a.m. until 6 p.m. Monday to Saturday – will usually work 40 hours across the week
Learning support assistant	£16,347 to £19,697	• Usually school hours five days a week

Table 6.4 Examples of pay and conditions for the health workforce

Job role	Pay range (2015–16)	Working conditions
Healthcare assistant	£15,000 to £20,000	• Usually 37 hours on shift/rota system including nights, weekends and bank holidays
Nurse (adult)	£21,909 to £41,000	• Usually 37.5 hours on shift/rota system including nights, weekends and bank holidays
Nurse (school)	£21,909 to £35,000	• Usually 37.5 hours during school hours
GP practice manager	£21,909 to £35,225	• Usually 37 hours on shift/rota system, including evenings and Saturday mornings
Hospital porter	£15,251 to £21,000	• 37.5 to 40 hours, including shifts and some weekends
Dietician	£21,909 to £35,225	• 37.5 hours, which could include some weekends
General practitioner (GP)	£23,00 to £84,500	• 50-hour week including evening and weekend work; rota for out-of-hours emergency work
Dentist	£30,732 to £82,295	• Usually work 9 a.m. to 5 p.m. weekdays but can work weekends on out-of-hours rota
Dental nurse	£16,000 to £22,000	• Usually work 9 a.m. to 5 p.m. weekdays

Table 6.5 Examples of pay and conditions for the social care workforce

Job role	Pay range (2015–16)	Working conditions
Social work assistant	£12,500 to £22,000	• Usually 37 hours on shift/rota system, including nights, weekends and bank holidays
Social worker	£19,500 to £40,000	• Usually work standard office hours with some nights on call on a rota basis
Care assistant	£12,500 to £18,000	• Working hours vary depending on job, but will be expected to work antisocial hours and public holidays
Care home advocate	£18,000 to £25,000	• 30 to 37 hours (weekdays)
Residential support worker	£17,000 to £21,000	• 37 to 40 hours on shift rota, including weekends, holidays and some sleep-ins
Family support worker	£18,000 to £24,000	• Usually 37 hours during the week
Family mediator	£20,000 to £30,000	• Standard office hours, although there could be some evening and weekend appointments

Challenges

Dealing with members of the public who are in stressful circumstances

When people are in stressful circumstances (for instance, being bullied at school or in the workplace, or they have been made homeless through a flood), they may feel that they have no say or control over a situation. This can cause them to become aggressive, because they feel helpless and find the situation challenging to deal with. For example, if a child has been in an accident and is brought by ambulance into A&E, the parents may feel that the medical staff are not doing enough to help. In these types of situations, emotions may run high and have the potential to become confrontational and aggressive.

Staff have to be very careful about how they deal with this kind of situation. They could easily respond in an equally aggressive tone and the situation could quickly get out of control. Staff are trained to realise that the aggressive person is vulnerable and that is why they are behaving in that manner. They must learn not to take the aggression personally and try to diffuse the situation by staying calm.

 Group activity

Can you stay calm?

In small groups, role play the following scenarios.

- A parent confronts a teacher about making her son, aged eight, continue to do PE after falling off a beam and breaking his arm.
- A daughter is very angry as she has been waiting more than two hours for her mother's GP to make a house call. Her mother is very poorly and in distress.
- An ambulance crew arrive at the home of a distressed husband three hours after he made a 999 call. His wife has had a stroke.

The impact of stressful situations on service workers

Careers in health, social care and the children and young people's workforce can be very challenging emotionally. Stressful situations can have a negative impact on service workers. If someone has been particularly aggressive towards them, the worker may feel shaken and scared. This could lower their self-confidence in dealing with other people. They may feel unable to return to work the next day as they are too worried and stressed.

In order to thrive in these sectors, workers need to have the ability to build relationships with service users. It is essential that people trust the worker, and so patience, friendliness and effective communication skills are needed. The worker needs to be genuinely compassionate and caring, but also thick-skinned.

Health and safety risks

Health and safety risks can occur when staffing levels are low, perhaps through stress. This can lead to staff having too much to do and not following correct procedures. For example, in a care home a member of staff might leave someone in the bath while they go to fetch a towel. Or in a hospital, care staff may not have time to ensure vulnerable patients are fed their meals. In a nursery, a member of staff may be out in the playground on their own and not see everything that is happening. A junior doctor doing too much overtime could also feel tired and, as a result, may lack concentration.

As mentioned earlier, many jobs in these sectors involve being physically fit, as carers may have to change beds, move patients using a hoist, or lift small children off apparatus. These types of activities can lead to injuries. There may also be the risk of physical attack, for example by a patient with dementia or an angry parent.

Upholding values

Pressure on staff or services can have an impact on upholding values. For instance, if there are excessive workloads (in other words, high levels of work), staff will be exceptionally busy. In order to get all the practical tasks finished, they may neglect to maintain confidentiality by leaving files out on a desk. They may feel they have not got time to promote individuals' rights and beliefs. For example, they might leave someone's door open while they are using a bedpan, leaving them without privacy or dignity.

It is understandable to feel overwhelmed by the tasks and responsibilities of a role but it is still important, no matter how busy you are, to uphold the principles and values of the sector in which you work.

Know it!

1 Explain why team working is important across health, social care and the children and young people's workforce.

2 Explain the advantage of avoiding conflict with others by dealing with it early.

3 Explain why there is a risk of workplace violence in health, social care and the children and young people's workforce.

4 Outline two rewards of working in the health, social care and children and young people's workforce.

5 List two challenges of working in the health, social care and children and young people's workforce.

Assessment guidance

Learning outcome 2: Understand the nature of working in health, social care or the children and young people's workforce

Marking criteria for LO2 Part A

Mark band 1	Mark band 2	Mark band 3
Demonstrates a **basic** understanding of the personal attributes and skills necessary for careers in health, social care or early years.	Demonstrates a **sound** understanding of the personal attributes and skills necessary for careers in health, social care or early years.	Demonstrates a **thorough** understanding of the personal attributes and skills necessary for careers in health, social care or early years.

 The OCR Model Assignment will ask you to:

● Show an understanding of the personal attributes and skills needed for working in your chosen career within one of the sectors.

 What do the command words mean?

● **Thorough understanding**: You will demonstrate an understanding of the personal attributes and skills necessary for careers in health, social care or early years that is extremely attentive to accuracy and detail.

You should check the glossary in the Introduction for the definitions of each of the command words from OCR.

Marking criteria for LO2 Part B

Mark band 1	Mark band 2	Mark band 3
Demonstrates a **basic** understanding of the rewards and challenges in health, social care or the children and young people's workforce with a **limited** understanding of the health and safety issues.	Demonstrates a **sound** understanding of the rewards and challenges in health, social care or the children and young people's workforce with a **detailed** understanding of the health and safety issues.	Demonstrates a **thorough** understanding of the rewards and challenges in health, social care or the children and young people's workforce, with a **thorough** understanding of the health and safety issues.
There will be **some** errors in spelling, punctuation and grammar.	There will be **minor** errors in spelling, punctuation and grammar.	There will be **few**, if any, errors in spelling, punctuation and grammar.

→

The OCR Model Assignment will ask you to:

- Show a thorough understanding of the rewards and challenges of working in your chosen sector.
- Show a thorough understanding of the health and safety issues in your chosen sector.

 What do the command words mean?

- **Thorough understanding**: Your understanding of the rewards and challenges in health and social care or the children and young people's workforce, and of the health and safety issues will be extremely attentive to accuracy and detail.
- **Few:** There will only be a small number of errors in spelling, grammar and punctuation. Not many, but more than one.

You should check the glossary in the Introduction for the definitions of each of the command words from OCR.

Learning outcome 3

Be able to plan for careers in health, social care or the children and young people's workforce

Getting started

How many learners in your class know which career they want to follow?

Have a discussion, then work out the percentage of you who know what you would like to do and the percentage who do not.

How to research career opportunities in health, social care or the children and young people's workforce

Speaking to careers advisors

It is the duty of a school to provide independent careers advice for all students from Year 8 to Year 13.

Careers advisors can:

- help with Cambridge Nationals/GCSE choices in Year 9 to ensure the learner chooses the right subjects for their career choice

- during Year 11, advise on the A-levels/Cambridge Technicals/BTECs that are required for certain jobs
- help a young person to look for a job or an apprenticeship.

Careers advisors can also talk through the different options that are available to a learner. They can help them build a CV (curriculum vitae) or explain how to use an action plan. They may have suggestions for work placements or experience.

Using recruitment material from organisations

Organisations use careers fairs to promote opportunities for new recruits to the sector. They often produce lots of useful information and guidance for people who want to work in their sector, including an application form.

Open days at residential homes, nursing homes and nurseries are also a useful source of material. Schools often have open days for graduates who might want to train as teachers.

Exploration of possible career leads by undergoing work placements/work experience

Nothing beats a work placement/experience for giving someone a true picture of the sector.

It may be that after a placement the person changes their mind and decides it is not the job for them. But it is better to find out before starting to train for that sector.

Advantages of work placements include:

- practical experience within the sector
- improved job opportunities, because the employer knows the learner has experience of the sector
- higher education opportunities, because the learner is able to discuss the sector in a knowledgeable way at interview, e.g. teaching applicants have to have classroom experience of teamwork
- development of interpersonal skills
- awareness of current developments in the sector
- the real chance of a job offer at the placement.

Desk research of industries, sectors, companies and organisations

There are many different ways to carry out desk research to help find out information about careers or jobs.

- Research the UK market for different careers by region using the National Careers Service website: nationalcareersservice.direct.gov.uk/Pages/Home.aspx
- Read job profiles: www.allaboutcareers.com/careers/industry/health-social-care
- Browse careers sections on websites representing the profession.
- Read job advertisements in newspapers and journals.
- Look at employers' websites, which sometimes have trainee videos.
- Help firm up career choices, e.g. by using www.careerpilot.org.uk/jobs, a website that gives advice on further qualifications, options, apprenticeships, etc.

Matching skills and attributes to jobs

It is important to understand your existing skills, knowledge and personal qualities so they can be matched to possible jobs. This will also help to identify the knowledge and skills that might need to be developed, or the personal qualities that might be needed to achieve career goals. An accurate and realistic assessment of these things is vital to an achievable career strategy.

One way of finding out if someone has the right skills and attributes for a certain job is to go to: https://nationalcareersservice.direct.gov.uk/advice/planning/jobprofiles/Pages/default/aspx.

Here, details about a job and all it entails (from entry requirements to work activities, working hours and conditions) are listed under job profiles.

For example, if someone wanted to be a play therapist, the website gives a list of skills and attributes needed (for this job, attributes such as empathy and an open and friendly manner, resilience and insight for working with children in emotional distress, and good spoken and written communication skills). If the person did not have these skills and attributes, then this would probably not be a suitable career for them.

The National Careers Service website also allows people to take a skills test.

How to prepare careers plans to inform development

Selecting a career

When selecting a career an individual should do the following.

- Reflect on themselves. What do they like or dislike, what are their interests, what subjects are they good at? What are their skills and personal qualities? It is also useful to know what type of learning suits them best. If they are good at traditional learning then traditional A-levels could be the best way for them. If they like the idea of hands-on work experience, then a vocational route such as Cambridge Technicals could suit them. If, however, they feel they would like to learn while being paid to do a job but still gain qualifications, then the answer could be an apprenticeship.
- Explore the different careers open to them. The first section of LO3 covers this.
- Make a plan. Could the person leave school at 16 and go straight into their chosen career?

Case study: Josh's medical career dilemma

Josh is 16. He has wanted to be a doctor since he was very young. He planned to return to sixth form to study A-levels. However, his GCSE results were very disappointing – he achieved a D in his maths and science, and Cs in the rest of his subjects. His teachers have told him that he cannot study A-levels in school as he does not have the entry requirements for the courses he wishes to follow. Josh knows that to do a medical degree he would have to have five GCSEs at A*/A, including maths and English, and a B in science. Josh is devastated.

Questions

1 What advice would you give Josh? Is he being realistic in his plans?

2 Explain which other careers Josh could pursue.

3 Explain how Josh could have avoided this disappointment.

(They would have to do some training as part of the job to meet the Raising of the Participation Age.) If they cannot get a job, perhaps they could do an apprenticeship? Do they need more academic qualifications for their career choice? Which skills do they need to develop? What about a work placement? It is good to be flexible and have other options in mind in case the original plan does not work out. This could be because of the lack of available jobs or apprenticeships. Or perhaps the grades needed for a career are not achievable for the individual.

Evaluating necessary experience

Most students at the end of Year 11 will have little job experience, except perhaps a two-week block placement in Year 10. This placement may have confirmed their career choice and they will have observed staff carrying out day-to-day procedures. Also, learners may have carried out informal care while helping to look after a parent, grandparent or sibling who has been in hospital. This is still useful and is worth noting on a career plan; it could be a discussion point at an interview for a job or apprenticeship.

The aim for a career plan would be to add to this experience. It could be a weekend role in a residential home or, if taking a vocational course, it could be weekly half-day or full-day work experience. By the time a learner has finished sixth form they should be able to list many more work experiences because they are over 16.

Identifying entry points/qualifications

It is important to identify entry points/qualifications so that you aim for what is achievable. For example, if like Josh in the case study above, As and A*s are impossible, then it is better to be realistic and recognise that medicine is not an appropriate career choice. This does not mean there can be no aspirations. In Josh's case, his entry point could be at 16 if he wanted to start a L2 nursing apprenticeship.

Considering health and safety/physical requirements

For information on considering health and safety/physical requirements in your plan, look back at the section on health and safety issues in LO2.

Consideration of development

People develop all the time, regardless of age. They gain new skills, for example they may learn to use a computer or play the piano. Skills gained since the beginning of the career plan should be added as they happen. For example, when Unit R031 is completed then you may have a recognised first aid certificate to add to your skills on the plan. You may have gained an achievement award for raising money for charity. This will have developed your organisational and interpersonal skills.

Requirements

Different jobs have different requirements in terms of qualifications, knowledge and experience, as well as skills and attributes. Although some of the skills needed for the sector are transferable, some are specific to the job role.

Research activity

Comparing requirements

1 Go to https://nationalcareersservice.direct. gov.uk
2 Research educational welfare officer and emergency care assistant roles. Compare the skills and attributes needed for these roles, and note down the different requirements.

Producing a career action plan/road map

A career plan is sometimes called a road map because it helps someone get to where they want to be. Producing a career action plan will help a learner to set their goals, to clarify the actions they need to take to achieve these goals, and to plan out activities that will help them meet their goals.

The learner must be actively involved in the plan, as it is theirs. There is no right or wrong way to draw up the plan. It is up to the learner to decide the best way forward. Parents, teachers and career advisors may comment on the plan, and offer advice and suggestions, but it needs to be owned by the learner.

How to plan developmental goals to improve behaviours, skills and attributes

Setting aims and objectives

An aim is the overall purpose of the plan. Objectives or development goals are statements of how the overall purpose/aim is going to be achieved.

Planning activities

Table 6.6 gives an example of the first stages of a career plan, for Poppy who is aged 14. She has decided that she wants to be a primary school teacher. Her goals/objectives explain her first stages in achieving this goal. These are as follows.

1 Find out the best GCSEs for teaching.
2 Work hard at GCSEs, especially maths.
3 Go to a primary school for her two-week placement.
4 Volunteer in a local nursery over the summer holidays and on Saturdays.
5 Work hard on the skills needed for teaching, especially time management.

The action column in Table 6.6 shows the planned activities that Poppy is planning to undertake to achieve her overall aim.

Poppy decided to start her career plan in table form as she felt she could see at a glance what needing doing and when. Obviously Poppy's plan is not complete and it started in Year 9, but it is one idea of how a plan may be set out.

Remember, you must create your own template rather than using one that has been given to you by your tutor. Table 6.6 is an example only and must not be used for the assessment.

Determining costs/allocating resources

Before starting any plan or project, it is important to determine costs. For example, Poppy's tutor is going to cost at least £25 each week. Some people could not afford to pay that amount. In this case, it may be possible to share the cost with another learner who also needs extra tutoring. This may make the cost more affordable and realistic.

As Table 6.6 shows, resources can be people as well as books, internet, school, etc. Time is also a resource.

Timescales

It is important to keep a note of timescales as some dates are quite specific. For example, in Poppy's plan she has to make her option choices by a set date. Also, some timescales must be in a set order, so deadlines need to take this into account. It can be motivating to see tasks being ticked off as they are completed. Deadlines can spur an individual to finish work.

Table 6.6 Example of the first stages of a career plan

Action	Target date	Cost/resources	Date completed
Research GCSEs needed for teaching	30/01/2017 before Year 9 options	Time to research on internet	04/02/2017
Ask H&SC teachers if Cambridge Nationals has work placement in primary school	30/01/2017 before Year 9 options	H&SC teachers	23/01/2017
Fill in options form after talking to form tutor	30/03/2017	Year 9 tutor	29/03/2017
Volunteer at nursery	13/06/2017	Time to go to nursery, plus bus fare	27/06/2017
Start at nursery to gain experience of working with children	30/07/2017	Time and bus fare	30/07/2017
Start GCSEs	04/09/2017	Time, textbooks	30/05/2019
Start working on time-management skills when planning homework	24/11/2017	Time (have researched this in library) School have shown us how to manage our time for revision	Ongoing
Develop impartiality	15/12/2017	Practise when at nursery	Ongoing
Struggling with maths ... will go to after-school classes	16/01/2018	Time after school (1 hour, lift home from school from Mum)	30/05/2019
Failed maths mock – will have to re-sit	23/02/2018	Maths tutor (one evening each week) Cost: 1 hour (approx. £25). Extra maths homework to do for tutor	Ongoing

Stretch activity

Development plan for Carrie

Carrie wants to be a social worker. However, she was cautioned by the police last year for anti-social behaviour. She has also been in trouble at school for poor attitude and behaviour.

Produce a plan of development goals to improve Carrie's behaviours, skills and attributes. The plan must be relevant to her career path and also realistic.

(Aim for a **thorough** plan. Look at the command word definitions to see what **thorough** means in the assessment.)

Know it!

1 Explain how recruitment material can help when researching careers.
2 Discuss the value of work placements when researching possible careers.
3 Explain what is meant by a career action plan.
4 Explain why timescales are necessary on a career plan.

Assessment guidance

Learning outcome 3: Be able to plan for careers in health, social care or the children and young people's workforce

Marking criteria for LO3 Part A

Mark band 1	Mark band 2	Mark band 3
Carries out limited research to identify **few** career opportunities in health, social care or the children and young people's workforce. Prepares **basic** career plans providing learner with **limited** scope to inform their development.	Carries out research to identify **some** career opportunities in health, social care or the children and young people's workforce. Prepares **detailed** career plans enabling learner to **adequately** inform their development.	Carries out **comprehensive** research to identify **many** career opportunities in health, social care or the children and young people's workforce. Prepares **thorough** career plans enabling learner to **appropriately** and **clearly** inform their development.

 ## The OCR Model Assignment will ask you to:

- Research and identify career opportunities in health, social care or the children and young people's workforce.
- Prepare your own career plan to inform your development.

 ## What do the command words mean?

- **Comprehensive research to identify many career opportunities**: You will carry out research that is complete and will include everything that is necessary (in terms of breadth and depth) to identify a large number of career opportunities in health, social care or children and young people's workforce.
- **Thorough career plans to appropriately and clearly inform development**: You will prepare a career plan that is extremely attentive to accuracy and detail and will enable you to inform your development in a relevant and focussed way.

You should check the glossary in the Introduction for the definitions of each of the command words from OCR.

Marking criteria for LO3 Part B

Mark band 1	Mark band 2	Mark band 3
Produces a **basic** plan of development goals to improve behaviours, skills and attributes. The detail within the plan has limited relevance to the job role/sector. Draws upon **limited** skills/knowledge/understanding from other units in the specification.	Produces a **reasonable** plan of development goals to improve behaviours, skills and attributes. The detail within the plan has **some** relevance to the job role/sector. Draws upon **some relevant** skills/knowledge/understanding from other units in the specification.	Produces a **thorough** plan of development goals to improve behaviours, skills and attributes. The detail within the plan is relevant and realistic. **Clearly** draws upon **relevant** skills/knowledge/understanding from other units in the specification.

→

The OCR Model Assignment will ask you to:

- Produce a plan of development goals to improve behaviours, skills and attributes, with detail that is relevant and realistic.
- Draw on relevant skills/knowledge/understanding from other units from specification.

 What do the command words mean?

- **Thorough plan**: You will produce a plan of development goals to improve your behaviours, skills and attributes that is extremely attentive to accuracy and detail. The detail will also be relevant and realistic.
- **Clearly draws on relevant skills**: In a focussed way, you will draw upon skills/knowledge/understanding from other units in the specification that will be correctly focussed on this activity. In other words, you will use accurately expressed ideas from your learning in other units.

You should check the glossary in the Introduction for the definitions of each of the command words from OCR.

Read about it

Weblinks

www.unison.org.uk Unison – advice on what unions do for members, etc.

www.hse.gov.uk Health and Safety Executive – advice on all aspects of health and safety

https://nationalcareersservice.direct.gov.uk National Careers Service – comprehensive careers advice

www.careerpilot.org.uk/jobs Careerpilot – advice about further qualifications, jobs, etc.

Reference books

Trotman Education (2017) *Careers 2017: The Bestselling Annual Jobs Directory*. Trotman Publishing.

R027 Creative activities to support individuals in health, social care and early years settings

About this unit

Creative activities with individuals and groups in health, social care and early years settings can encourage physical and mental well-being, provide stimulation and enjoyment, and develop communication and social interaction skills.

In this unit you will learn about the different types of creative activities that are available, and the different needs these activities address for children and young people, adults and older adults. You will also learn about the many benefits of participating in creative activities and how to encourage positive experiences for all those who take part in and support them.

Creative activities require careful planning and delivery if individuals and groups are to benefit from them. You will have an opportunity to plan and carry out a creative activity suitable for an individual or group in a health, social care or early years setting. You will also gain the knowledge and skills required to review a creative activity and make suggestions for improvements.

Learning outcomes

LO1: Understand the different types of creative activities available in health, social care and early years settings

LO2: Understand the benefits of participating in creative activities

LO3: Be able to carry out creative activities in a health, social care or early years setting

How will I be assessed?

You will be assessed through a series of assignment tasks, which are set by OCR. The assignment will be marked by your tutor and then moderated by OCR.

For LO1, you need to:

- demonstrate an understanding of the different types of creative activities available in health, social care and early years settings
- describe the different types of creative activities, with examples
- explain how the different types of creative activities meet the needs of different groups of individuals.

Note: SPAG is assessed in this learning outcome.

For LO2, you need to:

- demonstrate an understanding of the benefits of participating in creative activities

Make sure you refer to the current OCR specification and guidance.

- provide information, with examples, about the types of creative activity and their purpose
- explain the links between different types of creative activities and the relevant physical, intellectual, language, emotional and social (P.I.L.E.S.) benefits to the individual or group in a care setting.

For LO3, you need to:

- understand how to plan a creative activity to meet the individual or group's needs
- demonstrate how to carry out a creative activity in a health, social care or early years setting
- review the creative activity, with suggestions for improvement.

Links to other units

Unit R025 (optional unit): Understanding life stages (LO1, LO2) and **Unit R028 (optional unit): Understanding the development and protection of young children in an early years setting** (LO1):

When demonstrating your knowledge of the main characteristics of different types of creative activities, their purpose, benefits and the needs they can address you could apply your understanding of individuals' and groups' physical, intellectual, language, emotional and social needs (optional unit RO25, LO1, LO2) and their development (optional unit RO28, LO1).

Unit R024 (optional unit): Pathways for providing care in health, social care and early years settings (LO3):

When producing a plan for carrying out a creative activity with an individual or group you could also show your understanding of the purpose and the areas of content to be covered.

Unit R022: Communicating and working with individuals in health, social care and early years settings (LO3):

You must also include how you plan to communicate with all those involved to ensure that your communication is appropriate to their needs.

Unit R026 (optional unit): Planning for employment in health, social care and children and young people's workforce (LO3) and **Unit R028 (optional unit): Understanding the development and protection of young children in an early years setting** (LO3):

When delivering the creative activity, it is important that you apply your knowledge of the range of health and safety measures that are available to protect individuals and groups from danger, harm or abuse (optional unit RO26, LO3), including ensuring the activity takes place in a safe environment (optional unit RO28, LO3).

Unit R021: Essential values of care for use with individuals in care settings (LO3):

When reviewing the creative activity, you must also reflect on your approach, your application of the values of care and their impact on those who participated and were involved in supporting the activity.

Learning outcome 1

Understand the different types of creative activities available in health, social care and early years settings

'Creativity is the ability to challenge, question and explore. It involves taking risks, playing with ideas, keeping an open mind and making connections where none are obvious.'

Source: Victoria and Albert Museum of Childhood

Creativity involves:

- expressing yourself
- reflecting your individuality and your uniqueness
- being imaginative
- trying and exploring new activities
- enjoying and learning.

Different types of creative activities

Imaginative

'Imagination is more important than knowledge.'

Source: Albert Einstein

This type of creative activity encourages individuals to use their imaginations to act out, role-play and/or create different scenarios.

Getting started

Creative activities in health, social care and early years settings encourage individuals to express their thoughts and feelings, and provide enjoyment and stimulation.

Make a list of three of your favourite interests or hobbies. Then explain to a partner why you enjoy them. Next, ask your partner what their three favourite interests or hobbies are and listen to why they enjoy them. Compare and discuss your answers.

This can improve individuals' mental health and mood, and can enhance positive interactions with others. Imaginative creative activities can also help with developing children's and adults' language and communication skills.

Examples of this type of activity include:

- using puppets during songs with babies
- toddlers creating stories based on topics or interests
- young people dressing up and taking part in a role play
- dance and drama workshops
- older adults creating a display about their local area using photographs, paintings they have done and craft models they have made.

Physical

Physical activities involve individuals moving around and using their bodies and muscles to express themselves. Gardening, woodwork and dance can promote adults' gross motor skills, such as balance and co-ordination. Jigsaw puzzles are a good way to exercise the brain, increase cognitive function and develop motor skills.

Recreational activities are another type of physical activity that can take place both indoors and outdoors, with children and adults. Examples are music and movement, parachute games, ball games, trampolining, swimming, walking and cycling.

Intellectual

Intellectual activities can help to promote **language and cognitive development** in children and adults. Examples include:

- group of children reading stories
- group discussions
- doing crossword puzzles
- taking part in quizzes

 Key term

Language and cognitive development The learning of language and cognitive skills, such as understanding and using words, communicating, thinking, remembering and problem-solving.

Figure 7.1 Reading stories can help to promote language and cognitive development in children and adults

- poetry
- story-telling
- writing stories and plays.

Activities that enhance babies' language and cognitive development usually stimulate their senses. Examples include playing different types of music or animal sounds for recognition, reading stories with colourful pictures, or playing with toys that are made of different textures.

Medical

Medical creative activities can improve individuals' physical and mental health. For example, dancing and music and movement exercises for children and adults are good for improving the body's balance and co-ordination, and for creating feelings of well-being.

Activities such as knitting and crocheting can help with improving fine motor skills and ensuring that the joints in the hands remain healthy and pain-free. This in turn can lead to an improved sense of mental well-being.

Social

Social creative activities, such as singing, drama, **reminiscence therapy** and mime, encourage the building of positive relationships, and enable individuals to communicate, interact and meet with others, and exercise their bodies and minds. Group experiences such as painting, cooking and discussions can help with promoting social and mental well-being by encouraging individuals to interact with others and make new friendships.

 Key term

Reminiscence therapy An activity that involves the use of photographs, music or familiar objects to enable an individual to discuss and share their past life experiences.

Figure 7.2 How can group activities encourage positive interactions?

Figure 7.3 How do you express yourself?

Emotional

Emotional creative activities – for instance, story-telling, group discussions, painting, craft work and mime – can help individuals to understand and express their emotions or feelings. Not doing so can lead to individuals feeling frustrated and angry. This type of activity can also be a good way of exploring topics or areas that children and/or adults find difficult or too upsetting to talk about.

Developmental

Physical developmental activities, such as doing up buttons and being able to use a crayon, can encourage the development of fine motor skills in children.

Cognitive development activities, such as puzzles and quizzes, can help both children and adults to:

- problem-solve
- understand and interpret information
- improve their concentration levels
- listen to others' ideas and work together.

Creative development activities – for example, music and dance – provide individuals with opportunities to explore and express their thoughts, feelings, ideas and views.

The needs of individuals that creative activities address

Having learned about the different types of creative activities there are for individuals in health, social care and early years settings,

you will now find out more about the needs of individuals that these activities address. All individuals are different and therefore have diverse needs; this is why it is important to have a range of creative activities available that can be adapted to meet individuals' specific needs.

Children and young people

Physical needs

A child or young person who has cerebral palsy may have difficulties moving their body in a co-ordinated way when walking or running, and may have to use a wheelchair. Creative activities that encourage movement and co-ordination, such as dance and exercise, can help the child or young person to develop stronger muscles and improve their balance.

Learning difficulties

Creative activities can help children and young people with **learning difficulties** to become more independent and confident in their own abilities. Drama and role play, for example, can help a child or young person who has learning difficulties to interact with others and develop their communication and social skills. Trying new activities can also help children and young people to learn and develop new skills.

> ### Key term
>
> **Learning difficulties** Difficulties processing some types of information without an individual's general intelligence being affected, e.g. dyslexia.

Sensory impairment

Children and young people who have a visual or hearing impairment, or both, may have difficulties with (or lack confidence when) moving around in their environments. They may find it more difficult to explore and take interest in activities that are not known to them, but that does not mean that they cannot explore, be creative or use their imagination. Creative activities that have been designed to meet the visual, hearing and tactile (related to sense of touch) needs of children and young people who have sensory impairments can provide:

- a sense of achievement
- opportunities to learn a new activity
- opportunities to experiment with different textures and sounds
- opportunities to be with other children.

For example, painting a large-scale mural encourages children to use their hands, feet and whole bodies as the painting tools, rather than brushes. Similarly, woodwork can encourage young people with visual and hearing impairments to work together to create objects that can then be used by them and others. This fosters feelings of self-worth and purpose.

Figure 7.4 How can outdoor experiences benefit the senses?

 Key term

Obsessive compulsive disorder (OCD) An anxiety disorder characterised by obsessive thoughts and compulsive activities.

Behavioural conditions

Children and young people who have behavioural conditions such as **obsessive compulsive disorder (OCD)** or attention deficit and hyperactivity disorder (ADHD) can be difficult to engage due to their repetitive and disruptive behaviours. Creative activities such as painting and needlework can help children and young people who have OCD to relax and remain calm, reducing their anxiety levels and changing their focus onto more positive behaviours.

Children and young people with ADHD often have high energy levels. So physical activities that encourage high levels of activity, such as running, cycling and hiking, or team sports like football and basketball, will ensure the child moves around and is focused. Michael Phelps, the Olympic swimming gold medallist, was diagnosed with ADHD when he was a child. Taking part in swimming provided him with the focus and goals he needed to achieve.

Special needs

Children or young people who have special needs may need additional help because of:

- an illness or medical condition
- an emotional or learning difficulty or disability that prevents them from learning and developing in the same way as other children or young people of the same age who do not have special needs.

For example, art activities that enable children to use their creativity and explore their senses, such as clay and dough modelling, water and sand play, can provide a good focus for children who have difficulties concentrating and participating in activities.

Cinema groups, drama workshops and music activities that involve playing different instruments and creating a range of different rhythms and sounds can provide opportunities for young people to meet others of their age who have similar interests, and to relax and learn new skills.

Adults

Mental health needs

Adults with mental health needs and who may, for example, experience anxiety or **depression** can find that participating in creative activities such as photography, creative writing and poetry can help with building their confidence, interacting with others, making friendships and learning new skills. Other creative activities that can improve and maintain mental well-being by enabling individuals to regain their confidence and rebuild their skills include ceramics, painting and drawing.

Special needs

Adults who have special needs can also experience difficulties with communication, which can be related to speech and language, social skills and/or behaviour. Creative activities such as cooking, gardening, exercise and visiting cafés with friends can help to develop individuals' confidence, social skills and self-esteem.

Physical disabilities

Adults who have physical disabilities may want to maintain their physical health by keeping the muscles and joints in their body strong. Individuals participate in creative activities such as aerobic exercise, gym sessions, swimming and trampolining. Maintaining their mental well-being is also important and closely linked to good physical health and well-being.

Sensory impairment

Adults who have sensory impairments may benefit from a range of creative activities. Adults with visual impairments may benefit from music workshops where they can learn how to play an instrument, drama and dance, pottery and crafts. All of these activities provide mental and physical stimulation, and are good ways for individuals to continue enjoying their interests and hobbies while meeting other people. Adults who have hearing impairments may enjoy opportunities for creative expression that art activities such as pottery and ceramics, or acting and miming activities may bring.

Medical conditions

Adults may have a range of different medical conditions such as **diabetes**, obesity, high blood pressure, mobility difficulties, depression or anxiety, and may benefit from creative activities designed to improve and maintain good mental and physical well-being. This could include nature walks, specially designed gym sessions, relaxation and yoga classes.

Older adults

Memory loss

Older adults who experience memory loss can benefit from creative activities that encourage them to stay active and meet other people, such as going out to favourite places. Completing **life story work** with individuals, using photographs of the people and places that are important in their lives, can exercise the memory. Gardening activities, including indoor planting and window boxes, are also good for exercising the senses. Meeting with others to reminisce and creating memory boxes can be other creative activities that older adults with memory loss can enjoy.

Lack of mobility

Older adults who experience a lack of mobility, or limited mobility, find that physical creative activities are important to their overall physical and mental well-being, because they improve their self-esteem. For example, aerobic exercises in water can support individuals' bodies while reducing additional pressure on muscles and joints. Chair exercises, where the individual carries out exercises while sitting down, can strengthen bones and muscles, and can improve an individual's balance. Relaxation exercises, including yoga, can provide an overall sense of well-being.

Key terms

Depression A low mood that lasts for a long period of time and affects an individual's day-to-day activities.

Diabetes A condition where the amount of glucose in the blood is too high because the body cannot use it properly.

Life story work An activity that involves reviewing an individual's past life events and developing a biography to understand more about the individual and their experiences.

Sensory impairment, including hearing impairment
Older adults who have hearing and/or visual impairments may benefit from spending time in a sensory garden where they can experience an outside space using their senses. Some sensory gardens include scented plants, fruit that can be eaten, water features that can be listened to or sculptures that can be touched.

Group activity

How can creative activities meet the needs of older adults?

In small groups, find out how creative activities can address the different types of needs that older adults may have.

You may find it useful to reference:

- the Alzheimer's Society's website (for memory loss) – www.alzheimers.org.uk
- Sense's website (for hearing and sensory impairment) – www.sense.org.uk
- Age UK's website (for lack of mobility) – www.ageuk.org.uk

Stretch activity

Different types of creative activities

1 List the different types of creative activities that you know about.

2 Describe to a partner, in as much detail as possible, two different types of creative activities. Explain how they meet the needs of different groups.

(Aim to produce a **detailed** description and a **thorough** explanation. Look at the command word definitions to see what **detailed** and **thorough** means in the assessment.)

Case study: Meeting individuals' needs through creative activities

Sarah has cerebral palsy and is married to Geoff, who has learning difficulties. They have a daughter, Siobhan, who is four years old and has special needs relating to her speech and communication.

Sarah and Geoff attend a social group that meets once a week in their local area. The social group offers opportunities for making new friends, meeting lots of different people and trying out a range of activities. This evening, Sarah will be attending the dancing workshop and Geoff the poetry group.

Sarah and Geoff have made arrangements for Siobhan's childminder, who also has a child of her own, to look after Siobhan for one evening a week.

Bowling, parachute games and musical chairs are some of the group activities they have suggested Siobhan enjoys taking part in.

Questions

1 How many different types of creative activities are available to Sarah, Geoff and Siobhan?

2 What needs do you think the dancing workshop may address for Sarah? Why?

3 How can the poetry group address Geoff's learning difficulties?

4 What other types of creative activities may address Siobhan's speech and communication needs? Why?

Know it!

1 Name three different types of creative activities.

2 Give an example of a social creative activity.

3 What do you understand by the term 'developmental' creative activities?

4 Give two examples of how social creative activities can address the needs of adults with mental health needs.

5 List the needs of children with behavioural conditions that creative activities can address.

Assessment guidance

Learning outcome 1: Understand the different types of creative activities available in health, social care and early years settings

Marking criteria for LO1 Part A

Mark band 1	Mark band 2	Mark band 3
Provides a **basic** description of the different types of creative activities with **limited** explanation about how these meet the needs of different groups.	Provides a **clear** description of the different types of creative activities with **relevant** explanation about how they meet the needs of different groups.	Provides a **detailed** description of the different types of creative activities, with **thorough** explanation about how they meet the needs of different groups.
There is **limited** use of examples to illustrate practical understanding. There will be **simple** information about the **limited** range of activities included.	There is **sound** use of examples to illustrate practical understanding for some of the different creative activities. There will be **clear** information about the range of activities included.	There is **effective** use of examples to illustrate practical understanding for most of the different creative activities. There will be **detailed** information about the **wide** range of activities included.
There will be **some** errors in spelling, punctuation and grammar.	There will be **minor** errors in spelling, punctuation and grammar.	There will be **few**, if any, errors in spelling, punctuation and grammar.

The OCR Model Assignment will ask you to:

- Describe different types of creative activities.
- Include an explanation about how they meet the needs of different groups.
- Use examples to show practical understanding of the different creative activities. You will include information about the range of activities.

What do the command words mean?

- **Detailed description**: You will provide a description of the different types of creative activities and this will include a point by point consideration of each.
- **Thorough explanation**: You will provide an explanation about how the different types of creative activities meet the needs of different groups that is extremely attentive to accuracy and detail.

→

- **Effective**: You use examples to illustrate practical understanding for most of the different creative activities, which shows that you are able to apply skills appropriately to a task to achieve the desired outcome or result.
- **Detailed information and wide range**: the information you include will be a point-by-point consideration of a broad and comprehensive range of activities.
- **Few**: there may be a small number of errors in spelling, punctuation or grammar, if any.

You should check the glossary in the Introduction for the definitions of each of the command words from OCR.

Learning outcome 2

Understand the benefits of participating in creative activities

Getting started

Participating in creative activities can benefit children, young people, adults and older people in a variety of different ways.	What skills and abilities have you developed by taking part in creative activities? Make a note of these, then share your findings with a partner. Discuss and compare.

The benefits of creative activities can vary from one individual to another, depending on the individual's experience of the activity and the extent that the activity addressed their specific needs. Individuals can also experience different benefits at different times. Table 7.1 indicates the range of potential benefits that creative activities can bring.

Table 7.1 The benefits of participating in different types of creative activities

Type of creative activity	Skills and areas developed	Examples of benefits
Physical	<ul><li>Fine motor skills – small skilled actions that require the use of muscles, such as a child picking up a toy using the thumb and finger, or an adult cutting and sticking to create a collage.</li><li>Gross motor skills – large skilled actions that require the use of muscles, such as a child crawling or an adult jumping up and down.</li><li>Circulation – activities that increase the heart rate and improve the circulation of the blood around the body, such as walking, swimming and chair-based exercises.</li></ul>	<ul><li>Improved **dexterity**</li><li>Increased strength in muscles, i.e. in fingers, hands, wrists, toes</li><li>Improved hand to eye co-ordination</li><li>Improved **agility**</li><li>Improved mobility</li><li>Improved strength in muscles in the body</li><li>Increase in fitness</li><li>Exercises the heart, lungs and muscles of the body</li><li>Reduction of pain and discomfort, i.e. swollen feet and legs</li></ul>

→

Table 7.1 The benefits of participating in different types of creative activities *(continued)*

Type of creative activity	Skills and areas developed	Examples of benefits
Intellectual (cognitive)	● Mental stimulation – activities that exercise and stimulate the brain, such as doing crossword puzzles, taking part in a quiz or learning a new language. ● Work independently – activities that promote independent learning, such as role-play, making posters, creating 3D models. ● Creative skills – activities that encourage individuals to explore, experiment and promote self-expression, such as mixing paints, story-telling and dance.	● Prevent and/or slow down memory loss ● Relieve boredom ● Learn new skills ● Ability to plan daily activities ● Ability to make your own choices ● Problem solving ● Improved imagination ● Development of life skills ● Increased **self-awareness**
Language	● Communication – activities that enable individuals to engage and interact with others, such as visiting places, drama activities, painting and drawing. ● Language skills – activities that provide individuals with opportunities to develop their speech and language skills, such as reading, singing and story-telling.	● Improved verbal communication ● Improved written communication ● Ability to express how an individual thinks and feels ● Learning ● Improved speech ● Improved listening skills
Emotional	● Self-esteem – activities that enhance individuals' well-being and promote positive mental health such as walking, listening to music, dance. ● Express emotions – activities that provide opportunities for individuals to express and/or talk about their feelings, such as creative writing, poetry, drama and painting.	● Feeling valued ● Improved confidence and **self-worth** ● Having a sense of achievement ● Improved emotional stability ● Reduction in anxiety and low mood ● Relieves tension and stress
Social	● Social interaction – activities that provide opportunities for individuals to be actively involved in the lives of others, such as visiting family and friends, joining a group, going to the park. ● Developing friendships – activities that provide opportunities to interact and develop relationships with others, such as playing games, group story-telling and art projects.	● Being able to work in groups/teams ● Improved relationships ● Staying connected and sharing experiences with family and friends ● Being able to make friends and maintain friendships more easily ● Improved social network ● Experiencing how to receive and provide support can promote a sense of belonging

Key terms

Dexterity The ability to perform an action with the hands skilfully.

Agility The ability to move the body quickly and easily.

Self-awareness The ability to know one's own character and feelings.

Self-worth Confidence and value in one's own abilities and qualities.

Classroom discussion

The benefits of participation

As a whole group, discuss the top three benefits of participating in the following creative activities:

- dance (physical)
- quiz (intellectual)
- story-telling (language)
- painting (emotional)
- singing (social).

In small groups, discuss how these benefits may vary between the following groups of individuals: children and young people, adults and older adults.

Stretch activity

The skills and abilities developed by taking part in different types of creative activities

1 List the skills and abilities developed by taking part in the different types of creative activities that you know about.

2 Describe to a partner, in as much detail as possible, the skills and abilities developed by taking part in two different types of creative activities.

(Aim to produce a **detailed** description with **coherent** information and **appropriate** examples. Look at the command word definitions to understand the meanings of **detailed**, **coherent** and **appropriate**.)

Case study: The benefits of 'Right Now' for Stefan

Stefan is part of a youth production company called 'Right Now' – a theatre-based project aimed at 16–25 year olds who have, or are experiencing, mental health issues. The project encourages young people to be involved in all aspects of the development and performance of drama productions and plays, as a way of enabling them to express how they feel about the aspects of their lives that are affected by their mental health needs.

Stefan decided to join Right Now because his mental health had left him feeling isolated from other young people of his age. Participating in the group has enabled Stefan to feel more confident in his own abilities, make new friends with whom he feels relaxed and comfortable with, learn new skills, reduce his boredom, and

develop his imagination and creativity. Stefan has also noted that his periods of mental illness have reduced significantly.

Questions

1 How has participating in Right Now impacted positively on Stefan?

2 How may participating in creative activities improve young people's mental health needs?

3 Are there any other potential benefits to young people with mental health needs of participating in projects such as Right Now?

4 Participating in Right Now has enabled Stefan to learn new skills. What skills do you think he may have learned? Why?

Know it!

1 Name one benefit of participating in a physical creative activity.

2 Give an example of how participating in an intellectual activity can improve an individual's problem-solving skills.

3 What communication skills could be improved by participating in a creative activity?

4 Give two examples of creative activities that can enable individuals to express their emotions.

5 List the social benefits of participating in creative activities.

Assessment guidance

Learning outcome 2: Understand the benefits of participating in creative activities

Marking criteria for LO2 Part A

Mark band 1	Mark band 2	Mark band 3
Demonstrates a **basic** understanding of the benefits of participating in creative activities.	Demonstrates a **sound** knowledge of the benefits of participating in creative activities.	Demonstrates a **thorough** understanding of the benefits of participating in creative activities.
Provides **limited** information, with **few** appropriate examples, about the types of creative activity and their purpose.	Provides **clear** information, with **some** appropriate examples, about the types of creative activity and their purpose.	Provides **detailed** and **coherent** information, with **appropriate** examples, about the types of creative activities and their purpose.

 The OCR Model Assignment will ask you to:

- Show your understanding of the range of benefits of different creative activities.
- Include your knowledge, (with examples) about the types of creative activities and their purpose.

 What do the command words mean?

- **Thorough understanding**: You show an understanding of the benefits of participating in creative activities that is extremely attentive to accuracy and detail.
- **Detailed and coherent information, with appropriate examples**: Your work should consider logically and point by point the different types of creative activities and their purpose, with relevant examples.

You should check the glossary in the Introduction for the definitions of each of the command words from OCR.

Marking criteria for LO2 Part B

Mark band 1	Mark band 2	Mark band 3
Few **basic** links are made between different types of creative activities and relevant P.I.L.E.S. benefits to the individual or group in a care setting.	**Some** links are made between different types of creative activities and the relevant P.I.L.E.S. benefits to the individual or group in a care setting.	**Clear** links are made between the different types of creative activities and the relevant P.I.L.E.S. benefits to the individual or group participating in activity in a care setting.

 The OCR Model Assignment will ask you to:

● Make clear links between the different types of creative activities and the relevant physical, intellectual, language, emotional and social benefits to the individual or group taking part in the activity in a care setting.

 What do the command words mean?

● **Clear links**: your work shows focused and accurately expressed links/connections between different types of creative activities and the relevant P.I.L.E.S. benefits to an individual or group.

You should check the glossary in the Introduction for the definitions of each of the command words from OCR.

Learning outcome 3

Be able to carry out creative activities in a health, social care or early years setting

In order for creative activities to be successful in meeting individuals' needs and to be of maximum benefit, it is very important that they are planned and delivered in a structured way, and reviewed for their effectiveness on a regular basis.

Getting started

Individuals' experiences of creative activities will vary depending on how they are delivered and whether they had positive or negative impacts.

Think about a creative activity you or someone else you know participated in. Write down how this activity was experienced and the reasons why. Share your findings with a partner. Compare and discuss answers.

How to plan a creative activity

Good planning for a creative activity involves 12 steps.

Step 1: Choose the activity

Deciding on the type of creative activity to plan is very important, i.e. will it be an imaginative, physical, intellectual, social or emotional activity, or a combination of two or more of these? Determining the type of creative activity will very much depend on who the activity is for, its aim and objectives. Therefore, choosing the activity may involve consulting with others first, such as the individuals who the activity is for, your colleagues and others who know the individuals you are working with well, so that the type of activity reflects the individuals' needs, interests, wishes and preferences.

You should also think about planning a creative activity that interests you. Perhaps there is a particular topic or area that appeals to you, or a skill or area of knowledge that you can share with others?

Step 2: Set the aim for the activity

Next, you need to decide the purpose of the activity, in terms of what you would hope to achieve. For example, would you like the activity to improve a child's fine motor skills, or to provide a developmental opportunity for an adult with a learning disability to be able to read more confidently and independently?

Step 3: Set the objectives of the activity

Once you have set out the overall aim of the activity, you can begin to think about how you intend to achieve the aim by breaking it down into a series of objectives or targets that are realistic and achievable.

Examples are showing a child how to hold a crayon correctly, being able to support a young person with a learning disability to put on a sock correctly, and supporting an older adult to use a piece of equipment, such as a walking aid, accurately.

You may have heard of the acronym SMART (Specific, Measurable, Achievable, Relevant and Time bound). This is often used as a way of ensuring that all objectives set can be achieved and measured:

- **S**pecific – clear details about what you plan to do
- **M**easurable – clear outcomes that can be measured
- **A**chievable – realistic in terms of what can be achieved and agreed
- **R**elevant – relevant to the individual/s needs and overall aim
- **T**ime bound – achievable within the agreed timeframe.

Not having SMART objectives may lead to the activity not being achieved, individuals' needs remaining unmet and a negative experience.

Step 4: Agree the timescales for the activity

It is useful to agree on an overall timescale for the activity and a target timescale by which each objective should be achieved. Doing this will mean you can monitor closely whether each objective is

going to be achieved; if it is not, then you can take action early to make the necessary changes for the objective to be achieved. For example, each objective could be broken down into individual timescales of 10 to 15 minutes, with an agreed timescale for the whole activity of 45 minutes.

Not having enough time may create a sense of the activity being rushed and individuals may in turn feel that they have not had sufficient time to participate in a meaningful way. Having too much time can result in individuals feeling bored or getting distracted from the purpose of the activity.

Step 5: Organise the material resources for the activity

You must think about the materials and equipment you will need for the activity; this will depend not only on the chosen activity but also on the needs of the individuals.

For example, if you are supporting a group of four children to bake a cake, you will require a copy of the recipe for each of the children: one of these may need to be in large print for a child who has a visual impairment, and another may need to include photographs for a child who has learning difficulties. Utensils may have to be adapted with, for example, large handle grips.

You will also need:

- ingredients for the cake
- equipment for making the cake
- protective equipment like aprons
- access to tables and chairs
- access to a kitchen and an oven
- washing-up facilities
- a cloth to wipe the tables clean
- a broom to sweep the floor afterwards
- plates to put the cake on.

The materials need to be ready to use and in sufficient supply. Not having the correct materials, or not having enough materials, can prevent the activity from taking place or mean it takes too long to achieve within the agreed timescales. It may also reduce the time available to deliver the activity.

Step 6: Protect individuals from harm

Although it is very important for activities to be enjoyable and successful, they must also be safe and protect individuals and others involved in the activity from actual and potential harm, danger or abuse. Considering what might go wrong during the activity, or what may cause a potential danger or harm, is good planning. Taking this into account before the activity minimises the risks of any danger, harm or abuse occurring.

It is important that all individuals, including you and others participating in the activity, have access to clear information about what dangers, harm and/or abuse may exist, how to recognise the signs, and what organisational procedures must be followed if and when these do arise, including who to approach for help and advice.

How to minimise risks

A risk assessment is a method used to protect individuals from harm. It should help you think about:

- what could go wrong with an activity
- how to identify suitable ways of controlling risks by eliminating, reducing or minimising the risks of harm occurring to individuals and others present when the activity is taking place.

The Health and Safety Executive (HSE) recommends an approach where you carry out the risk assessment process in five steps, as follows.

- Step 1: Identify the hazards associated with work activities.
- Step 2: Identify who could be harmed by the hazards.
- Step 3: Identify the control measures; how you manage the risks and whether the risks can be further reduced.
- Step 4: Record the findings of your risk assessment and inform those at risk of the controls that you have put in place.
- Step 5: Review the risk assessment on a regular basis.

Key term

Health and Safety Executive (HSE) The official supervisory body for the health, safety and welfare of people in work settings in the UK.

It is important that you carry out a risk assessment every time you carry out an activity, even if it is the same activity. Figure 7.5 shows a risk assessment for an arts and crafts activity carried out in a care setting with young people.

Safety of equipment

It is very important that any equipment you use for the activity is:

- maintained correctly, so it is safe for you and others to use

Activity	Hazards identified	Controls to eliminate or reduce the risk	Likelihood of an accident happening	Risk rating
Painting	Spillage of paint on floor	• Young people work in small groups, with one volunteer and one support worker per group. • All spillages are cleaned immediately.	Likely	Medium
Sticking – using glue	Contact with skin, mouth and eyes	• One glue stick to be made available per group. • Glue stick use to be supervised for every young person. • Precautions to be explained to young people.	Not likely	Low
Cutting – using scissors	Cuts	• Approved craft scissors to be made available per young person. • Scissor use to be supervised for every young person. • Precautions to be explained to young people.	Not likely	Low

Risk assessment signed by: M Hayes (Support Worker)
Risk assessment agreed with: D Mills (Manager)
Date of risk assessment: 10/01/17
Review date of risk assessment: 10/4/17

Figure 7.5 Example risk assessment for an arts and crafts activity

- used safely by trained people and in line with the manufacturer's instructions
- appropriate for the job.

Not doing so may result in accidents and/or injuries.

Contingency plans for emergencies

Making plans for what to do in the event of an emergency during an activity is very important, so that you can respond effectively.

Contingency planning for emergencies involves asking yourself the following three questions.

1   What might happen? (e.g. a fire, an accident.)

2   What do I need to do if it happens? (e.g. follow the fire/accident procedure.)

3   What can I do to prepare for the emergency? (e.g. attend training, read through policies and procedures, simulate a fire emergency or accident scenario, inform individuals and others at the beginning of the activity.)

Step 7: Know the legal requirements

It is important to follow safe working practices in accordance with legal requirements, in order to safeguard not only individuals but also your own and others' safety and well-being. The Health and Safety at Work Act 1974 (HASAWA) is the main piece of health and safety legislation that applies and forms the basis of all health and safety legislation.

The aims of the Act are:

- to protect the health and safety of employees
- to protect others who may be affected by work activities.

Being aware of the legal requirements is very important so that you can:

- protect individuals, yourself and others' well-being
- provide a safe environment free from harm, danger and abuse.

 Key term

Contingency planning A process that takes account of possible future events, i.e. emergencies.

 Research activity

Health and safety legal requirements for creative activities

Research the health and safety legal requirements for protecting individuals from danger, harm and abuse when carrying out creative activities.

You will find the HSE's website a useful source of information: www.hse.gov.uk.

You could also find out more information from staff who work in care settings.

Step 8: Know the costs of the activity

Costs for running an activity must be taken into account. Not doing this may mean that you do not have the materials and people you need for the activity to be effective and run smoothly. For example, how much do the materials cost? How many people will you need to run the activity? Will you need to pay for a venue? If so, how much?

You will also need to know what the total budget available for the activity is and ensure that you remain within this. It could be that you are able to use some materials (such as paper, crayons, printing, ink, cooking ingredients) for more than one activity. If so, you will need to proportion out the cost.

Stretch activity

Health and safety considerations for creative activities

1   Describe the health and safety issues that may arise during the delivery of creative activities.

2   For two health and safety issues, explain to a partner, in as much detail as possible, how to protect individuals from harm.

(Aim to produce a **detailed** description and a **thorough** explanation. Look at the command word definitions to see what **detailed** and **thorough** means in the assessment.)

Table 7.2 Costing for an activity with an older man who has mobility difficulties

Type of cost	Actual cost
Carer (2 hours)	£19.80 × 2 = £39.60
Car travel (mileage)	0.45p/mile × 5 miles = £2.25
Lunch	£10.80 **Total cost: £52.65**

For example, Table 7.2 shows a costing that has been done by a domiciliary agency worker. She is planning an activity with an older man who has mobility difficulties. They are going out for lunch to build his confidence while walking supported.

Step 9: Measure the success of the activity

Pre-set criteria must be in place before you deliver the activity, so that you can measure its success. There are different ways to do this. For example, at the end of the activity you could consult with the individuals and those who supported the activity in groups, you could interview participants on a one-to-one basis, or give out questionnaires posing questions such as:

- What worked well, and why?
- What didn't work well, and why?
- Was the aim of the activity met?
- Were the objectives of the activity met?
- What could have been done differently?
- What progress/development did you make?
- What were the benefits of the activity for you?
- How do you think you performed? How could you improve on this?

Step 10: Be clear about roles and responsibilities

It is very important to be clear about your role and responsibilities, as well as those of others who are supporting you to deliver the activity. It is useful to have these written down and to explain them to all involved. This ensures that everyone is clear about not only their role and responsibilities, but also those of others. Here are some areas to think about.

- Who is going to plan the activity and how?
- Who is going to lead the activity and be the lead person responsible?
- Who is going to support the activity and how?
- What are the general responsibilities everyone will have?
- What are the individual responsibilities different people will have?

Step 11: Know what methodology to use

Leading by example in a demonstration can be motivating for children, as you can demonstrate how to do the different aspects of the activity. Is the activity going to involve individuals working on their own, in pairs or in small groups? (If in pairs or groups, how long for and why?) Group work lends itself well to role-playing. It provides opportunities for individuals to work together with others as a team, interact and appreciate one another's points of view, and provides an opportunity to practise skills. Asking individuals to work on their own when painting a picture, and then to share this with the person sitting next to them, can be useful for encouraging individuals to be creative and original, and then take into account another individual's perspective.

Step 12: Communicate

The final step – communication – is very important. It is, in effect, what underpins the success of all activities: without good communication even the best of activities will not be a success. Good communication will inspire others to achieve and do their very best. You must take into account verbal and non-verbal communication methods, as well as written and electronic communication.

Ask yourself the following questions when planning a creative activity.

- How appropriate is it for participants? In other words, will participants be able to understand it? Does it meet everyone's needs? Will participants receive the message you are communicating in the way it is intended?
- How clear is the information provided? Will participants understand the purpose of the activity? Will individuals understand what they are required to do?
- Is communication encouraging and motivational? This includes what is spoken,

what is conveyed without words, what is expressed, how questions are answered. You can make sure your communication is encouraging and motivational by:

- communicating about what is important to others
- communicating positively by using words, expressions and non-verbal communications that are positive and empowering.

How to carry out the creative activity

Carrying out a creative activity requires a good knowledge of who the activity is aimed at, along with a range of skills and qualities to make it effective, safe and enjoyable for everyone. The following aspects must be included.

- An introduction, which provides an overview of the tasks, demonstrates how to carry out the activities and shows how to use any equipment that will be needed.
- The main content, which includes ensuring the individuals are settled and prepared to carry out the activity, knowing about any support needed and how to provide it, and ensuring that all health and safety requirements are met, and that further action to support the activity is encouraged.
- The closing stages, which include ensuring that agreed timescales are adhered to, that the environment is left clean and tidy, and that all equipment used is cleared away, allowing for time at the end of the activity to have an end-of-session discussion and exchange feedback.

Case study: Dee's best practice guide

Dee is an activities co-ordinator in a day service and has many years of experience in carrying out creative activities with older people. She has provided a document with the best practice principles of how to carry out creative activities, to help guide her team.

Read through the best practice guide in Figure 7.6 and consider how you can use it to guide you with your practice when carrying out a creative activity.

Questions

1 Summarise the best practice principles to follow when introducing a creative activity.

2 Give two examples of how you can make individuals feel comfortable during a creative activity.

3 What are the potential consequences of not following health and safety requirements during a creative activity?

4 Give two reasons why it is important to obtain feedback at the end of an activity.

→

Introducing the activity

To try to grab participants' attention straight away, have an introduction activity that shows the group the equipment they are going to use. Ask them to guess what activity they think it might be and why. Then encourage them to look at the equipment and pick it up. For example, place pens, paper, scissors and glue on each table and then ask each group to guess what they are going to do.

Then outline what the creative activity is and what it is going to involve. You can check individuals' understanding of this and show them what the end product may look like – for example, a collage. Next, explain that you are going to demonstrate each of the tasks first so they can model your actions. You can use pictures, photographs and diagrams to help to convey your message about what each task involves and/or the equipment to use, such as, for instance, craft or cookery utensils.

Delivering the activity: the main content

It is really important that individuals feel settled and comfortable so that they are prepared to carry out the activities. You could sort individuals into smaller groups and check with each of them that they have everything they need. Checklists are a useful tool to make sure that participants are clear about what they are doing.

Make sure the participants have sufficient space, lighting, are not too hot or too cold, and are not in an environment that is too noisy. This will help to focus their minds. Start the activity by showing the group a picture or singing a song.

Close supervision of the activity is important to ensure that it is going to plan, and health and safety requirements are being met. It is important to observe participants' behaviour and amend activities as and when needed, For instance, if a participant is not enjoying an activity, then support them to choose another activity while the remaining participants in the group continue with their activity.

Always make sure that health and safety requirements are being met, i.e. that all areas are kept hazard-free, and that the risks of danger, harm and abuse are avoided.

If participants wish or need to do more on the creative activity, encourage them by suggesting ideas, appropriate demonstration and effective communication.

Closing stages of the activity

The end of the activity is just as important as the beginning. You want each participant to go away having enjoyed the activity and feeling that they achieved what they set out to do. Not doing so can be frustrating for participants, so it is vital to keep to timescales. It is important to leave enough time to clear away; this could be incorporated into the end of the activity and participants should be encouraged to have an active role in this. Also, at the end of the activity it is important to discuss with the participants how they found the session: what worked and what didn't. Observe too what participants' body language is telling you, i.e. do they look happy and like they've had fun?

Figure 7.6 Best practice guide for creative activities

How to review the benefits to the participants of the creative activity

The quality and value of a creative activity will depend on how it is reviewed. Reviewing a creative activity can help to measure whether and how its objectives have been met, increase your awareness and learning of the positive and negative aspects that have been experienced, and help you with developing even better and more enjoyable activities in the future. Table 7.3 provides more information about what is involved in reviewing creative activities.

Table 7.3 Suggestions and questions to ask when reviewing a creative activity

Reflect on the activity	• Think back over the creative activity and review its aim and objectives. • Were these met? • To what extent and how?
Examine how the activity worked	• What worked well in the activity and why? • What didn't work well and why? • Did you experience any difficulties? • Did you experience any positive developments that you were not expecting?
Value skills, knowledge and strengths	• What skills did the leader and support staff have? • What specific areas of knowledge and strengths did the leader and support staff have? • What specific areas of knowledge and strengths did the individuals have?
Investigate options	• What could have been done differently and/or better? • How would this benefit the participants? • How would this benefit the overall running of the activity?
Explore ideas	• What ideas did leaders, support staff and individuals share with you for next time the activity is delivered? • Were there any common themes or comments shared?
Welcome improvements	• Agree on improvements to be made. When delivering the activity again put these improvements into practice. Then start the REVIEW cycle again by comparing the second time you deliver the activity with the first time, and think about what improved as a result. • What evidence do you have that the activity improved? How are you going to capture this evidence (i.e. comments, photographs of individuals, products displayed)? • What benefits resulted from the improvements? Consider whether any further improvements need to be made to the activity if delivered again.

Know it!

1 Name two important aspects to consider when planning a creative activity.

2 Give two examples of how to communicate the aims of a creative activity to a group of children.

3 Describe two ways of ensuring that a creative activity is going to plan.

4 List the key stages involved when closing a creative activity.

5 Give two examples of the benefits of reviewing a creative activity.

Assessment guidance

Learning outcome 3: Be able to carry out creative activities in a health, social care or early years setting

Marking criteria for LO3 Part A

Mark band 1	Mark band 2	Mark band 3
Produces a **basic** plan for a creative activity, providing a **simple** solution to meet the individual/group's needs. Demonstrates a **limited** understanding of what the objective of the creative activity is, with **few** success measures. May need guidance and support to produce the plan. A **limited** explanation is given for why the activity chosen may be suitable for the individual or group.	Produces a **clear** plan for a creative activity, providing a **sound** solution to meet the individual/group's needs. Demonstrates a **thorough understanding** of what the objective of the creative activity is, with **clear** success measures. **Relevant** explanation is given for why the activity has been chosen and is suitable for the individual or group.	Produces a **comprehensive** plan for a creative activity, providing a solution, which shows originality and creativity, to meet the individual/group's needs. Demonstrates a **comprehensive** understanding of what the objective of the creative activity is, with **clear** success measures. **Detailed** explanation, with justification, is given for why the activity chosen is suitable for the individual or group.

 The OCR Model Assignment will ask you to:

- Produce a plan for a creative activity for an individual or a group, providing a solution, showing originality and creativity, to meet the individual's/group's needs.
- Show an understanding of what the objective of the activity is and how you will measure success.
- Include an explanation of the reasons why the creative activity you have chosen is suitable for the individual or group.

 What do the command words mean?

- **Comprehensive plan**: You will produce a plan for a creative activity, providing a solution to meet an individual's or group's needs. The plan will show originality and creativity, and will include everything that is necessary to evidence your understanding in terms of both breadth and depth.
- **Comprehensive understanding and clear success measures**: Your plan shows your understanding of the objective or purpose of the creative activity. This will include everything that is necessary to evidence your understanding in terms of both breadth and depth. You will include how you will measure its success and these measures will be focussed and accurate.
- **Detailed explanation**: The explanation will be a point-by-point justification of why the chosen activity is suitable for the individual or group.

You should check the glossary in the Introduction for the definitions of each of the command words from OCR.

→

Marking criteria for LO3 Part B

Mark band 1	Mark band 2	Mark band 3
Demonstrates **limited** consideration of health and safety issues. There may be a **simple** explanation of how to protect individuals from harm. Carries out a **simple** activity. There may be **limited** structure. Demonstrates a **limited** confidence when delivering the creative activity, and may need guidance and support to complete.	Demonstrates **sound** consideration of health and safety issues, with some explanation for their choices. There will be a **clear** description of how to protect individuals from harm. Carries out an **appropriate** creative activity, which is structured and mostly follows to time. **Confidently** delivers the creative activity, with no support necessary.	Demonstrates **comprehensive** consideration of health and safety issues, with detailed explanation for their choices. There will be a **thorough** explanation of how to protect individuals from harm. Carries out a **well-structured** creative activity **effectively**, which meets time requirements. **Confidently** and **effectively** delivers the creative activity, engaging their participants and adapting to ensure that the individual's/group's needs are met.

 ## The OCR Model Assignment will ask you to:

- Include an explanation that shows how you took into account health and safety issues. Make sure to include an explanation of how to protect individuals from harm.
- Using your plan, carry out and deliver a creative activity for an individual or group which meets time requirements.
- Deliver the creative activity, engage your participants and adapt to ensure that the needs of the individual/group are met.

 ## What do the command words mean?

- **Comprehensive consideration and thorough explanation**: You will demonstrate consideration of health and safety issues with detailed explanation for their choices. The consideration will be comprehensive which means that you will include everything that is necessary to evidence understanding in terms of both breadth and depth. Your explanation of how to protect individuals from harm will be extremely attentive to accuracy and detail.
- **Well-structured and effectively**: You will successfully carry out a creative activity which is well-structured and meets time requirements. You will appropriately apply your skills to the task.
- **Confidently and effectively**: You will deliver the creative activity, engaging your participants and adapting to ensure that the individual's/group's needs are met. You will do this showing certainty and applying your skills appropriately to the task and do this successfully.

You should check the glossary in the Introduction for the definitions of each of the command words from OCR.

Marking criteria for LO3 Part C

Mark band 1	Mark band 2	Mark band 3
A **basic** review of the activity is included, which may give **limited** suggestions for improvement. Draws upon **limited** skills/knowledge/understanding from other units in the specification.	A **review** of the activity is included, with **some** relevant suggestions for improvements. Draws upon **some relevant** skills/knowledge/understanding from other units in the specification.	A **thorough** review of the activity is included, which gives **relevant** suggestions for improvements, with justification for these changes. **Clearly** draws upon **relevant** skills/knowledge/understanding from other units in the specification.

→

The OCR model assignment will ask you to:

- Complete a review of the creative activity you've carried out.
- Include suggestions for improvement in your review.
- Draw on skills/knowledge/understanding from other units you have studied on the course.

 What do the command words mean?

- **Thorough and relevant**: The review of your creative activity is extremely attentive to accuracy and detail, and includes correctly focused suggestions for improvements, with justifications.
- **Clearly and relevant**: In a focussed way, you will draw upon skills/knowledge/understanding from other units in the specification that will be correctly focussed on this activity.

You should check the glossary in the Introduction for the definitions of each of the command words from OCR.

Read about it

Weblinks

www.ageuk.org.uk Age UK – information about activities for older adults

www.alzheimers.org.uk Alzheimer's Society – information about activities for individuals who have dementia

www.bhf.org.uk British Heart Foundation – information about staying active

www.hse.gov.uk Health and Safety Executive – information about risk assessment

www.mind.org.uk Mind – information about how to maintain good mental health and well-being

www.sense.org.uk Sense – information about activities for children and adults who have sight and hearing loss

Information guides online

www.nurseryworld.co.uk/art-in-the-early-years Art in the Early Years – best practice guides in helping young children to develop their creativity through art published (Nursery World, 2011)

www.bhf.org.uk/heart-matters-magazine/ medical/diabetes Living with Diabetes – guide about how to live healthily and manage diabetes (British Heart Foundation, 2016)

www.nurseryworld.co.uk/outdoors-in-winter Enabling Environment – Outdoors – best practice guides about outdoor play for children (Nursery World, 2013)

www.alzheimers.org.uk/site/scripts/ documents_info.php?documentID=115 Staying Involved and Active – information guide about staying involved and active for individuals who have dementia (Alzheimer's Society, 2016)

www.alzheimers.org.uk/site/scripts/ documents_info.php?documentID=2195 Taking Part: Activities for People with Dementia – information booklet about activities for people who have dementia (Alzheimer's Society, 2016)

www.bhf.org.uk/heart-health/preventing- heart-disease/10-minutes-to-change-your-life Time to Get Moving – information guide about why it is important to be active (British Heart Foundation, 2016)

Reference books

Agar, K. (2008) *How to Make Your Care Home Fun: Simple Activities for People of All Abilities*. Jessica Kingsley Publications.

Bowden, A. and Lewthwaite, N. (2009) *The Activity Year Book: A Week by Week Guide for Use in Elderly Day and Residential Care*. Jessica Kingsley Publications.

Frankel, J., Hobart, C. and Walker, M. (2009) *A Practical Guide to Activities for Young Children* (4th edn). Nelson Thornes.

R028 Understanding the development and protection of young children in an early years setting

About this unit

All areas of development happen rapidly from a child's birth up to five years. Knowing what is the average development for a child helps parents and care workers to know what to expect at different stages. They can then identify any potential problems. Keeping a child safe, at home or in a nursery, is very important. It is the role of anyone working with children to keep them in a safe, secure environment.

In this unit you will be able to identify the key milestones of child development between 0–5 years and understand the early years values that apply to this setting. You will learn how to carry out a risk assessment on an early years setting and how to create a safe environment.

Learning outcomes

LO1: Understand the key milestones of physical, intellectual and language development between 0–5 years

LO2: Understand the key milestones of emotional and social development between 0–5 years

LO3: Be able to create a safe environment to protect children (in an early years setting)

How will I be assessed?

You will be assessed through a series of assignment tasks, which are set by OCR. The assignment will be marked by your tutor and then moderated by OCR.

For LO1, you need to:

- demonstrate an understanding of the physical, intellectual and language developmental milestones in children between 0–5 years
- explain, with comparisons, the key physical, intellectual and language development milestones of a child aged 0–5 years.

For LO2, you need to:

- demonstrate an understanding of the emotional and social development milestones in children between 0–5 years

Make sure you refer to the current OCR specification and guidance.

- explain, with comparisons, the key emotional and social development milestones of a child aged 0–5 years
- draw on skills/knowledge/understanding from other units in the specification.

Note: SPAG is assessed in this learning outcome.

For LO3, you need to:

- explain the types of risks and hazards in an early years setting from which young people need to be protected
- carry out a risk assessment
- produce a plan of how to promote and maintain a safe environment for children in an early years setting.

Links to other units

Unit R021: Essential values of care for use with individuals in care settings (LO2): This unit will help you to understand the early years values which apply to this age group.

Unit R022: Communicating and working with individuals in health, social care and early years settings (LO1): Communication skills learned will allow you to communicate in an early years setting.

Unit R025 (optional unit): Understanding life stages (LO3): You will have an understanding of physical, intellectual, language, emotional and social stages of development.

Unit R026 (optional unit): Planning for employment in health, social care and the children and young people's workforce (LO2): You will have covered how personal hygiene, safety and security measures protect individuals.

Unit R027 (optional unit): Creative activities to support individuals in health, social care and early years settings (LO1): You will have learned about the needs of individuals and the value of creative activities.

Understand the key milestones of physical, intellectual and language development between 0–5 years

Getting started

When a baby is born it is helpless. It is totally dependent on the care given to it by its mother/carer.

As a group, list all the physical, intellectual and language skills a new baby is likely to develop by the age of two years. When you have completed this learning outcome, have a look back at your list. Did you miss anything?

The key milestones of a child's physical, intellectual and language development from birth to five years

Children acquire a certain set of skills at roughly the same age, although not all children develop at the same rate. These skills are referred to as milestones. Health professionals recognise and use milestones as a way of assessing and monitoring a child's development. This helps them to evaluate the child's progress.

The normal development stages and sequences

Physical development

Physical development involves developing control over the body, particularly muscles and physical co-ordination.

Gross and fine motor skills

Gross motor (physical) skills require whole-body movement and involve the large muscles of the body to perform everyday functions, such as standing, walking, running and sitting upright. Gross motor skills include hand–eye co-ordination skills such as ball skills (e.g. throwing, catching, kicking).

Fine motor skills are finger and hand skills such as writing, cutting, opening lunchboxes and tying shoelaces. The development of these skills relies on the age-appropriate development of physical skills providing the stable base from which the arm moves with control. Fine motor skills also involve hand–eye co-ordination skills such as handwriting or drawing.

Table 8.1 summarises the development of gross and fine motor skills from birth to five years.

Table 8.1 Development of gross and fine motor skills

Age	Gross motor skills	Fine motor skills
0–6 months		• Holds small object in hand • Reaches for toy • Holds toy, e.g. rattle, for a short time • Follows object with eyes in all directions
6–12 months	• Crawls forwards on belly • Assumes a seated position unaided • Creeps (moves forward slowly near to the ground) on hands and knees • Transitions into different positions: sitting, all fours, lying on tummy • Pulls self to stand • Walks while holding on to furniture • Takes 2–3 steps without support • Rolls a ball, copying an adult	• Reaches, grasps, puts object in mouth • Controlled release of object • Picks things up with pincer grasp (thumb and one finger) • Transfers object from one hand to the other • Drops and picks up toy

→

Table 8.1 Development of gross and fine motor skills (*continued*)

1–2 years	• Sits, crawls, walks • Still has wide gait but walking/running is less clumsy • Pushes against a ball (does not actually kick it) • Walks smoothly and turns corners • Begins running • Able to pull or carry a toy while walking • Climbs on to/down from furniture without assistance • Walks up and down steps with support • Picks up toys from the floor without falling over	• Builds tower of three small blocks • Places five pegs in pegboard • Turns pages two or three at a time • Scribbles • Turns knobs • Paints with whole arm movement, shifts hands, makes strokes • Self-feeds with minimal assistance • Able to use signing to communicate • Brings spoon to mouth • Holds and drinks from cup independently
2–3 years	• Imitates standing on one foot • Imitates simple bilateral movements of limbs (e.g. arms up together) • Climbs jungle gym and ladders • Pedals on tricycle • Walks up/down stairs, alternating feet • Jumps in place with two feet together • Able to walk on tiptoes • Catches using body	• Strings four large beads • Turns single pages • Snips with scissors • Holds crayon with thumb and fingers (not fist) • Uses one hand consistently in most activities • Imitates circular, vertical, horizontal strokes • Paints with some wrist action; makes dots, lines, circular strokes • Rolls, pounds, squeezes and pulls play dough • Eats without assistance
3–4 years	• Stands on one foot for up to 5 seconds • Kicks a ball forwards • Throws a ball overarm • Catches a ball that has been bounced • Runs around obstacles • Able to walk on a line • Able to hop on one foot • Jumps over an object and lands with both feet together	• Builds tower of nine small blocks • Copies circles • Manipulates play dough material (rolls balls, makes snakes, cookies) • Uses non-dominant hand to assist and stabilise the use of objects • Snips paper using scissors
4–5 years	• Able to walk upstairs while holding an object • Walks backwards, toe–heel • Jumps forward 10 times without falling • Hangs from a bar for at least 5 seconds • Steps forward with leg on same side as throwing arm when throwing a ball • Catches a small ball using hands only	• Cuts on line continuously • Copies cross and square shapes • Writes name • Writes numbers 1–5 • Copies letters • Left-/right-handedness established • Dresses/undresses independently

Hand/eye development

Hand/eye development (otherwise known as hand–eye co-ordination) milestones occur alongside gross and fine motor skills development.

Between birth and three years of age, infants:

- start to develop vision that allows them to follow slowly moving objects with their eyes
- begin to develop basic hand/eye skills, such as reaching, grasping objects, feeding and dressing
- begin to recognise concepts of place and direction, such as up, down and in
- develop the ability to manipulate objects with fine motor skills.

Between three and five years of age, children continue to develop hand–eye co-ordination.

- They develop a preference for left- or right-handedness.
- They continue to understand and use concepts of place and direction, such as under, beside.
- They develop the ability to climb, balance, run, gallop, jump, push and pull, and take stairs one at a time.
- They develop eye/hand/body co-ordination and depth perception.

Balance

Balance is a fundamental skill necessary for maintaining controlled positions, such as sitting in a chair, or engaging in physical activities such as running or riding a bike. Having balance makes motor skill development easier, reduces the risk of injury and helps children focus on academic tasks.

Balance is about making connections between the part of the brain that controls balance and the limb movements needed to stay upright. This takes lots of practice and time under many different conditions.

There are two types of balance that children should master:

1 the ability to balance when standing still (stationary balance)

2 the ability to balance when moving around (dynamic balance).

Stationary balance can be developed by simple activities, such as standing on one foot, balancing on both knees, or balancing without moving on a narrow line or fallen log. Dynamic balance develops along with agility as the child learns to walk and run. Activities that develop agility will also develop dynamic balance. This moving type of balance is also developed with learning new skills such as riding a scooter, tricycle or bike, or learning to skate or ski.

Physical appearance

A child's physical appearance changes massively between 0–5 years. Physical growth refers to an increase in body size (length or height and weight) and in the size of organs. From birth to about age one or two years, children grow rapidly. After this time, growth slows.

Doctors measure length in children that are too young to stand. They measure height once the child can stand. In general, length in normal-term infants increases about 30 per cent by the age of five months and more than 50 per cent by 12 months. Infants typically grow about 10 inches (25 centimetres) during the first year, and the height at five years is about double the birth length.

By four to six months, an infant's weight should be double their birth weight. During the second half of the first year of life, growth is not as rapid. Weight gain is usually about 2.2 kilograms (five pounds) per year between ages two to five.

Mobility

Table 8.1 shows that babies become mobile at around six months when they crawl and creep. During this 6–12 month stage, a baby's mobility increases rapidly as they learn to crawl or effectively roll to where they want to get to. Some babies even take their first steps before they turn 12 months. They use this mobility to discover the world around them, picking up interesting things and exploring them with their mouth. Table 8.1 provides specific examples of babies' movement and motion from six months to five years.

Intellectual development

Intellectual development is about how individuals organise their minds, ideas and thoughts to make sense of the world they live in.

Learning

Intellectual development begins shortly after birth. Babies learn to use their brains to play, respond to carers, and familiarise themselves with objects and other people in order to try to learn about the world around them. The process continues as children go to school, form intellectual relationships with others and learn new skills. Intellectual development means being able to think creatively, to pay attention, solve problems and develop judgement skills along with a lifelong readiness to learn.

Books are very important for learning. A book provides a child with valuable vocabulary, starting from simple basic words to whole sentences. A child's imagination is stimulated and they can understand better the world they are living in. Social skills are developed through storybooks, and children learn about relationships and emotions. In this way, a child can recognise different situations as they grow up, and be better prepared to deal with or understand them. Different types of books offer children a breadth of knowledge and experience. This can help children be better prepared for school and enhance their curiosity for deeper subjects or abstract ideas.

Perception

Perception is making sense of what you see, hear, smell, touch and taste. As a result of children's experiences, they start to make sense of the world around them. Their perception is affected by their previous experiences and knowledge, and also by their emotional state at the time.

When children's experiences are repeated, they can then form concepts. Understanding concepts is a gradual process and an important part of a child's development. Concepts can include number, speed, volume and colour. Children playing in a sand pit in a nursery, for example, are learning about concepts such as mass and volume. Children frequently ask difficult questions, to which the answers involve some complicated concepts.

Thinking

The following bullet lists summarise the normal development stages and sequences of thinking between 0–5 years.

A newborn baby:

- uses their senses (sight, touch, taste, smell, hearing) to explore and experience their world
- uses their reflexes, such as sucking, to stimulate brain activity
- cries when they need to be fed or changed.

At one month, a baby:

- shows interest in sounds, turning their head towards the noise
- starts to recognise their mother/carer.

At three months, a baby:

- recognises their mother's/carer's face
- shows excitement by kicking their feet in the air
- listens and smiles when spoken to
- grasps a rattle
- takes an interest in their surroundings.

At six months, a baby:

- becomes aware of their own fingers
- responds to speech by making noises
- uses eyes a lot to follow movement
- holds toys
- explores using their hands.

 Group activity

Favourite books

In small groups, discuss your favourite book from your childhood. Explain why this book appealed to you. What did you get out of the book? Did your vocabulary improve?

Then discuss the following questions in small groups.

- Has a book helped you with your relationships or your emotions?
- Has a book encouraged you to do further investigation or research?

Once you have discussed these questions in your small groups, share your thoughts with the rest of the class.

At nine months, a baby:

- shouts for attention
- understands 'No'
- can play 'peekaboo'
- can look for fallen toys
- has a memory of events such as bath and bedtime routines.

At 12 months, a baby:

- knows their own name
- obeys simple instructions
- watches and copies adults
- repeats actions – such as dropping a rattle so someone will pick it up
- knows what some things are, for example, dog, teddy, spoon.

At 18 months, a child:

- enjoys and tries to join in with nursery rhymes
- picks up named toys
- enjoys looking at simple picture books
- builds a tower of three or four bricks
- develops a preference for using their right or left hand.

At two years, a child:

- understands many more words than they can say
- puts two or three words together to form simple sentences
- refers to themselves by name
- asks names of objects and people
- can build a tower of six or seven bricks
- has established their hand preference.

At two and a half years, a child:

- knows their full name
- continually asks questions
- likes stories
- recognises themselves in photographs
- can build a tower of seven or more bricks.

At three years, a child:

- can state their full name, gender and age

Research activity

Developing thinking skills for a two to three year old

In pairs, look back at the thinking skills lists for two to three year olds.

Design a game, activity, book or puzzle that would help a two- to three-year-old child to develop thinking skills appropriate to their age. Explain and justify your design to the rest of the group.

- carries on simple conversations
- constantly asks questions
- demands their favourite story over and over again
- can count up to ten
- can thread wooden beads on string
- can name colours.

At four years, a child:

- enjoys dramatic play
- enjoys more realistic play, e.g. school, shops
- classifies objects by purpose, e.g. 'to play with', 'to wear'
- understands the order of daily routines
- sorts objects by colour and size
- counts objects.

At five years, a child:

- understands how to sort objects by characteristics
- enjoys games that require matching items
- recognises and identifies 'bigger', 'biggest', 'smaller' and 'smallest'
- identifies and names different colours
- understands the order of numbers.

Language

Humans are the only species that have the ability to use language. Language is an organised system of symbols that humans use to communicate and connect with the world, and establish relationships with one another.

Communication and expression

Young children learn to talk very early. This is called verbal communication. Although talking with others is a very important aspect of language development, there is more to communication than using language. Babies communicate before they can speak by using non-verbal communication such as eye contact, body language, gestures and facial expressions. They also use noises such as babbling, crying, laughing, etc.

Speech development

A baby learns to talk by making sounds. These sounds are then put in order to shape recognisable words.

Speech and language develop through a child's interaction with the people around them. The process is a natural one and can be helped by the parent/carer reading to the child or playing games with them. Repeating nursery rhymes will give a child the opportunity to learn new words and practise by repetition. The child should always be encouraged to speak even if their speech is not very clear, as constant correction could put them off trying.

Table 8.2 summarises language development between 0–5 years.

Table 8.2 Milestones in expression and speech development between 0–5 years

Age	Comprehension	Expression	Sentences
0–6 months	• Is aware of sounds and voices • Recognises facial expressions and tones of voice	• Cooing – practising sounds needed to make speech	• No specific milestones
6–12 months	• Responds to familiar requests (e.g. 'Come here.') and own name • Understands gestures (e.g. wave for 'bye')	• Babbling (e.g. mama, dada) • Takes turns vocalising with others • Extensive echoing • Recognises names of a few objects	• No specific milestones
1–2 years	• Follows simple instructions, e.g. 'Give the ball to daddy' • Obeys simple commands with gesture, e.g. 'Give me the cup' • Can understand approximately 50 words • Identifies body parts	• First words, e.g. mine, no, mum, dad, ta • Able to point to common objects when named • By 24 months (two years), has approximately 50–100 words • Saying nouns, pronouns and verbs	• By two years is joining two words together
2–3 Years	• Follows two-part instructions (e.g. 'Go to your room and get your shoes') • Points to main body parts, clothing items, toys and food when asked • Obeys simple command without gesture • Responds to who, why, what and where? • Identifies objects by name and function	• Names actions (e.g. go, run) • By 30 months, vocabulary is 250–300 words • By 36 months (three years), uses 1,000 words • Intelligible vocabulary • Using adjectives, plurals and prepositions	• Minimum of two to three words in a sentence (e.g. 'Daddy go work') • Still talks to self in long monologues
3–4 years	• Follows three-part instructions (e.g. 'Point to the cat, the dog and the monkey' • Understands longer, more complex sentences • Identifies three colours and numbers	• By 48 months (four years) uses nearly 1,500 words • Can give name and address	• Minimum of three- to four-word sentences • Tells you what they are doing • Tells you the function or use of an object

→

Table 8.2 Milestones in expression and speech development between 0–5 years (*continued*)

4–5 years	• Follows the meaning of others' conversations • Can listen and accurately retell a story	• Continuing to expand vocabulary to approximately 2,000-plus words • Can generally understand colour and shape words (e.g. red, square) • Can sort objects into simple categories (e.g. animals, food) • Asks meaning of abstract words • Gives age and birthday • Speech fully intelligible	• A minimum of four- to five-word sentences

Case study: Matthew's speech development

Matthew started to babble when he was nine months old. He continued to babble but did not say any words apart from 'mama' or 'dada'. His parents were concerned about him as his first and then second birthdays went by without a word. He was healthy enough and thriving in other ways. Physically, he was slightly ahead of the milestones. His parents mentioned his lack of speech to their GP, who reassured them that there was nothing to worry about. Matthew would talk when he was ready to.

Suddenly, just before his third birthday he said, 'Matthew going to grandma's today.' That was the beginning of Matthew's communication. He missed out all the stages between babbling and talking in sentences.

Questions

1 In pairs, find out how common it is for children to miss the communication milestones.
2 What can parents do to help their child to talk?

Stretch activity

Sammie's physical milestones

Sammie is five. She did not go to nursery but is now at primary school. Her teachers have noticed that she does not join in the physical activities, such as rounders, as she is unable to catch a ball. When they do apparatus work she is unable to hang from the bars despite being encouraged by her friends. Sammie is also unable to hop. After swimming she is unable to dress herself. In the classroom, she cannot cut out shapes properly and cannot write her own name.

Provide a written explanation of the physical development milestones for Sammie compared to the normal development stages.

(Aim for a **thorough** and **clear** understanding. Look at the command word definitions to see what **thorough** and **clear** means in the assessment.)

Know it!

1 Explain what is meant by gross motor skills.
2 What is meant by fine motor skills?
3 Summarise which language milestones should be achieved by the time a child is three years old.
4 With examples, explain what is meant by perception.
5 Why are books important for a child's development?

Assessment guidance

Learning outcome 1: Understand the key milestones of physical, intellectual and language development between 0–5 years

Marking criteria for LO1 Part A

Mark band 1	Mark band 2	Mark band 3
Demonstrates a **basic** understanding of the physical, intellectual and language developmental milestones in children between 0–5 years.	Demonstrates a **sound** understanding of the physical, intellectual and language developmental milestones in children between 0–5 years.	Demonstrates a **thorough** and **clear** understanding of the physical, intellectual and language developmental milestones in children between 0–5 years.

 The OCR Model Assignment will ask you to:

● Demonstrate an understanding of the physical, intellectual and language developmental milestones between 0–5 years.

 What do the command words mean?

● **Thorough and clear understanding**: You will show an understanding of the physical, intellectual and language developmental milestones for children between 0–5 years that is focussed and extremely attentive to accuracy and detail.

You should check the glossary in the Introduction for the definitions of each of the command words from OCR.

Marking criteria for LO1 Part B

Mark band 1	Mark band 2	Mark band 3
Provides a **basic** explanation, including a **few** comparisons, of the key milestones of a child aged between 0–5 years. Demonstrates **some** understanding of the normal development stages, which will partly follow the correct sequence.	Provides a **clear** explanation, including **some** comparisons, of the key milestones of a child aged between 0–5 years. Demonstrates an understanding of the normal development stages in correct sequence.	Provides a **detailed** explanation, including **detailed** comparisons, of the key milestones of a child aged between 0–5 years. Demonstrates a **clear and thorough** understanding of the normal development stages in correct sequence.
A **limited** range of examples are given for **few** of the key milestones.	A range of relevant examples are given for **many** of the key milestones.	A range of relevant examples are given for **most** of the key milestones and the relevance of their use is justified.

→

The OCR Model Assignment will ask you to:

- Provide an explanation, including comparisons, of the key milestones of a named child aged 0–5 years.
- Show an understanding of the normal development stages in the correct order.
- Provide examples for the key milestones and you will justify the relevance of their use.

What do the command words mean?

- **Detailed explanation including detailed comparisons**: Provide an explanation, including comparisons of the key milestones of a child aged between 0–5 years. Your explanation and comparisons will be a point-by-point consideration of the key milestones between 0–5 years.
- **A clear and thorough understanding**: You will demonstrate a focussed understanding of the normal development stages in the correct sequence, that is extremely attentive to accuracy and detail.
- **Most of the key milestones**: You will include a range of relevant examples for the majority (at least 75%) of the key milestones and explain the reasons for the relevance of their use.

You should check the glossary in the Introduction for the definitions of each of the command words from OCR.

Learning outcome 2

Understand the key milestones of emotional and social development between 0–5 years

Getting started

Are you usually confident? Which situations leave you feeling insecure? What helps you to feel more confident?

Discuss these questions in small groups. Do others in your group have similar feelings?

The key milestones of a child's emotional and social development from birth to five years

In addition to rapid physical, intellectual and language development between 0–5, a child also has a range of emotional and social development milestones during this time. This section looks at these milestones in detail.

The normal development stages and sequences

Emotional development

Emotional development refers to a child's growing ability to control emotions and to form secure relationships.

The bullet lists below summarise the normal stages and sequences of emotional development between birth and five years.

At one month, a baby:

- cries when hungry, thirsty or in pain.

At three months, a baby:

- loves attention, being cuddled or played with
- cries if their mother/carer leaves them.

At six months, a baby:

- starts to show anger and frustration

- prefers to be with their mother/carer
- is anxious with strangers.

At nine months, a baby:

- recognises family, e.g. parents, brothers, sisters, grandparents
- is still anxious with strangers
- likes a routine.

At 12 months, a baby:

- returns kisses and cuddles
- is less worried about strangers
- shows affection
- loves to see familiar people.

At 18 months, a child:

- enjoys being the centre of attention
- starts to develop confidence
- is still reserved with strangers.

At two years, a child:

- will have temper tantrums
- can show negative behaviour, such as biting or nipping
- plays beside other children but not with them
- constantly demands their mother's/carer's attention.

At two and a half years, a child:

- does not want to share toys
- likes their own way
- is still dependent on their mother/carer
- is very active and restless.

At three years, a child:

- begins to understand sharing
- is less prone to temper tantrums
- is able to understand other people's feelings
- experiences a broad range of emotions, e.g. anger, joy, happiness, worry, etc.

At four years, a child:

- becomes more imaginative in play

- experiences positive self-esteem and feels good about themselves
- does what their parents asks them to do more often
- feels a valued member of their family
- is aware of themselves and their gender.

At five years, a child:

- stays with a difficult task for a longer period of time
- starts to develop friendships
- is more able to control emotions
- understands right from wrong.

Bonding with the mother/primary carer

Bonding is the intense attachment that develops between parents and their baby. Scientists are still learning a lot about bonding. They know that the strong ties between parents and their child provide the baby's first model for close relationships, and give them a sense of security and positive self-esteem. Parents' responsiveness to an infant's signals can affect the child's social and intellectual development.

Most infants are ready to bond immediately. Parents, on the other hand, may have a mixture of feelings about it. Some parents feel an intense attachment within the first minutes or days after their baby's birth. For others, it may take a bit longer.

Inborn temperament

Most parents believe that babies are born with very different behavioural styles. Some are relaxed and easy-going, while others appear more intense and dramatic. Some seem to move constantly, others are more docile. Some are cheerful most of the time, while others are more serious.

These differences in how a child responds to the world and to their own body are called **inborn temperament** (see page 218 for definition). The idea of temperament helps explain how children growing up in the same family often have such different personalities. It also explains why some parents have difficulty raising certain children compared to others.

Key terms

Inborn temperament Personality traits or characteristics that a child is born with; these are genetically determined.

Unconditional positive regard Letting children know that they are cared about, accepted and approved of no matter what.

Self-concept and self-esteem

Self-concept develops very early in life. From the very beginning, a baby learns from how people respond to them and how people see them. By about 18 months of age, a child has a clear notion that they have a separate and specific identity.

Children who have self-confidence have a belief in themselves that enables them to welcome challenges and work co-operatively with others. When children don't develop self-confidence, they tend to focus on failure instead of success, problems instead of challenges, and difficulties instead of possibilities. There is no single way to enhance self-esteem, but one way is to show children **unconditional positive regard**.

Shyness is a recognised milestone in emotional and social development, and is clearly recognised by parents and carers. Shyness can be a useful protective response to unfamiliar people and situations. Parents and carers can offer reassurance and comfort. Playing with other children and meeting adults in a safe, secure environment can help.

Group activity

Design stickers for nursery children

You are a nursery nurse at Busy Bunnies Nursery. The manager is concerned that some of the children seem to be lacking in self-confidence and has asked you to design some stickers that will praise and reward the children for good behaviour.

- In groups, design some stickers. Then share your designs with the rest of the class. Justify your group's designs – explain why the stickers will help to raise self-confidence.
- As a class, evaluate all of the stickers that have been produced. You could take the best ones to a nursery and ask for their opinion.

Fears

Children are imaginative and their fears can seem very real to them. They can be frightened of the dark, of monsters hiding under the bed or in the wardrobe, and of spiders, among other things.

Children can also have nightmares, and can wake up screaming and in an agitated state. It is important to reassure the child and gently help them to go back to sleep.

Feelings

As we have seen in this section, emotions are feelings such as love, happiness, sadness, anger and joy. Young children can have very strong emotions, and emotional development is about understanding, making sense of and exercising some control over these emotions. Emotional development is linked to all other areas of development, especially socialisation.

Case study: Desai's nightmares

Desai is four and has just started primary school. Recently he has been waking up during the night screaming and crying after a nightmare. He takes some time to settle back down. He is now so scared he does not want to go to bed at night. His parents are really worried about him.

Questions

1 Do Desai's parents have any cause for concern?

2 What advice would you give them?

Social development

Social development includes all the skills required to build relationships, such as making friends and getting along with others by sharing, observing rules and taking turns. These skills are built on self-confidence, co-operation and trust.

Development of social skills

It is widely accepted that the development of social and emotional skills in early childhood benefits all aspects of children's learning, development, mental health and well-being. This is because, throughout life, learning happens within and through relationships.

Social interaction

Table 8.3 outlines the social development milestones between 0–5 years, including how social interaction develops.

The role of play in development

During play, children increase their social skills and emotional maturity. Play helps them to feel good about themselves. A good deal of children's important early learning about how to express and manage their feelings takes place through play. As well as contributing to emotional development and building confidence in their own ability, children's play is important for developing

Table 8.3 Social development milestones between 0–5 years

Age	Social development
0–6 months	• Establishes eye contact for a few seconds • Responds with a smile when socially approached • Recognises parent visually • Discriminates strangers • Distinguishes between friendly and angry voices
6–12 months	• Plays peekaboo • Participates in clapping when prompted • Lifts arms to parent • Responds to facial expressions • Extends toys to others • Imitates an adult's actions
1–2 years	• Identifies self in mirror • Imitates adult behaviour • Unable to share; competes with other children for toys • Observes other children playing around them but will not play with them (solitary play) • Begins to play next to other children (parallel play) • Says 'Hi', 'Bye' and 'Please' without prompting
2–3 years	• Has a strong sense of ownership • May begin co-operative play • Has an awareness of a parent's approval or disapproval of their actions • Will express emotions • Will verbalise their desires/feelings (e.g. 'I want a drink') • Begins to obey and respect simple rules
3–4 years	• Takes turns with other children • Talks about their feelings • Feels shame when caught doing the wrong thing
4–5 years	• Begins taking turns and negotiating • Plays together with shared aims of play with others (co-operative play) • Usually prefers playing with other children than playing by themselves

Research activity

Observing play

Arrange a visit to a local nursery to observe different types of play. Before you go to the nursery, explain what you are hoping to achieve and get permission from the nursery manager.

- Observe the children playing. How many different types of play can you see?
- Write down the context for the type of play and explain the reasons for your categorisation. What age are the children? Do they fit in to the suggested age groups for the different types of play?

Stretch activity

Maz's emotional and social development

Maz is five and has recently started primary school. He is not settling in. He will not play with the other children in his class or share his toys. At playtime he watches the others playing but will not join in. He likes to play by himself and has made no friends. When asked why he doesn't join in with the other children, he flies into a tantrum.

Provide a written explanation of the emotional and social developmental milestones for Maz compared to the normal developmental milestones.

(Aim for a **thorough** and **clear** understanding. Look at the command word definitions to see what **thorough** and **clear** means in the assessment.)

and learning the skills that will be the foundation for their future relationships.

These skills develop over time and through different types of play, as shown in Table 8.3.

- **Solitary play** is when a child plays alone. This type of play is important because it teaches children how to entertain themselves. Any child can play independently, but this type of play is the most common in children around one to two years of age.
- **Parallel play** is when two children are having fun, playing side by side in their own little world. They could be playing two totally different games. Despite having little social contact with their playmate, children who parallel play actually learn quite a bit from each other, such as taking turns. Even though it appears that they are not paying attention to each other, they often copy each other's behaviour. As such, this type of play is viewed as an important bridge to the later stages of play.

- **Co-operative play** is where children start playing together, usually at around four to five years. Co-operative play brings together all of the social skills the child has been working on and puts them into action. Whether they are building a puzzle together, playing a board game or an outdoor group game, co-operative play sets the stage for future interactions as the child matures into an adult.

Moral development
Most **moral** (see page 221 for definition) development comes from children watching other people and adults. It is important that the main adults in a child's life are able to set a good moral example for them. Parents should be able to teach their children what is right and what is wrong, starting from the time they are born.

Children should be allowed to have social interactions with other children where they can exercise what is right and what is wrong. These social interactions will set the stage for the way they develop their morals as older children and adults.

Key term

Moral Concerned with the principles of right and wrong behaviour.

Group activity

What is the correct sequence?

● In groups, photocopy all of the social development bullet points from Table 8.3, then cut out each bullet point.

● Share the bullet points within the group (making sure they are not in the correct order).

● Arrange the bullet points in the correct chronological age group, explaining why each bullet point belongs where it has been placed.

Know it!

1 Using examples, explain what is meant by inborn temperament.

2 Define social development. You do not have to cover milestones.

3 Define emotional development. You do not have to cover milestones.

4 Describe how play helps children to develop and learn.

5 Explain what is meant by 'unconditional positive regard'.

Assessment guidance

Learning outcome 2: Understand the key milestones of emotional and social development between 0–5 years

Marking criteria for LO2 Part A

Mark band 1	Mark band 2	Mark band 3
Demonstrates a **basic** understanding of the emotional and social developmental milestones in children between 0–5 years.	Demonstrates a **sound** understanding of the emotional and social developmental milestones in children between 0–5 years.	Demonstrates a **thorough** and **clear** understanding of the emotional and social developmental milestones in children between 0–5 years.

 The OCR Model Assignment will ask you to:

● Demonstrate an understanding of emotional and social developmental milestones between 0–5 years.

 What do the command words mean?

● **Thorough and clear understanding**: You will demonstrate an understanding of the emotional and social developmental milestones in children between 0–5 years that is focussed and extremely attentive to accuracy and detail.

You should check the glossary in the Introduction for the definitions of each of the command words from OCR.

→

Marking criteria for LO2 Part B

Mark band 1	Mark band 2		Mark band 3
Provides a **basic** explanation of the key milestones of a child aged between 0–5 years. Demonstrates **some** understanding of the normal development stages, which will partly follow the correct sequence.	Provides a **clear** explanation, including some comparisons, of the key milestones of a child aged between 0–5 years. Demonstrates an understanding of the normal development stages in correct sequence.		Provides a **detailed** explanation, including some comparisons, of the key milestones of a child aged between 0–5 years. Demonstrates a **thorough** understanding of the normal development stages in correct sequence.
There will be **some** errors in spelling, punctuation and grammar.	There will be **minor** errors in spelling, punctuation and grammar.		There will be **few**, if any, errors in spelling, punctuation and grammar.
A **limited** range of examples are given for **few** of the key milestones.	A range of relevant examples are given for **many** of the key milestones.		A range of relevant examples are given for **most** of the key milestones and the **relevance** of their use is **justified**.
Draws upon **limited** skills/knowledge/understanding from other units in the specification.	Draws upon **some relevant** skills/knowledge/understanding from other units in the specification.		**Clearly** draws upon **relevant** skills/knowledge/understanding from other units in the specification.

 The OCR Model Assignment will ask you to:

- Provide an explanation, including comparisons, of the key emotional and social milestones of a named child aged 0–5 years.
- Show an understanding of the normal development stages in the correct order.
- Proofread your work carefully and check for spelling, punctuation and grammar errors.
- Provide examples for the key milestones and justify the relevance of their use.
- Draw on your skills/knowledge from other units in the specification.

 What do the command words mean?

- **Detailed explanation including some comparisons**: You will provide an explanation, including some comparisons of the key milestones of a child aged between 0–5 years. The explanation will be a point-by-point consideration.
- **A thorough understanding**: You will demonstrate an understanding of the normal development stages in the correct sequence that is extremely attentive to accuracy and detail.
- **Few**: There will only be a small number of errors in spelling, punctuation and grammar, if any.
- **Most, relevance, justified**: A range of the relevant examples are given for the majority of the key milestones. You will give the reasons for their relevance in a focussed way.
- **Clearly and relevant**: You will draw upon focussed skills/knowledge/understanding from other units in the specification in a focussed way.

You should check the glossary in the Introduction for the definitions of each of the command words from OCR.

Learning outcome 3

Be able to create a safe environment to protect children (in an early years setting)

Getting started

Did you know that every time a teacher takes a group of learners out of school they have to complete a risk assessment to assess any dangers that may occur?

Think of the last school trip you went on and list the possible risks.

How to carry out a risk assessment on an early years setting

Figure 8.1 shows the five main steps involved in carrying out a risk assessment on an early years setting – this could be a nursery, a childminder's, a play school or crèche.

1 **The first step in a risk assessment is to identify the hazards.** This involves walking around the early years setting and assessing what could cause serious harm or could impact people. This could include the equipment in a nursery (e.g. a damaged cot), the physical environment (e.g. a cracked pane of glass in a door) or security (e.g. the possibility of intruders, or violent and aggressive behaviour of visitors).

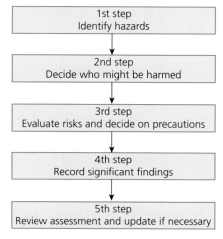

Figure 8.1 How to carry out a risk assessment

2 **The second step is to decide who might be harmed.** All employees must be taken into account when making a risk assessment. In the case of an early years setting the children, their carers and any visitors must also be considered.

3 **The third step is to evaluate risks and decide on precautions.** The first consideration should be if the hazard can be eliminated. For example, if there was a cracked pane of glass in a door, this could be removed and replaced without too much trouble. In the meantime, it could be covered with cardboard and taped over. Priority should be given to any risk that remains high or affects most people.

4 **The fourth step is to record significant findings.** If there are five or more employees, then significant findings (hazards and conditions) from the risk assessments must be recorded. Insignificant risks do not need to be recorded. Staff must be told about the findings.

5 **The final step is to review the assessment and update it if necessary.** Few workplaces stay the same. New equipment is brought in and new hazards could appear, so it is important to undertake regular reviews.

The types of risk from which young children need to be protected

Children are vulnerable and when they are young they have limited understanding of danger, so it is up to parents or carers to look after their safety at all times. However, they also need to explore their environment in order to gain self-confidence. Every precaution should be taken to remove hazards without taking away children's freedom to explore.

In an early years setting, the environment can pose different types of risk.

● All doors in a nursery should have adult-height door handles so children are unable to reach and open them. There should be finger/hinge guards on all the doors to prevent fingers from being trapped. The front and back doors should be double locked and have adult-height handles.

223

- Outdoor space should be secure – it is also good practice to supervise young children at all times. Adult supervision can help prevent injuries by making sure children use playground equipment correctly and do not engage in unsafe behaviour around it. If an injury does occur, an adult can assist the child and administer first aid straight away. Nursery staff should ensure the garden is secure, with no damaged fencing, so that the child cannot get out on to a busy road where they may be knocked over. There should also be a safety lock on the garden gate. If there is a pond in the nursery, young children will be safer if it is filled in, fenced off or securely covered. Even if it is a shallow pond, a small child can drown in a small amount of water.

- Fixtures and fittings – it is important that staff check and maintain playground equipment. This should be carried out at least once a week on a scheduled basis, but if staff are outside with the children it is easy to see if there are any obvious signs of wear and tear. The outdoor sand pit should always be covered when not in use to prevent contamination from animals, such as cats. The surface under and around play equipment should be soft and shock absorbent, and be covered with specifically approved surface materials. This will prevent many injuries if children fall off the equipment. Children should play on age- and weight-appropriate equipment so, for instance, a small child does not use a swing without the safety bars to hold them in. High-risk play areas (e.g. slides, swings and water play) should receive the most staff attention as these activities have the highest number of falls. Falls are the single greatest cause of injury in the childcare environment and the most common injury requiring medical care. Although many of the injuries resulting from falls are minor (cuts and scrapes), many others, such as heavy bleeding, broken bones, and head and eye injuries, may be more severe and could be potentially life threatening. Staff should check that a child is dressed appropriately to avoid strangulation (no drawstrings on jackets, etc.). This should happen before the child goes out to play.

The types of hazard from which young children need to be protected

As well as environmental risks, there are many hazards indoors. This section looks at some examples.

Broken toys

Toys bring fun and can be a learning aid, but they can also be a source of injury. Toys should be in good repair and free of sharp edges, splinters or broken parts. Staff should be vigilant in looking for broken toys, which should be repaired or discarded immediately so that scratches, cuts and scrapes are avoided.

Broken lock on cleaning material cupboard

If the lock is broken on the cleaning materials cupboard, it must be fixed straight away. If this is not possible, then all cleaning materials must be removed from the cupboard. Small children can easily mistake liquid dishwasher and washing machine detergent capsules for toys or sweets. If eaten, the tablets will poison the child. Other cleaning materials are also dangerous, for instance sprays could be sprayed into a child's eyes causing severe irritation, as well as eye damage or burns. Some chemicals, if inhaled, can cause asthma.

Upturned carpets and rugs

Floors should be clean and free of debris or tripping/falling hazards. Some children may have just learned how to walk; they may be unsteady on their feet and hurt themselves on an upturned rug. Carpet tape or rubber backing should be used to prevent rugs from curling or slipping. It should be firmly stuck to the floor to avoid accidents. An upturned stair carpet could cause a serious fall down the stairs.

Staff should carefully check for pins, staples, paperclips, toy parts or other small items that can hide in the carpet's pile, in corners and under furniture. They should also check floor tiles and floorboards for loose material, protruding nails (nails that are sticking out) or splinters.

Blocked fire exit

In a nursery or play school setting, the manager should check every morning that there is nothing blocking the fire exit. Fires can break out at any time, so it is vital that the fire exit is kept clear at

Case study: Food poisoning at Osbourne Otter's Nursery

There has been an outbreak of vomiting at Osbourne Otter's Nursery. The cause is suspected to be the cold roast beef salad that was served for the children's lunch. The roast beef had been cooked the day before and because it came out of the oven at home time, it had been left uncovered on a window sill to cool down. The next day, a warm summer's day, it was sliced, covered and left out in the kitchen as there was no room in the fridge. The children and staff became ill later that day.

Questions

1 What do you think caused the outbreak of food poisoning at the nursery?
2 What should have happened to the meat?

all times, including the area around the exit. This may be the only escape route in the event of a fire. The exit should be clearly marked.

Correct storage of food

Young children are susceptible to food poisoning so it is very important that food is stored correctly. Here are some recommendations:

- The fridge should be washed and cleaned regularly, and kept at 0–5°C for safe food storage.
- If the food has a use-by date then it should be eaten on or before that date.
- When chilled food arrives it should go into the fridge as soon as possible, particularly if the weather is warm.
- If a tin of food is opened but all of the contents are not used, then the remaining food should be removed from the tin and placed in a suitable container in the fridge.
- Raw and cooked food should be stored separately in the fridge. Bacteria from raw food can contaminate cold cooked food, and the bacteria can multiply to dangerous levels if the food is not cooked thoroughly again. Raw food should be stored in sealed or covered containers at the bottom of the fridge. Keep raw foods below cooked foods, to avoid liquid such as meat juices dripping down and contaminating the cooked food.
- Food-poisoning bacteria grow and multiply fastest in the temperature danger zone between 5°C and 60°C. It is important

to keep high-risk food – for example, yoghurt, meats, custard, seafood, salads and cooked rice – out of this temperature zone. Generally, tinned and dried food can be stored in a clean, dry cupboard or larder until it is needed.

The different ways of protecting children through safety features

This section looks at a range of different ways in which children can be protected through safety features and procedures.

Electric socket covers

Electric covers used to be considered safe. Now there is a campaign that claims they are unsafe and make it more likely for a child to have an electric shock.

Classroom discussion

Socket covers

Read this article: www.childalert.co.uk/article.php?articles_id=28

As a class, decide if you think there is a case for electric socket covers.

- Would you recommend the use of these in a nursery?
- What facts would you present to a nursery manager? Justify your argument.

Keypad on entrance doors

Most schools and nurseries have a keypad entry system on their main entrance. This is to prevent unauthorised access into the building. Access to the building is usually through a single point of entry, preferably near an administrative office. This helps to supervise the admission of all visitors.

Only authorised staff have the entry code for the door. Everyone else, including parents and visitors, has to press the buzzer or intercom and state their reason for visiting before staff decide if they can come in to the building. There is sometimes closed-circuit television (CCTV) for monitoring purposes. During normal hours of operation, additional required entry and exit doors should remain locked to the exterior (in other words locked from the inside), allowing people to exit only.

Signing in and out for visitors

Once in the building, visitors have to sign in. They are given a visitor's badge and are escorted by a member of the office staff to where they need to go. When they have completed their visit they return to the office (escorted) and sign out. The school then has a record of all visitors and the length of time they have spent in the building.

Fire extinguishers

Fire extinguishers are not meant for putting out a serious fire but rather for trying to put out minor fires before they become too serious. Fire extinguishers should be placed around the nursery. They should be serviced every year by a competent person, to ensure they would work were there a fire. There are different types of fire extinguisher for different fires, for example, water, foam and dry powder.

Smoke alarms

Smoke alarms are essential in a nursery as they give a warning of a fire. This would allow staff to clear the building, leading the children to safety before the fire takes hold. Smoke alarm batteries should be checked at least once every half term on a scheduled test.

In some nurseries, the fire alarm links automatically to the local fire station, so if it goes off the fire brigade come straight out to the nursery. Smoke alarms are impossible to ignore as they beep very loudly.

Window safety and locks

There are a few key safety precautions relating to windows.

- Curtains and blinds should be used without potentially hazardous cords.
- Windows should be fitted with locks to prevent a child from opening them from the bottom.
- Make sure that windows cannot open more than 12.5 centimetres (5 inches).
- Keep furniture and other items the child may be tempted to climb on away from windows.

Building security

CCTV cameras are sometimes placed around the outside of a nursery. This allows staff to identify any sources of concern, for instance someone climbing over the fence. A nursery can lock its gates so no one can access nursery grounds without ringing a buzzer. This provides added security.

Personal security

Staff must make sure that they do not give out any personal information relating to any of the children. If someone unknown rings up asking for information about a child (saying they are a social worker, for example) then the member of staff should ask their name and say they will ring back. They should then contact the local authority (or other appropriate organisation) asking to speak to this person, to check their identity. With young children, staff should also know who will be collecting the child from nursery.

 Classroom discussion

Safety

As a group, discuss why it is necessary for staff to always know who will be collecting a child from nursery.

Hand washing

Regular hand washing is the best way of preventing infection. If possible, use antibacterial soap from a dispenser and dry hands on a disposable paper towel.

It is important that children are taught to wash their hands correctly; Figure 8.2 shows the correct hand-washing technique. Seeing staff washing their hands regularly sets a good example to children.

Washing hands properly ensures that dirt and germs are removed from the skin. All areas of the hands must be washed as the backs of the hands, between the fingers and the fingertips are often missed. Hands should be wet before adding the soap to make sure the soap works effectively. Rinsing the hands washes off the soap, dirt and germs. Using the elbow to turn off the tap ensures that clean hands are not re-contaminated with any germs or dirt on the taps. A single use towel makes sure that the hands are dried on a clean, dry and germless towel.

Protective clothing

Disposable gloves are worn when there is:

- a risk of being contaminated by body fluids, e.g. a child could have vomited or wet themselves or had diarrhoea
- contact with an open wound or cut, e.g. a child could have fallen off a swing and cut themselves.

Disposable aprons are not needed to carry out many normal aspects of day-to-day care with nursery children, but they will be needed for helping in a procedure that might involve contamination by body fluids, for example, helping

Wet hands with water

Apply enough soap to cover all hand surfaces

Rub hands palm to palm

Rub back of each hand with palm of other hand with fingers interlaced

Rub palm to palm with fingers interlaced

Rub with back of fingers

Rub each thumb clasped in opposite hand using a rotational movement

Rub tips of fingers in opposite palm in a circular motion

Rub each wrist with opposite hand

Rinse hands with water

Use elbow to turn off tap

Dry thoroughly with a single-use towel

Hand washing should take 15–30 seconds

Source: NHS

Figure 8.2 Hand-washing technique with soap and water

Group activity

Hand washing poster

In small groups, design a hand washing poster. It should be suitable to put above the wash basins in a nursery to remind children how to wash their hands correctly. Remember, some of the children will be unable to read.

Research activity

Are your hands as clean as you thought?

1 Wash your hands the way you normally would.
2 Then use a hand inspection cabinet to see if your hands are really clean. (You may be surprised to find your hands are not as clean as you thought.)
3 Now wash your hands again, following the instructions in Figure 8.2.
4 Re-test your hands using the cabinet. Are you surprised at the results?

Stretch activity

Risk assessments

1 For an example of risk assessment documentation, go to www.hse.gov.uk. On the home page, click on 'Risk assessment' under the 'I am interested in ...' heading. Then click on 'Classroom checklist' under the 'Interactive tools' heading.

2 In small groups, go around your centre and identify any classroom hazards. Decide who could be harmed. Could the risk/hazard be dealt with easily to prevent accidents? If not, what precautions could be taken to lessen the risk?

3 Present the information to the centre's health and safety officer and ask for comments. Evaluate the risk assessment form you used from the HSE website – was it fit for purpose?

(Aim to carry out a **detailed** and **thorough** risk assessment **independently** completing the documentation with **detailed** information. Look at the command word definitions to see what **thorough**, **detailed** and **independently** mean in the assessment.)

---

the child with personal hygiene tasks after they have vomited, had diarrhoea or wet themselves.

The gloves and aprons should be thrown away after use, reducing the chance of cross-infection.

How to design a safe environment for an early years setting considering design features

Use of spaces

The use of internal and external space should allow children and adults to move safely and freely between activities. There must be adequate space for the children to play and interact both inside and outside. If there is too little room to move around or the space is cluttered then there are likely to be accidents.

Space and its uses must be planned carefully. The space should be divided into activity areas so the purposes of use are clear. Staff must make sure that they can see every part of the space they are supervising. This helps to prevent potential accidents.

Ergonomics

Ergonomics is the science of equipment design, aimed at maximising efficiency for users. In an early years context, this means making sure that children have age- and size-appropriate equipment to use, such as washbasins, toilets and chairs.

As mentioned above, the layout of an early years setting should be divided into different areas. Outside, the big equipment such as swings and slides should be used for that purpose only. There should not be anyone playing underneath or near them. The rest of the outdoor area should be split into a quiet space where children can read or sit with friends, an area for more active games such as ball games, and another area for less active games such as skipping. Creating different areas for different activities provides additional interest and helps avoid conflict or accidents.

Indoors, it is sensible to have wet and dry areas. This means that all the areas using water (for example, for painting, the sand pit and the nature table) are together. The dry area would accommodate the quiet area, dressing-up area, etc.

There should be a separate base room for children under two.

Equipment and resources

Equipment and toys offered to children should be developmentally appropriate. Materials that are suitable for an older child may be a risk to younger or less mature children. For example, small building blocks would not be suitable for very young children. There should be some domestic furniture to allow children to continue normal life experiences. All furniture and equipment must be well maintained and conform to safety standards in order to prevent accidents.

Research activity

Safety symbols

What do the following safety symbols on children's equipment mean?

- CE marking
- Kitemark
- Lion Mark
- Fire safety

Sleeping

It is important that provision is made within the nursery to allow small children to sleep or nap if they need to. This should be a quiet area which needs to be fully equipped with comfortable cots or similar.

Food and hygiene

Food should be nutritious and meet the child's dietary and religious needs. Children should be offered regular drinks. All food should be served and eaten in a separate area to the rest of the nursery. Children should be encouraged to wash their hands before eating any food.

Staff should practise good hygiene when preparing and serving food. When preparing food, they should wash their hands before touching cooked food and after handling raw food. It is important to ensure that all work surfaces and equipment are clean before and after use. Good hygiene practices will ensure there is a clean workplace and will reduce the risk of infections spreading.

All workers should be aware of the basic guidelines relating to the hygienic production of meals and snacks. Protective clothing should be worn in the kitchen. Staff should have hair tied back and all jewellery should be removed. Cuts and grazes should be covered with a clean blue plaster.

You may find it useful to look back at the sections on the correct storage of food and on hand washing.

Safety

Safety issues are covered in the risks and hazards sections earlier in LO3.

Know it!

1 Outline briefly the five steps involved in carrying out a risk assessment.
2 Explain the importance of correct hand washing.
3 What does ergonomics mean?
4 Describe the usefulness of disposable aprons and gloves in a nursery.
5 Explain why the nursery should be divided into different areas.

Assessment guidance

Learning outcome 3: Be able to create a safe environment to protect children (in an early years setting)

Marking criteria for LO3 Part A

Mark band 1	Mark band 2	Mark band 3
Provides a **basic** explanation of types of risks and hazards to be considered in an early years setting, and includes some ways of protecting early years children. **Few** are supported with relevant examples.	Provides a **clear** explanation of the types of risks and hazards to be considered in an early years setting, and includes different ways of protecting early years children. **Some** are supported with relevant examples.	Provides a **detailed** explanation of the types of risks and hazards in an early years setting, and effectively considers different ways early years children need to be protected. **Most** are supported with relevant examples.
Carries out a **basic** risk assessment on an early years setting with support. Completes documentation with **basic** information.	Carries out a **sound** risk assessment on an early years setting with **limited** support. Completes documentation with **sound** information.	**Independently** carries out a **detailed** and **thorough** risk assessment. Completes documentation with **detailed** information.

→

The OCR Model Assignment will ask you to:

- Provide an explanation of the types of risks and hazards in an early years setting. The explanation will consider the ways that early years children need to be protected, and you will include relevant examples.
- Carry out a risk assessment in an early years setting and complete documentation with information.

 What do the command words mean?

- **Detailed explanation and most**: You will explain the types of risk and hazards in an early years setting, point by point, and effectively consider the different ways early years children need to be protected. The majority of these will be supported with relevant examples.
- **Independently, detailed, thorough and detailed**: Without relying on others, you will carry out a point-by-point risk assessment that is extremely attentive to accuracy and detail. You will complete documentation with information point-by-point.

You should check the glossary in the Introduction for the definitions of each of the command words from OCR.

Marking criteria for LO3 Part B

Mark band 1	Mark band 2	Mark band 3
Produces a **basic** plan of how to promote and maintain a safe environment for children in an early years setting, including **limited** features, **few** of which will have examples and purposes of use explained.	Produces a **clear** plan of how to promote and maintain a safe environment for children in an early years setting, including **some** features, **some** of which will have examples and purposes of use explained.	Produces a **detailed** and **thorough** plan of how to promote and maintain a safe environment for children in an early years setting, including **many** of the features, **most** of which will have examples and purposes of use explained.

 The OCR Model Assignment will ask you to:

- Produce a plan of how to promote and maintain a safe early years environment, including the features.
- Explain the purposes of use and features, with examples.

 What do the command words mean?

- **Detailed and thorough**: Your plan will be a point-by-point consideration and will be extremely attentive to accuracy and detail with regards to how to promote and maintain a safe environment for children in an early years setting.
- **Many and most**: Your plan will include a large number of the features, the majority of which will have examples and purposes of use explained.

You should check the glossary in the Introduction for the definitions of each of the command words from OCR.

Read about it

Weblinks

www3.imperial.ac.uk/pls/portallive/docs/1/46973696.PDF Full Day Care (National Standards for Under 8s Day Care and Childminding) – information on national standards

www.nhs.uk/Tools/Pages/birthtofive.aspx NHS Choices – birth-to-five development timeline

www.ican.org.uk/~/media/Ican2/Book%20Shop/Downloads/GPChecklistA5.ashx I Can – information on speech, language and communication

www.ichild.co.uk/tags/browse/365/Personal-Social-Emotional-Development-1-3-Years iChild – information on emotional and social development (you need to register on the website to obtain some information)

www.education.gov.uk/publications/eOrderingDownload/eyfs_cards_0001207.pdf Child Development Overview – all areas of development from physical to safety to health and well-being, etc.

www.kidsdevelopment.co.uk/childrensintellectualdevelopment.html 'Intellectual development in children' – article about intellectual development in children (from 3–12 years)

Reference books

Minett, P. (2010) *Child Care and Development* (6th edn). Hodder Education.

Sharma, A. and Cockerill, H. (2014) *Mary Sheridan's From Birth to Five Years: Children's Developmental Progress* (4th edn). Routledge.

R029 Understanding the nutrients needed for good health

About this unit

Food is essential for life and necessary for health and well-being. By studying this unit you will learn how nutritional requirements vary throughout the different life stages and how government guidelines help to promote healthy eating.

You will learn about the various factors that can influence what we eat, ranging from cost, personal preferences and health conditions, to religious and cultural influences.

You will explore the dietary needs of individuals with a specific dietary condition and learn how to meet those nutritional needs by creating a suitable dietary plan. You will also have the opportunity to demonstrate how to produce a nutritious meal for an individual with a specific dietary requirement.

Learning outcomes

LO1: Know the dietary needs of individuals in each life stage

LO2: Be able to create dietary plans for specific dietary needs

LO3: Be able to produce nutritional meals for specific dietary requirements

How will I be assessed?

You will be assessed through a series of assignment tasks, which are set by OCR. The assignment will be marked by your tutor and then moderated by OCR.

For LO1, you need to:

- demonstrate knowledge of the dietary needs of the different life stages (young people 5–16 years, adults and older adults) with reference to the importance of nutrients and the nutritional function of each nutrient
- provide a description of government guidelines and dietary requirements.

Note: SPAG is assessed in this learning outcome.

For LO2, you need to:

- understand the factors that influence diet
- create a dietary plan that meets the needs of an individual
- include information on how the plan reflects the needs of the individual and their condition(s), and how food choices can address their condition(s) and symptoms
- understand the sources and functions of different types of nutrients, and give examples
- provide information on how to achieve a balanced diet
- draw on relevant skills/knowledge/understanding from other units in the specification.

For LO3, you need to:

- produce a nutritional meal for an individual with specific dietary needs
- select ingredients demonstrating consideration of dietary requirements and nutritional value
- carry out an analysis of the meal with reference to government dietary guidelines and assess how well it meets the needs of the individual
- follow hygiene and safe food preparation procedures.

Make sure you refer to the current OCR specification and guidance.

Links to other units

Unit R022: Communicating and working with individuals in health, social care and early years settings (LO3): You could explain how you used your written communication skills when creating a dietary plan for an individual with specific dietary needs.

Unit R024 (optional unit): Pathways for providing care in health, social care and early years settings (LO3) and **Unit R025 (optional unit): Understanding life stages** (LO4): You could explain how you used your knowledge of care planning and creating eating plans to inform your choice of a nutritional meal to support an individual's specific needs.

Unit R027 (optional unit): Creative activities to support individuals in health, social care and early years settings (LO3): You could describe how planning and carrying out a creative activity such as cooking has helped you to know about how to select appropriate ingredients and equipment, to be aware of and follow hygiene and safety procedures when preparing a meal.

Unit R028 (optional unit): Understanding the development and protection of young children in an early years setting (LO3): You could describe how your knowledge of health and safety and food hygiene procedures in an early years setting has informed your preparation and production of a nutritional meal.

Unit R030 (optional unit): Research – a project approach (LO3 and LO4): You could explain how your experience of planning, carrying out and reviewing a research project has influenced your planning, preparation and analysis of a nutritional meal, and your assessment of how well it meets government guidelines.

Learning outcome 1

Know the dietary needs of individuals in each life stage

Good food and nutrition are essential for everyone. Figure 9.1 outlines some reasons why.

Growth and repair	• Body tissues are constantly replaced throughout life and food is needed to make this take place. • When someone is ill their nutritional needs increase.
Energy	• Food provides energy for physical activity. • The amount needed depends on how active the person is.
Body processes	• Half the calories we eat are used up just to keep us alive and regulate metabolism: breathing, digestion, transmitting nerve impulses and maintaining body temperature.
Prevention of disease	• Some foods are known to help prevent or reduce the risk of disease. • Good nutrition is needed to stay healthy.

Figure 9.1 Why do we need food and drink?

Getting started

In small groups discuss the following questions.
● What do you know about the dietary needs of individuals at different life stages? Can you give some examples?
● Can you name any current dietary guidelines?
Share your findings and discuss with the rest of the class.

The dietary needs of the different life stages

A diet that is suitable for a child will not be suitable for an adult or an older adult because they have different nutritional needs. Growth and development, ageing, activity levels, and illness or a health condition will all affect an individual's dietary needs. So, for the purposes of this unit, dietary needs have been split into three main groups:

● young people (5–16 years)
● adults
● older adults.

Key term

Dietary needs An individual's food and nutrition requirements to maintain their good health and well-being.

Young people

Children require nutrition that will:

● sustain rapid growth
● promote good health for developmental changes
● support gains in bone and muscle.

Children between the ages of 5 and 16 are growing fast and are very active, so their nutritional needs are high. They need to have healthy, balanced meals with a variety of food groups providing **nutrients** (see page 235 for definition) that will give energy and support growth. Examples include bread, potatoes, dairy, meat, fish, fruit and vegetables.

Adolescents will experience a growth spurt during puberty; growth at this time is faster than at any other life stage. Protein is needed to support growth of muscle and bones, and for the repair and maintenance of body tissues. Energy requirements are also high because of increased activity and growth.

Fatty foods and those high in sugar should be avoided as they can lead to excessive weight gain and cause problems such as type 2 diabetes in later life.

Figure 9.2 summarises the specific dietary needs of children and teenagers.

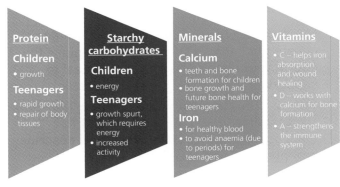

Figure 9.2 Specific dietary needs of young people

Research activity

The School Food Plan

Find out about the School Food Plan: www.schoolfoodplan.com/standards

This was introduced by the Department for Education in 2015 to set out the standards for food provided for children in all schools.

Key terms

Nutrients The individual components of the food we eat. Examples are vitamins, protein, fats and carbohydrates.

Metabolism Chemical processes and reactions that take place in the body.

Sedentary A lack of physical activity. A person with a sedentary lifestyle spends a lot of time sitting and does little, if any, exercise.

Antioxidants Protect the body from damage caused by harmful molecules called free radicals. Many experts believe this damage is a factor in the development of blood vessel disease (atherosclerosis), cancer and other conditions. Vitamins A, C and E are antioxidants.

Adulthood

An adult needs a healthy diet to:

● prevent disease

● regulate **metabolism**

● maintain normal growth and function, and promote healthy lifestyles.

Adults need a well-balanced diet to ensure they have the correct nutrients in the right amounts to stay healthy. Poor diet can lead to obesity and ill-health.

The amount of food an adult requires will be affected by their body size, height, their gender and the amount of physical activity they do. Adults who are **sedentary**, perhaps working in an office and sitting at a desk all day, will burn less energy than someone who does manual work and is active all day. Pregnant women and those who are breast-feeding require a nutritious diet that provides nourishment for themselves and the growing baby.

Figure 9.3 summarises the specific dietary needs of adults.

Older adults

An older adult needs a healthy diet to:

● maintain both mental and physical health

● preserve muscle tissue and strength.

Older people still need a balanced diet that provides all the nutrients in the correct amounts. They do not require as many calories, though, because an individual's metabolism slows down with age. Smaller portions of nutritionally dense foods are needed.

Figure 9.4 summarises the specific dietary needs of older adults.

The importance of nutrients

Nutrients are the component parts of the food we eat. They are chemicals that provide energy,

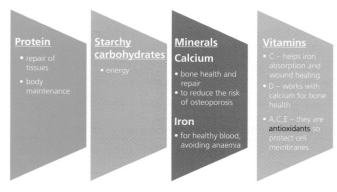

Figure 9.3 Specific dietary needs of adults

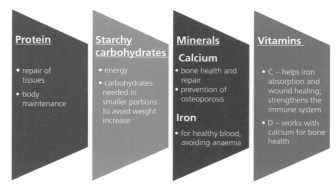

Figure 9.4 Specific dietary needs of older adults

support growth and repair, and support the normal functioning of the body. It is important to have the correct quantities of each nutrient so that individuals do not become undernourished, suffer deficiencies, or become over-nourished and obese. This is called a balanced diet and contains a variety of different foods. Figure 9.5 shows an example of the ingredients for a balanced diet.

Figure 9.5 A balanced diet is important for good health at all life stages

Vegetarians and vegans need to eat vegetable sources of protein instead of meat and fish to achieve a balanced diet. These include nuts, quinoa and soya products.

Macronutrients

Macronutrients are foods such as protein, fat and starchy carbohydrates, which are needed by the body in relatively large amounts.

Micronutrients

Vitamins and minerals are called micronutrients. This is because they are required in much smaller quantities than macro nutrients. They include, for example, vitamins A, B group, C, D, E and K, and the minerals calcium and iron.

The function of each nutrient

Table 9.1 summarises the functions of the main nutrients.

Table 9.1 The functions of nutrients

Function	Nutrient	What it does
Producing energy	Starchy carbohydrate	• Provides energy for the body • Provides vitamins, minerals and fibre
Growth and repair	Protein	• Helps to build, maintain and repair body tissues • Makes hormones, enzymes and antibodies • Provides energy, if not enough provided by carbohydrates
Prevention of disease	Calcium	• Helps to maintain and build strong bones and teeth
	Vitamin C	• Helps heal wounds • Helps to fight infection • Helps to maintain healthy teeth, bones and blood vessels
	Vitamin E	• Prevents heart disease
	Vitamin K	• Needed for blood clotting; helps wounds heal properly and prevents osteoporosis
Aid nerve function	B12 B6 Minerals	• Help brain, nerves and muscles to function • Help the body use the energy from the foods we eat
Aid the excretion process	Fibre	• Aids digestion • Helps avoid constipation; contributes to maintaining bowel health
To act as a carrier for other nutrients	Fat	• Carries fat-soluble vitamins A, D, E and K throughout the body in the bloodstream for use (absorption)
For cell formation	Vitamin E	• Helps form red blood cells, muscles and other tissues
To protect and maintain cell **homeostasis**	Vitamins Minerals	• Help regulate the many chemical processes in the body • Iron helps make haemoglobin in red blood cells and helps cells use oxygen

Key term

Homeostasis How the body adjusts to maintain a constant and steady state. For example, blood sugar levels are kept constant by the supply of insulin from the pancreas.

Dietary requirements and guidelines

The government provides a range of diet-related advice, guidance and recommendations for healthy eating to help individuals maintain their health and well-being throughout their lives.

Dietary Reference Values (DRVs)

The Dietary Reference Values (DRVs) are recommendations made by the UK government for males and females of different ages. They are estimates of the amount of energy and nutrients needed by different groups of people in the UK population. They are not goals or targets for individuals. They are based on the range of different requirements for each group. For example, nutrients to support growth are more relevant for young children than for older adults.

Reference Nutrient Intake (RNI)

Reference Nutrient Intake (RNI) is an estimate of the amount of energy, and macronutrients, vitamins and minerals needed per day for a healthy balanced diet, to meet the needs of the group to which it applies. It is not intended to be a target but an indication of how much the 'average' person needs.

Table 9.2 outlines the government's recommendations for dietary intake at each life stage.

Table 9.2 Government recommendations for dietary intake

Age (years)	4–6		7–10		11–14		15–18		19–64		65–74		75+	
Gender	M	F	M	F	M	F	M	F	M	F	M	F	M	F
Energy (Kcal/day)	1,482	1,378	1,817	1,703	2,500	2,000	2,500	2,000	2,500	2,000	2,342	1,912	2,294	1,840
Macronutrients														
Protein (g/day)	19.7	19.7	28.3	28.3	42.1	41.2	55.2	45.0	55.5	45.0	53.3	46.5	53.3	46.5
Fat (g/day) [less than]	58	54	71	66	97	78	97	78	97	78	91	74	89	72
Carbohydrate (g/day) [at least]	198	184	242	227	333	267	333	267	333	267	312	255	306	245
Free sugars (g/day) [less than]	20	18	24	23	33	27	33	27	33	27	31	26	31	25
Salt (g/day) [less than]	3.0	3.0	5.0	5.0	6.0	6.0	6.0	6.0	6.0	6.0	6.0	6.0	6.0	6.0
Dietary fibre (g/day)	15 (4y) 20 (5–6y)		20	20	25	25	30	30	30	30	30	30	30	30
Micronutrients														
Vitamin A (µg/day)	400	400	500	500	600	600	700	600	700	600	700	600	700	600
Vitamin B6 (mg/day)	0.9	0.9	1.0	1.0	1.2	1.0	1.5	1.2	1.4	1.2	1.4	1.2	1.4	1.2
Vitamin B12 (µg/day)	0.8	0.8	1.0	1.0	1.2	1.2	1.5	1.5	1.5	1.5	1.5	1.5	1.5	1.5
Vitamin C (mg/day)	30	30	30	30	35	35	40	40	40	40	40	40	40	40
Vitamin D (µg/day)	10	10	10	10	10	10	10	10	10	10	10	10	10	10
Iron	6.1	6.1	8.7	8.7	11.3	14.8	11.3	14.8	8.7	14.8 8.7(50+)	8.7	8.7	8.7	8.7
Calcium (mg/day)	450	450	550	550	1,000	800	1000	800	700	700	700	700	700	700

Source: Public Health England, 2016. Crown Copyright. www.gov.uk/government/uploads/system/uploads/attachment_data/file/547050/government__dietary_recommendations.pdf

Current government dietary guidelines

Fruits and vegetables

The current government recommends that everyone should eat at least five portions of fruits and vegetables a day. The '5 A DAY' campaign is based on advice from the World Health Organization, which recommends eating a minimum of 400 grams of fruits and vegetables a day to lower the risk of serious health problems such as heart disease, strokes and some cancers. Fruits and vegetables are low in fat and **calories** (as long as they are not fried or roasted in oil) and so can help individuals maintain a healthy weight. Fruits and vegetables are also an important source of fibre, vitamins and minerals.

Research activity

Why eat five fruits and vegetables a day?

1 Can you think of five reasons to eat five fruits and vegetables each day?

2 Make a list and then share your ideas with a partner.

3 Once you have a final list, compare it with the list of reasons on the NHS website: www.nhs.uk/Livewell/5ADAY/Pages/Why5ADAY.aspx

Key term

Calories A calorie is a measurement of the energy provided by food. Energy-dense foods contain a high number of calories per gram.

The Eatwell Guide

Public Health England, a government body, has introduced the Eatwell Guide to provide information to the population about how to achieve a healthy, balanced diet. It shows how much of what we eat overall should come from each of the main four food groups. The breakdown is:

● fruit and vegetables (approximately 40 per cent)

● starchy carbohydrates (approximately 38 per cent)

● dairy and alternatives (approximately 8 per cent)

● protein (approximately 12 per cent).

The final small segment (about 1 per cent) of the guide includes unsaturated oils and spreads. These are vegetable, rapeseed, olive and sunflower oils. All types of fat are high in energy (calories) and so should be eaten sparingly.

The recommendations shown for a healthy, balanced diet are for food consumption over a day, or a week, not for each individual meal.

Figure 9.6 shows an illustration of the Eatwell Guide.

Group activity

5 A DAY: what counts?

In groups, answer the following questions.

1 Which of the following count as one of your 5 A DAY?

● sweet potatoes

● potatoes

● frozen blueberries

● carton of fruit juice

● a yam

● dried apricots

2 How big is one portion of:

● raw carrot

● frozen peas

● broccoli

● apple

● satsumas

● pineapple chunks?

3 What does the 5 A DAY portion indicator look like on food packet labels?

You can check your group's answers by reading the NHS 'Just Eat More' 5 A DAY leaflet at: www.nhs.uk/Livewell/5ADAY/Documents/Downloads/5%20A520DAY%20z%20card.pdf

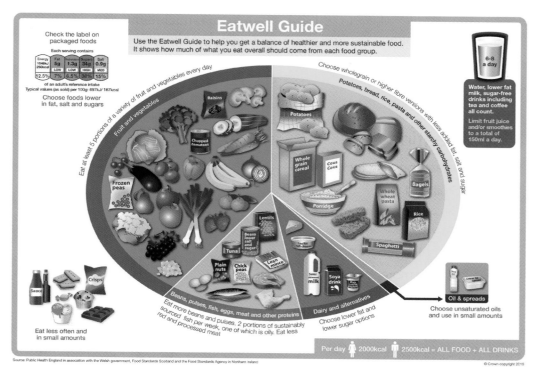

Figure 9.6 The Eatwell Guide

To use the Eatwell Guide, individuals should try to choose a variety of different foods from each of the groups to help get the wide range of nutrients the body needs to stay healthy. Foods that are unhealthy (contain a lot of fat, salt or sugar) have been placed around the outside of the main picture. They are not considered necessary for a healthy, balanced diet and most people need to cut down on them. Foods containing **free sugars** – such as cakes, biscuits and sweets – should be avoided.

The Eatwell Guide also recommends that six to eight cups or glasses of fluid should be consumed each day. These should be water, lower-fat milks, and low-sugar or sugar-free drinks. Guidance is also given on the total number of calories that adults should consume: 2,000 for women and 2,500 for men.

An example of a food label is shown in the top-right corner of the Eatwell Guide (see Figure 9.6). This is intended as a quick guide to the energy, fat, salt and sugar content of the item. It shows red, amber and green colour coding: red means high, amber medium and green low. It also provides nutritional information by stating the percentage of reference nutrient intake (see

Table 9.2), to indicate how much the maximum daily intake of a portion accounts for. This front of packet (FOP) labelling is used by most of the major food retailers and manufacturers.

Eight tips for eating well
The government has eight practical tips to cover the basics of healthy eating (see Figure 9.7). These tips aim to help individuals make informed, healthier choices. In the 'Live Well' section, the NHS Choices website provides detailed information about how to follow the advice provided by the eight healthy tips: www.nhs.uk/Livewell/Goodfood/Pages/eight-tips-healthy-eating.aspx.

As shown in Figure 9.7, as part of the Eatwell Guide, the government also recommend eating 'leaner, lower, less'.

> ## 🔑 Key term
>
> **Free sugars** Sugars that are added to food – for example, the sugar content of a fizzy drink or the sugar you would add to a cup of tea. The sugar is not part of the cell structure of the food.

Look through the Eatwell Guide, which explains the government's dietary guidelines in more detail: www.gov.uk/government/uploads/system/ uploads/attachment_data/file/528200/Eatwell_guide_booklet.pdf.

8 tips for eating well

1. Base your meals on starchy foods
2. Eat lots of fruit and veg
3. Eat more fish – including a portion of oily fish each week
4. Cut down on saturated fat and sugar
5. Eat less salt – no more than 6g a day for adults
6. Get active and be a healthy weight
7. Don't get thirsty
8. Don't skip breakfast

Remember fruit juice and/or smoothies should be limited to no more than 150ml per day in total.

Leaner	Choose leaner cuts of meat and poultry, remove any visible fat.
Lower	Go for lower fat, salt and sugar products - especially dairy and starchy carbohydrate foods.
Less	Use less oils and spreads. Choose foods high in fat, salt and sugar less often.

Source: Public Health England, 2016. Crown Copyright.

Figure 9.7 Government dietary guidelines

Stretch activity

The Eatwell Guide

The Eatwell Guide has been developed from previous government guidelines called the Eatwell Plate.

Research the development of the Eatwell Guide so that you can describe it in as much detail as possible.

(Aim to produce a **thorough** description. Look at the command word definitions to see what **thorough** means in the assessment.)

You may find it useful to reference this link from the British Nutrition Foundation's website: www.nutrition.org.uk/healthyliving/eatwellguide/eatwell.html

Case study: Jamie

Jamie, aged 16, is an active teenager. He loves sport and plays for the school football team. He also enjoys running and belongs to a local running club.

Jamie is always hungry, and often snacks between meals on sweets and crisps. He sometimes buys a burger on his way home from school. He doesn't worry about eating all this extra food as well as the meals his mum provides. Jamie thinks he gets so much exercise he will not put on excess weight, so he doesn't need to watch what he eats.

Questions

1 What are the dietary needs of an average teenager?

2 Is Jamie correct – does it matter what he eats as long as he exercises? Give reasons for your answer.

3 Using the Eatwell Guide or other government dietary guidelines, recommend healthy options that Jamie could eat in between meals.

Know it!

1 Give three examples of nutrients needed by children and young people. Why are they needed?

2 Name and give the function of three vitamins and two minerals needed by adults.

3 What do the initials DRV and RNI stand for? What do they mean?

4 What is '5 A DAY'?

5 Name the two largest sections of the Eatwell Guide and give some examples of foods from each of the sections.

Assessment guidance

Learning outcome 1: Know the dietary needs of individuals in each life stage

Marking criteria for LO1 Part A

Mark band 1	Mark band 2	Mark band 3
Demonstrates **basic** knowledge of the nutritional requirements of the different life stages (young people, adults and older people) with **limited** reference to the function of each nutrient.	Demonstrates **sound** knowledge of the nutritional requirements of the different life stages (young people, adults and older people) with **detailed** reference to the function of each nutrient.	Demonstrates **thorough** knowledge of the nutritional requirements of the different life stages (young people, adults and older people) with **comprehensive** reference to the function of each nutrient.

 The OCR Model Assignment will ask you to:

- Provide information about the nutritional requirements of young people, adults and older adults.
- Provide information about the function of each nutrient.

 What do the command words mean?

- **Thorough knowledge**: You will demonstrate knowledge of the nutritional requirements of the different life stages (young people, adults and older people) that is extremely attentive to accuracy and detail.

- **Comprehensive reference**: Your work will reference functions of each nutrient which will include everything that is necessary to evidence your understanding in terms of both breadth and depth.

You should check the glossary in the Introduction for the definitions of each of the command words from OCR.

Marking criteria for LO1 Part B

Mark band 1	Mark band 2	Mark band 3
Provides a **limited** description of government guidelines and dietary requirements.	Provides a **detailed** description of government guidelines and dietary requirements.	Provides a **thorough** description of government guidelines and dietary requirements.
There will be **some** errors in spelling, punctuation and grammar.	There will be **minor** errors in spelling, punctuation and grammar.	There will be **few**, if any, errors in spelling, punctuation and grammar.

→

The OCR Model Assignment will ask you to:

- Provide a description of current government guidelines and dietary requirements.
- Ensure that your spelling, punctuation and grammar are error free.

What do the command words mean?

- **Thorough description**: Your description of government guidelines and dietary requirements will be extremely attentive to accuracy and detail.
- **Few**: There will only be a small number of errors in spelling, punctuation and grammar, if any.

You should check the glossary in the Introduction for the definitions of each of the command words from OCR.

Learning outcome 2

Be able to create dietary plans for specific dietary needs

Now that you have learned about dietary needs at different life stages and explored government guidelines, let's find out about the different factors that can influence individuals' food choices. You will also learn how to create dietary plans for specific conditions.

The factors that influence diet

Many factors influence people's diets, not just the nutritional needs of the body. Some of these factors are illustrated in Figure 9.8 and are discussed in more detail below.

Income

The amount of money available in a household can have a direct influence on the type of food purchased. If a family is short of money, special offers such as the burger meal shown in

Getting started

In small groups discuss what influences your food choices. Why do you eat what you eat?

Make a list. Share and discuss your list of influences with the rest of the group.

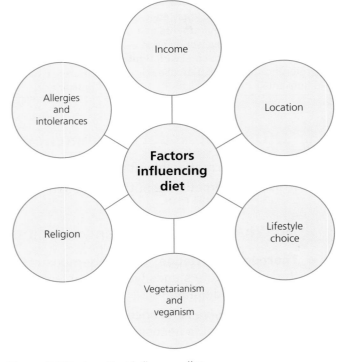

Figure 9.8 Factors that influence diet

Figure 9.9 can seem to be an affordable way to feed everyone. Foods high in healthy nutrients, such as fresh fruits, fresh vegetables, fish and lean meat can be more expensive.

Knowledge of healthy eating, understanding of dietary issues and being able to afford some foods and not others have all been linked to social class. Research studies (such as the National

A burger and chips meal
from a fast food restaurant £1.99

Fresh blueberries
£8.75 per kg

Free-range chicken
breast fillets
£15.45 per kg

Organic broccoli
£4.47 per kg

Figure 9.9 The cost of food

Food Surveys) have found that poorer people are more likely to eat processed food that has a higher fat and sugar content, whereas more affluent social classes eat healthier food. The graph in Figure 9.10 shows that, in 2014, lower-income households purchased four per cent less fruits and vegetables, and three per cent more food and drink high in fat or sugar, compared to higher-income households.

Location

The availability of food can vary depending on where you live. In some developing countries people suffer from malnutrition due to lack of food because of drought, flooding and failed harvests. In most developed countries there is no shortage of food and people have access to a wide variety of different food shops. This gives individuals the opportunity to have a balanced, healthy diet, but can also lead to overeating and obesity.

Eatwell plate comparison for low income and all households

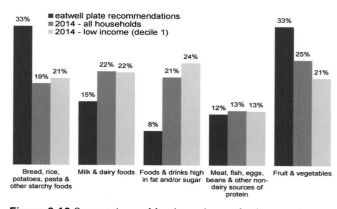

Legend:
- eatwell plate recommendations
- 2014 - all households
- 2014 - low income (decile 1)

Bread, rice, potatoes, pasta & other starchy foods: 33%, 19%, 21%

Milk & dairy foods: 15%, 22%, 22%

Foods & drinks high in fat and/or sugar: 8%, 21%, 24%

Meat, fish, eggs, beans & other non-dairy sources of protein: 12%, 13%, 13%

Fruit & vegetables: 33%, 25%, 21%

Figure 9.10 Comparison of food purchases for low- and average-income households. You should also look at the Eatwell Guide on page 239.

However, an individual's location, even in a developed country such as the UK, can still affect the availability of food. Sometimes, in poorer, deprived areas, people have to shop at small

Table 9.3 Ethical food choices

Food label	What it means
Fairtrade	Provides farmers with fair prices and better conditions for farm workers.
Farm Assured	Farms and food companies meet high standards of food safety and hygiene, animal welfare and environmental protection.
Free range	A method of farming where animals are provided with enough space to roam freely.
Sustainable	Food production methods are used that aim to preserve the world's natural resources for future generations, for example sustainably caught fish.

convenience stores where there is limited choice of fresh foods. This can result in having to rely mainly on ready meals and packets of food, or on take-away meals. It can be difficult to get to better shops if these are some distance away, as individuals might not have the time to travel to them if they are at work, or they may not drive, so public transport has to be used at an added cost. Most areas these days, though, do have a number of different food shops, market stalls and supermarkets where a wide range of different foods can be bought.

Another aspect that affects people's food choices is how far food has to be transported. Some people choose to buy only locally produced, **seasonal** food that does not have to be transported as far. This lowers the **food miles** and reduces the impact on the environment.

Lifestyle choice

The attitudes and values individuals have can affect the food choices they make. Personal preferences can be developed over time from experiences of meal times as a child. People tend to eat what they are used to eating.

Being brought up in a family with specific cultural or religious beliefs can have a huge influence on the types of food that are consumed. Experience of eating out at restaurants and travelling abroad can expose individuals to different foods, which they then try at home.

Some individuals take an **ethical** (see page 245 for definition) approach to the food that they purchase and consume. They will only have foods that meet certain conditions and will look for

specific labelling on their foods. Table 9.3 shows some examples.

Enjoyment or dislike of cooking can also influence the type of food that individuals consume. Someone who is really interested in food and enjoys cooking may buy fresh ingredients and cook everything themselves. Other individuals may lack interest, do not have the food preparation skills, or work long hours and haven't got the time or energy to cook, and so will prefer to buy ready meals or take-aways.

Media and celebrity endorsements can influence individuals' food choices and cause certain foods to become a trend. For example, Gwyneth Paltrow's 'Goop' website includes recipes to detox and cleanse, and has information on how to use superfoods. Jamie Oliver has a website that provides advice and recipes for feeding a family, and information about healthy eating. Other examples include Gary Lineker advertising crisps, Beyoncé and Katy Perry endorsing Pepsi products, and Justin Timberlake, McDonald's. The availability of new food preparation tools can start trends, for example juicing or spiralising vegetables.

Vegetarians and vegans

Vegetarians do not eat meat and fish, but will eat dairy and eggs. Vegans eat no animal products at all. Being vegetarian or vegan is a personal choice. An individual may decide not to eat meat because they do not believe in killing animals for food, or because it is a requirement of their religious faith.

Religion

Many religions and cultures have strict dietary traditions and restrictions. They have a huge influence on what individuals eat, and also on the methods that are used to slaughter animals and how meals are prepared. Some religions have beliefs and traditions that have been followed for centuries and are a well-established way of life. Some of these dietary restrictions and beliefs are shown in Table 9.4.

 Key terms

Ethical Something that is seen as morally right.
Halal In Islam, an animal can be eaten only if it has been slaughtered in a particular way.
Haram In Islam, this means forbidden.
Kosher In Judaism, this is used to describe something that is 'correct', i.e. an animal can be eaten only if butchered in a particular way.
Ovo-lacto vegetarian Will not consume any animal flesh, but will consume dairy and egg products.

Table 9.4 Religion and diet

Religion	Influence on diet
Buddhism	No meat or fish. Most Buddhists eat a vegetarian diet; some are vegan. Natural foods from the earth are considered most pure. Buddhists fast on the anniversary of the birth, enlightenment and death of Buddha.
Catholicism (Christianity)	Fish on Fridays, no meat. Feasting at Christmas and Easter, fasting during Lent.
Hinduism	Vegetarian diet, though some eat restricted amounts of lamb, chicken and fish. No beef – cows are considered to be sacred. Feasting on major Hindu holidays.
Islam	Food must be **halal**. No pork or birds of prey can be eaten; no alcohol; they are **haram**. Fasting during Ramadan, no food or drink (including water) from dawn until sunset.
Judaism	Food must be **kosher**. No pork or shellfish. Meat and dairy foods must be prepared and cooked separately and cannot be eaten together at the same meal. Fasting is practised during Yom Kippur and other festivals.
Rastafari movement	Most Rastafarians are vegetarian or vegan. They eat approved foods called Ital; these are natural and pure without artificial colourings, flavourings or preservatives. They avoid alcohol and caffeinated drinks.
Seventh-day Adventist Church	No beef, pork or lamb. Many Adventists are **ovo-lacto vegetarians**. Some Adventists avoid food and drink that contains caffeine, so no tea or coffee. They also avoid alcohol.
Sikhism	Sikhs do not eat halal or kosher meat because, according to the Sikh Rehat Maryada (code of conduct), they are not meant to take part in such rituals.

Key terms

Allergic reaction An unpleasant physical reaction to a particular substance.

EpiPen A device that auto-injects adrenaline if someone has anaphylactic shock due to an allergic reaction (to peanuts, for example).

Anaphylactic shock A sudden, life-threatening reaction to a substance. Common causes are peanuts and shellfish.

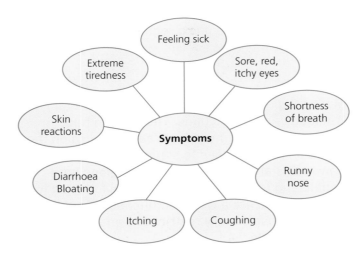

Figure 9.11 Allergic reactions to food

Allergies and intolerances

A food allergy is a reaction produced by the body's immune system when it encounters a normally harmless food. This reaction tends to happen very quickly and will happen even with a tiny amount of that food. Examples are peanut and shellfish allergies.

An intolerance doesn't usually involve the immune system and takes place when a food causes an unpleasant reaction (such as diarrhoea). Unlike an allergic reaction, effects are rarely immediate and can develop over a period of time. Examples are lactose, wheat and gluten intolerance.

Allergic reactions

An allergy is when someone has a sensitivity to something that causes a reaction. These reactions can be very serious. Individuals with a peanut or shellfish allergy, for example, have to carry an **EpiPen** to be used if they accidentally eat peanuts or shellfish – this can save their life as the reaction is extreme and can cause **anaphylactic shock**. Individuals with these types of allergies have to avoid the foods that trigger the reactions.

Figure 9.11 shows a range of symptoms that individuals can experience when they have allergic reactions to foods.

Food intolerances

Some individuals have a sensitivity to certain foods. This can cause a severe reaction, with a range of symptoms such as nausea, tiredness and stomach pains. Examples of food intolerance conditions are described in the next section. Further information about

all of the conditions can be found on the NHS Choices website (Health A–Z of conditions and treatments).

Creating dietary plans considering dietary needs for specific conditions

As mentioned above, not everyone can choose to eat exactly what they want, due to allergies or intolerances. Some individuals have special dietary requirements due to conditions such as coeliac disease, irritable bowel syndrome, diabetes and wheat intolerance. Some people develop conditions such as high cholesterol; this affects their dietary choices as they need to reduce their cholesterol levels. Others are obese and need to change their diet in order to achieve a healthy weight. Some people are vegetarians or vegans – a lifestyle choice rather than a specific condition (see above).

The specific requirements of individuals have to be considered when creating a dietary plan so that it meets their needs. Having to avoid certain foods because of a dietary condition or choice can result in a lack of some nutrients. It is important to ensure that any deficiencies are taken into account by substituting them with alternative foods, so that the individual has a healthy, balanced diet.

When creating a dietary plan for an individual, you should take into account the total dietary intake for each day and over a whole week. This should include all meals, drinks and also snacks. It is a good idea to include portion sizes for each part of the meal, for example how many slices of toast. The importance of the nutrients in each meal or snack should be considered in detail and matched to the individual's specific dietary needs.

Coeliac disease

Coeliac disease is an autoimmune condition where the immune system mistakes substances found inside gluten as a threat to the body and attacks them. Gluten in the diet triggers various symptoms such as diarrhoea, tiredness, bloating of the stomach, wind and constipation. People with this condition have to avoid gluten in their diet. This can have quite a significant effect on what they can eat, as gluten is found in many foods. For example:

- bread
- pasta
- cereals
- biscuits and crackers
- cakes and pastries
- pies
- gravies and sauces.

These foods are generally good sources of starchy carbohydrate, and dietary guidelines state that 38 per cent of food energy should be provided by starchy carbohydrate. If all of the above foods are excluded from an individual's diet this could cause a nutrient deficiency. Alternate sources of carbohydrate need to be included in the dietary plan to avoid this.

Fibre is another nutrient that could be in short supply if an individual's diet is restricted. Wholemeal bread, high-fibre breakfast cereals and wholemeal pasta are all excluded from a coeliac diet. So fibre intake will be affected and needs to be taken account of in a dietary plan if the recommended 25–30 grams per day is to be achieved.

Having a restricted diet excluding cakes, bread, pasta and pastries could be very difficult for an individual to cope with. Imagine never being able to eat cake! It is therefore important to provide occasional treats, and also variety, in a coeliac diet to make it seem less restrictive and boring. From a psychological point of view, simply cutting out all the foods listed above would be very tedious.

Figure 9.12 Gluten-free food labelling

Gluten-free versions of the restricted foods are available and can be included in a dietary plan. Figure 9.12 shows the Crossed Grain symbol which is a licensed scheme used to confirm that a labelled food product is gluten-free.

Many basic foods, such as meat, fish, fruits, vegetables, cheese, eggs, milk, potatoes and rice, are naturally free from gluten so can still be part of the diet. This means that all of the other food groups in the Eatwell Guide are covered, ensuring that micro nutrients (such as vitamins and minerals) and macro nutrients (such as protein and fats) can be included in sufficient quantities.

Coeliac UK, the charity that provides information and services for individuals with coeliac disease, has devised an app to help check foods for gluten when shopping. It is called the Gluten Free Food Checker and it enables individuals to search thousands of food products suitable for a gluten-free diet: www.coeliac.org.uk/gluten-free-diet-and-lifestyle/gluten-free-food-checker-app.

The app includes:

- a barcode scanner
- lists of ingredients and nutritional information for products
- ready-made product lists
- a labelling video to help make choices in the main supermarkets.

They also produce a Food and Drink Directory listing thousands of products suitable for a gluten-free diet.

Irritable bowel syndrome (IBS)

Irritable bowel syndrome (IBS) is a condition with a range of symptoms such as frequent abdominal cramps, bloating, diarrhoea and constipation. With IBS, food moves through the digestive system either too quickly or too slowly. The symptoms are usually worse after eating and tend to come and go. In many people the symptoms seem to be triggered by something they have had to eat or drink, and changes in diet and lifestyle can be important in managing and controlling the condition.

The foods that are most commonly reported to cause IBS symptoms in the UK are:

- wheat (in bread and cereals)
- rye
- barley
- dairy products
- coffee (and other caffeine-rich drinks such as tea and cola)
- onions.

There is evidence that taking probiotics may help to ease symptoms in some people with IBS. Probiotics contain 'good bacteria', i.e. bacteria that normally live in the gut and seem to be beneficial. Eating probiotics may increase the good bacteria in the gut, which may help to ward off bad bacteria that cause IBS symptoms. Various foods are available that contain probiotic bacteria, such as certain milk drinks, yoghurts, cheeses, frozen yoghurts and ice creams. They may be labelled as 'probiotic', 'containing bacterial cultures' or 'containing live bacteria'.

Here is some advice for individuals living with irritable bowel syndrome.

- Have regular meals and take time to eat at a leisurely pace.
- Avoid missing meals or leaving long gaps between eating.
- Drink at least eight cups of fluid per day, especially water or other non-caffeinated drinks. This helps to keep the stools (faeces) soft and easy to pass along the gut.
- Restrict tea and coffee to three cups per day (as caffeine may be a factor for some people).
- Restrict the amount of fizzy drinks that you have to a minimum.
- Don't drink too much alcohol. (Some people report an improvement in symptoms when they cut down from drinking a lot of alcohol.)
- Consider limiting intake of high-fibre food (although an increase may help in some cases).

- Limit fresh fruit to three portions (of 80 g each) per day.
- If you have diarrhoea, avoid sorbitol, an artificial sweetener found in sugar-free sweets (including chewing gum) and drinks, and in some diabetic and slimming products.
- If you have a lot of wind and bloating, consider increasing your intake of oats (for example, oat-based breakfast cereal or porridge) and linseeds (up to one tablespoon per day). You can buy linseeds from health food shops.

Source: http://patient.info/health/irritable-bowel-syndrome-leaflet

Diabetes

Diabetes is a lifelong condition that causes a person's blood sugar level to become too high.

The hormone insulin – produced by the pancreas – is responsible for controlling the amount of glucose in the blood. It allows glucose to enter the body's cells, where it is used as fuel for energy so we can work, play and generally live our lives. It is vital for life.

Glucose comes from digesting carbohydrate and is produced by the liver. If you have diabetes, your body cannot make proper use of this glucose so it builds up in the blood and can't be used as fuel.

There are two main types of diabetes:

- type 1 – where the pancreas doesn't produce any insulin
- type 2 – where the pancreas doesn't produce enough insulin or the body's cells don't react to insulin.

Type 2 diabetes can be caused by lifestyle. It usually appears in people over the age of 40. It is, however, becoming more common in children and young people. Type 2 diabetes accounts for between 85 and 95 per cent of all people with diabetes, and is treated with a healthy diet and increased physical activity. Medication and/or insulin are often required.

The Diabetes UK website at www.diabetes.org.uk provides extensive advice and guidance about healthy eating for individuals with diabetes.

Group activity

Tips to help prevent type 2 diabetes

1 In small groups, make a list of up to ten dietary recommendations to help prevent type 2 diabetes.

2 Share your findings with the rest of the class.

3 Then compare your lists with the British Nutrition Foundation recommendations: www.nutrition.org.uk/nutritionscience/health-conditions/diabetes.html?limit=1&start=4

Lactose intolerance

Lactose intolerance causes people to suffer from flatulence (wind), bloating, diarrhoea and stomach cramps. This is caused by undigested lactose. Lactose is a sugar found in milk and milk products. Some people cannot digest lactose properly and so it affects their digestion.

As well as milk and dairy products, other foods and drinks sometimes contain lactose. These include:

- salad cream, salad dressing and mayonnaise
- biscuits
- chocolate
- boiled sweets
- cakes
- some types of bread and other baked goods
- some breakfast cereals
- packet mixes to make pancakes and biscuits
- packets of instant potatoes and instant soup
- some processed meats, such as sliced ham.

If the symptoms are severe, individuals have to follow a diet without milk or milk-based products. If the condition is mild they can tolerate some milk taken with or in meals. Other changes to the diet must be made to make up for the lack of nutrients such as calcium and riboflavin in the diet due to lack of milk products.

There are a number of alternative foods and drinks available to replace the milk and dairy products that may have to be avoided.

Classroom discussion

Lactose intolerance

1 Read the following menu, which has been created for someone who is lactose intolerant.

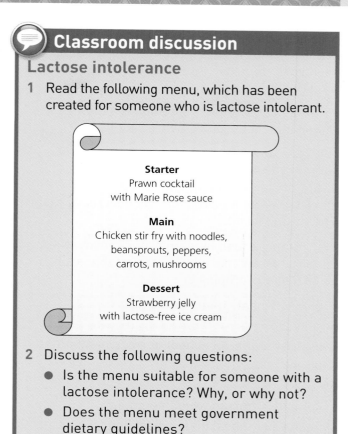

Starter
Prawn cocktail
with Marie Rose sauce

Main
Chicken stir fry with noodles, beansprouts, peppers, carrots, mushrooms

Dessert
Strawberry jelly
with lactose-free ice cream

2 Discuss the following questions:

- Is the menu suitable for someone with a lactose intolerance? Why, or why not?
- Does the menu meet government dietary guidelines?
- How could the menu be improved?

Food and drinks that don't usually contain lactose include:

- soya products – milks, yoghurts and some cheeses
- milks made from rice, oats, almonds, hazelnuts, coconut, quinoa and potato
- foods that carry the 'dairy-free' or 'suitable for vegans' signs
- carob bars.

It is possible to buy cow's milk containing additional lactase (the enzyme used to digest lactose). This means the individual still gets the nutritional benefits of milk, but is less likely to experience any symptoms after consuming it.

Wheat intolerance

Wheat intolerance:

- is different from coeliac disease, as the symptoms experienced by individuals vary considerably from one person to another

- causes a range of symptoms that can be very unpleasant, including abdominal discomfort, nausea, tiredness, bloating and altered bowel habit
- is not caused by an immune reaction in the body
- cannot cause life-threatening reactions or consequences, unlike wheat allergies.

For a wheat-free diet, individuals need to make sure they check all ingredient labels and be aware of hidden wheat. This can be found in many convenience products such as ready meals, sauces and so on.

Sometimes, a food label may not specify wheat but another form of wheat product that must also be avoided. Examples are:

- durum wheat, spelt, kamut
- couscous
- bran, wheat bran, wheat germ, wheat gluten
- farina
- rusk
- semolina, durum wheat semolina
- flour, wholewheat flour, wheat flour, wheat starch
- starch, modified starch, hydrolysed starch, food starch, edible starch
- vegetable starch, vegetable gum, vegetable protein
- cereal filler, cereal binder, cereal protein.

There are, however, many alternatives to wheat that can be used when preparing meals.

Alternatives for cereal and grains include:

- maize (corn), maize (corn) flour, potato, potato flour, rice, rice flour, soya beans, soya flour, millet, buckwheat, sago, tapioca, quinoa, chickpea flour and lentil flour

- chickpeas, beans and lentils (good fillers and can be added to soup)
- wheat-free pasta (available in large supermarkets and health food stores).

Individuals on a wheat-free diet can eat all fresh and frozen meat and fish without coatings.

Wheat-free alternatives for desserts include rice or sago puddings, jellies, sorbets, gelatine or veggie-gel based desserts.

Alternatives for seasonings, sauces and condiments include:

- pure spices
- salt
- freshly ground pepper
- French mustard
- home-made mayonnaise and dressings
- sauces prepared with corn flour or another alternative flour.

The sources of nutrients

When creating a dietary plan it is important to consider the nutrients that the individual requires at their life stage and how they can be provided, taking into account any specific dietary need(s).

Sources of protein

Every cell in the body contains some protein. It is needed for growth and repair of blood cells, body tissues and muscles. Proteins are available from animal and plant sources.

Table 9.5 shows sources of the different types of protein.

Table 9.5 Sources of protein

Animal/fish/dairy sources of protein HBV – high biological value	Vegetable sources of protein Generally LBV – low biological value (but with some HBV)
- Beef, lamb, pork, venison, sausages, bacon - Fish – cod, salmon, haddock, plaice - Seafood – prawns, scampi, scallops, crab - Milk, yoghurts, cheese, eggs	- Cereals – wheat, rice, oats, barley - Cereal products – bread, pasta, chapattis, flatbreads - Sweetcorn, peas, beans, lentils, chickpeas - Nuts and nut products, such as peanut butter, seeds - HBV – quinoa, soya beans and soya products such as TVP (textured vegetable protein)

Proteins are made up of chains of **amino acids**. The high biological value (HBV) sources contain all of the essential amino acids the body needs. The low biological value (LBV) sources do not, except for quinoa and soya products.

Those who choose to follow a vegetarian diet often use two types of protein in a meal to obtain the full range of amino acids. This is called 'protein complementation'; examples are beans on toast or hummus with pitta bread.

 Key term

Amino acids Essential nutrients that the body cannot make, so they have to be eaten as part of an individual's diet.

Sources of carbohydrates

Carbohydrates can be divided into three groups:

1 **starches** – sometimes called complex carbohydrates or starchy carbohydrates; they release energy slower than sugars so keep your appetite satisfied for longer

2 **sugars** – quickly digested and provide instant energy; excess energy is converted into fatty acids and stored as body fat

3 **dietary fibre** – aids the digestive process by helping prevent constipation and disorders of the digestive system; fibre makes people feel full so they are less likely to overeat.

Table 9.6 shows sources of each of the three types of carbohydrate.

Table 9.6 Sources of carbohydrates

Starchy carbohydrates	Sugars	Dietary fibre
• Bread • Pasta • Potatoes • Pulses, e.g. lentils, chickpeas **Beans** • Runner beans, broad beans, kidney beans • Baked beans • Butter beans, pinto, cannellini, borlotti, haricot and edamame beans **Cereal products** • Barley • Corn • Quinoa • Tapioca • Wholewheat breakfast cereals (porridge, oats and oatmeal) **Rice and grains** • All kinds of rice – Arborio, basmati, brown, long grain, short grain and white • Couscous • Bulgur wheat	**Fruit sugar** Found naturally in fruit and vegetable cells **Free sugar** Added to food or drinks • Granulated • Caster • Icing • Demerara • Golden syrup • Treacle • Honey **Processed foods with hidden sugar** • Ready-made pasta sauces • Tomato ketchup • Ready-made soups • Ready-meals • Canned fruit • Breakfast cereals • Sweetened fruit juice • Fizzy drinks Always check the list of ingredients on a food packet or jar – look for sugar, glucose, dextrose, fructose, glucose syrup and invert sugar	**High in dietary fibre** • Wholemeal bread • Wholemeal pasta • Brown rice • Couscous • High-fibre breakfast cereals • Wholemeal flour • Beans • Lentils • Sweet potato • Broccoli • Brussels sprouts • Artichokes • Jacket potatoes **Lower in dietary fibre** • White bread • White pasta • Cornflakes • White flour • White rice

Sources of fat

Fat supplies a concentrated source of energy and the essential fatty acids omega 3 and 6. However, too much fat in the diet can lead to obesity. Fats can be hard fats or oils.

Table 9.7 shows sources of animal and vegetable fats.

There are saturated fats and unsaturated fats.

- Most saturated fats come from animal sources. Too much saturated fat can increase the amount of cholesterol in the blood, which increases the risk of developing heart disease.

Table 9.7 Sources of fat

Animal sources of fat	Vegetable sources of fat
• Milk • Cream • Butter • Cheese • Oily fish (salmon, tuna, sardines, mackerel, trout) • Fat in meat	• Avocados • Nut oils • Seeds • Vegetable oils (olive oil, sunflower oil) • Margarine • Spreads such as Benecol • Soya milk, yoghurts and cheeses

- Unsaturated fats can reduce cholesterol levels. Good sources of unsaturated fat include olive oil and spreads made from monounsaturated fat.

To enjoy the health benefits of dairy without eating too much fat, it is recommended to use semi-skimmed, 1 per cent fat or skimmed milk, as well as lower-fat hard cheeses or cottage cheese, and lower-fat, lower-sugar yoghurt. Unsweetened, calcium-fortified dairy alternatives like soya milks, soya yoghurts and soya cheeses also count as part of this food group and can make good alternatives to dairy products.

Sources of vitamins

The B group of vitamins and vitamin C are water soluble and cannot be stored in the body. This means that they have to be eaten regularly. Vitamins A, D, E and K are fat soluble (in other words they can be dissolved in fats) and can be stored in the body for months, even years. They do not have to be eaten in large amounts.

Table 9.8 shows the sources of the different vitamins we need.

Research activity

Assessing nutritional content

Access a supermarket website and find four different food products that you like to eat.

1 Examine the labelling for the nutritional content relating to:
   - protein
   - carbohydrates
   - fat
   - salt
   - sugar.
2 Which is the most healthy product and why?
3 Which is the least healthy product and why?

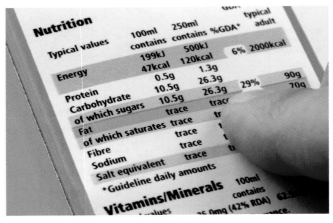

Figure 9.13 Reading a food label

Table 9.8 Sources of vitamins

Vitamin	Sources
A	• Eggs, full-fat milk, butter and cheese • Oily fish (e.g. mackerel), liver, kidneys • Yellow, red and green leafy vegetables such as spinach, kale, carrots, sweet potatoes, red peppers • Yellow fruit such as mangos and apricots • Fortified breakfast cereals
B1	• Liver • Milk, cheese, eggs • Bread, fortified breakfast cereals and flour • Dried fruit, nuts • Potatoes, peas, broccoli
B2	• Red meat, liver, chicken • Fish • Milk, yoghurt • Fortified breakfast cereals • Bread, rice • Yeast extract, e.g. Marmite • Soya beans
B6	• Red meat, liver • Fortified breakfast cereals • Potatoes • Eggs • Yeast extract, e.g. Marmite
B12	• Red meat is a major source, other meats • Salmon, cod • Milk, eggs • Fortified breakfast cereals • Yeast
C	• Fruit (e.g. strawberries), and especially citrus fruit such as oranges, lemons, grapefruits • Green vegetables, e.g. broccoli, sprouts • Tomatoes, red and green peppers • Potatoes
D	• Sunlight • Milk, butter, eggs • Fortified breakfast cereals • Margarine with added vitamin D • Fortified fats, e.g. soft spreads • Lean red meat
E	• Nuts and seeds • Cereals and cereal products • Sunflower and olive oil • Egg yolk, milk • Soya
K	• Leafy green vegetables such as spinach, broccoli, peas and beans • Vegetable oils • Cereals

Sources of minerals

Minerals are needed in small amounts. Calcium ensures that blood clots normally. Iron helps make red blood cells.

Figure 9.14 Sources of calcium

Figure 9.15 Sources of iron

The main functions of minerals are to:

• build strong bones and teeth
• turn food into energy.

Figures 9.14 and 9.15, and Table 9.9 on page 254 show examples of the food sources of calcium and iron.

Table 9.9 Sources of minerals

Mineral	Source
Calcium	• Milk, cheese • Oily fish (sardines and pilchards) • Soya beans, tofu • Nuts • Bread and fortified cereals • Broccoli, cabbage, okra
Iron	• Liver, meat • Salmon • Beans, nuts, dried fruit • Whole grains such as brown rice • Fortified breakfast cereals • Soybean flour • Most dark green leafy vegetables, e.g. curly kale, broccoli, watercress • Good-quality dark chocolate

Case study: Chantelle's dietary plan

Chantelle has been diagnosed with coeliac disease. She has reviewed what she eats and has started to work out a gluten-free dietary plan using basic foodstuffs and gluten-free products from her local supermarket. She has planned two days so far.

Read Chantelle's plan and then answer the questions.

Questions

1 Has Chantelle included all the main food groups? If so, give some examples. If not, which ones has she left out?

2 What makes this coeliac plan suitable for someone with lactose intolerance?

3 How could the plan be improved?

Day 1			
Breakfast	**Lunch**	**Dinner**	**Drinks and snacks**
Gluten-free oatcakes with cottage cheese and grapes Cup of tea	Tuna and sweetcorn sandwich made with gluten-free brown bread	Chicken curry with wild and white rice Natural yoghurt with sliced pear and strawberries	Orange juice Gluten-free cup cake Apple

Day 2			
Breakfast	**Lunch**	**Dinner**	**Drinks and snacks**
Boiled egg with gluten-free brown bread Cup of tea	Hummus with celery, carrot sticks and gluten-free high-fibre crackers	Home-made fish pie with mashed potato and cheese topping, green beans and broccoli Apple pie and custard	Apple juice Dried fruit and nuts, e.g. apricots, pecans, coconut Gluten-free mixed berry cereal bar

Stretch activity

Days three and four of Chantelle's dietary plan

Complete another two days of the dietary plan for Chantelle.

The plan must include suggested meals, snacks and drinks that could be eaten over the next two days.

(Aim to produce a **detailed** plan. Look at the command word definitions to see what **detailed** means in the assessment.)

Know it!

1   Give two examples of how religion can affect an individual's choice of food.

2   (a) Name two dietary conditions that affect an individual's food choices. (b) For each condition you named in part (a) give two examples of how the condition can affect what they eat.

3   What do the initials HBV and LBV stand for? What do they mean?

4   What is the difference between a food 'allergy' and a food 'intolerance'?

5   Name two source foods for (a) vitamin A, (b) calcium, (c) dietary fibre and (d) protein.

Assessment guidance

Learning outcome 2: Be able to create dietary plans for specific dietary needs

Marking criteria for LO2 Part A

Mark band 1	Mark band 2	Mark band 3
Makes **limited** references to the factors that influence diet.	Makes **detailed** references to the factors that influence diet.	Makes **thorough** references to the factors that influence diet.
Creates a **basic** dietary plan that enables the learner to **partly** meet the needs of individuals.	Creates a **sound** dietary plan that enables the learner to **mostly** meet the needs of individuals.	Creates a **detailed** dietary plan that enables the learner to **fully** meet the needs of individuals.

 The OCR Model Assignment will ask you to:

● Provide information about the factors that influence diet.

● Create a dietary plan that meets the needs of an individual.

 What do the command words mean?

● **Thorough reference**: You make references to the factors that influence diet and these will be extremely attentive to accuracy and detail.

● **Detailed plan and fully meets needs**: You should produce a point-by-point dietary plan that enables you to completely meet the needs of the individual. The plan you create will take into account the individual's specific dietary requirements.

→

255

You should check the glossary in the Introduction for the definitions of each of the command words from OCR.

Marking criteria for LO2 Part B

Mark band 1	Mark band 2		Mark band 3
The plan includes **basic** information on how it reflects the needs of the individual and their condition(s), and how it can address their condition(s) and symptoms.	The plan includes **clear** information on how it reflects the needs of the individual and their condition(s), and how it can address their condition(s) and symptoms.		The plan includes **detailed** information on how it reflects the needs of the individual and their condition(s), and how it can address their condition(s) and symptoms.
It shows **basic** understanding of the importance of nutrients and their functions to the individual and **limited** reference to the main nutrients required in the diet and sources described in a **basic** way. There is **some** understanding of the importance of a balanced diet.	It shows a **sound** understanding of the importance of nutrients and their functions to the individual and **some** relevant references to the main nutrients required in the diet and sources described in a **clear** manner. There is **clear** understanding of the importance of a balanced diet.		It shows a **thorough** understanding of the importance of nutrients and their functions to the individual, and **many** relevant references to the main nutrients required in the diet and sources described in a **detailed and coherent** manner. There is **detailed** information of how to achieve a balanced diet.
Draws upon **limited** skills/knowledge/understanding from other units in the specification.	Draws upon **some relevant** skills/knowledge/understanding from other units in the specification.		Clearly draws upon **relevant** skills/knowledge/understanding from other units in the specification.

 ## The OCR Model Assignment will ask you to:

- Provide an explanation of how the plan meets the needs of the individual and their conditions, and how it can address their conditions and symptoms.
- Provide information about the importance of nutrients and their functions. Include relevant references to the main nutrients required in the diet and describe the sources. Include information on how to achieve a balanced diet.
- Include some supplementary written work about skills, knowledge or understanding you have used from other units.

 ## What do the command words mean?

- **Detailed information**: Your plan includes point-by-point information on how it reflects the needs of the individual and their condition(s), and how it can address their condition(s) and symptoms.
- **Thorough understanding**: Your plan shows an understanding of the importance of nutrients and their functions to the individual that is extremely attentive to accuracy and detail.
- **Many relevant references**: Your work will include a large number of references to the main nutrients required in the diet.

→

- **Detailed and coherent**: Your descriptions of the sources will be set out point-by-point, in a logical way.
- **Detailed information**: There will be information of how to achieve a balanced diet, again set out point-by-point.
- **Relevant skills/knowledge/understanding from other units**: You will clearly draw upon correctly focussed skills/knowledge/understanding from other units in the specification.

You should check the glossary in the Introduction for the definitions of each of the command words from OCR.

Learning outcome 3

Be able to produce nutritional meals for specific dietary requirements

Getting started

Write down a list of five points you think should be taken into account when planning a meal for someone.

Share and discuss your ideas with the rest of your class.

Creating a meal for specific dietary needs

A meal consists of at least two courses or dishes. It could include a starter and a main course, or a main course and dessert. Recipes are the starting point when planning a meal.

The nutritional requirements of the specific dietary need and the life stage of the individual should be taken into account when deciding on the dishes to prepare.

Consider the government's nutritional recommendations and guidelines when planning dishes (look back at LO1 for details of these).

A meal should form part of a healthy balanced diet. If an individual cannot eat certain foods due to a dietary condition, they may develop deficiencies of some nutrients, so substitutes should be included.

Ingredients

To decide on a suitable meal to prepare for an individual, carefully consider the ingredients.

Are they:

- appropriate for the specific dietary need, e.g. gluten-free
- nutritious
- part of a healthy balanced diet?

Sometimes a recipe will need to be adapted. You may need to change ingredients to improve its nutritional value or to meet current healthy eating guidelines. Examples include:

- reducing the amount of sugar
- swapping saturated fat with unsaturated fat, e.g. sunflower spread instead of butter
- using herbs or spices instead of salt for seasoning
- using wholegrain versions of ingredients, e.g. flour, rice, pasta
- using low-fat yoghurt or fromage frais instead of cream.

Combining nutrients in a meal

Many foods, such as casseroles and stews, pizzas, pasta dishes and sandwiches, are combinations of the food groups in the Eatwell Guide. These types of meals can be a useful method of ensuring that an individual obtains the full range of nutrients they need in a healthy diet.

Example meals include:

- cheese on toast, with a glass of fruit juice or piece of fruit (suitable for a vegetarian if vegetarian cheese is used, this combines protein, carbohydrate and fat)
- cottage pie made using TVP protein, served with peas and carrots (suitable for a vegetarian as it replaces meat with HBV protein from soya, and includes starchy carbohydrate, vitamins and fibre)
- lamb and vegetable casserole with a baked potato, followed by fresh fruit salad and yoghurt (this combines protein, starchy carbohydrate and fat, suitable for an active, growing teenager or an adult).

Portion size

The term 'portion size' refers to the amount of food that is recommended for one person to eat in one sitting. The portion size of a meal should be adjusted to the individual. For example, a young child will need a smaller portion than an adult.

Some research has indicated that increased portion size, packaging and the size of a plate can lead to people choosing larger amounts of food and eating more. This suggests a possible link between portion size and overeating.

Assessing meal choices in relation to government guidelines

Carrying out an analysis of a meal is necessary to establish its nutritional value. Nutritional analysis can help you to decide if a recipe, meal or diet is suitable for the target group and if it is healthy.

Assessing the nutritional value of a meal can be carried out in different ways.

- The ingredients of the meal could be examined by looking at the labelling of the food products. This gives information about the nutrients contained in each food and what percentage of RNI (reference nutrient intake) it provides.

- The information obtained from food labelling could then be compared with the sections of the Eatwell Guide or DRVs (dietary reference values) to check if the food groups are in the correct proportions to provide a healthy meal.
- Computer software can also be used to carry out nutritional analysis of a meal. Free software (Explore Food) can be accessed from the British Nutrition Foundation:

explorefood.foodafactoflife.org.uk. This tool enables a step-by-step analysis of a recipe or a day's diet. It provides data that can then be used to inform conclusions when assessing the nutritional value of a meal.

Whatever method of analysis you use, the data should inform the assessment of a meal's nutritional value. The data on its own is not an assessment. Conclusions need to be drawn about how the meal meets an individual's dietary needs and the government dietary guidelines.

Case study: A nutritional meal?

Harry, aged 52, has been diagnosed with high cholesterol. Cholesterol builds up in the artery walls, so having high cholesterol can increase the risk of narrowing of the arteries (atherosclerosis), strokes and heart disease, because the flow of blood is restricted. Harry's GP has advised him to eat a diet low in saturated fat.

Harry has carried out some research about high cholesterol on the NHS Choices website. He knows that it is important to keep his diet low in fatty foods (especially food containing saturated fat) and to eat plenty of fruits, vegetables and wholegrain cereals.

Based on this advice, Harry has chosen the following recipes for one of his meals.

Chicken with a lentil and green bean salad
Ingredients:
1 skinless chicken breast
1 tablespoon roasted pepper and almond pesto
40 g fine green beans
60 g puy lentils
50 ml vegetable stock
3 spring onions
1 tablespoon extra-virgin olive oil
Grated zest and juice of ½ lemon
¼ teaspoon ground cumin

Nutritional value:

24.0 g protein	2.0 g saturated fat
16.0 g carbohydrates	5.7 g fibre
2.7 g sugars	1.0 g salt
12.2 g fat	

Fruit kebabs
Ingredients:
1 piece melon
1 peach
1 kiwi fruit
Raspberries for decoration

Nutritional value:
10.0 g protein
19.6 g carbohydrates
7.6 g sugars
0.0 g fat
18.0 g fibre
trace salt

→

259

The hygienic and safe preparation of food

There are many ways that food can become contaminated. Food poisoning bacteria can enter food during the storage, preparation, cooking and serving of food. Figure 9.16 summarises the main causes of food contamination.

Figure 9.16 How does food become contaminated?

Preparing the environment and yourself

Do the following to ensure the hygienic and safe preparation of food.

- Wash tables and work surfaces down before use: worktops should be washed down with hot, soapy water, using a clean cloth; anti-bacterial spray can be used afterwards to destroy any remaining bacteria.
- Ensure that equipment and utensils are clean: dirty equipment can cross-contaminate food; any equipment that has been in contact with raw meat and poultry must be thoroughly cleaned with hot, soapy water before being used again.
- Wear an apron/tie long hair back: this protects the food from bacteria on clothes and hair.
- Cover wounds: use a coloured waterproof plaster to stop the spread of infection.
- Wash your hands properly: use the correct hand-washing procedure. Hands carry bacteria so should be washed before and after working with food, and after going to the toilet.

Using colour-coded boards for food preparation
Colour-coded chopping boards can be useful to avoid cross-contamination of food as they can prevent the transfer of bacteria between different foods. Raw meat and cooked meat, or other cooked food, should never be prepared using the same board.

The colour-coded boards are used as follows:

- white – bread and dairy
- red – raw meat and poultry
- yellow – cooked meat
- brown – vegetables
- blue – fish
- green – salad and fruit

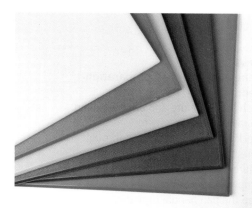

Figure 9.17 Colour-coded chopping boards can help prevent cross-contamination

How to check if food is cooked properly

Bacteria are destroyed at high temperatures, so if food is cooked at the correct temperature it will be safe to eat. A food temperature probe or meat thermometer should be used to check that food has reached 75°C or above. Frozen food must be completely defrosted before cooking.

How to put the hygienic and safe preparation of food into practice

Figure 9.18 shows hygienic and safe food preparation procedures to follow when preparing chicken with a lentil and green bean salad.

Know it!

1 Give an example of how to combine nutrients in a meal.

2 Describe two ways of carrying out a nutritional analysis of a meal.

3 How can using different-coloured chopping boards prevent cross-contamination?

4 Give three ways that food could be contaminated during preparation and cooking.

5 Give three ways of using equipment safely when cooking vegetables in a saucepan.

- Preparing and cooking the green beans – rinse, and then top and tail the green beans while the puy lentils are cooking, then steam the beans.

Hygiene and safe food preparation procedures:
- ensure the saucepan handle is not sticking out

when lentils are cooking on the hob
- rinse green beans thoroughly
- handle knife with care

When steaming the green beans:
- keep face away from pan when removing lid
- do not allow pan to boil dry

Figure 9.18 Hygienic and safe food preparation procedures for chicken with a lentil and green bean salad →

Brush both sides of the chicken breast with the pesto and cook in a griddle pan for about 8 minutes, until well browned.

Hygiene and safe food preparation procedures
- Wash hands before and after handling the raw chicken.
- Check the chicken is cooked through – there should not be any pink meat.
- Ensure the heat is at the required temperature, not too high.
- Keep the pan handle turned inwards.

While the chicken is cooking, drain the green beans and refresh under cold water. Pat them dry and then place in a bowl with the lentils and sliced spring onions.

For the dressing, whisk together the oil, lemon juice and zest, cumin and seasoning.

Hygiene and safe food preparation procedures
- Be careful of steam and boiling water when draining the green beans.
- Use oven gloves if needed.
- Place the hot pan on a trivet.

Put the sliced spring onions in a bowl with the cooked lentils. Pour over the dressing and mix together.

Hygiene and safe food preparation procedures
- Handle knife with care when chopping the onions. Make sure it is clean and has not been used to prepare raw food.
- Use a clean chopping board
- Cover the bowl with cling film and place in fridge until needed.

Serve the salad with the chicken.

Hygiene and safe food preparation procedures
- Check the chicken is cooked through – there should not be any pink meat.
- Use a spoon to serve the salad and tongs to serve the hot chicken.
- Serve straight away.

Hygiene and safe food preparation procedures after cooking
- Place all dishes, pans and utensils in the dishwasher and wash on the appropriate programme, or wash by hand in hot soapy water.
- Thoroughly clean all work surfaces with hot soapy water and antibacterial spray.
- Ensure any food waste is wrapped and placed in a closed bin.

Figure 9.18 Hygienic and safe food preparation procedures for chicken with a lentil and green bean salad (*continued*)

Assessment guidance

Learning outcome 3: Be able to produce nutritional meals for specific dietary requirements

Marking criteria for LO3 Part A

Mark band 1	Mark band 2	Mark band 3
Selection of ingredients demonstrates **basic** consideration of dietary requirements and nutritional value.	Selection of ingredients demonstrates **some** consideration of dietary requirements and nutritional value.	Selection of ingredients demonstrates **thorough** consideration of dietary requirements and nutritional value.
Carries out a **basic** analysis of the meal, with **limited** reference to government dietary guidelines and meeting the specific dietary needs of the individual.	Carries out a **detailed** analysis of the meal, with **some** reference to government dietary guidelines and meeting the specific dietary needs of the individual.	Carries out a **thorough** analysis of the meal, with **comprehensive** reference to government dietary guidelines and meeting the specific dietary needs of the individual.

The OCR Model Assignment will ask you to:

- Plan a meal using ingredients suitable for a specific dietary need, and also consider the nutritional value of the ingredients.
- Carry out an analysis of the meal, refer to the government dietary guidelines and meet the specific dietary needs of the individual.

What do the command words mean?

- **Thorough consideration**: You should take into account all the necessary information about your chosen individual's condition and nutritional needs when choosing ingredients for a meal. Your selection of ingredients will show that you have been extremely attentive to accuracy and detail when considering their dietary requirements and nutritional value.
- **Thorough analysis**: You will carry out an analysis of the meal that is extremely attentive to accuracy and detail.
- **Comprehensive reference**: You will include references to government dietary guidelines and meeting the specific dietary needs of the individual which will be complete and include everything that is necessary to evidence your understanding in terms of both breadth and depth.

You should check the glossary in the Introduction for the definitions of each of the command words from OCR.

Marking criteria for LO3 Part B

Mark band 1	Mark band 2	Mark band 3
Creates a meal with **some** support and guidance, which meets a **few** of the dietary needs of the individual.	Creates a meal with **minimal** support and guidance, which meets **some** of the dietary needs of the individual.	Creates a meal **independently**, which meets **most** of the dietary needs of the individual.
Follows hygiene and safe food preparation procedures with **some** support.	Follows hygiene and safe food preparation procedures with **minimal** support.	Consistently and effectively follows hygiene and safe food preparation procedures **independently**.

→

The OCR Model Assignment will ask you to:

- Cook a meal which meets the dietary needs of the individual.
- Follow hygiene and safe food preparation procedures.

 What do the command words mean?

- **Independently create a meal, and most of the dietary needs of the individual**: Without relying on others, you will create a meal which meets the majority of the dietary needs of the individual.
- **Independently follow safe and hygienic procedures**: Without relying on others you will consistently and effectively follow hygiene and safe food preparation procedures.

You should check the glossary in the Introduction for the definitions of each of the command words from OCR.

Read about it

Weblinks

www.allergyuk.org/home/home Allergy UK – comprehensive information about food allergies and intolerances (the causes and symptoms, and how to live with them)

www.coeliac.org.uk/home Coeliac UK – information about the services and support provided by the UK's charity for people with coeliac disease

www.diabetes.org.uk Diabetes UK – information about the causes, symptoms and effects of diabetes; plus advice, services and support

www.nutrition.org.uk British Nutrition Foundation – detailed and up-to-date information about healthy living and nutrition

www.foodafactoflife.org.uk British Nutrition Foundation – has a free nutritional analysis tool, and provides a wealth of free resources about healthy eating, cooking and food

www.theibsnetwork.org IBS Network – has extensive information about IBS, provides advice on diet and has a recipe section

www.nhs.uk/livewell/healthy-eating/Pages/Healthyeating.aspx NHS Choices – extensive information about healthy eating; guidelines, dietary conditions and case studies

www.nutritionprogram.co.uk The Nutrition Program – a nutritional analysis programme by Jenny Ridgwell (requires an annual subscription)

www.gov.uk/government/uploads/system/uploads/attachment_data/file/547050/government__dietary_recommendations.pdf Public Health England's 'Government dietary recommendations: government recommendations for food, energy and nutrients for males and females aged 1–18 years and 19+ years', 2016

Reference books

Rickus, A., Saunder, B. and Mackey, Y. (2016) *AQA GCSE Food Preparation and Nutrition*. Hodder Education.

Ridgwell, J. (2009) *Examining Food and Nutrition for GCSE* (2nd edn). Heinemann.

R030 Research – a project approach

About this unit

This unit will help you develop your planning, researching, presenting and analysing skills through an individual project in the context of a health, social care or early years setting.

You will be planning and carrying out research to answer a question (set by yourself, from the model assignments or from suggestions in the specifications) and test a hypothesis. You can extend your learning from units you have already covered or you may wish to choose a new area related to health, social care or early years.

As you are working your way through this unit, remember to look for skills, knowledge and understanding that you have gained from other units you have studied. You will have to produce a written piece of work to demonstrate this.

Learning outcomes

LO1: Be able to create project plans for a specific purpose

LO2: Know how to conduct research for projects

LO3: Be able to carry out projects

LO4: Know how to review projects

How will I be assessed?

You will be assessed through a series of assignment tasks, which are set by OCR. The assignment will be marked by your tutor and then moderated by OCR. For this unit, you will be given a list of suggested project titles in the model assignment or you can use your own.

For LO1, you need to:

- understand the different forms that the project output might take
- know how to choose a project topic independently
- understand how to set objectives and identify success criteria for your project
- know how to use planning tools and techniques to create your project plan.

For LO2, you need to:

- understand how to find information in different ways and from a range of sources (primary and secondary)
- know how to choose sources that are relevant to your project
- understand how to check that information is accurate and appropriate
- choose information that is relevant to your project
- understand how to check the reliability of your chosen sources
- know how to acknowledge other people's ideas and work
- understand how to produce a reference list appropriately.

For LO3, you need to:

- produce content that is based on the agreed project topic
- understand how to record and monitor the progress of the project
- know how to produce the project record while carrying out the different project stages
- understand how to ask for and act on feedback during the project
- know how to maintain project records so you can check your progress
- incorporate what you have learned into the next stage of the project.

Note: SPAG is assessed in this learning outcome.

For LO4, you need to:

- understand the difference between the actual outcome of the project and what was anticipated
- know the difference between what was planned and the actual process of completing the project
- describe what went well and what lessons can be learned for next time
- review the actual project timeframe compared to the planned timeframe
- understand how to measure the project against its objectives
- describe what has been learned from completing the project.

Make sure you refer to the current OCR specification and guidance.

Links to other units

Unit R022: Communicating and working with individuals in health, social care and early years settings (LO1, LO2 and LO3): All your communication skills will be used as you will need to write a report. You will also have to write a questionnaire and interview individuals.

Unit R024 (optional unit): Pathways for providing care in health, social care and early years settings (LO1 and LO2): You may choose to carry out an investigation into the different forms of support available in health and social care or look at the barriers to care pathways.

Unit R025 (optional unit): Understanding life stages (LO1): You may examine factors that have influenced an individual's development. For example you may look at the issues surrounding an individual's culture e.g. looking at arranged marriages.

→

Unit R026 (optional unit): Planning for employment in health, social care and children and young people's workforce (LO1 and LO2): You may use information about a career as a basis for a project.

For example you could find out if all the controversy surrounding doctors' hours etc in the NHS has put individuals off from training as a doctor.

Unit R027 (optional unit): Creative activities to support individuals in health, social care and early years settings (LO1, LO2 and LO3): Skills learned in this unit could help you to examine how certain activities are popular for individuals

with for example mental health needs or behavioural conditions.

Unit R028 (optional unit): Understanding the development and protection of young children in an early years setting (LO1, LO2 and LO3): You could use all the knowledge gained from this unit to develop a game or toy for a child which would help with their development.

As you are working your way through this unit remember to look for skills/knowledge and understanding that you have gained from other units that have been studied. You will have to produce a written piece of work to demonstrate this.

Learning outcome 1

Be able to create project plans for a specific purpose

Getting started

Which areas of health, social care and early years have you really enjoyed learning about?

Is there a topic that you haven't studied that you think you would like to examine in more detail?

Look at the model assignment suggested tasks, to give you an idea of what is required and what is a realistic topic/question.

As a group, make some suggestions for possible projects. Are they all realistic?

The different forms the project could take

All good projects, whatever form they take, should answer a question or respond to a **hypothesis**. Examples of questions include the following:

- For a report focussed on health: 'What is the average waiting time at Accident & Emergency departments in the .... area?'
- For a report focussed on social care: 'Are older individuals aware of the social care facilities available in the local area?'
- For a report focussed on early years: 'Are early years meals at a chosen nursery as healthy as they should be?' This topic could also be adapted for a social care report by changing the question to 'Are meals in a chosen residential home as healthy as they should be?'

The project could take the form of:

- a report
- an investigation
- an artefact (accompanied by a report)
- a presentation (accompanied by a report).

You must also produce a project record for assessment. The finished project must cover all the assessment criteria.

 Key term

Hypothesis A statement that makes a prediction about what will be found out in the research.

Report or investigation

Before starting to write the report or investigation it is important to understand exactly what is required. It is not an essay. It should have a formal format with headings so that other people can access and understand the work. See LO3 for more detailed information.

Artefact

An artefact is something you make. Let's look at how one learner used an artefact for their project.

Lola really enjoyed studying Unit R028 (Understanding the development and protection of young children in an early years setting). She decided she would take some finger puppets she had made into the primary school where she did her work placement. She had noticed there were two very shy children in the class. She read that puppets can support children emotionally by giving them a 'friend' to talk to, or a way to talk to other children without having to speak directly. She decided her question for her project would be: 'Can finger puppets help children to develop social skills?' As well as creating the puppets (which she had made as part of a textiles project), Lola still had to produce a report/investigation and project record about her topic. Another artefact could be a board game for early years (made in technology), perhaps to help teach young children the alphabet.

Presentation

You could do your presentation using PowerPoint slides, so you would deliver your project research to an audience. The presentation could be used to advance your communication skills and share the project skills that you developed throughout the project management. The presentation could also be a display, including photographs, video recordings or posters. As with the artefact, you would still need to write a project report.

How to choose a project topic

Here are some pointers to help you decide what project topic to choose.

- The project must be in the context of a health, social care or early years setting.

- The project should be of a realistic size, with enough time factored in to plan, research and finish it.
- Avoid a topic that would need a lot of tutor input, as this will lose marks.
- Make sure the topic is something that interests you, as you have to carry out the research!

As a starting point, you may find it useful to make a list of topics that are of interest. A list of broad topics is fine. They can be narrowed down later so that the project is specific and manageable. Spider diagrams and mind maps are great tools for planning and helping you see an overall picture of your ideas.

For example, to help Lola decide on her project she made a spider diagram of how finger puppets can help with development (see Figure 10.1). She knew they could help development in many different ways. From her diagram she decided that she was going to research social skills because she could see this would help the two shy children at her placement. She knew she would be able to narrow her topic down to a question. Remember, if you use a spider diagram or a similar project tool, only one area in the diagram should be made into the question or hypothesis. Otherwise, the subject to be covered will be huge and impossible to cover in the amount of time available.

Before you finalise your project topic, check that there are plenty of available resources for your research. If there are very few existing resources, then the topic is going to be difficult to work on. It would then be a good idea to change to a different topic.

It is also important to narrow down the topic so it does not cover too wide an area. In the case of Lola's project, she is going to look at the finger puppets in her own placement with a specific age group (three to four years). She is not looking at the whole country or at all age groups.

Once the topic is chosen, write the question or hypothesis. If you choose a hypothesis, you will need to test it and find evidence to support or contradict it. You may therefore find it simpler to ask a question, as it does not make any predictions. It allows the research to be broader.

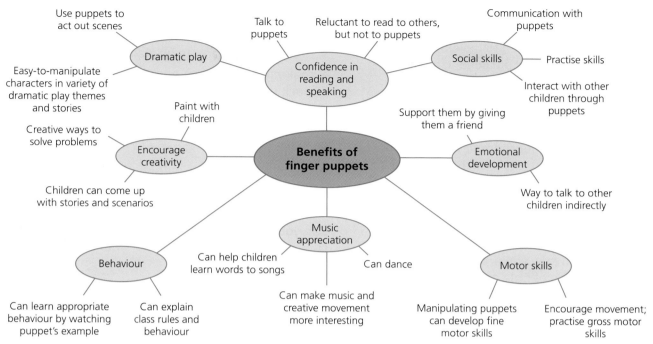

Figure 10.1 Lola's spider diagram

 Case study: Helping Ruby choose a project topic

Ruby would like to train as a nursery nurse. She thinks a project on play may help her get into college to follow her chosen course. She can't decide on how to narrow down her topic choice, so she chooses to do a project on all aspects of play.

Questions

1 Explain to Ruby why her idea of covering all aspects of play may not be a good idea.

2 Suggest a way forward for Ruby that may help her to narrow down her topic to a manageable question.

Rationale

The rationale is an introductory statement about the research. It expands on the reason why the topic was chosen and why the research question or hypothesis was set.

Lola's rationale was that she had noticed the two shy children on her work placement. She wanted to do something positive to help them. However, a topic may be chosen because of a recent newspaper or media interest in a subject. Or it could be that you are thinking about going to work in a particular career and the topic is related to that career. Or you might just have an interest in that subject and want to follow it through.

How to set objectives and identify success criteria

Once you have decided on a topic, you need to set objectives and identify success criteria for the project. But first, look at the project's overall **aim**. This should clarify the question or hypothesis. It sets out the reason for your project, while making links to the purpose for the research.

 **Key term**

Aim The intention of the project.

269

For Lola's research, her aim could be that she wants to research the effectiveness of finger puppets in helping children to develop social skills. This links in to her purpose, which is to help two shy children in her nursery class to communicate with other children in the group through the use of finger puppets. First, she would have to encourage them to communicate with the puppets and get them to practise their new skills. Then the children could use the medium of the puppets to build up their confidence to speak to other children.

Setting objectives

Objectives explain how you are going to achieve your aim. Examples of Lola's objectives could be to:

- produce a timeline for the project
- research sources for the use of toys in helping with building social skills
- observe the two children in group sessions (to try to understand their lack of social interaction with other children)
- introduce the children to the puppets and see if they are interested in talking to them
- question teachers about children's social interactions.

These are a few examples of Lola's objectives but you should have a longer list for your project.

Identifying success criteria

When carrying out research for a project, success criteria could be:

- achieving your objectives
- delivering an answer to the set question
- meeting time targets or plans
- making the best use of resources, such as your work placement
- managing any unplanned issues and adapting your time plan accordingly
- staying realistic
- carrying out research independently
- developing new skills during the process of the project.

Can you think of any others? What are the success criteria going to be for your project?

How to use planning tools and techniques to create plans

Time management is a very important part of project management. This section looks at two planning techniques for creating plans: timelines and dividing a project into manageable chunks.

Use timelines for planning a project, and the need to amend and review plans

There is no right or wrong way of writing a time plan or timeline. It is entirely up to you to decide which type of timeline suits you best. Whichever timeline you go for, a useful approach is to first set out all the tasks so that you can see what needs to be done. You can then work out which tasks need to be done first to allow the project to succeed. It is a good idea to start with the finish date and work backwards.

Setting out a timeline gives you a clear direction and purpose. It is important to stick to the research topic and not get side-tracked onto something else, even if there is a slight overlap. For example, Lola could easily fall into the trap of looking at other benefits of finger puppets instead of keeping to her narrow boundaries. But it is important to stay on track; otherwise the project loses its focus and becomes too big to handle in the amount of time available. Figure 10.2 shows a simple linear timeline that Lola used.

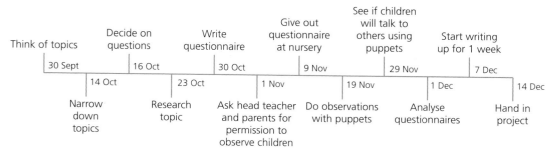

Figure 10.2 Simple linear timeline for Lola's project

Table 10.1 More detailed time plan for Lola's project

Goal	Goal target date	Actual date goal achieved	Notes
Think of topics	30 September	30 September	I had a good idea I'd be looking at finger puppets before I started but didn't know which area of development.
Narrow down topics	14 October	14 October	Right on time. Difficult, as I was interested in all my glove puppet ideas but shy children were a good opportunity for me to try out social interaction.
Decide on question	16 October	20 October	Found it difficult to narrow it down as there were so many questions related to the topic.
Research topic	23 October	30 October	Huge amount of information out there. Have made notes of sources I'm going to use.
Write questionnaire	30 October	3 November	Research had knock-on effect on writing questionnaire, so I was delayed writing questionnaire.
Ask head teacher and parents for permission to observe children	1 November	8 November	Head teacher out of school; therefore, I had to ask her a week after I planned to. But managed to ask parents and receive written permission from them after school on the set date.
Give out questionnaire at nursery	9 November	9 November	Gave questionnaires to both sets of parents and classroom teacher, and asked them to return them to me by next week. It isn't very long but I'm worried they'll not return them if I give them longer.
Do observations with puppets	19 November 23 November 26 November	19 November 23 November 26 November	I had already observed children without puppets for several weeks on work placement.
See if children will talk to others using puppets	29 November	29 November	Yes they did, although they were not aware that this was the date I'd set.
Analyse questionnaires	1 December	4 December	Had a lot of homework this week. Parents and teacher did return questionnaires; I only had five to collect so this helped.
Start writing up for 1 week	7 December 10 December 12 December 14 December	7 December 10 December 12 December 14 December	Had to happen as planned lessons to write up findings.
Hand in project	14 December	14 December	Deadline date.

Classroom discussion

Timelines

As a class, look at Figure 10.2 and Table 10.1.

1 Which timeline do you prefer?
2 Explain why and justify your answer.

Know it!

1 Outline three different forms your project could take.
2 Explain what is meant by hypothesis.
3 What is a rationale?
4 Explain why it is important to plan out the time available when starting a project.

Before Lola started her timeline, she wrote down all the tasks she had to carry out. As Figure 10.2 shows, Lola only planned out her time; she did not include any review dates or dates when the actual goals were achieved. Remember, this is only a very basic plan for Lola's use of time and there would need to be further evidence of use of time, review and so on, in her final project.

Lola could have prepared a more detailed time plan, such as the one in Table 10.1. More columns could be added to suit her needs.

Remember, you must create your own template rather than using one that has been given to you by your tutor. Table 10.1 is an example only and must not be used for the assessment.

Divide a project into manageable stages

Here are some useful points to follow when dividing your project into stages.

- Divide the project into manageable chunks, as this is more achievable than trying to do too much all at the same time.
- Set time spans that are realistic.
- Sometimes research takes a lot longer than first planned because the information is not readily available. It is therefore better to allow too much time than too little.

In Lola's case she had to ask the head teacher and the parents if the two shy children could be observed. This took longer than she had planned as the head teacher could not see Lola on the day she planned. She was able to get the parents' written permission when they came to meet their children after school.

Assessment guidance

Learning outcome 1: Be able to create project plans for a specific purpose

Marking criteria for LO1

Mark band 1	Mark band 2	Mark band 3
Gives a **simple** reason for doing the project, making **few** links to a specific purpose.	Gives a **clear** reason for doing the project, making **some** links to a specific purpose.	Gives a **clear** and **detailed** rationale for doing the project, making **clear** links to a specific purpose.
Gives a **limited** description of project objectives with **limited** clarity.	Gives a **detailed** description of project objectives with **some** clarity.	Gives a **thorough** description of project objectives. Objectives are stated **clearly** and **precisely**.
Produces a **basic** project plan with **limited** detail of what is to be done and a very **brief** outline of timelines.	Produces a project plan, which is **detailed**, and assigns timelines to the tasks.	Produces a **comprehensive** project plan showing clearly the realistic expected timelines for all of the tasks.
Support and guidance needed in identifying and scoping a project topic related to a health, social care or early years setting.	**Some** support and guidance needed in identifying and scoping a project topic related to a health, social care or early years setting.	Works **independently** in identifying and scoping a project topic related to a health, social care or early years setting.

→

The OCR Model Assignment will ask you to:

- Give reasons for doing the project, making links to a specific purpose.
- Give a description of project objectives.
- Produce a project plan with clear and realistic timelines for all of the tasks.
- Identify and scope a project topic related to a health, social care or early years setting.

 What do the command words mean?

- **Clear, detailed and clear links**: You will produce a focussed and point-by-point rationale or reason for doing the project, which makes focussed links to a specific purpose.
- **Thorough description**: You will give a description of your project objectives which will be extremely attentive to accuracy and detail.
- **Clearly and precisely**: Your objectives will be focussed and precise.
- **Comprehensive project plan**: Your plan is complete and includes everything necessary to show understanding in terms of breadth and depth showing clearly the realistic expected timelines for all of the tasks.
- **Works independently**: You work without relying on anyone else in identifying and scoping a project topic related to a health, social care or early years setting.

You should check the glossary in the Introduction for the definitions of each of the command words from OCR.

Learning outcome 2

Know how to conduct research for projects

Getting started

If a parent were looking for a toy to help with their child's development, how would they research different options? Discuss this question in small groups, using the bullet points below to help you. Then share your findings with the rest of the class.

- Would they use secondary research – for example, would they look online or in magazines? How would they begin their online research?

- Would they go to a toyshop in town and ask for advice? Or would they use primary research, in other words ask their friends or other parents?

- Who would they trust to give them the best advice? Do you think some advice may be biased? (For example, will a retailer always give reliable information or might they want to sell a particular brand of toy?)

How to find information in different ways and from a variety of sources, both primary and secondary

When you are conducting the research for your project, you will find information in a range of ways and from different sources, both primary and secondary.

Primary research

Primary research is research that you carry out for yourself. The research is original and new but may already have been carried out in other contexts, for instance in other geographical areas or across a different target group.

For example, you may wish to find out if new mothers feel supported by midwives to breastfeed after they have left hospital. Out of this idea the possibilities for original research are endless (the age groups could be varied as could the cultures and geographical range).

Figure 10.3 shows the different methods of collecting primary research. We will discuss each of these in turn.

Questionnaires

Questionnaires are a popular method of collecting primary data. A questionnaire is a series of questions designed by the researcher.

Figure 10.3 Methods of collecting primary research

 Key terms

Quantitative data Data that records quantities and from which numbers or numerical data (e.g. charts, graphs etc.) result.

Qualitative data Data that is based on people's views, opinions and beliefs; usually written in words rather than numbers or figures.

Questions are usually closed, open or give a forced choice.

- A closed question generally has an answer of 'yes' or 'no'. For example, 'Do you exercise every day?' This is **quantitative** data; the data is number or quantity related.
- An open question gives the participant the opportunity to answer the question fully. An example of an open question would be: 'What do you think about exercising every day?' This is **qualitative** research as the participants qualify or give a reason for their answer.
- Questions with a forced choice give the participant a limited range of answers to choose from. Opinions are not asked for. Figure 10.4 is an example of a forced choice question.

Questionnaires should:

- be as short as possible
- have a logical order
- make sense
- be clear and unambiguous
- be written in simple language.

Table 10.2 outlines the advantages and disadvantages of questionnaires.

Do you exercise:
- every day?
- every other day?
- at weekends?
- once a week?
- once a month?

Figure 10.4 Example of a forced choice question

Table 10.2 Advantages and disadvantages of questionnaires

Advantages of questionnaires	Disadvantages of questionnaires
Cheap and easy to produce	Can have a poor return rate
A lot of data produced in a short amount of time	No opportunity to ask further questions
Participants answer at their own pace	If a question isn't understood (because it is poorly written) it can affect the results of the questionnaire
Participants can remain anonymous	It takes time to write a good questionnaire
Researcher's time used effectively	

Observations

This method of research involves watching people to observe their behaviour. Observations are often used to watch young children who would be unable to answer questionnaires or take part in meaningful interviews. Children's physical, intellectual, language, emotional and social development is often observed. There are two types of observation:

1 participant
2 non-participant.

Participant observation is used when the researcher joins in with the individuals she or he is observing. For example, a researcher could be helping children in a physical education lesson while observing them at the same time.

Non-participant observation is where the observer has no interaction with the individuals he or she is observing. This could encourage the individuals to change their behaviour as they recognise that they are being observed.

Table 10.3 outlines the advantages and disadvantages of observations.

Interviews

Generally, interviews provide more detailed information than questionnaires but they can be very time-consuming. They can provide both qualitative and quantitative data. There is a high response rate as the researcher speaks to the

Table 10.3 Advantages and disadvantages of observations

Advantages of observations	Disadvantages of observations
You can observe body language/non-verbal behaviour as well as verbal	Time consuming
Able to collect detailed data	Small groups are observed; therefore, behaviour might not be representative of other similar groups
Researcher can narrow down research as she or he observes	Observer can get too involved and get distracted from task
Data can be collected immediately as and when it happens	Behaviour may be affected by having an observer present in the group

 Research activity

Break time observation

Plan an observation for break time. Plan what you want to observe, why you want to observe it and what you hope to get out of it.

For example, Fiona and Diane decided they would like to observe how many girls washed their hands after using the toilet in school. They were surprised by what they observed.

participants individually on a one-to-one basis. The researcher writes down the interviewee's answers but can influence the participant by the body language they use, so this may distort the findings.

There are three types of interview:

1 structured or formal
2 unstructured or informal
3 semi-structured.

A structured interview is where the participants are asked a series of closed questions. Everyone is asked the same questions and they are not allowed to expand their replies. It is a good way of collecting quantitative data.

An unstructured interview is where the researcher has a list of subjects they would like to cover during the interview, but they don't have a list of pre-set questions. Participants are allowed to expand their answers.

A semi-structured interview is a mixture of structured and unstructured questions. The researcher does have a list of pre-set questions but is allowed to expand on them.

Table 10.4 outlines the advantages and disadvantages of interviews.

Table 10.4 Advantages and disadvantages of interviews

Advantages of interviews	Disadvantages of interviews
High response rate	Time consuming as one to one
More information collected as participants talk rather than write	Researcher's body language may influence replies

Key term

Plagiarise Copy or use someone else's work as your own without acknowledging or giving credit to the original author.

Case studies

Case studies can be both primary and secondary research (we look at secondary research below).

Primary case studies are where the researcher knows the case study individual. For example, if the researcher were to look at the question of breastfeeding new mothers and whether they felt supported by midwives, they may know someone with a relevant story that could add weight to their study. The case study individual has to be known personally to the researcher for it to be primary research. However, if the case study came from an online source, then it would be secondary research.

Secondary research

Secondary research is research that has been produced by someone else. It can save a lot of time as the material already exists and is readily available, for instance in books, magazines or on websites. However, remember the following points when using secondary sources.

- Note down all sources (in your jotter) as you work through information.
- Never **plagiarise**.
- Always credit other people's ideas.
- Use trusted, accurate and reliable websites, e.g. BBC News.
- Use published books that are current and up to date.

To summarise: find it, check it, credit it.

Figure 10.5 shows the different methods of doing secondary research. We will discuss each of these in turn (case studies are covered above).

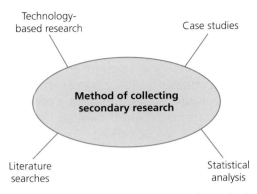

Figure 10.5 Examples of secondary research methods

Research activity

Office for National Statistics

Visit www.ons.gov.uk and make a note of the types of information available.

How might this information help you with your project?

Statistical analysis

Statistical analysis involves collecting, analysing and examining large amounts of data in order to find out about trends and patterns.

Statistical data is produced by local and national government, as well as many other sources. The census that takes place every ten years produces information on housing, employment, income, health statistics, etc. This helps the government and local authorities decide on their priorities for health, housing, and so on. A great deal of statistical information is available from the Office for National Statistics: www.ons.gov.uk.

Technology-based research

Technology-based research includes the internet, CDs and social media.

The internet has many search engines and there is a huge amount of information readily available at your fingertips. Remember, though, that not everything online is fact! Anyone can set up a website so it is important to use reputable sites. BBC News is online and so too are many of the national newspapers. There are also online libraries and encyclopaedias.

When using the internet, remember that:

- anyone can publish online
- sources may be untrue
- sources may be inaccurate.

You should:

- always check the relevance of the content
- always check the reliability of the content
- always check the accuracy of the content
- be critical of all content you find.

CDs are usually available in libraries and cover all different types of information. The discs are capable of storing huge amounts of information, but they are easy to use and access. Make a note of any resources that may be of use.

Social media is online communication that allows people to share information, views, opinions, images and so on. Examples include Facebook, Instagram, LinkedIn and Twitter. There are forums such as discussion boards, which allow questions to be put up for discussion. This can allow you to reach a global audience.

Literature searches

A literature search is the traditional method of secondary research. Sources include:

- newspapers
- magazines
- specialist journals
- books.

Make sure that the newspapers, magazines and journals you source are up to date and fit for purpose (for instance, a tabloid newspaper might not be the best source of reference for a scientific study and a specialist journal article might include technical language that is difficult to understand).

Research activity

Library visit

Visit your school library and see which publications would be useful for your research project. Were you surprised by the number of relevant magazines, journals and other resources?

When choosing books, always make sure you have the most recent edition. As with specialist journals, specialist books can include jargon and be difficult to follow. You may find that a textbook is simpler to understand and therefore more fit for purpose for this type of research.

Remember to take note of the sources you use, as it can be difficult to remember the publication details at a later date. Use UK-based books for this project; you can then be sure that they are referring to what happens in this country.

How to select sources that are relevant to the project

As we have seen, there is a wealth of different sources to choose from for your research. So how do you decide which sources to select?

A literature review is where you examine all the sources that could be useful for the project. Look for sources that contain key phrases from the topic. These can then be skimmed and scanned to check their relevance to the project. Some of the sources may be too academic and technical, making them difficult to understand. These should be rejected. You also need to check reliability and validity.

Rebecca decided to answer this question for her project: 'How have treatments and attitudes to mental illness changed over the past ten years?' Table 10.5 shows how Rebecca decided to record her resources and how their reliability was checked.

Table 10.5 An example of a literature/resource review

Resource	Brief summary	Reliability	Used in project
www.nice.org.uk/guidance/cg185	Background in treatments of a mental illness	This is published by the National Institute for Health and Care Excellence – a government website used by healthcare professionals	Yes
www.nhs.uk/Conditions/Pages/BodyMap.aspx?Index	Summary of a range of treatments	Published by the NHS	Yes
No Going Back: Forgotten Voices from Prudhoe Hospital, by Keilty, T. and Woodley, K. (2013) The Centre for Welfare Reform.	History of treatment of mentally ill people	Historian backed by Skills for People	Yes
https://en.wikipedia.org	Has interesting information on mental illness	May not be reliable (anyone can post on this website)	No

How to check for bias and accuracy of information

Bias

Secondary source information can be **biased**. Biased information can be avoided by checking the following.

- Who produced the information?
- What is the purpose of the information?
- Is the information trying to influence people?
- Does the information give just one viewpoint?

Consider why a person or organisation is writing on this topic. For instance, if you are looking for information about global warming, these people are likely to offer different points of view:

- a leading scientific research council
- a personal blog from a climate change protestor
- a company offering carbon-neutral flights.

Primary research can also be biased if the researcher is not impartial to the answers given by the interviewee. The researcher's body language can give clues to the interviewee on how to answer the question, for example, if they are nodding or smiling when a certain answer is given. It is important that the questions are carefully worded and not biased in any way.

Accuracy

One way to check if a secondary source is accurate is to use other secondary sources to confirm the information. Then check the list of references used by the author. The reference list can tell you the types of sources used and how they can be verified. If a secondary source does not have references, it may be best not to use it.

Key term

Biased Information that gives one particular opinion.

Group activity

Who's telling the truth?

In small groups, do the following.

1 Collect a selection of newspapers from the same date. Ensure you have a selection from the tabloids and broadsheets.

2 Find a health, social care or early years related article and look at the coverage of that topic across the newspapers. Pull out the main points made by each newspaper and compare them.

3 What do you notice? Is there evidence of factual accuracy in all the reports? Is there any evidence of bias?

4 Which newspaper's report would you use if you were doing a project on that subject? Justify your answer.

Now share your findings with the rest of the class. Did everyone feel the same?

How to select information that is relevant

Make sure that the information you select is directly relevant to the project topic. It is a good idea to scan or skim-read any possible articles to ensure the material is relevant. Once relevant materials have been found, it is useful to highlight the points relating to the subject.

For example, in Lola's project the information would have to be directly related to finger puppets and how they can help young children to socialise. Lola would have found lots of materials about socialisation of children and separate information about the use of finger puppets. These sources would be useful to her only if they related specifically to finger puppets helping children to socialise.

How to check the reliability of information selected

When checking the reliability of information, here are some key questions to ask.

- Who wrote the information?
- Why did they write the information?
- When was the information written?
- Where was the information written?
- Was the information written at an appropriate level for me to understand?
- How can this information help me?

Case study: Malik's project

Malik has decided to base his project on an interesting article he read in a tabloid newspaper. So far he has been able to find little verification for the article in other publications.

Questions

1. Do you think the tabloid newspaper is a reliable source?
2. What would your advice to Malik be?

How to acknowledge other people's ideas and written work

Whenever secondary sources are used, they must be acknowledged. Failure to acknowledge sources is plagiarism, which is a form of malpractice.

At Cambridge National/GCSE level, a bibliography or resources list at the end of the work is sufficient. It shows knowledge, understanding and planning skills to acknowledge where the source has been used within the text. You should never copy text directly from a secondary source without acknowledging it. If direct quotations are taken from textbooks or websites, use quotation marks around the direct quote. After the quotation, include in brackets the author's name, date of publication and the page number that the quotation was taken from.

How to record sources of information using formal referencing systems

This section looks at how to record the reference information for a book, web article, newspaper or magazine article, and journal. In addition to the information below, you may find the following weblink helpful when you are putting together the bibliography for your project: www.neilstoolbox.com/bibliography-creator/reference-book.htm.

Books

In the Harvard system for referencing books, authors are listed in alphabetical order using the format below.

1. Name of the author(s) (surname first, followed by their initial/initials)
2. Year the book was published, in brackets
3. Title of book, in italics
4. Edition of book
5. City it was published in
6. Publisher
7. Pages you used

Here is an example of a book reference:

Nolan, Y. (2011) *Health and Social Care (Adults)* (3rd edn). London: Heinemann, pages 10–11.

If there is more than one author, include all of them or add et al.

Websites

To reference an article from a website, follow the following steps.

1   Name of the author(s) (surname first, followed by their initial/initials)
2   Year published, in brackets
3   Title, in italics
4   'Available at', then include full website URL
5   Date accessed

Here is an example of a web reference:

Stanbridge, N. (2016) *DNA confirms cause of 1665 London's Great Plague*. Available at: www.bbc.co.uk/news/science-environment-37287715 (last accessed 23 September 2016).

Newspapers or magazines

To reference a newspaper or magazine, follow these steps.

1   Name of the author(s) (surname first, followed by their initial/initials)
2   Year published, in brackets
3   Article title, in single quotation marks
4   Newspaper/magazine title, in italics
5   Day and month
6   Page or pages

Here is an example of a reference from a newspaper article:

Cochrane, K. (2014) 'The fightback against gendered toys', *Guardian*, 22 April, p. 23.

Stretch activity

Bibliography

Produce a bibliography for a piece of work you have already completed, for example, for another unit for this course, which shows evidence of the use of relevant resources.

(Aim for a **wide range** of relevant resources showing evidence of **extensive**, **relevant research**. Look at the command word definitions to see what **wide range**, **extensive** and **relevant research** mean in the assessment.)

Know it!

1   Explain what is meant by secondary sources.
2   Explain how a case study can be both primary and secondary research.
3   Briefly outline how you can check for bias and accuracy of information.
4   List the advantages and disadvantages of a questionnaire.
5   What are the advantages and disadvantages of interviews?

Assessment guidance

Learning outcome 2: Know how to conduct research for projects

Marking criteria for LO2

Mark band 1	Mark band 2	Mark band 3
There is evidence of **basic** research.	There is evidence of **relevant** research.	There is evidence of **extensive**, **relevant** research.
Produces a bibliography that shows a **limited** range of resources, **some** of which may not have relevance to the project.	Produces a bibliography that shows a **reasonable** range of relevant resources.	Produces a bibliography that shows evidence of the use of a **wide** range of relevant resources.
Gives a **basic** justification for the choice of resources and **partly** checks on the reliability of the resources used.	Gives **sound** justification for the choice of resources and **mostly** checks the reliability of the resources used.	Gives a **clear** and **effective** justification for the choice of resources, and **fully** checks the reliability of the resources used.

→

The OCR Model Assignment will ask you to:

- Show evidence of researching the chosen topic.
- Produce a bibliography that shows evidence of a range of relevant resources.
- Justify your choice of resources.
- Check the reliability of the resources you have used.

 What do the command words mean?

- **Extensive relevant research:** You will provide evidence of extensive and correctly focussed research.
- **Wide range:** You will produce a bibliography which shows that you have used a comprehensive range of relevant resources and have not taken a narrow approach.
- **Clear and effective justification:** You will give a focussed justification, for the choice of resources, that is successful.
- **Fully:** You will check completely the reliability of the resources used.

You should check the glossary in the Introduction for the definitions of each of the command words from OCR.

Learning outcome 3

Be able to carry out projects

Getting started

Do you plan out big events in your life? For example, imagine if you were planning your eighteenth birthday party – would you start planning the week before? If you were going on a holiday of a lifetime, what would you have to consider? When would you start planning? Would you make a written plan so you could record your progress?

As a group, discuss big events that have taken place in your life and the way you planned for them. Did you stick to the plan, or adapt it as the event unfolded?

How to write up a project on your chosen topic

It is a good idea to follow a standard format for writing up a project so that there is a recognisable outcome at the end of the process.

One suggested order is:

1 the research question/hypothesis (see page 267 for definition)
2 the rationale or reason why this is the chosen project and the purpose behind it
3 the aim and the objectives
4 the methods of research to be used, which you need to justify
5 analysis of primary and secondary research
6 conclusion
7 evaluation (review of the project)
8 bibliography.

For example, Lola decided to do observations with the children because questionnaires and interviews were not fit for purpose for this age group. But she produced questionnaires for the parents and the teacher. After analysing the primary and secondary information, she decided to use pie charts or bar charts to display the analysis of the data. She then wrote a conclusion, where all the findings of the project were brought together. Next, the evaluation reflected on all aspects of the research project, from the initial planning stage to the final completion. She also completed a bibliography, which listed all the sources she used, and she checked their reliability.

Remember, it is also vital to have a timeline or equivalent project plan, which you can refer to as you work through the project.

Evaluation – how did the project go?

In the evaluation section, there should be a full review of all aspects of the project. Here are some examples of questions to ask yourself.

- Did the timeline work well? If not, why not?
- Was the project question answerable?
- Were the aim and objectives achievable?
- Was the project well planned?
- Did you choose the most appropriate primary and secondary methods?
- Were sources recorded as and when they were used?
- Did you check the reliability of sources before you used them?
- Did you keep records throughout the project?
- Which skills did you develop during the project?
- What worked well and what did not?

If you had to repeat the project, what changes would you make?

How to record and monitor project progress

It is vital to record and monitor the progress of your project, to make sure you keep on track and to manage any setbacks you might have.

Project plan, record of investigation and diary of progress

As we saw in LO1, a project or time plan is essential to the process of completing a project. Here are the different ways you will record and monitor your project progress.

- **Project plan** – this is completed at the beginning of your project. You plan out all the tasks that need to be completed within the time available, from the beginning of the project up until the end date. This plan should allow time for everything, from deciding on the topic to the final write-up. Remember, some dates, for example, may have to change due to circumstances.
- **Record of investigation** – this is a record of all your research, both primary and secondary.
- **Diary of progress** – this is a record of your progress throughout the project. Just like a daily diary, it will record the highs and lows of completing the work. You need to record anything that happens, whether it is positive or negative.

One option is to combine your project plan, record of investigation and diary of progress. This means that everything project related can be recorded on one chart. Table 10.6 shows how Perla chose to do this for part of her project. Note that it does not start from the beginning of her project.

Remember, you must create your own template rather than using one that has been given to you by your tutor. Table 10.6 is an example only and must not be used for the assessment.

 Group activity

Perla's plan

In small groups, discuss Perla's combined project plan, record of investigation and diary of progress.

1. Do you think it is a good idea?
2. Discuss the positive and/or negative points of Perla's format.

After 10 minutes, share your thoughts with the rest of the group.

Table 10.6 An example of a combined project plan, record of investigation and diary of progress

Activity	Date	Details	Problems encountered	Solution to problems
Changing project title	23/11/2016	I looked at my original list of titles and decided to change the title after having problems collecting resources. This means having to research all topics again to refresh my memory. This time I made a pros and cons list to make sure I had the right title.	Research showed there were few secondary sources.	Change to title where there are plenty of resources.
Talk to H&SC teacher	03/12/2016	I talked to my teacher again and presented him with my new title: 'How effective is chemotherapy and radiotherapy in alleviating pain?' He thought it was better than my last title, as he knew I had problems finding resources for it.	Chemotherapy is often coupled with radiotherapy so it would be hard to separate them. I wouldn't know if it was the chemotherapy or radiotherapy that was most effective. Plus I needed to think of whether to do the research in terms of alleviating pain or curing cancer.	I decided to do both chemo- and radiotherapy, and to do the research in terms of pain alleviation because I believe the responses I would get would be more interesting and make questionnaires easier to do.
Start researching	15/12/2016	Started researching and listed all websites I visited and the dates I visited them. I made a note of the websites I found most useful, to save time in the future.		
Continue research	16/12/2016 to 02/01/2017	I went to the school library to get more secondary sources. I made a list of all the books I looked at and made a copy of the pages useful to me.	Some books I found were outdated so the information may be outdated too.	I cross-referenced the information I found in the books with information found on the internet. If they disagreed with each other, I disregarded the information. I cross-checked the key information to make sure it was accurate and up to date.
Start writing possible questions for questionnaire	20/12/2016 06/01/2017 – Amended questions after nurse's advice	I started to compose a list of possible questions. I made sure they weren't too intrusive, refined them and produced the final questionnaire.	It was difficult to decide if some of the questions were too intrusive for the patients, as I didn't know the patients' conditions and what they had already experienced.	If I had to debate whether the questions were suitable or not, I decided it would be better to either change the question or take it out. I asked the nurse at my placement to check the questions. She suggested a couple of changes as the questions were too probing.
Write aim and objectives	15/01/2017 16/01/2017 – Had to rewrite	I broke down my aim, deciding what I needed to do to meet it. From that I was able to write the objectives.	The computer froze and I had to shut it down, managing to lose everything as I hadn't saved my work!	I had to rewrite the aim and objectives again, but this time I saved it as I went along.
Write up results from primary research questionnaires	22/02/2017 26/02/2017 – Now had software loaded	I started practising writing up the results for my primary research. I hadn't used spreadsheets yet and wanted to know I could use them. I created various spreadsheets based on the questionnaires I got back. I presented them as bar and pie charts to make my project interesting.	I didn't have the spreadsheet program on my home computer and the login for school didn't work because of a new system, so I was unable to start practising the write-up when I had planned to.	I downloaded new software on to my computer, which was similar to the spreadsheet program. But it took me a while to find the tools I needed, since it was all new to me and the layout was different to what I was used to. This proved especially difficult when creating graphs because the process was different, but after watching an online tutorial I managed.

The importance of producing the project record while carrying out various stages of the project

As you can see, Perla's project record is a working document. Perla updated it at every project stage, and as she encountered problems and found solutions.

It is vital to record issues and problems as and when they happen during the project. The project record provides evidence, for the assessor, of your problem-solving skills. If there have been issues that are not of your making then the project record should record these. You should also explain how you tried to overcome the issues.

Stretch activity

Why reviews are so important

For his project Bharti decided to look at the meals in a local residential home to see if they were healthy. Bharti produced a detailed original plan but he did not review it at all during the project. He encountered several problems during his research but these were not recorded in his plan.

Explain to Bharti why it is essential to have evidence of a review of his original plan and to record any consequent amendments made as a result of problems encountered.

To obtain and act on feedback while completing a project

Feedback is important during a project as it can help you to stay focussed and prevent time-wasting mistakes. Acting on feedback can keep you motivated, as you know you are going in the right direction with your research.

As can be seen in Table 10.6, Perla took advice from her health and social care teacher about her new project title. She had already chosen a title but she wanted to run it past him to see if he thought it was realistic. She was reassured by his response.

Perla also asked the nurse on her work placement if she would check her questionnaire. The nurse gave Perla the benefit of her

Case study: Isaac's refusal to act on feedback

Isaac has decided to focus his project on child abuse. He has decided to interview some children who were abused. His health and social care teacher tells him it is not a good idea as he will not be able to do a work placement with abused children (he is too young and inexperienced). Isaac has ignored this advice and started to write a questionnaire for abused children to answer.

Questions

1 Do you think Isaac is right to ignore his teacher's advice? Why, or why not?
2 Can you think of any other topics that might be difficult to work on?

experience and suggested a couple of changes. This advice positively altered the outcome of her questionnaire results – if the patients had thought the questions were too probing or intrusive, they might have refused to answer them and she would have had to rethink her questionnaire.

To keep records in order to look back and check progress

Regular monitoring is important to keep you focussed on the research question or hypothesis and mindful of the project deadlines. It is reassuring to look back and see how many tasks have been ticked off the list. This is a good indicator of the progress that has been made to date.

Keeping records can also help you identify any issues so that they can be addressed before they cause too much time to be wasted. For example, in Table 10.6, Perla had an issue with her home computer, which she solved before she wasted too much time.

To learn from work already completed and incorporate learning into the next stage of the project

As the project develops, you will gain many skills. Here are some examples.

- You will develop communication skills through writing a questionnaire, and through interviews and observations.
- You should become better at time management, decision making and problem solving.
- You may gain independence through carrying out the different parts of the project.
- Your literacy, numeracy and IT skills should improve.

All of these new skills can be transferred to other subject areas. They can also be used to further the progress of the project you are working on. For example, the improved literacy skills should mean better grammar, vocabulary and use of English in the finished report.

Know it!

1 List the usual order of content when writing up your project.
2 Explain why it is important to produce a project record while carrying out the project.
3 Outline why advice and feedback should be obtained and followed during the project process.
4 List three skills that could be developed throughout the course of the project.

Assessment guidance

Learning outcome 3: Be able to carry out projects

Marking criteria for LO3

Mark band 1	Mark band 2	Mark band 3
An attempt has been made to meet project objectives.	Some of the project objectives are met.	**Most** of the project objectives have been met.
The project record contains:	The project record contains:	The project record contains:
• a **basic** description and explanation of the development of the project	• a **sound** description and explanation of the development of the project	• a full and **clear** description and explanation of the development of the project
• **limited** evidence of review of the original plan and any consequent amendments made as a result of feedback	• **some** evidence of review of the original plan and any consequent amendments made as a result of problems encountered or feedback	• **clear** evidence of review of the original plan and any consequent amendments made as a result of problems encountered or feedback
• progress of project objectives are **partly** articulated	• project objectives are **mostly** articulated	• project objectives are **clearly** and fully articulated
• **limited** use made of technical language	• **some** use made of technical language	• **appropriate** and **accurate** use made of technical terminology
• **some** errors in spelling, punctuation and grammar, which may be sufficient to detract from the clarity of the record.	• **minor** errors in spelling, punctuation and grammar but insufficient to detract from the clarity of the record.	• **few**, if any, errors in spelling, punctuation and grammar so that the record is clear and coherent.
The information in the project record is **partly** relevant and presented in a format with a **basic** structure.	The information in the project record is **mostly** relevant and presented in a structured and **clear** format.	The information in the project record is relevant, clear, organised, and presented in a structured and **coherent** format.
Draws upon **limited** skills/knowledge/understanding from other units in the specification.	Draws upon **some relevant** skills/knowledge/understanding from other units in the specification.	**Clearly** draws upon **relevant** skills/knowledge/understanding from other units in the specification.

→

The OCR Model Assignment will ask you to:

- Produce a project record.
- Meet the project objectives.
- Give a description and explanation of the project development.
- Include evidence of review of the original plan and any amendments made as a result of problems encountered or feedback.
- Fully articulate your project objectives.
- Use technical terminology where project appropriate.
- Check the spelling, punctuation and grammar in your work to ensure your record is clear and coherent.
- Present information in your project record and ensure it is relevant, clear, organised and presented in a structured and coherent format.
- Draw on skills/knowledge/understanding from other units.

 What do the command words mean?

- **Most**: You will meet or fulfil the majority of the project objectives.
- **Full and clear description**: Your project record contains a complete, focussed and accurately expressed description and explanation of the development of the project.
- **Clear evidence**: The project record will contain focussed evidence of the review of the original plan and any consequent amendments made due to problems or feedback that you may have come across.
- **Clearly articulated**: The project objectives are focussed, accurately expressed, have no ambiguity and are fully articulated.
- **Appropriate and accurate**: Technical terminology that you use will be relevant to the purpose or task and accurate.
- **Few**: There will only be a small number of errors in spelling, punctuation and grammar in your work, if any, so that the record is clear and coherent.
- **Coherent format**: The information in the project record is relevant, clear, organised and presented in a structured, logical and consistent format.
- **Clearly draws upon relevant skills/knowledge/understanding from other units in the specification**: In a focussed way, you will draw upon skills/knowledge/understanding from other units in the specification that are also focussed on this activity.

You should check the glossary in the introduction for the definitions of each of the command words from OCR.

Learning outcome 4

Know how to review projects

To differentiate between the actual project outcome and the anticipated outcome

To differentiate between the actual project outcome and the anticipated outcome relates to the difference between what you thought would happen and what actually did happen.

The outcomes are the overall achievements of your project and whether the project accomplished what it intended to do. If the project has been well planned, with an achievable question, a realistic aim and objectives, then the actual outcome should be similar to the anticipated outcome. This is particularly true if the project has been monitored throughout the whole process.

However, this may not always be the case. For example, in Lola's study of finger puppets she obviously hoped that the children's social skills would improve. Perhaps they did not and the problem with the shyness was not solved by the puppets. This lack of change is the actual outcome rather than Lola's anticipated outcome of improving the children's social skills.

To differentiate between the actual process of completing the project and the planned process

Many factors can alter the planned process of completing a project. Here are a few examples, but you may be able to think of others.

- If the project question has been set without too much thought or research, then this can result in having to start the project again. This could cause timescales to be totally changed as you will be behind schedule before you start!
- There may be setbacks caused by poor organisation, for instance leaving it too late to find resources. Again, timescales would have to be adjusted to accommodate finding different resources.
- You may have planned the wrong primary research or your questionnaire does not provide the answers you thought it would. The primary data might have been more difficult to analyse than you thought it would be.
- Your questionnaire may have used closed questions throughout so no qualitative data is collected.
- Secondary resources may be hard to find or be out of date, so are unusable.
- You may not have found many resources, or checked their reliability.
- You may have difficulty using new software or have other IT issues, like Perla did (see Table 10.6).
- If you were relying on other people, were they reliable and available for interview when they said they would be? Or did they hold up the process by repeatedly cancelling appointments?
- Was time management an issue or had you produced a realistic time plan?
- Did you record all the references as and when they were used, or was time wasted trying to look back for them?

It is always difficult to estimate timeframes in a plan. Tasks can take longer than hoped and unexpected events can happen. For example, Perla's evaluation of her project said that she underestimated the length of time required for each task. This was because she had failed to factor in her mock GCSEs and other school commitments.

To describe what went well and what could be improved

All aspects of the project need to be examined in the evaluation section. Start from the very beginning of the project, work through all the processes and decide what could have been improved and what went well. Here are the types of questions you could ask yourself.

- Did the initial stages of choosing a project topic take too long?
- Was too much time spent narrowing the topic down to the final question/hypothesis?
- Was the question answerable?
- Were others supportive of the ideas?
- Was your time well planned?
- Were the aims and objectives achieved?
- Was the secondary research carried out thoroughly?
- Was the primary research chosen to collect evidence to meet the question/hypothesis?
- Did you fill in the project progress plan regularly?
- Were plans adapted when lessons were learned?
- Was feedback obtained and acted on?
- Were the resources checked for reliability?
- Was Harvard referencing used for the bibliography?

 Case study: Frankie's review

Frankie has just finished her project. She feels it went so well that she does not need to review it, as she cannot think of any improvements she needs to make.

Questions

1 Do you think Frankie can leave out the evaluation section of her project? Why, or why not?
2 What advice would you give to Frankie?

To review the actual project timescale compared to the planned timescale

As discussed above, it is difficult to estimate exact timescales when you plan out your time at the start of the project. For various reasons, there are likely to be changes to the original plan as you work through the tasks.

Review any issues as they happen and adjust timescales accordingly, rather than leaving this to the end of the project.

For further ideas regarding time see the section above entitled 'To differentiate between the actual process of completing the project and the planned process'.

To measure the project against its objectives

Measuring the project against its objectives is a good way to identify how successful it has been. If the project is well planned, then the objectives should help you to achieve your aim. For example, in LO1, Lola hoped to observe the two children in group sessions to see how they interacted with the other children. She then wanted to introduce the children to the puppets to see if they helped them in social situations. If these and her other objectives were achieved then the project could be said to be successful.

However, it is insufficient for the review just to say that the objectives were achieved. There must be an explanation and justification for each objective

 Group activity

Lola's project

The parents of the children taking part in Lola's project decided to withdraw the children from the project at the last minute. It was too late for Lola to find other children to take part.

In small groups, discuss the following.

1 Do you think Lola's project will now be unsuccessful? Or can she redeem the project because she has put a lot of effort into recording all aspects of her work?
2 What advice would you give Lola?

to say how it was achieved. Detailed reasons should be given if objectives were not achieved.

To describe the learning achieved as a result of completing the project

As we have discussed, completing a project develops a lot of new skills as well as existing ones. You may have learned how to:

- monitor your own progress and adjust your project plan accordingly
- prioritise to ensure certain tasks were completed before others
- organise yourself and the progress of the project
- problem solve if things did not go according to plan
- communicate with individuals outside of school
- work independently
- act on constructive criticism to change plans, for example questions in questionnaires
- use different IT packages
- write up a project report
- think creatively by exploring your own ideas
- show self-motivation by carrying through the project
- research and make effective use of the materials found
- review and evaluate your own work
- benefit from your own experiences, both successful and not so successful

- write references, using the Harvard method
- manage your time effectively
- gain confidence in your own ability.

Can you think of anything else you have learned from completing the project?

Stretch activity

Review your work

Produce a review of a piece of coursework you have completed, with an indication of how it went and what could be improved.

(Aim for a **thorough** review with a **clear** indication of what went well and what could be improved. Look at the command word definitions to see what **thorough** and **clear** mean in the assessment.)

Know it!

1 Why might your planned timescales have to be adjusted once the project is under way?
2 List three questions you could ask to help determine what went well and what could be improved while carrying out this project.
3 Describe three things that you would hope to learn from carrying out this project.
4 Outline what is important to include in your writing when you are measuring a project against its objectives.

Assessment guidance

Learning outcome 4: Know how to review projects

Marking criteria for LO4

Mark band 1	Mark band 2	Mark band 3
Produces a **basic** review of the project, which makes **limited** reference back to the project objectives and identifies **some** issues but with a **limited** attempt to identify solutions.	Produces a **sound** review of the project, which makes **some** reference back to the project objectives and shows **some** indication of what went well and what could have been improved.	Produces a **thorough** review of the project, which refers back to the project objectives with a **clear** indication of what went well and what could have been improved.
Demonstrates a **limited** understanding of the learning achieved as a result of completing the project, with a **limited** understanding of the process.	Demonstrates **some** understanding of the learning achieved as a result of completing the project, with **some** understanding of the process.	Demonstrates a **clear** understanding of the learning achieved as a result of completing the project, with clear understanding of the process.

→

The OCR Model Assignment will ask you to:

- Produce a review of the project that refers to the project objectives, indicating what went well and what could have been improved.
- Show an understanding of the learning you achieved by completing the project, showing a clear understanding of the process.

 What do the command words mean?

- **Thorough review**: You will produce a review of the project that is extremely attentive to accuracy and detail and which refers back to the project objectives.
- **Clear indication**: There will be a focussed and accurately expressed indication of what went well and what could have been improved.
- **Clear understanding**: Your writing gives an accurately expressed account of what you have learned as a result of completing the project, i.e. you are able to accurately express your understanding of the process.

You should check the glossary in the introduction for the definitions of each of the command words from OCR.

Read about it

Weblinks

www.ons.gov.uk Office for National Statistics – census, demographic, economic, social statistics, etc.

http://library.bcu.ac.uk/learner/writingguides/1.02%20Reports.htm Guidance on how to write a report

www2.le.ac.uk/offices/ld/resources/writing/writing-resources/reports Guidance on writing a report

Reference books

Bell, J. and Waters, S. (2014) *Doing Your Research Project: A Guide for First-time Researchers* (6th edn). Open University Press.

Denscombe, M. (2014) *The Good Research Guide: For Small-scale Social Research Projects* (5th edn). Open University Press.

Mukherji, P. (2014) *Research Methods in Early Childhood* (2nd edn). Sage Publications.

Pears, R. and Shields, G. (2016) *Cite Them Right: The Essential Referencing Guide* (Palgrave Study Skills) (10th edn). Palgrave.

Thomas, G. (2013) *How To Do Your Research Project*. Sage Publications.

R031 Using basic first aid procedures

About this unit

In an **emergency** situation, would you know what to do? Sometimes a qualified first aider is not available, so it is useful for everyone to be aware of the standard response procedures that should be followed to protect casualties, yourself and others. Basic knowledge of first aid procedures can make a big difference in any emergency situation.

By studying this unit you will find out how to assess the scene of an accident and what immediate actions should be taken. You will learn about the information that it is important for the emergency services to have.

You will also learn about the different types of health emergency that can occur in health and social care and develop an understanding of how to carry out first aid procedures for those health

emergencies. You will have the opportunity to demonstrate basic first aid procedures.

Studying this unit does not make you a qualified first aider, but it will help to develop your confidence, and your knowledge and understanding of what should be done if you ever experience an emergency situation. If you wish to become a first aider, you will need to complete a first aid course provided by an organisation such as the British Red Cross or St John Ambulance. Your work for this unit can only be evidenced in the context of adult first aid, not with children. Information about practical first aid procedures must be delivered by a suitable qualified first aider, that is, someone who is the holder of a current first aid certificate and is a qualified teacher or trainer.

Learning outcomes

LO1: Be able to assess scenes of accidents to identify risks and continuing dangers

LO2: Understand the first aid procedures for a range of injuries

LO3: Be able to apply basic first aid procedures

Key term

Emergency An unexpected event that needs prompt action.

How will I be assessed?

You will be assessed through a series of assignment tasks, which are set by OCR. The assignment will be marked by your tutor and then moderated by OCR.

For LO1, you will be able to:

- demonstrate how to assess dangers to the casualty, first aider and others at the scene of an accident
- consider how the area can be made safe
- demonstrate obtaining informed consent
- demonstrate an understanding of how to communicate clearly
- describe when and how to seek additional support, and why the people you are reporting to are appropriate
- provide detailed, appropriate information to emergency services.

For LO2, you need to:

- demonstrate understanding of how to identify the nature and severity of a range of injuries, and be able to list the possible causes

- describe symptoms that relate to the injury, with examples to illustrate practical understanding
- describe the current first aid procedures, giving information on the correct sequence of steps
- provide a rationale for the procedures you recommend, with examples to illustrate understanding.

For LO3, you will be able to:

- apply basic first aid procedures
- carry out the steps involved in certain first aid procedures, demonstrating understanding of practical application
- provide a review of your practical activities and consider your competency
- describe your strengths and weaknesses, and suggest improvements relevant to your performance
- draw on relevant skills/knowledge/ understanding from other units in the specification.

Note: SPAG is assessed in this learning outcome.

Make sure you refer to the current OCR specification and guidance.

Links to other units

Unit R021: Essential values of care for use with individuals in care settings (LO4): You could explain how your knowledge of how personal hygiene and emergency procedures protect individuals in care settings has helped you to apply first aid procedures safely and hygienically.

Unit R022: Communicating and working with individuals in health, social care and early years settings (LO1): You could explain how you used your verbal skills such as tone of voice, empathy and clarity when administering first aid procedures; and also when calling the emergency services.

Unit R023 (optional unit): Understanding body systems and disorders (LO2): You could explain how you used your understanding of special dietary requirements for different dietary conditions to help explain links between disorders and the functioning of the digestive system.

Learning outcome 1

Be able to assess scenes of accidents to identify risks and continuing dangers

Getting started

In small groups, do the following.

- Suggest some personal qualities or skills needed to deal with an emergency situation.
- Discuss whether you have ever been in an emergency situation, either helping to give **first aid** or receiving it.

Share with the rest of the class.

How to assess the scene of an accident within health, social care or early years settings

In an emergency it is important to act calmly and quickly. As Figure 11.1 illustrates, there are four main steps to follow.

Figure 11.1 What to do in an emergency

Assess the situation

Before approaching the **casualty**, and before any first aid help can be given, look around the scene of the incident. You must quickly check for any potential danger to the casualty or anyone else at the scene.

Dangers could include tripping hazards such as fallen objects, furniture or water spills. There might be sharp objects such as knives (if someone has cut themselves preparing food), or hot cooker hobs and boiling water, which can cause burns or scalds. An accident could result in chemical spills, electrocution **risks**, a fire or gas leaks. Moving traffic and fuel spills could be hazards if there is an accident on the road.

In any emergency situation, consider the following.

- Are there any bystanders who could help?
- Does anyone appear to be in a life-threatening condition?
- Is professional help needed, e.g. police to manage traffic, an ambulance, a qualified first aider?
- Is there a first aid kit available?

Make the area safe

You should try to make the area safe appropriately before giving first aid. If possible, quickly remove any hazards, without putting yourself in danger.

- You need to check the area around the casualty. This could be as simple as moving a sharp knife or a fallen chair out of the way, or switching off a cooker or a plug socket.
- If it is a car accident, turn off the ignition to reduce the risk of a spark causing a fire. Ask bystanders to warn approaching traffic (standing in a safe place), put out a warning triangle and call an ambulance.
- If someone has been electrocuted and is still in contact with the source of electricity, switch it off at the mains or plug socket. Alternatively, stand on wood, a plastic mat or a telephone directory, and with a wooden broom push the casualty's limb away from the electrical source. Do not touch the casualty as they could be 'live' and you would risk being electrocuted.

Give emergency aid

If there is more than one casualty, they need to be assessed to decide who is a priority for treatment. Anyone with a life-threatening condition should be treated immediately.

Key terms

First aid Urgent treatment given to an individual who has suffered a sudden injury or an unexpected health problem.

Casualty Someone who has suffered an injury.

Risk Something that could cause harm to individuals.

Key terms

Conscious Awake and aware of surroundings.
Airway The passageway through which air reaches a person's lungs.
Pulse The pumping action of the heart that can be felt at the wrist or neck.

The key signs that need to be checked are:

- Are they **conscious**?
- Is their **airway** open?
- Do they have a **pulse**?

Get help

Call 999 in a medical emergency – in other words, when someone is seriously ill or injured and their life is at risk.

Medical emergencies include:

- heart attacks
- strokes
- serious head injuries
- loss of consciousness
- someone in a very confused state
- fits that are not stopping
- persistent, severe chest pain
- breathing difficulties
- severe bleeding that cannot be stopped
- severe allergic reactions
- severe burns or scalds.

For minor injuries, a qualified first aider, if one is available, will be able to provide treatment, and will be able to assess whether a trip to a GP, a walk-in centre or a hospital is necessary.

For other injuries, 999 should be called to obtain urgent medical help. Dialling 999 does not always result in an ambulance being sent; the call handler will decide what is needed.

Response units that could be sent include:

- an emergency ambulance
- a rapid response vehicle or motorbike

Case study: A cycling accident

As you are walking home you see a cycling accident. A man stops to help the cyclist, who appears to be injured. You also decide to assist.

Assess the scene of the cycling accident shown in Figure 11.2, then answer the questions below.

Figure 11.2 A cycling accident – assessing the scene

Questions

1 What are the dangers to the casualty and others at the scene?
2 How can the area be made safe?
3 Do you need to call 999? Why, or why not?

- a community first responder
- a combination of the above.

How to obtain informed consent when possible

Consent means that permission is given for something to happen. For consent to be 'informed', the person giving permission needs to be provided with information so that they understand what they are giving consent for, what is going to happen and why. When dealing with a casualty, it is important that you obtain 'informed consent' when possible before starting to give first aid.

If the casualty is conscious it helps to establish trust if you introduce yourself, and offer help and assistance. As mentioned above, always ask permission before starting any first aid procedures, explaining what you need to do and asking if it is OK to help. The casualty is then informed about what will happen and knows what treatment they are giving consent for. The casualty should be treated with dignity and respect, and you should always say what you are going to do before you do it. Give choices, such as asking if they need help to sit up or lie down. Remain calm and do not try to do anything without explaining first. You should also try to honestly answer any questions they may have.

How to communicate clearly

Effective communication can be achieved by treating people as individuals with different needs. For example, simple words are needed for a child; if someone speaks a different language you may need to use gestures and body language. It is important to communicate with all the appropriate people at the scene of an accident; in other words not just the casualty but also the bystanders and the emergency services or first aider.

It is vital to help the casualty understand what is happening and to reassure them so that they remain calm. Figure 11.3 shows different ways to communicate effectively with a casualty.

Figure 11.3 How can you communicate effectively with a casualty?

Group activity

Role play: good communication

Work in pairs. Sit back to back with your partner.

Learner 1

Think of an incident scenario where first aid is necessary. You are the casualty and your partner will offer first aid.

Learner 2

Playing the role of a first aider, find out what has happened to learner 1 and what type of injury they have.

Use effective communication skills such as listening, questioning and reassurance to demonstrate the importance of listening and talking effectively to gain the information needed.

Reverse the roles and use another scenario.

Afterwards, give each other feedback on your communication skills as a first aider.

When and how to seek additional support/report issues to the appropriate people

Earlier in this section, we covered what might constitute a medical emergency and the key signs to check for if you think the casualty is in a life-threatening condition.

We also looked at how to seek additional support if casualties are injured. If you need to call the emergency services, it is important to listen carefully so you clearly answer any questions with the correct information. The emergency services need this information to get to the scene quickly and to be as well prepared for the casualty as possible. The next section looks at how to provide appropriate information to the emergency services.

How to provide information to emergency services

When you call 999, the information you give to the call handler enables them to provide the appropriate response as quickly as possible.

It is vital that you stay calm and listen carefully so that you can clearly give the information the call handler needs.

What information to give

Table 11.1 summarises the information you should provide to the emergency services and why it is important.

Table 11.1 999: what do I have to tell the call handler?

Information	Why it is important
Exact location/address and postcode if known	So they can find you quickly.
Your telephone number	In case they need to ring you back.
The name of the person making the call	So they have a contact person, and to check it's not a hoax call.
Type of emergency: ● exactly what has happened (road traffic accident, heart attack fall at a care home or down stairs, garden accident with hedge cutters, etc.) ● how many casualties	So appropriate help can be provided/appropriate advice given over the telephone.
Age, gender and current condition of the casualty: ● Are they awake/conscious/breathing? ● Is there any serious bleeding or chest pain?	To inform paramedics and help them prepare if the casualty is in a life-threatening condition.
Details of the injury and how it happened	Broken limb, heart attack, asthma attack, bleeding cut, etc.
Fire/leaking gas or other hazards	So that other emergency services can be alerted.
Name of casualty	So they can be identified on arrival, and so they can look up medical notes.

Stretch activity

What should I say?

Revisit the case study earlier in this section and look again at Figure 11.2. The man who is helping the injured cyclist tells you that he thinks she may have broken her leg. He asks you to call an ambulance.

1 Write a script for your call to the emergency services. The script should provide all the information that the emergency services would need.

2 Explain why each piece of information is needed, so that you know how to provide **thorough** and **wholly** appropriate information to emergency services.

(Look at the command word definitions to see what **thorough** and **wholly** mean in the assessment.)

Know it!

1 List the four main steps to follow in an emergency situation where someone has been injured.

2 Give three examples of how to make the area at the scene of an accident safe.

3 Give two examples of injuries or conditions for which assistance from the emergency services would be urgently required.

4 State four pieces of information you should give when calling the emergency services, and explain why each piece of information is needed.

5 What is the meaning of 'informed consent'?

Assessment guidance

Learning outcome 1: Be able to assess scenes of accidents to identify risks and continuing dangers

Marking criteria for LO1 Part A

Mark band 1	Mark band 2	Mark band 3
Requires guidance and support when demonstrating how to assess dangers to the casualty, first aider and others at the scene of an accident. **Basic** consideration is given on how the area can be made safe, which demonstrates **limited** understanding.	Requires **limited** guidance and support when demonstrating how to assess dangers to the casualty, first aider and others at the scene of an accident. **Clear** consideration is given on how the area can be made safe, which demonstrates **sound** understanding.	**Independently** demonstrates how to assess dangers to the casualty, first aider and others at the scene of an accident **Thorough** consideration is given on how the area can be made safe, which demonstrates **thorough** understanding.

The OCR Model Assignment will ask you to:

- Give a practical demonstration of how to assess the scene of an accident.
- Include some supplementary written work about how to make the area safe.

What do the command words mean?

- **Independently demonstrate**: Without relying on others, you will show how to assess dangers to the casualty, first aider and others at the scene of an accident.
- **Thorough consideration**: You will consider how the area can be made safe and this will be extremely attentive to accuracy and detail.
- **Thorough understanding**: You will demonstrate an understanding of all of this which will be extremely attentive to accuracy and detail.

You should check the glossary in the Introduction for the definitions of each of the command words from OCR.

Marking criteria for LO1 Part B

Mark band 1	Mark band 2	Mark band 3
Demonstrates **limited** confidence when obtaining informed consent. Demonstrates **basic** understanding of how to communicate clearly. Provides a **basic** description of when and how to seek additional support, with a **basic** description of why the people they are reporting to are appropriate. Provides **limited** information to emergency services, which is **partly** appropriate.	Demonstrates **confidence** when obtaining informed consent. Demonstrates **sound** understanding of how to communicate clearly. Provides a **detailed** description of when and how to seek additional support, with a **detailed** description of why the people they are reporting to are appropriate. Provides **detailed** information to emergency services, which is **mostly** appropriate.	Demonstrates **confidence and competence** when obtaining informed consent. Demonstrates **thorough** understanding of how to communicate clearly. Provides a **thorough** description of when and how to seek additional support, with a **thorough** description of why the people they are reporting to are appropriate. Provides **thorough** information to emergency services, which is **wholly** appropriate.

→

The OCR Model Assignment will ask you to:

- Give a practical demonstration of using good communication skills to obtain informed consent before starting first aid procedures.
- Write a description of when, how and from whom to get additional support and a description of why the people they are reporting to are appropriate.
- Give a practical demonstration of providing information to the emergency services.

 What do the command words mean?

- **Demonstrates confidence and competence**: You will demonstrate certainty and evidence that meets the necessary standard for the task when obtaining informed consent.
- **Thorough understanding**: Your demonstration shows that you understand how to communicate clearly and this understanding is attentive to accuracy and detail.
- **Thorough description**: Your work will include a description that is attentive to accuracy and detail about when and how to seek or find additional support. You will also include a description of why the people you report to are appropriate, which will also show that you are attentive to accuracy and detail.
- **Thorough information**: You will provide extremely accurate and detailed information that is required by the emergency services.
- **Wholly appropriate**: The information you provide will be completely appropriate.

You should check the glossary in the Introduction for the definitions of each of the command words from OCR.

Learning outcome 2

Understand the first aid procedures for a range of injuries

Getting started

What do you think is meant by the term 'first aid'? Discuss with a partner and then share your thoughts with the rest of the group.

First aid procedures: ABC check and recovery position

The aims of first aid are to:

- preserve life – your own, the casualty's and bystanders'
- prevent deterioration – stop the casualty getting worse
- promote recovery – help them get better.

ABC check

After checking an accident scene for danger (covered in LO1) you should carry out an 'ABC' check, unless the casualty is conscious and talking (if this is the case you know that their airway and breathing are ok).

- **A = Airway**: check for any obstruction in the mouth or throat (such as a piece of food, a foreign object or the tongue) that is stopping breathing. If the airway is not cleared the individual will not be able to breathe. Open the airway by tilting the head back, placing your fingertips on the point of their chin and lifting the chin.
- **B = Breathing**: look for chest movements and listen for breathing sounds. You can feel air being exhaled by putting your cheek close to the casualty's mouth. If the casualty is breathing, put them into the recovery position (described below), which will keep their airway open and clear.

Research activity

Finding out about CPR

1 Watch this St John Ambulance video clip which shows how to give CPR: www.sja.org.uk/sja/first-aid-advice/loss-of-responsiveness/unresponsive-not-breathing/adult.aspx.

2 Write a set of step-by-step instructions for giving CPR.

Key terms

CPR Cardiopulmonary resuscitation – i.e. giving someone chest compressions to keep their heart and circulation going, in order to save their life. Can also be done in combination with 'rescue breaths' by first aiders trained to do this.

Unconscious Unresponsive to any sound or touch.

- **C = Circulation**: now you need to check that the casualty has got a pulse. Check this at the wrist or neck. Are there any life-threatening injuries affecting circulation, such as severe bleeding? If there is no breathing or pulse, **CPR** chest compressions will need to be carried out to keep the person alive until the emergency services arrive.

Recovery position

If a casualty is **unconscious** but breathing they should be put in the recovery position, unless there is a suspected spine or neck injury, or other life-threatening condition, in which case the casualty should not be moved. The recovery position keeps the casualty's airway clear and open, and also prevents them choking on any vomit.

Figure 11.4 and the text below, adapted from the NHS Choices website, show how to put someone in the recovery position.

- Once the casualty is lying on their back, kneel on the floor at one side of them.

Figure 11.4 How to put someone in the recovery position

- As the photograph shows, place the arm nearest you at a right angle to their body, with their hand upwards. This will keep it out of the way when you roll them over.
- Tuck their other hand under the side of their head. The back of their hand should be touching their cheek.
- Bend the knee furthest from you at a right angle.
- Carefully pull on the bent knee and roll the person on to their side, facing you. Their top arm should be supporting the head and their bottom arm will stop you rolling them too far.
- Move the bent leg, which is nearest you, away from their body so it is resting on the floor.
- Gently tilt the person's head back and lift their chin, in order to open their airway. Check that nothing is blocking their airway.
- Monitor the casualty's condition until help arrives.

How to identify the nature and severity of a range of injuries, the current first aid procedures for the injuries and the rationale

In this section, Tables 11.2–11.7 outline first aid procedures for a range of common injuries and health emergencies.

Conscious, unconscious and breathing or not breathing

Whether a casualty is conscious and breathing, or not, will help to identify the **severity** of an injury, as Table 11.2 shows.

Group activity

Can you put someone in the recovery position?

Watch the video clip on this web page, which provides guidance on how to put someone into the recovery position: www.nhs.uk/Conditions/Accidents-and-first-aid/Pages/The-recovery-position.aspx

- In small groups, take it in turns to put one another in the recovery position, as shown in Figure 11.4, and described in the text and video.
- If you are observing, provide feedback on technique – how well did everyone do?
- Create a flow chart that shows the correct sequence for putting someone in the recovery position.

 Key terms

Severity How serious an injury is (i.e. is it life threatening, a minor superficial injury, or something in between?).

Hypoglycaemia A condition that occurs due to a lack of glucose in the bloodstream, which is essential for proper brain function. Symptoms include sweating, nausea, pale colour, being cold to the touch and unconsciousness.

AED Automated external defibrillator, which is used by qualified first aiders to deliver electric shocks to a casualty whose heart has stopped.

Rationale A set of reasons for a course of action.

Table 11.2 First aid procedure when assessing consciousness and breathing

Possible causes	Heart attack, shock, severe bleeding, drowning, choking, stroke, head injury, electric shock, alcohol poisoning, **hypoglycaemia**, etc.	
What should you do first?	• Find out whether the casualty is conscious or unconscious by gently shaking their shoulders. • Say 'What's happened?' or 'Open your eyes'. • Speak loudly and clearly.	
Severity	• Life threatening if unconscious and not breathing. • If conscious and breathing, severity depends on the nature of the injury.	
Symptoms	• Unresponsive and no movement if unconscious • Shallow, rapid breaths and unconscious • Responds normally to sound and to touch if conscious	
Correct sequence of steps	If the casualty is conscious …	• Check for injuries and place in the recovery position.
	If the casualty is unconscious …	• Check their airway, breathing and circulation (ABC check). • Shout for help and call 999.
	If the casualty is breathing …	• Check for injuries and place them in the recovery position.
	If you think the casualty may not be breathing …	• Open the airway by tilting the head back, placing fingertips on the point of their chin and lifting the chin. • Look and listen for no more than 10 seconds for signs of chest movement, and feel for breaths on your cheek; check for pulse.
	If the casualty is not breathing and has no pulse …	• Obtain and use an **AED** if available. • Begin CPR with chest compressions; continue until the emergency services arrive and take over.
Rationale	The aim is to: • prevent unconsciousness (tilt head to open the airway) • detect shock developing (by monitoring breathing and pulse) • keep airway open, and maintain circulation and breathing (recovery position) • ensure any vomit or fluid will not cause choking (recovery position) • enable breathing (AED/CPR) • transfer to hospital for specialist treatment if necessary (call 999).	

Research activity

What is the Heimlich manoeuvre?

The photograph in Figure 11.5 shows a lady who is choking. The person helping her is carrying out the Heimlich manoeuvre.

1 Find out what the Heimlich manoeuvre involves and how it can help someone who is choking.

2 An interesting starting point could be this BBC News article and video about Dr Heimlich saving the life of a choking woman with the manoeuvre he invented: www.bbc.co.uk/news/world-us-canada-36400365

Figure 11.5 The Heimlich manoeuvre

Choking

Table 11.3 outlines the first aid procedure for choking.

Table 11.3 First aid procedure for choking

Possible causes	A foreign object (e.g. food, peanut, fish bone, small toy) that gets stuck in the throat, blocks it and prevents breathing.	
Severity	• If mild, the casualty may be able to clear the blockage. • If severe, the casualty will be unable to speak, cough or breathe, and will eventually lose consciousness.	
Symptoms	• Coughing, spluttering and gasping for breath • Difficulty in speaking, coughing and breathing	
Correct sequence of steps	Encourage casualty to cough	• If the casualty can breathe, give them encouragement to cough in order to move the obstruction. • If this is not successful, go to next step.
	Give up to five back slaps	• If the casualty is unable to cough or breathe, bend them forward and give five sharp blows with the heel of your hand between their shoulder blades; check the casualty's mouth. • Then move to next stage.
	Give up to five abdominal thrusts	• Stand behind the casualty; put both arms around them; put one fist between their navel and the bottom of their breastbone; grasp your fist with your other hand and pull sharply inwards and upwards; repeat up to five times. • Re-check the mouth.
	Repeat and then if necessary call for emergency help	• Repeat the back blows and then the abdominal thrusts until the obstruction clears. • If after three repeats it has still not cleared, call 999. • Continue the cycles of repeats until help arrives or until the casualty loses consciousness.
	If casualty loses consciousness	• Open the airway – tilt head back, lift the chin and check breathing; give CPR.
Rationale	The aim is to: • dislodge and remove the obstruction (through coughing, back blows or abdominal thrusts) • enable breathing and prevent unconsciousness (tilt head and open the airway) • transfer to hospital for specialist treatment if thrusts are unsuccessful (call 999) • re-start breathing (CPR).	

An asthma attack

Table 11.4 outlines the first aid procedure for an asthma attack.

Table 11.4 First aid procedure for an asthma attack

Possible causes	Triggers can be allergies, a cold, cigarette smoke, poor air quality	
Severity	• A mild attack may need an inhaler. • A severe attack may cause exhaustion. • If the attack worsens the casualty may stop breathing and lose consciousness.	
Symptoms	• Difficulty in breathing, especially out • Wheezing and difficulty in speaking • Cyanosis (grey-blue colouring in skin, lips, earlobes and nail-beds) • Distress and anxiety	
Correct sequence of steps	Help casualty use inhaler	• If this is the first attack and the casualty has not got an inhaler, call 999 immediately. • If the casualty is unconscious, check airway and breathing. • If the casualty has an inhaler, keep calm and reassure them; sit them down; help them to find and use the inhaler; this should take effect within minutes.
	Encourage slow breaths	• Help the casualty into a comfortable breathing position, sitting slightly forwards. • Within a few minutes a mild attack should ease; if it does not, ask the casualty to take another dose from the inhaler.
	Call for emergency help	• Call 999 if the inhaler has no effect, breathlessness makes talking difficult, or the casualty is becoming exhausted.
	Monitor casualty	• Monitor the casualty's vital signs (level of response, breathing and pulse) until they recover or the emergency service arrives. • Help them to use their inhaler as required.
	If casualty loses consciousness	• Open the airway and check breathing. • Give CPR.
Rationale	The aim is to: • ease breathing (use of inhaler, move to comfortable breathing position) • detect shock developing (by monitoring breathing and pulse) • enable breathing and prevent unconsciousness (administer inhaler/move to comfortable breathing position) • transfer to hospital for specialist treatment if necessary (call 999).	

Burns or scalds

Table 11.5 outlines the first aid procedure for burns or scalds.

Table 11.5 First aid procedure for burns or scalds

Possible causes	• Dry burn: fire, contact with hot objects (e.g. saucepan, oven, cigarettes); friction (e.g. rope burns) • Scald: steam/boiling water, hot liquids such as tea or coffee, or hot fat • Electrical burns: current from electrical appliances • Cold injury: frostbite, contact with freezing meals, or vapours such as liquid nitrogen • Chemical burn: paint stripper, oven cleaner • Radiation burn: sunburn, sunlamp overexposure
Severity	• Could range from minor burns/scalds to major life-threatening burns/scalds
Symptoms	• Pain • Reddening, swelling or blistering of the skin • Areas of superficial, partial thickness or full-thickness skin damage • Breathing difficulties, if airway is affected • Signs of shock

→

Correct sequence of steps	Start to cool the burn	• Help the casualty be comfortable by aiding them to sit or lie down.
		• Flood the injury with cold water; cool for at least 10 minutes or until pain is relieved.
	Call for emergency help	• Call 999 for help if necessary; tell the ambulance control that the injury is a burn, explain what caused it, the size and depth of the burn.
	Remove any constrictions	• While cooling the burn, remove any clothing or jewellery from the area before the area starts to swell.
		• Do not remove anything that is stuck to the burn; do not touch the burn or burst any blisters.
	Cover burn	• Cover the burn with kitchen film placed lengthways over the injury, or use a plastic bag.
		• Monitor the casualty's level of response, breathing and pulse for signs of shock while waiting for help.
Rationale	The aim is to:	
	• stop the burning and remove the pain (cool injury with running cold water)	
	• minimise the risk of infection and prevent further damage (nothing that is sticking to the burn should be removed, blisters should not be burst and the burn should not be touched; instead cover with cling film)	
	• minimise the risk of shock (monitor consciousness, breathing, pulse)	
	• transfer to hospital for specialist treatment if necessary (call 999).	

Bleeding

Table 11.6 outlines the first aid procedure for bleeding.

Table 11.6 First aid procedure for bleeding

Possible causes	• Incised wound: straight cut from a sharp-edged object, e.g. knife
	• Stab wound: knife penetrating the body
	• Puncture wound: standing on a nail or other sharp object (which may be embedded), pricked by a needle
	• Graze: caused by a fall
Severity	• Incised wound: could be a straight, deep cut; stitches may be needed; blood vessels cut straight across so the bleeding can be profuse; tendons or nerves may be damaged
	• Stab: danger of injury to vital organs; life threatening
	• Puncture: could be deep; dirt and germs could be introduced; high infection risk
	• Graze: usually superficial, raw and tender; if there are embedded particles they may cause infection
Correct sequence of steps	Apply direct pressure to the wound	• Use a sterile wound dressing.
		• Apply firm pressure with palm of hand; add another dressing if blood seeps through.
	Raise and support the arm	• While maintaining pressure on the wound, raise the arm above the level of the heart.
	Lay casualty down	• Help the casualty lie down with their legs raised.
	Bandage dressing in place	• Secure a pad over the wound with a bandage.
		• Check circulation around the bandage every 10 minutes; loosen and reapply if necessary.
	Continue to apply direct pressure to the wound	• Reapply a new sterile wound dressing if the blood continues to seep through.
		• Apply firm pressure with palm of hand; add another dressing if blood seeps through.
	Call for emergency help	• Call 999 if bleeding cannot be controlled; give the address; inform them about what has happened, the position of the cut, how much it is still bleeding and whether the casualty is conscious and breathing.
		• Keep monitoring breathing and pulse until emergency help arrives.

→

Rationale	The aim is to: ● control bleeding (applying pressure on either side if there is an object in the wound) ● control blood flow (by raising the arm) ● prevent or minimise the risk of shock (by laying the casualty down) ● detect shock developing (by monitoring breathing and pulse) ● make sure no food or drink is provided for the casualty (in case anaesthetic needs to be given) ● minimise infection or cross-infection (sterile dressing) ● transfer to hospital for specialist treatment if necessary (call 999).

Stretch activity

What would you do?

James, aged 85, is preparing a meal. He has arthritis in his hands, which makes it difficult for him to hold a knife. As Figure 11.6 shows, his hand slips and he cuts himself. His left hand is now bleeding very heavily.

You are visiting James and arrive just after he has cut his hand. Give a detailed description of your first aid response. Make sure you include the following information.

● What type of cut is it?

● How serious is the cut?

● How would you treat the wound? Give step-by-step instructions in the correct order.

● Give detailed reasons for each of the steps in your treatment of the cut.

● Would you seek additional support? Why, or why not?

Figure 11.6 A kitchen accident

(The rationale will be **thorough** with **detailed** examples to illustrate understanding. Look at the command word definitions to see what **detailed** and **thorough** mean in the assessment.)

Shock

Table 11.7 outlines the first aid procedure for shock.

Table 11.7 First aid procedure for shock

Possible causes	● When you are in shock, the circulatory system fails so vital organs are deprived of oxygen. ● Causes can be severe trauma (e.g. severe burns), severe blood loss (which can be external or internal), allergic reaction (e.g. anaphylactic shock), severe vomiting and diarrhoea, causing fluid loss, hypothermia, heart attack, acute heart failure and drug overdose.
Severity	● Can be life threatening, as vital organs do not get enough oxygen due to reduced blood circulation resulting from trauma →

Symptoms	• Rapid pulse and sweating; skin is pale, cold and clammy
	Other possible symptoms:
	• rapid and shallow breathing
	• grey-blue skin (cyanosis), especially inside the lips
	• when a fingernail or earlobe is pressed it will not regain its colour immediately
	• weakness and dizziness
	• low blood pressure
	• weak pulse
	• nausea and vomiting
	• thirst
	• loss of consciousness.

Correct sequence of steps	Treat any possible cause of shock	• Treat injury, bleeding, burns, etc.
	Get the casualty into a position that is appropriate for the type of shock they have	• For example, for physiological shock help the casualty to lie down on their back, with legs raised and supported; for anaphylactic shock, help the casualty to sit up if they are having trouble breathing. • Keep the casualty's head low.
	Loosen tight clothing	• Loosen any constricting clothing that could affect the blood flow.
	Keep casualty warm	• Cover the casualty with, ideally, a blanket.
	Call for emergency help	• Call 999 giving ambulance control full details of the situation, including the cause of shock if known.
	Monitor vital signs until help arrives	• Monitor the level of response, breathing and pulse.
Rationale	The aim is to:	
	• treat the cause appropriately (sitting or lying, depending on the type of shock)	
	• improve the blood flow, minimising the risk of shock developing (by lying the casualty down with raised legs, head low and loosened clothing)	
	• reduce the risk of losing consciousness (by keeping the head low)	
	• keep warm, minimise effects of shock (cover with a blanket)	
	• make sure no food or drink is provided for the casualty (in case anaesthetic needs to be given).	

 Case study: Students save the day

Teenagers Ella, Isaac and Ria are walking home from school when they see a lady in her sixties fall to the ground.

Fortunately, the teenagers have recently been on a first aid course and are able to use the skills they have learned. Isaac runs to find a first aid kit and Ria uses her mobile phone to call 999. Ella starts to help the lady, Fatima, who is slipping in and out of consciousness.

Ella controls the blood coming from a head wound Fatima has and makes sure her airway is clear. She puts a blanket under her head and bandages up her wounds. Ria puts her in the recovery position.

The training they have all received helps them to stay calm until help arrives.

Questions

1 Describe how the students took control of the situation.

2 Write an explanation of the following, giving a rationale (reasons) for each action:
   • dealing with Fatima's head wound
   • keeping her airway clear
   • putting her in the recovery position.

Know it!

1. What are the three main aims of providing first aid?
2. What do 'ABC' and 'CPR' stand for?
3. Describe how to check whether someone is breathing.
4. Describe how to put someone in the recovery position.
5. How many minutes, at least, would you run cold water over a burn?

Assessment guidance

Learning outcome 2: Understand the first aid procedures for a range of injuries

Marking criteria for LO2 Part A

Mark band 1	Mark band 2	Mark band 3
Demonstrates a **basic** understanding of how to identify the nature and severity of a range of injuries, with **few** causes listed.	Demonstrates a **sound** understanding of how to identify the nature and severity of a range of injuries, with **some** causes listed.	Demonstrates a **thorough** understanding of how to identify the nature and severity of a range of injuries, with **most** causes listed.
Provides a **limited** description of symptoms. **Few** symptoms will relate to the injury, **basic** examples will be given to illustrate practical understanding.	Provides a **detailed** description of symptoms. **Most** symptoms will relate to the injury, **detailed** examples will be given to illustrate practical understanding.	Provides a **thorough** description of symptoms. Symptoms will **wholly** relate to the injury. **Comprehensive** examples will be given to illustrate practical understanding.

The OCR Model Assignment will ask you to:

- Describe a range of different types of injury that require first aid.
- Show an understanding of how to identify the nature and severity of a range of injuries and list causes.
- Provide a description of symptoms that relate to the injury and give examples to illustrate your practical understanding.

What do the command words mean?

- **Thorough understanding**: Your work shows that you have an understanding of how to identify the nature of a range of injuries, their severity and their causes. This understanding will be extremely attentive to accuracy and detail.
- **Most causes**: You will list the majority of causes.
- **Thorough description and wholly**: You will provide a description of symptoms that is extremely attentive to accuracy and detail and will relate to the injury to the whole amount.
- **Comprehensive examples**: You will include examples to illustrate practical understanding and this will include everything that is necessary to show you understand this in terms of breadth and depth.

You should check the glossary in the Introduction for the definitions of each of the command words from OCR.

→

Marking criteria for LO2 Part B

Mark band 1	Mark band 2	Mark band 3
Provides a **simple** description of the current first aid procedures; **limited** information is given on the correct sequence of steps.	Provides a **sound** description of the current first aid procedures; **detailed** information is given on the correct sequence of steps.	Provides a **detailed** description of the current first aid procedures; **comprehensive** information is given on the correct sequence of steps.
The rationale will be **limited**, with **basic** examples to illustrate understanding.	The rationale will be **sound**, with **clear** examples to illustrate understanding.	The rationale will be **thorough**, with **detailed** examples to illustrate understanding.

 ## The OCR Model Assignment will ask you to:

- Describe current first aid procedures for a range of injuries and give information on the correct sequence of steps.
- Give information and reasons for each step of the first aid procedures.

 ## What do the command words mean?

- **Detailed description**: You will provide a description that will include a point-by-point consideration of the current first aid procedures.
- **Comprehensive information**: All the steps of each procedure will be given. The steps will be in the correct order with no omissions. You will provide information on the correct sequence of steps, which will include everything that is necessary to evidence understanding in terms of both breadth and depth.
- **Thorough rationale with detailed examples**: Your rationale of reasons for each of the steps of the first aid response will be extremely attentive to accuracy and detail and you will include examples, which show you have considered point-by-point the argument to show your understanding.

You should check the glossary in the Introduction for the definitions of each of the command words from OCR.

Learning outcome 3

Be able to apply basic first aid procedures

Getting started

What could be the consequences of an untrained person giving first aid?

Share and discuss your thoughts with the rest of your class.

 ## Classroom discussion

Should everyone be trained in first aid?

One view is that all children should learn basic first aid at school (for instance, how to deal with shock, bleeding and choking), as it could save hundreds of lives.

What do you think? Discuss the following questions with the rest of your class.

- Is it a good idea for everyone to be trained in first aid?
- What would be the benefits of providing the training in schools?
- Do you think first aid should be made compulsory?
- Would there be any disadvantages or difficulties in making this happen?

How to apply the steps involved in certain first aid procedures

This section of the unit requires you to perform six first aid procedures, where the casualty:

- is conscious/unconscious and breathing/not breathing
- is choking
- is having an asthma attack
- has suffered burns or scald
- is bleeding
- is in shock.

You will need to be familiar with the correct procedures and the sequence of carrying them out (look back at LO2). You will need to think about how you will use appropriate communication skills for the different scenarios provided by your tutor.

How to review your performance

After you have carried out the first aid procedures, you will need to review your performance.

This means you will need to look carefully at how you completed the task of demonstrating the first aid procedures – to reflect on how it went. How well did you plan, prepare and perform the procedures?

Reviewing your own performance involves thinking about what went well and what could be done better next time. The next step is to think about what you have learned from the experience and what you would do to improve your performance if you repeated the task.

Professor Graham Gibbs created a 'reflective cycle'. Figure 11.7 illustrates how thinking about what you have done helps you to identify what you have learned, and how this knowledge informs your thoughts about doing things differently and what could be improved next time. Gibbs' reflective cycle should help you to review your own performance if you examine it at different stages.

Stretch activity

Getting it right

Choose three of the following six scenarios.

1 A 15 year old has fallen off his skateboard and banged his head on the pavement.
2 James has burned his hand quite badly while doing the ironing.
3 Leila collapses during a netball match. She is wheezing and finding it difficult to breathe.
4 Ethan is having lunch with friends and suddenly has difficulty breathing; his skin is red and blotchy.
5 Noah is mowing his lawn. He accidentally mows over an electric cable. His son hears a shout and goes outside to find his father lying on the lawn.
6 While emptying the dishwasher, Judith accidentally picks up a sharp knife by the blade and gets a deep cut to the palm of her hand.

Now do the following.

- **Independently** create a flow chart for each of your three chosen scenarios. Each flow chart should show the step-by-step first aid procedures for the injury, in the correct order.
- Annotate each flow chart with reasons for each of the actions. This will enable you to show **thorough** understanding of each procedure

(Look at the command word definitions to see what **independently** and **thorough** mean in the assessment.)

Source: adapted from Gibbs, G. (1988) *Learning by Doing*. Oxford.

Figure 11.7 Gibbs' reflective cycle

Competency

You need to consider how much support, if any, you required to complete your first aid procedure demonstrations. Consider whether you remembered all the steps in the correct order. Did you use appropriate communication skills with the casualty and others at the scene; were you calm and reassuring, for example?

Strengths and weaknesses

To decide on your strengths and weaknesses, you could try making a list under the two headings. Then you could write in more detail about the specific things that you did well and other tasks that could perhaps be improved.

These are the sorts of questions you could ask yourself:

● Did you have confidence?
● Did you work independently or need a bit of help?
● Did you perform some first aid procedures better than others. If so, why?
● Were communication skills a strength? Why, or why not?

Suggest improvements to your performance

Use your reflections on your performance of the first aid procedures to help you suggest improvements.

For example, if you needed support at certain points, think of how you could perform independently if you performed the procedures again. This might mean becoming more familiar with a sequence of steps for a particular procedure, or practising more.

Case study: Reviewing performance

Read this case study about four friends helping an elderly man who falls over.

Four school friends were in their local shopping centre when they saw an elderly man fall over. Luckily the students had completed a first aid course at school just a few weeks earlier.

Sarah said, 'He just fell down right in front of us, so straight away we checked if he was OK. He had knocked himself unconscious and his forehead was bleeding.'

Gennelle recalled, 'I checked that he was breathing, just like we were trained to do on the first aid course.'

Maria called an ambulance: 'I was really upset and a bit frightened because he was unconscious, but I remembered the training and

tried to stay calm. I talked as calmly as I could, though it was difficult, and I was probably talking a bit too fast! I answered all the questions and gave the information the call handler needed.'

Priya added: 'If I hadn't done the first aid course I would have panicked, I know I would. But I was able to help Gennelle to put the man in the recovery position because of what I learned on the course.'

Using information from the case study, carry out a review of the students' performance when carrying out the first aid procedures. Use the following points as headings to write up the review:

● Competency
● Strengths and weaknesses
● Suggest improvements.

Group activity

How well did I do?

- Write a scenario for a situation that requires first aid assistance.
- Each member of the group takes turns to be a character in the scenario: first aider, bystander, casualty, emergency services and observer.
- Each member of the group takes a turn at observing one 'first aider' carry out the procedures, and writes a performance review using the headings:
  - Competency
  - Strengths and weaknesses
  - Suggest improvements.
- Discuss your performance with the group member who observed you as the first aider and identify areas that could be improved next time.

Know it!

1 Give four examples of health emergencies where first aid treatment would be required.

2 How can you check whether someone is conscious or unconscious?

3 What is the first aid procedure for someone who is choking?

4 Give three health emergencies where you would immediately call an ambulance.

5 Identify four aspects of your performance that you would consider in a review of carrying out first aid procedures.

Assessment guidance

Learning outcome 3: Be able to apply basic first aid procedures

Marking criteria for LO3 Part A

Mark band 1	Mark band 2	Mark band 3
First aid procedures are carried out with support and guidance, demonstrating **limited** confidence. Carries out the correct sequence of steps with **some** guidance, demonstrating a **basic** understanding of practical application.	First aid procedures are carried out with **limited** support and guidance, demonstrating **some** confidence. Carries out the correct sequence of steps with **limited** guidance, demonstrating a **sound** understanding of practical application.	First aid procedures are carried out **independently**, **confidently** and **effectively**. **Independently** carries out the correct sequence of steps, demonstrating a **thorough** understanding of practical application.

 The OCR Model Assignment will ask you to:

- Give a practical demonstration of first aid procedures.
- Carry out the correct sequence of steps.

→

What do the command words mean?

- **Independently, confidently and effectively**: You will carry out first aid procedures without relying on others, showing certainty and applying your skills appropriately to the task.
- **Independently and thorough understanding**: Without relying on others, you will carry out the correct sequence of steps. Your practical demonstration shows that you have an understanding of this that is extremely attentive to accuracy and detail.

You should check the glossary in the Introduction for the definitions of each of the command words from OCR.

Marking criteria for LO3 Part B

Mark band 1	Mark band 2	Mark band 3
Provides a **basic** review of the practical activities, with **limited** consideration of their competency.	Provides a **detailed** review of the practical activities, with **some** consideration of their competency.	Provides a **comprehensive** review of the practical activities, with **thorough** consideration of their competency.
Descriptions of their strengths and weaknesses are **limited**, improvements have **limited relevance** to their performance.	Descriptions of their strengths and weaknesses are **detailed**, improvements are **partly relevant** to their performance.	Descriptions of their strengths and weaknesses are **thorough**, improvements are **mostly relevant** to their performance.
Information provided will have **some** errors in spelling, punctuation and grammar, which may be sufficient to detract from the clarity.	Information provided will have **minor** errors in spelling, punctuation and grammar but insufficient to detract from the clarity.	Information provided will have **few**, if any, errors in spelling, punctuation and grammar so that it is clear and coherent.
Draws upon **limited** skills/knowledge/ understanding from other units in the specification.	Draws upon **some** relevant skills/ knowledge/understanding from other units in the specification.	Draws upon **relevant** skills/knowledge/ understanding from other units in the specification.

 ## The OCR Model Assignment will ask you to:

- Provide a review of your performance in your practical first aid demonstrations.
- Include some supplementary written work about skills or knowledge you have used from other units.
- Ensure that your spelling, punctuation and grammar are error free.

 ## What do the command words mean?

- **Comprehensive review and thorough consideration**: Your review of the practical activities will include everything that is necessary to evidence understanding in terms of both breadth and depth, and your consideration of their competence will be extremely attentive to accuracy and detail.
- **Thorough and mostly relevant**: Your descriptions of the strengths and weaknesses of the activities will be extremely attentive to accuracy and detail. The improvements you suggest will mostly be focussed on the activity and performance.

→

- **Few**: The information that you provide will only have a small number of errors in spelling, punctuation and grammar, if any, so that it is clear and coherent.
- **Draw upon relevant skills/knowledge/understanding from other units**: You will draw upon skills / knowledge / understanding from other units in the specification that are correctly focussed on this activity.

You should check the glossary in the Introduction for the definitions of each of the command words from OCR.

Read about it

Weblinks

www.redcross.org.uk/What-we-do/First-aid/Everyday-First-Aid British Red Cross – comprehensive information about first aid procedures

www.sja.org.uk/sja/default.aspx St John Ambulance – extensive information about all aspects of first aid

www.nhs.uk/conditions/Accidents-and-first-aid/Pages/Introduction.aspx NHS Choices – detailed information about first aid procedures

Reference books

St John Ambulance, St Andrew's First Aid and British Red Cross (2016) *First Aid Manual* (10th edn). Dorling Kindersley.

Stretch, B. (2007) *Core Themes in Health and Social Care*. Heinemann.

Thomson, H. and Aslangul, S (2009) *OCR Health and Social Care for GCSE*. Hodder.

Walsh, M. (2009) *GCSE Health and Social Care for OCR*. Collins.

Glossary

Abstract thinking Being able to solve problems using concepts and general principles.

Adaptive switch A device that allows an individual to use assistive technology.

Advocacy Getting support with safeguarding your rights and expressing your views and wishes.

AED Automated external defibrillator, which is used by qualified first aiders to deliver electric shocks to a casualty whose heart has stopped.

Agility The ability to move the body quickly and easily.

Aim The intention of the project.

Aims Desired outcomes, i.e. what you want to achieve.

Airway The passageway through which air reaches a person's lungs.

Allergic reaction An unpleasant physical reaction to a particular substance.

Amino acids Essential nutrients that the body cannot make, so they have to be eaten as part of an individual's diet.

Anaesthetist A doctor who specialises in pain relief.

Anaphylactic shock A sudden, life-threatening reaction to a substance. Common causes are peanuts and shellfish.

Antioxidants Protect the body from damage caused by harmful molecules called free radicals. Many experts believe this damage is a factor in the development of blood vessel disease (atherosclerosis), cancer and other conditions. Vitamins A, C and E are antioxidants.

Assistive technology Devices or technologies that support individuals to maintain or improve their independence and safety.

Attention deficit hyperactivity disorder (ADHD) A group of behavioural symptoms that include inattentiveness, hyperactivity and impulsiveness.

Attribute A feature or characteristic of a person.

Autism A lifelong developmental disability that affects how people perceive the world and interact with others.

Bereavement Coping with change following the loss of someone very close, such as a partner, wife, husband, etc.

Biased Information that gives one particular opinion.

Birth defects Problems that affect the structure or function of organs or systems in the body from birth.

Calories A calorie is a measurement of the energy provided by food. Energy-dense foods contain a high number of calories per gram.

Carbohydrates Essential nutrients from food that provide energy.

Cardia Where the contents of the oesophagus empty into the stomach.

Cardiovascular system Cardio = heart and vascular = blood vessels. The heart pumps blood around the body, which is transported by blood vessels.

Cartilage A strong and stretchy connective tissue between bones. It is not as hard and rigid as bone, but is stiffer and less flexible than muscle tissue.

Casualty Someone who has suffered an injury.

Cerebral palsy Affects body movement, muscle control, muscle co-ordination, muscle tone, reflex, posture and balance. It can also impact fine motor skills, gross motor skills and oral motor functioning.

Cognitive development The construction of thought processes (including remembering, problem-solving and decision-making) from childhood through to adulthood.

Communication book A way for individuals to communicate through the use of pictures, photographs, signs, symbols and words.

Conscious Awake and aware of surroundings.

Contingency planning A process that takes account of possible future events, i.e. emergencies.

CPR Cardiopulmonary resuscitation – i.e. giving someone chest compressions to keep their heart and circulation going, in order to save their life. Can also be done in combination with 'rescue breaths' by first aiders trained to do this.

CT scan A computerised tomography scan used for internal organs, blood vessels or bones (sometimes called a CAT scan).

DBS checks Criminal record checks carried out by the Disclosure and Barring Service (DBS) to help to prevent unsuitable people working with vulnerable adults or with children.

Dementia A condition that causes memory loss, confusion and difficulty with daily living tasks.

Deoxygenated blood Blood that has no oxygen, but does contain carbon dioxide.

Depression A low mood that lasts for a long period of time and affects an individual's day-to-day activities.

Designated child protection officer A named individual who is the first point of contact for staff in a care setting if they have any concerns about a child or need advice about the welfare of a child.

Dexterity The ability to perform an action with the hands skilfully.

Diabetes A condition where the amount of glucose in the blood is too high because the body cannot use it properly.

Diagnosis An investigation of the symptoms of an illness to identify what is the cause of the problem.

Diaphragm A muscle anchored to the lower ribs, which separates the chest from the abdomen.

Dietary needs An individual's food and nutrition requirements to maintain their good health and well-being.

Disabilism Behaviour that is abusive or discriminatory based on the belief that people with disabilities are inferior or less valued members of society.

Discrimination When people judge others based on their differences, and use these differences to create disadvantage or oppression. Discrimination could be based on race, disability or gender.

Disorder A state where part of the body is not functioning correctly and is causing ill-health.

Diversity Involves recognising and appreciating differences. Valuing diversity means accepting and respecting individual differences such as faith, diet, ethnicity and customs, for example.

Domiciliary care agency An organisation that provides care and support to individuals in their own homes.

Domiciliary care services Care services that are provided to individuals in their homes.

Down's syndrome A genetic condition that typically causes learning disabilities and some physical characteristics.

Dynavox Speech-generating software. By touching a screen that contains text, pictures and symbols the software then converts those symbols touched into speech.

Emergency An unexpected event that needs prompt action.

Empower To give someone the authority or control to do something. The way a health, social care or early years worker encourages an individual to make decisions and to take control of their own life.

Enzymes Chemical substances found in the body; they cause key chemical reactions to happen, such as during the digestion of food.

EpiPen A device that auto-injects adrenaline if someone has anaphylactic shock due to an allergic reaction (to peanuts, for example).

Equality Promoting equality means ensuring that people are treated equally. For example, ensuring individuals are treated fairly and given the same choices and opportunities regardless of differences. They are not discriminated against due to their age, race or sexuality, for example. People are treated according to their own, individual needs.

Ethical Something that is seen as morally right.

Fine motor skills Smaller actions, such as grasping an object between the thumb and a finger when holding a paintbrush or pencil.

First aid Urgent treatment given to an individual who has suffered a sudden injury or an unexpected health problem.

Free sugars Sugars that are added to food – for example, the sugar content of a fizzy drink or the sugar you would add to a cup of tea. The sugar is not part of the cell structure of the food.

Genetics The study of the traits people inherit from their family through DNA.

Gross motor skills The larger movements of arms, legs, feet or the entire body (for walking running, skipping and jumping).

Halal In Islam, an animal can be eaten only if it has been slaughtered in a particular way.

Haram In Islam, this means forbidden.

Harassment Unwanted behaviour that has the purpose or effect or violating a person's dignity, or intends to intimidate or humiliate them.

Health and Safety Executive (HSE) The official supervisory body for the health, safety and welfare of people in work settings in the UK.

Hearing loop system A specialist type of equipment that transmits sounds to individuals who use hearing aids or cochlear implants.

Homeostasis How the body adjusts to maintain a constant and steady state. For example, blood sugar levels are kept constant by the supply of insulin from the pancreas.

Hospice A service that provides treatment and support to patients who have a life-limiting illness and/or palliative care needs, and their families.

Hypoglycaemia A condition that occurs due to a lack of glucose in the bloodstream, which is essential for proper brain function. Symptoms include sweating, nausea, pale colour, being cold to the touch and unconsciousness.

Hypothesis A statement that makes a prediction about what will be found out in the research.

Inborn temperament Personality traits that a child is born with; these are genetically determined.

Informal carer Usually a family member or friend who provides care and support to an individual without getting paid.

Intercostal muscles Muscles found between the ribs.

Interpreter Converts a spoken or signed message from one language to another.

Jargon The use of technical language or terms and abbreviations that are difficult for those not in the group or profession to understand.

Kosher In Judaism, this means 'correct', i.e. an animal can be eaten only if butchered in a particular way.

Language and cognitive development The learning of language and cognitive skills, such as understanding and using words, communicating, thinking, remembering and problem-solving.

Learning difficulties Difficulties processing some types of information without an individual's general intelligence being affected, e.g. dyslexia.

Legislation A collection of laws passed by Parliament, which state the rights and entitlements of the individual. Law is upheld through the courts.

Life story work An activity that involves reviewing an individual's past life events and developing a biography to understand more about the individual and their experiences.

Lightwriter A text-to-speech device. A message is typed on a keyboard, is displayed on the screen and then converted into speech.

Mental health crisis house Residential setting that offers intensive, short-term support for individuals experiencing a crisis and who are not able to remain living safely in their own homes.

Metabolism Chemical processes and reactions that take place in the body.

Monitor The independent regulator of NHS foundation trusts.

Moral Concerned with the principles of right and wrong behaviour.

MRI scan A magnetic resonance imaging scan; a strong magnetic field and radio waves are used to produce detailed images of almost all parts of the body.

National insurance contributions Money deducted and paid to the government for the cost of state benefits such as the state pension.

Neural growth Refers to any growth of the nervous system.

Nutrients The individual components of the food we eat. Examples are vitamins, protein, fats and carbohydrates.

Objectives How you intend to meet desired outcomes, i.e. how you are going to achieve what you want.

Obsessive compulsive disorder (OCD) An anxiety disorder characterised by obsessive thoughts and compulsive activities.

Obstetrician A doctor who specialises in the care of women during pregnancy, childbirth and after birth.

Ofsted (the Office for Standards in Education, Children's Services and Skills) Inspects and regulates services that care for children and young people, and services providing education and skills for learners of all ages.

Ovo-lacto vegetarian Will not consume any animal flesh, but will consume dairy and egg products.

Oxygenated blood Blood that contains oxygen.

Paediatrician A doctor who specialises in the care of babies and children.

PECS Stands for 'Picture Exchange Communication System'. It is a specialist method of communication. It was developed for use with children who have autism and helps them learn to start communicating by exchanging a picture for the item or activity that they want.

Peer group A group of people (usually of similar age, background and social status) with whom a person associates, and who are likely to influence the person's beliefs and behaviour.

Plagiarise Copy or use someone else's work as your own without acknowledging or giving credit to the original author.

Protected characteristic Refers to nine characteristics identified by the Equality Act. It is unlawful to discriminate against someone on the basis of a protected characteristic.

Psychological therapies Techniques used to support individuals to manage their mental health and overcome any difficulties they are experiencing.

Puberty The process of physical changes through which a child's body matures into an adult body capable of sexual reproduction.

Pulse The pumping action of the heart that can be felt at the wrist or neck.

Qualitative data Data that is based on people's views, opinions and beliefs; usually written in words rather than numbers or figures.

Quality An expression of personality and temperament, e.g. honesty.

Quantitative data Data that records quantities and from which numbers or numerical data (e.g. charts, graphs etc.) result.

Radiography assistant A practitioner who works under the supervision of a radiographer to diagnose a patient's illness, disease or condition, and treat medical conditions through the use of x-rays and imaging.

Rationale A set of reasons for a course of action.

Redress To obtain justice after being discriminated against or receiving inadequate care. This may take the form of compensation awarded by the courts or having your rights restored in some way.

Reminiscence therapy An activity that involves the use of photographs, music or familiar objects to enable an individual to discuss and share their past life experiences.

Residential short break A holiday where children can socialise and take part in activities to give their family or carers a break from caring.

Risk Something that could cause harm to individuals.

Seasonal Buying foods that are naturally growing in their season. This reduces food miles, as food does not need to be imported from abroad so that it can be eaten out of season.

Sedentary A lack of physical activity. A person with a sedentary lifestyle spends a lot of time sitting and does little, if any, exercise.

Self-awareness The ability to know one's own character and feelings.

Self-esteem How much a person values themselves and the life they live. High self-esteem is associated with people who are happy and confident. An individual with low self-esteem experiences feelings of unhappiness and worthlessness.

Self-worth Confidence and value in one's own abilities and qualities.

Sessional day care services Day care offered to pre-school children for a total of not more than 3.5 hours per session.

Severity How serious an injury is (i.e. is it life threatening, a minor superficial injury, or something in between?).

Sexualism Discrimination or negative attitudes towards a person or group on the basis of their sexual orientation or sexual behaviour – for example, against lesbian or bisexual individuals.

Sharps injury When the skin is punctured by a needle, blade (such as scalpel) or any other medical instrument.

Social services A range of public services provided by the UK government and private organisations, such as in relation to housing, healthcare and social care.

Sonographer Specially trained to carry out ultrasound scans.

Sphincter A circular muscle that narrows a body passage. Examples are the pyloric sphincter at the lower end of the stomach and the anal sphincter.

Spina bifida A type of birth defect called a neural tube defect; it occurs when the bones of the spine (vertebrae) don't form properly around part of the baby's spinal cord.

Sternum A narrow bone connected with the ribs, also known as the breastbone.

Stools Body waste called faeces.

Symptoms An indication of a disease or disorder.

Taxes Money deducted and paid to the government for services funded by the government.

Thorax The part of the body just above the abdomen and below the neck; it includes the ribcage, which encloses the heart and lungs.

Translator Converts a written message from one language to another.

Transphobia Discriminatory behaviour against transgender or transsexual individuals on the basis that they do not conform to society's gender expectations.

Unconditional positive regard Letting children know that they are cared about, accepted and approved of no matter what.

Unconscious Unresponsive to any sound or touch.

Valves Valves are found in veins and ensure a one-way flow of blood.

Victimisation Bad treatment directed towards someone who has made a complaint or taken action under the Equality Act.

Vulnerable An individual who is unable to take care of themselves against significant harm or exploitation. This may be because of mental or physical disability or illness.

Whistleblower Someone who reveals wrongdoing within an organisation to the public or to those in positions of authority.

Index

Note: page numbers in **bold** refer to key word definitions.

Index